Foundations of
Corporate Success

How business strategies add value

JOHN KAY

OXFORD
UNIVERSITY PRESS

OXFORD

UNIVERSITY PRESS

Great Clarendon Street, Oxford OX2 6DP

Oxford University Press is a department of the University of Oxford.
It furthers the University's objective of excellence in research, scholarship,
and education by publishing worldwide in

Oxford New York

Athens Auckland Bangkok Bogotá Buenos Aires Calcutta
Cape Town Chennai Dar es Salaam Delhi Florence Hong Kong Istanbul
Karachi Kuala Lumpur Madrid Melbourne Mexico City Mumbai
Nairobi Paris São Paulo Singapore Taipei Tokyo Toronto Warsaw
with associated companies in Berlin Ibadan

Oxford is a registered trade mark of Oxford University Press
in the UK and in certain other countries

Published in the United States
by Oxford University Press Inc., New York

© John Kay 1993

Hardback edition first published 1993
Paperback edition first published 1995

British Library Cataloguing in Publication Data
Data available

Library of Congress Cataloging in Publication Data
Kay, J. A. (John Anderson)
Foundations of corporate success: how business strategies add
value / John Kay.
Includes bibliographical references.
1. Corporate planning.   2. Corporations—Finance.
3. Organizational effectiveness.   4. Success in business.
I. Title.
HD30.28.K387   1993   658.4'012   92-33883
ISBN 0-19-828781-X
ISBN 0-19-828988-X (Pbk)

10 9 8 7 6

Printed in Great Britain
on acid-free paper by
Biddles Ltd.
Guildford and King's Lynn

FOREWORD

I$_T$ is a common fate of business authors to find that their admired corporations are no longer so widely admired when their books come to be reprinted. Notoriously, several of the firms picked out in Peters and Waterman's *In Search of Excellence* appeared as laggards not leaders in the decade that followed.

My approach in *Foundations of Corporate Success* helped me to finesse that problem. I argued that corporate success is based on the distinctive capabilities of the firm—those things, often the product of its particular history, which competitors cannot reproduce even after others realize the benefits these capabilities bring to the company that enjoys them. Corporations add value when they successfully match these distinctive capabilities to the external environment they face. It follows that there are not, and could never have been, any generally applicable strategies for corporate success. It also follows that the futures of individual corporations are bound to wax and wane, as capabilities become more or less distinctive and more or less relevant to the market which the company faces. So I have no difficulty in understanding why BMW or IBM, Disney or Liverpool Football Club, should experience both extraordinary success and traumatic failures.

So to see which companies will be successful in the next century, we need to look away from a projection of today's trends. It is a frequent mistake in looking forward to think that current performance and above all current size are the most important elements in future success. Size offers no long-term protection for those who have no true distinctive capability: lack of it proves no obstacle to those who genuinely enjoy one. The rise in industrial concentration in the twentieth century was driven by economics of scale based on low unit costs from long mass production runs. But today concentration is falling, with the growth of flexible manufacturing, and as the production of undifferentiated manufactured goods becomes a steadily diminishing proportion of the output of advanced economies.

There are many people in government and business who still look forward to production concentrated in fewer and fewer hands until a few large multinational businesses, with powers rivalling or exceeding national governments, dominate the world economy. They fail to appreciate that size is mostly the result of competitive advantage, not its cause, and that because competitive advantage must be based on distinctive capability it can rarely be sustained indefinitely.

The appropriate sporting analogy is not the knock-out competition, in which a defined group of entrants is reduced to a single winner, but the league, in which clubs play for each other repeatedly and all experience promotions and regulations from time to time. The successful companies of the next century will certainly include many of which we have not yet heard. There will be many more Nintendos and Microsofts—large and exceptionally successful companies, unknown a decade ago, and by no means assured of a future a decade hence.

Microsoft's competitive advantage rests on its proprietary standards in MS-DOS and Windows. Its strength is not derived from its manufacturing capability, but on its capacity to add value to these capabilities in others. Coca-Cola, Nintendo, Glaxo, Benetton, Reebok are all manufacturing firms; but for all of them making things is not an important part of what they do. The added value corporation—of which these are all examples—may or may not build the products sold under its name. Some do, some do not. But for all, their success lies not so much on the efficiency of the process of manufacture, but on their control of a key element of it—the syrup (Coke), the standard (Nintendo), the patent (Glaxo), the co-ordinating function (Benetton), the marketing (Benetton). That is another reason why tomorrow's corporations will be smaller than today's. None of these firms need employ many people to earn substantial profits.

There are many ways in which firms can add value; but the competitive advantage of a firm like Microsoft can be eroded by those who emulate its distinctive capability. Where success is based on positioning, as for Body Shop or Wal-Mart, that position can be replicated. Some companies—like Glaxo, or Xerox have accomplishments which have been based on extraordinary products, but ones which others will in due course match. All these are companies of their time. They will attain continued success only if they establish new sources of competitive advantage as potent as those they initially enjoy. Some may achieve it. Most will not.

Other competitive advantages are easier to sustain. Some firms have unique, and carefully protected, products for which future demand seems assured. Look at Coca-Cola, Mars, Disney—the tastes of children are somehow more enduring than the preferences of adults or the needs of business. When adults buy brands they look to the supplier's assurance that his ever-changing product range is well adapted to their needs. That is why they buy from Price Waterhouse, JP Morgan, or Marks & Spencer. Coke, Mars and Disney need only protect and preserve their products; JP Morgan and M&S must protect and preserve their ability to meet the requirements of their customers in new ways. Yet these companies have done so for decades, and new firms may hope to do so in the same areas where brands are needed, but not yet established. Distinctive capabilities based on well-managed reputation are more often enduring than those which result from positioning, or innovation, or from standards.

Companies whose success is derived from strategic assets—from the absence of effective competition rather than the presence of competitive advantage—face a more difficult problem. It is most acute for the great utilities—some of them long-established as private corporations, others newly transferred, or to be transferred, from the public sector, as technology, deregulation and internationalization change their markets fundamentally. AT&T is a radically different company from that of a decade ago, and European telecommunications companies face a choice between adjustments equally radical, and oblivion. If fragmentation is making the national PTT irrelevant in telecommunications, concentration is making the national flag carrier irrelevant in airlines. Sometimes, as in telecoms, technology and liberalization allow more players; sometimes, as in aviation, it requires fewer. And in all these markets there will be once great companies which suffer the fate of PanAm by failing to redefine their roles.

Since the publication of the first edition of *Foundations of Corporate Success*, it has become more and more clear that the resource-based theory of business strategy, to which it is intended as a contribution, is becoming the dominant paradigm in this area of business research. It is fashionable to argue that the pace of change in modern business is such that today's wisdom is immediately outdated. I believe, on the contrary, that the next century will continue to demonstrate that there are indeed some unchanging 'Foundations of Corporate Success'.

PREFACE

In 1986 I was offered the opportunity, and substantial resources, to answer the question, 'What are the origins of industrial success?' There are, perhaps, more important questions, but not many, and that was certainly the most important question I felt in any way equipped to try to answer. So I accepted the challenge.

It was obvious that there was no shortage of data. Every corporation is required to file detailed returns of its activities. In all Western economies there are several journals which track the performance and activities of leading companies. Case studies, business histories, and business biographies describe how decisions were made and problems overcome. I began to understand that what was needed was not to collect new information, but to establish a framework for understanding what was already known. The development of such a framework became my primary goal, and the purpose of this book is to describe that framework. I will have succeeded if the thoughtful senior executive thinks less often, 'That is something new,' than, 'That makes sense of my experience.'

There were those who told me that the task I had set myself could not be done, or was not worth doing. Business problems were too complex to be susceptible to the use of analytic techniques. Every situation was unique and there could be no valid generalizations. It had even been argued by some (as in Abernathy and Hayes, 1980) that the attempt to apply analytic methods to business issues is at the heart of Western economic decline.

It might be true that there can be no valid generalizations about business, and that there can be no general theories of the origins of corporate success or failure. But it does not seem very likely that it is true. It is not just that similar observations were made ahead of much greater leaps in scientific knowledge. How could we hope to understand something so complex, and so subject to change, as the motion of the planets or the make-up of genetic material? The issues considered in this book seem, on the face of it, to be ones that could respond to analytic tools. I believe that the tools presented in this book do give real help in handling these questions. If they fail to do so, it is more likely that they are the wrong tools than that no tools will ever become available.

One paradox was immediately apparent. If I asked what was meant by corporate success, many different answers were proposed. Some people emphasized size and market share, others stressed profitability and returns to shareholders. Some people looked to technical efficiency and innovative capability. Others stressed the reputation that companies enjoyed among their customers and employees, and in the wider business community.

Yet this disagreement was hardly reflected at all in disagreement about which companies were successful. Whatever their criteria of success, everyone seemed to point to the same companies—to Matsushita and to Hewlett-Packard, to Glaxo and to Benetton, to BMW and to Marks & Spencer. I formed the view that the achievement of any company is measured by its ability to add value—to create an output which is worth more than the cost of the inputs which it uses. These different opinions on how success should be measured were partly the result of disagreement about how added value was created, but rather more the product of different views as to how, once created, added value should be used. Successful companies, and successful economies, vary in the relative emphasis to be given to returns to shareholders, the maximization of profits, and the development of the business. Different firms, and different business cultures, gave different weights to these purposes. But the underlying objective of adding value was common to all.

I began by asking the managers of successful companies to explain the sources of their success. They told me that success depended on producing the right product at the right price at the right time. It was essential to know the market, to motivate employees, to demand high standards of suppliers and distributors. I recognized that all these things were true, but those who emphasized them were describing their success, not explaining it.

I found that much had been written on strategic management. But stripped of rhetoric, most strategy texts offered checklists of issues that senior executives needed to address in considering the future of their business. That literature posed questions but yielded few answers.

Economists had studied the functioning of industry, but their concerns were mostly with public policy, not business policy, and I was sure that industrial success was founded on the behaviour of firms, not on the decisions of governments. Sociologists had studied the functioning of organizations, but only a few had matched the characteristics of the firm to the economic environment that determined its competitive performance.

I came to see that it was that match between the capabilities of the organization and the challenges it faced which was the most important issue in understanding corporate success and corporate failure. That perception led directly to the primary themes of this book. These begin from a recognition that there are no recipes, and generic strategies, for corporate success. There cannot be, because if there were their general adoption would eliminate any competitive advantage which might be derived. The foundations of corporate success are unique to each successful company.

The uniqueness is a product of the firm's contracts and relationships. I see the firm as a set of relationships between its various stakeholders—employees, customers, investors, shareholders. The successful firm is one which creates a distinctive character in these relationships and which operates in an environment which maximizes the value of that distinctiveness. The rest of this book is concerned with the nature of these relationships, the ways in which they achieve distinctiveness, and how effective companies select and manage their environment in the light of these capabilities. I am convinced that description of that process illuminates the origins of success in firms, in industries, and in national economies.

The book is divided into seven parts. Parts I and II establish building blocks for the later analysis. Part I is concerned with what is meant by corporate success and corporate failure, and presents a clear objective for the firm—adding value. A firm adds value through the distinctive character of the relationships it establishes with its stakeholders—its employees, customers, shareholders, and suppliers. These relationships, and the variety of forms they take, are the subject of Part II.

That unique set of relationships gives the successful firm a distinctive capability—something it can do which its potential competitors cannot. Part III is concerned with the forms which such distinctive capabilities might take. But a distinctive capability becomes a competitive advantage only when it is applied in a relevant market. The matching of markets to capabilities is the subject of Part IV. Parts III and IV define the central issues of corporate strategy. They describe how the firm should answer the familiar question, 'What business are we in?'.

Part V examines business and competitive strategy. It analyses relationships with competitors in the chosen market. So Part V is concerned with problems of pricing, positioning, advertising and branding, and with vertical relationships—the firm's dealings with its suppliers and distributors. Firms add value by creating a distinctive capability through a unique set of relationships, establishing a competitive advantage based on that distinctive capability in relevant markets, and maximizing the value of that advantage through the firm's business strategy. Part VI—the strategic audit—pulls these strands together at the levels of firm, industry, and nation. For many readers, the book can finish there, but Part VII is designed for those who wish to understand how this analysis relates to other approaches to the understanding of business behaviour.

A book such as this is synthetic in objective. It seeks to draw ideas from a wide range of sources, and any claims to originality rest on the way in which it brings a variety of different approaches from business history, economics, law, and sociology to bear on a specific group of issues rather than on the novelty of these ideas themselves. Instead of attributing each of these strands

---

1 I have also taken the opportunity to overcome the problem of different monetary units by expressing cash amounts in Ecus, except in some cases where it would be absurd to convert from the original currency. A list of conversion factors is to be found on p. 369.

of thinking fully as they arise, I have been sparing with references in the text, but have provided relatively full bibliographical notes which are designed to serve the twin purposes of acknowledgement of sources and guide to further reading. Chapter 21, a brief history of the subject of business strategy, is designed to relate the analysis here to the existing management literature, and there a different and more conventional style is appropriate.

In writing Chapter 21 I became very conscious that virtually all the references were to articles or books written in English, at least of sorts, and that the vast majority of them came from the United States. This would have been almost as true, although I believe less true, if I had chosen to survey modern physics or chemistry (and been competent to do so). But while the United States contains a disproportionate fraction of the world's talent and resources in physics and chemistry, it is less apparent that this is true of business strategy. And while the laws of physics and chemistry know no national boundaries, there is much that is culturally specific in strategy and in approaches to strategy. The perspective of this book is European and the examples and illustrations it uses are mostly European.[1]

A European perspective bears directly on the issue of how commercial relationships are established and managed. The business culture of the United States is a strongly individualistic and opportunistic one, where hard bargains are driven and expressed in concrete contractual form. It is an environment in which firms have no hesitation in looking to legal process to enforce the terms of these contracts—and may, indeed, do so without jeopardizing a continuing commercial association. The Japanese way of doing business is characterized by complex but informal networks of relationships, where many of the rules are implicit and may be evident only to the parties to the relationship themselves. Europe lies somewhere in between. I believe that few American management writers have understood the significance of these cultural differences, or their relevance to the competitive advantages of firms and of nations, and that if Europeans fail to do so there is a danger that we will end up with a combination of the worst aspects of these two business styles rather than with the best, as we have an opportunity to do. I return to these themes in Chapters 20 and 22.

I should like to thank the many people who have helped with this book. In particular, I am indebted to David Sainsbury, who set the challenge, and the Gatsby Foundation, which provided financial support; to Evan Davis, who contributed greatly to developing the ideas it contains; to Jonathan Star, who acted as a highly effective research assistant throughout the preparation of the manuscript; and to Barbara Lee, who managed endless versions and revisions of a complex manuscript. The Economic and Social Research Council's technology initiative provided additional research support which is particularly reflected in chapters 5 and 7. Stefan Szymanski and David Thompson were responsible for the preparation of substantial pieces of analysis contained here, and Matthew Bishop, Michael Cronshaw, Stephanie Flanders, Esther Perkins, and Laura Rovizzi all gave research assistance in particular subject areas. I can identify ideas which derive from conversations with Charles Baden Fuller, Richard Brealey, Romano Dyerson, Paul Geroski, Peter Grindley, Michael Roper, and Paul Willman, and I am sure there are many others. Comments on earlier versions of the manuscript were provided by Andrew Dilnot, Simon Domberger, Leslie Hannah, Robert Laslett, Geoffrey Owen, George Richardson, Nigel Savage, Bettina von Stamm, and John Vickers. Hayley Bell prepared the first version of the manuscript. The editors, Herb Addison, David Musson, and Andrew Schuller, provided helpful advice and comments and necessary support and encouragement. The Coca-Cola Company and Bells assisted with original artwork.

CONTENTS

LIST OF FIGURES

LIST OF TABLES

LIST OF ILLUSTRATIONS

I

CORPORATE SUCCESS

1

The Structure of Strategy

In this chapter I describe three legendary stories of business success. In 1959 BMW was on the edge of bankruptcy. The company recovered to become one of the world's most profitable automobile manufacturers. Honda became the leading supplier of motor cycles in the United States within five years of entering the market. That example proved the prototype of Japanese attacks on many established Western industries. Glaxo, a British company best known for its baby foods, discovered what was to prove the best-selling drug in the history of the pharmaceutical industry, and marketed it around the world.

But success is most illuminating when contrasted with failures. So I also tell how Saatchi & Saatchi tried to create the world's first multinational, multidisciplinary consultancy business, how Groupe Bull sought to be a European rival to IBM, and how EMI exploited the most important advance in radiography since the discovery of X-rays; and how each of these endeavours brought the major companies concerned close to financial collapse.

These histories illustrate how corporate success is based on an effective match between the external relationships of the firm and its own distinctive capabilities. BMW, Honda, Glaxo are all firms which identified their distinctive capabilities, selected the markets best suited to these strengths, and built effective competitive strategies to exploit them. They did so sometimes belatedly and not always consciously, but it was that process which formed the basis of their subsequent success.

The other three firms exemplify the most common causes of failure. Bull simply lacked capabilities sufficient for its aspirations. Saatchi misunderstood the nature of its own competitive strengths and entered, expensively, markets in which its capabilities had no value. EMI, with the most distinctive capability of any of these six firms, failed to gain any long-run benefit from it by mishandling its relationships with its competitors and customers. It pursued a mistaken competitive strategy.

Corporate success, of the kind achieved by BMW, Honda, and Glaxo, is not the realization of visions, aspirations, and missions—the product of wish-driven strategy. It is the result of a careful appreciation of the strengths of the firm and the economic environment it faces. But nor is success often the realization of a carefully orchestrated corporate plan. The strategy of successful firms is adaptive and opportunistic. Yet in the hands of a successful company an adaptive and opportunistic strategy is also rational, analytic, and calculated. Adaptiveness does not mean waiting for something to turn up. Opportunism is only productive for a firm which knows which opportunities to seize and which to reject.

This chapter introduces the central themes of the book. Corporate success derives from a competitive advantage which is based on distinctive capabilities, which is most often derived from the unique character of a firm's relationships with its suppliers, customers, or employees, and which is precisely identified and applied to relevant markets. The remainder of the book develops these arguments and explains the various types of distinctive capability which successful firms hold and how they are effectively identified, developed, and exploited.

Did it make sense for Benetton, an Italian knitwear manufacturer, to move into retailing, and was it right to decide to franchise most of its shops to individual entrepreneurs? Should Saatchi & Saatchi have attempted to build a global advertising business? What segment of the car market was most appropriate for BMW? These are typical issues of corporate strategy. Corporate strategy is concerned with the firm's choice of business, markets, and activities.

Should Eurotunnel offer a premium service or use its low operating costs to cut prices? How should Honda have approached the US motor-cycle market? Faced with three different standards for high definition television, and a market potentially worth tens of billions of pounds, what stance should a television manufacturer adopt? What will be the future of European airlines as deregulation progresses? These are typical issues of business, or competitive, strategy. Competitive strategy is concerned with the firm's position relative to its competitors in the markets which it has chosen.

The strategy of the firm is the match between its internal capabilities and its external relationships. It describes how it responds to its suppliers, its customers, its competitors, and the social and economic environment within which it operates. The analysis of strategy uses our experience of the past to develop concepts, tools, data, and models which will illuminate these decisions in future. Taking corporate and business strategy together, we learn why some firms succeed and others fail. Why did EMI fail to profit from its body scanner while Glaxo succeeded brilliantly in marketing its anti-ulcer drug, Zantac? Why has Philips earned so little from its record of innovation? Why has Marks & Spencer gone from strength to strength when so many other retailers have enjoyed spectacular, but purely transitory, success?

The object of this chapter is to understand how successful companies established successful strategies by understanding their own distinctive capabilities and relating them to the business environment they faced.

BMW

Few who drive a BMW car know what the initials stand for, or realize that the distinctive blue and white propeller badge reproduces the colours of the state flag of the State of Bavaria. The Bayerische Motoren Werke were established during the First World War. They specialized in the manufacture of engines. The company subsequently diversified into what are now its two principal product ranges: automobiles and motor cycles. Today BMW is one of Germany's largest and most successful companies.

BMW cars are not the most powerful, or the most reliable, or the most luxurious on the market, although they score well against all these criteria. No one has ever suggested that they are cheap, even for the high level of specification that most models offer. Although BMW rightly emphasizes the quality and advanced nature of its technology, its products are not exceptionally innovative. The design of the company's cars is conventional and the styling of its models is decidedly traditional.

The achievements of BMW are built on two closely associated factors. The company achieves a higher quality of engineering than is usual in production cars. While most car assembly has now been taken over by robots or workers from low-wage economies, BMW maintains a skilled German labour force. The company benefits, as many German firms do, from an educational system which gives basic technical skills to an unusually high proportion of the population. Its reputation has followed from these substantial achievements. In this, BMW is representative of much of German manufacturing industry.

Yet BMW's success was neither easy nor certain. In 1945, the company was Germany's leading manufacturer of aeroengines. Its primary market and its capital equipment were both in ruins. Its principal factory at Eisenach was across the border in the Soviet occupation zone. While German recovery through the 1950s occurred at a pace which attracted the title of economic miracle, BMW did not prosper. Uncertain of its future, the company emphasized automobiles but its products ranged from tiny bubble cars, manufactured under licence, to limousines. In 1959, the firm faced bankruptcy and a rescue by Mercedes seemed its only hope of survival.

Instead, BMW found a powerful shareholder—Herbert Quandt—who perceived the company's inherent strengths. The turning-point came when the firm identified a market which most effectively exploited its capabilities—the market for high-performance saloon cars, which has since become almost synonymous with BMW. The BMW 1500, launched in 1961, established a reputation for engineering quality in the BMW automobile brand. The brand in turn acquired a distinctive identity as a symbol for young, affluent European professionals. That combination—a system of production which gives the company a particular advantage in its chosen market segment, a world-wide reputation for product quality, and a brand which immediately identifies the aims and aspirations of its customers—continues to make BMW one of the most profitable automobile manufacturers in the world.

Today, the BMW business is structured to maximize these advantages. Retail margins on BMW cars are relatively high. The company maintains tight control over its distribution network. This control supports the brand image and also aids market segmentation. BMW cars are positioned differently and priced very differently in the various national markets. The same tight control is reflected in BMW's relationships with suppliers, who mostly have continuing long associations with the company. BMW's activities are focused almost exclusively on two product ranges—high-performance saloon cars and motor bikes—which reflect its competitive strengths. The company also uses the brand to support a range of motoring accessories.

BMW is a company with a well-executed strategy. It is a company which came—after several false starts—to recognize its distinctive capabilities and choose the market, and subsequently markets, which realized its full potential. Its dealings with its suppliers and distributors, its pricing approach, its branding and advertising strategies, are all built around that recognition and these choices. There was no master plan, no single vision which took BMW from where it was in 1959 to where it is today. There was a group within the company which believed strongly that a model like the 1500 was the firm's main hope of survival. There were other views, other options. No one had more than partial insight into what the future would hold. But BMW's success was no accident either.

Strategic planning

Businesses have had strategies since the earliest days of commerce. But only since the 1960s has it been common to address explicitly the question of what their strategy should be. Since then, strategy has been studied, taught, and discussed interminably.

Early strategic thinking was equated with medium- and long-term planning. The corporate plan would provide projections of sales, revenues, costs, and profits for the company's businesses. Increasingly, firms came to recognize that these exercises had little influence on their actual operating decisions, and the fashion for planning gradually receded. While many companies still continue a formal planning cycle, few now set the same store by it or devote the same resources to it.

Intriguingly, it is modern developments in mathematics which have demonstrated what most practical businessmen long suspected. Attempts to forecast the evolution of a firm for more than a short period ahead are fundamentally useless. Two decades ago it seemed possible to believe that technology would ultimately conquer these problems. With sufficient information, and infinitely powerful computers, the uncertainties of business behaviour would gradually be resolved. We know now that this will never be true. Like the weather, business is a chaotic system in which small differences in the starting-point can translate into large divergencies in final outcomes. That means that we cannot expect that better and better, but still imperfect, information will lead us to convergence on the true outcome. We can never hope to know what the weather will be ten years from today, and we will never be able to forecast what profits will be in ten years' time either.

Yet, as the analogy makes clear, we can learn a great deal once we recognize the limitations of our knowledge. If we do not know what the weather will be like ten years hence, we certainly know that it is likely to be hotter in summer than in winter, and wetter in Bergen than in Madrid, and that tomorrow's weather is not only influenced by today's but influenced in ways that are largely, if never completely, predictable. This knowledge has important effects on our behaviour. The recurrence of patterns and the assurance of trends are central in the structured accumulation of experience. In just the same way, the evolution of a business can never be wholly predictable or controllable, but it is not a chance process either.

Honda

Honda's redefinition of the US motor-cycle market is a classic case in corporate strategy. Motor bikes in the United States in the 1950s were associated with a subculture now best recalled through movies, leather jackets, the smell of oil, and teenage rebellion. In 1964, five years after its entry into the United States, one in three motor cycles sold there were Hondas. The best-selling product was a 50 cc supercub, marketed under the slogan, 'You meet the nicest people on a Honda.'

There are two views of this achievement. In one, Honda's strategy was an archetype of Japanese penetration of Western markets. The aggressive pursuit of domestic volume established a low-cost base for expansion overseas. This was the conclusion of a Boston Consulting Group study for the British government (BCG, 1975). A rather different account was given by Richard Pascale, who went to Tokyo to interview the elderly Japanese who had brought the first Honda machines to the United States. As they recalled it, Honda had aimed to secure a modest share of the established US motor-cycle market.

Mr Honda was especially confident of the 250 cc and 350 cc machines. The shape of the handlebar on these larger machines looked like the eyebrows of Buddha, which he felt was a strong selling point. (Pascale, 1984: 54.)

These hopes were not realized. The eyebrows of Buddha had little attraction for the leather-jacketed Marlon Brando.

We dropped in on motor-cycle dealers who treated us discourteously and, in addition, gave the general impression of being motor-cycle enthusiasts who, secondarily, were in business. (Pascale, 1984: 54.)

The first supercubs exported to the United States were used by Honda employees for their own personal transport around the concrete wastes of Los Angeles. It was only when these caught the attention of a Sears buyer and the larger machines started to show reliability problems that Honda put its efforts behind the 50 cc machines. The 'nicest people' slogan was invented by a University of California undergraduate.

Neither of these accounts is entirely convincing. The BCG account is an expression of the near paranoia created for many Westerners by Japanese achievement. But Pascale's suggestion that Honda's success was simply the result of good fortune would be more persuasive if the company had not been blessed by such good fortune quite so often in the course of its spectacular rise. The 'eyebrows of Buddha' are all too reminiscent of the South Sea island girls who teased Margaret Mead with ever more extravagant accounts of their sexual exploits.

We shall never know the extent to which Honda's success was truly the result of chance or rational calculation. But while knowing may be important to the business historian, it is of little significance to the corporate strategist.[1] Honda effected a brilliantly successful market entry. Like all successful strategies, it was based on a mixture of calculation and opportunism, of vision and experiment. Like all successful corporate strategies, it was centred on Honda's distinctive capability—an established capacity to produce an innovative but simple, low-cost product. Its realization depended on a successful competitive strategy, which made full use of segmentation and involved the creation of a distinctive distribution network which bypassed the traditional retail outlets of the enthusiasts. The lessons we can learn from that strategy are much the same whether Honda conceived it by grand design or stumbled on it by accident.

The nature of strategy

The issues that BMW and Honda handled so successfully are the central questions of strategy. BMW and Honda had to consider what markets to enter, how to position their products within these markets, how to build relationships with dealers and component manufacturers. The subject of strategy analyses the firm's relationships with its environment, and a business strategy

1 Quinn, Mintzberg, and James (1988)—in what is perhaps the best of recent strategy texts—pose for their readers the question (p. 81), 'Ask yourself while reading these accounts, how the strategic behaviour of the British motorcycle manufacturers who received the BCG report might have differed if they had instead received Pascale's second story.' The correct answer, of course, is 'Not at all.' Suppose it were shown conclusively that Honda's success was the result of purest chance. It would not then follow that the right approach for British firms was to wait for similar good fortune to fall on them. This was what they in fact did, with notable lack of success.

is a scheme for handling these relationships. Such a scheme may be articulated, or implicit, pre-programmed, or emergent. A strategy—like that of BMW or Honda—is a sequence of united events which amounts to a coherent pattern of business behaviour.

All firms are part of a rich network of relationships. They must deal with customers and suppliers, with competitors and potential competitors. For many firms, the relationship with the government is also critical to their strategy. The government may buy the firm's products or regulate many of its activities. The objective of Chapters 3 and 4 is to define and analyse the different types of relationships which firms build.

These relationships may be *classical* and *contractual*—elaborately articulated in legal documents—or they may be *informal* and *relational*, and enforced primarily by the need the parties have to go on doing business with each other. They are designed to secure outcomes in which all parties win, because in commerce, as in life, relationships are rarely of the type in which one party gains what the other loses. They are designed to deal with problems of co-operation, of co-ordination, and of differentiation. The unique structure of these relationships, their architecture, is the source of some firms' competitive advantage, and this is explored in Chapter 5.

If the subject of business strategy focuses on the relationship between the firm and its environment, there are many key management issues which it does not address. Strategy is not principally concerned with employee motivation, or with finance, or with accounting, or with production scheduling and inventory control, although these may influence the firm's strategy and be influenced by it. In the last two decades, the pretensions and prestige of the subject of strategy have been such that strategists have stressed not only the central importance of the issues with which they deal but also the relevance of strategy to all aspects of business behaviour. For the same reasons, everyone involved in business—from the personnel manager to the public relations consultant—has asserted a right to contribute to the strategy process.

But strategy is not simply another word for important. There are many aspects to good management, and to say that strategy and operations management are distinct facets of it is not to disparage either. Yet there is a difference between strategy and these other elements of management practice which illuminates the nature of strategy itself and may partly explain its supposed primacy. In most industries, there are many firms which have their finance and accounting right, their human relations right, their information technology adapted to their needs. For one firm to succeed in these areas does not damage others. In implementing finance and accounting, human relations, and information technology, it is right, and normal, to look to the best practice in other firms.

But strategy is not like that. Honda and BMW did not establish their market positions by methods which built on the best practice of their competitors. For both companies, attempts to match their rivals' strategies failed. BMW's bubble cars were not as well regarded as Innocenti's, and its limousines were inferior to those of Mercedes. Honda was able to sell powerful motor bikes in the US only after its success with quite different products had destroyed its competitors' finances and established its own reputation. Successful strategy is rarely copycat strategy. It is based on doing well what rivals cannot do or cannot do readily, not what they can do or are already doing.

Groupe Bull

IBM has strong claims to be regarded as the most successful company in the world during the last three decades. It has dominated a large, rapidly growing, and profitable market and its products have changed every aspect of business behaviour. IBM is a high tech company but its strength is not simply derived from its technology, where it has often chosen to follow rather than to lead. IBM's most famous advertising slogan—'No one ever got fired for choosing IBM'—was not devised or used by the company but by its customers. It reflects the company's true distinctive capability—its ability to deliver not just hardware but solutions to its clients' problems, and its reputation for having that ability.

European politicians and businessmen have long dreamt of creating a European IBM. The British government promoted ICL, the Germans Nixdorf and Siemens, the Italians supported Olivetti. These companies have succeeded only in subsectors of the computer market. The European government most determined to resist IBM's hegemony across the full range of computers has been the French, and the European company most determined to resist it has been Groupe Bull.

Bull is, curiously, named after a Norwegian whose patented punch card system proved popular with French banks before the Second World War. But Bull's greatest success came when its gamma 60 range offered perhaps the most advanced and innovative machines available as the computer age dawned in the 1960s. That gave the company a world-wide name, and marketing capability, but the 90 range which followed failed to live up to specifications. The company recognized that it lacked the technical capacity to challenge IBM alone and that the United States would be by far the largest geographic market for computers. It looked for a US partner, and found a strong one in General Electric. De Gaulle, outraged by the dilution of the vision of a French world leader in computing, first blocked the deal. When it eventually went ahead, the irate President established a state-owned, and wholly French, competitor, Cii. Cii was less successful than Bull and in 1976 the two companies merged. The firm soon reverted to its original name but the French state now had a majority stake.

General Electric came to an early conclusion that the computer business was IBM's, and quit it completely. Bull found a new American partner in Honeywell. The company enjoyed a captive market in the French public sector, and did well more generally in Francophone countries, but elsewhere the gap between IBM and either Honeywell or Bull continued to widen. Through the 1980s Bull struggled, surviving only on the continued support of its indulgent principal shareholder. Eventually Honeywell too gave up the chase, and Bull bought out its partner.

In 1989, Groupe Bull acquired a new chief executive, Francis Lorentz, who reasserted the company's primary objective—'To become the major European supplier of global information systems'. (*Financial Times*, 30 June 1989, p. 29). The emphasis had shifted slightly from a French to a European base, but the central message remained the same. But by now even IBM was faltering. IBM's distinctive capabilities remained strong, but markets had changed. A computer had become a commodity, not a mystery, and there could be one on every manager's desk. In 1990 Bull posted large losses, and 1991 was a worse year still. Early in 1992, Bull announced an alliance with IBM.

For thirty years Groupe Bull has been a company driven not by an assessment of what it is but by a vision of what it would like to be. Throughout it has lacked the distinctive capabilities which would enable it to realize that vision. Bull—and the other attempts at European clones of IBM—epitomize wish-driven strategy, based on aspiration, not capability. Effective strategy, like that of BMW or Honda, starts from what the company is distinctively good at, not from what it would like to be good at, and is adaptive and opportunistic in exploiting what is distinctive in these capabilities.

Creating strategy

There is nothing new in saying that strategies should be adaptive and opportunistic, or that planning should start with an assessment of the firm's distinctive capabilities. Yet these observations are often misinterpreted. Adaptive strategy is contrasted—quite mistakenly—with analytical approaches to strategy, while the real contrast is with the vision, the mission, and the wish-driven strategy about which there is nothing analytical at all. To say that we cannot forecast where our organizations will be in five years' time is not to say that we cannot plan for the future. To say that successful businesses, and successful entrepreneurs are opportunistic, like Honda, is not to say that firms and managers should, like the British motor-cycle industry, wait to see what turns up.

When strategists talk of distinctive capabilities they quickly turn to talk of how to build them. This is evidently important, and most distinctive capabilities have, in some sense or other, been created by the firms which hold them today. Yet the attempt to establish distinctive capabilities confronts its own version of wish-driven strategy. Building distinctive capabilities must be a task of exceptional difficulty because, if it were not, the capability would soon cease to be distinctive. The story of Komatsu's conquest of Caterpillar—how a small Japanese company took on the world's largest producer of earth-moving equipment, and won—has become the business equivalent of 'from log cabin to White House'. But, like the epic of Abraham Lincoln, it is often misinterpreted.[1] The lesson of Lincoln's success is not that anyone can become President of the United States if they try hard enough, but that in an open society exceptional talent can thrive however humble its origins. The lesson of Komatsu is that the internationalization of modern business creates commercial opportunities as wide-ranging as the political opportunities offered by the democratization of the United States. Komatsu succeeded because of the quality and competitive price of its products. Its achievement was the product of its competitive advantage, not the strength of its will.

So the emphasis in this book will be more on the definition and identification of distinctive capabilities than on their creation. Although it is possible to create distinctive capabilities, success is more often based on exploitation of those capabilities which the firm already enjoys. These may derive from its history or from its location, or they may be capabilities which it has already established in related markets or industries. Strategy begins with an understanding of what these distinctive capabilities are.

Saatchi & Saatchi

Saatchi & Saatchi was, for a time, the best known advertising agency in the world. An advertisement devised to promote birth control, which showed a picture of a pregnant man, created a mixture of controversy and envy which catapulted a small agency controlled by Charles and Maurice Saatchi to national fame. The agency's contribution to Margaret Thatcher's first successful election campaign in 1979 turned that domestic reputation into an international one.

But international recognition was not enough. The Saatchis determined to create an international business. In 1983, it is reported (by Fallon, 1988: 203), Maurice Saatchi read a famous article in the *Harvard Business Review* on the development of global markets (Levitt, 1983). Inspired by the vision it held out, he flew the Atlantic to learn the full details of the new doctrine. These transatlantic flights were to become more frequent as the operating companies within Saatchi & Saatchi came to span not just Britain and the United States but other continents and other markets.

By the end of the decade, Saatchi & Saatchi was, as the brothers had intended, the world's first truly international, interdisciplinary, marketing and consultancy organization. It was also in serious financial difficulty. Under

---

1 And, like much written about Lincoln, largely apocryphal. Komatsu entered the US market with a very aggressive pricing strategy, and imposed massive losses on Caterpillar, which was unwilling to cede market share, and ready to cut prices to retain it. Komatsu's price policy proved difficult for the Japanese company itself to sustain, and in the end it allowed prices to drift upwards and has settled for a modest share of the US market.

pressure from bankers and stockholders, the Saatchis relinquished executive control and a new management team set to work dismantling the empire which the brothers' vision had put together.

Saatchi & Saatchi began with a reputation that was unmatched in its business, and a creative team that was almost equally admired. These are characteristic assets of the highly successful professional service firm. The firms it bought were firms which had precisely these assets themselves. Its largest acquisition, Ted Bates, was itself one of the largest and most respected advertising agencies in the United States and had no need of the Saatchi label. It already enjoyed an equivalent reputation in its own market and there was never any suggestion that it would trade under the Saatchi name. International customers did not bring their business to the new merged agency. They took it away, fearing conflicts of interest as the enlarged concern was often already handling the accounts of its competitors. Ted Bates was worth less to Saatchi & Saatchi than to almost any other purchaser. Saatchi already had those things which made Bates valuable and they were worth less, not more, under Saatchi ownership.

But in the grip of the strategic objective of internationalization, Saatchi paid a large premium to gain control of that and other businesses. For a time, the inherent weaknesses of the strategy were concealed by the growth in the underlying earnings of the businesses and the capacity of the Saatchi share price to drift ever upwards on a cushion of hot air. Eventually, earnings faltered and the hot air escaped. The company was left with a mountain of debt and a collection of businesses that, while sound in themselves, were not worth the prices that had been paid for them.

Wish-driven strategy failed for Groupe Bull because the goal was unattainable. Wish-driven strategy failed for Saatchi & Saatchi because the goal, although attainable and attained, was not a sensible one for that particular company to pursue. Wish-driven strategy emphasizes the importance of the corporate vision, frequently starts with an assertion of the mission statement, and creates a company driven by a view of what it would like to be. The Saatchi strategy was based on a dream, rather than an analysis of the competitive strengths of the business, and the company adapted to market realities only when corporate collapse was staring it in the face.

Sustainability and appropriability

A capability can only be distinctive if it is derived from a characteristic which other firms lack. Yet it is not enough for that characteristic to be distinctive. It is necessary also for it to be *sustainable* and *appropriable*. A distinctive capability is sustainable only if it persists over time. Honda's achievement was not only to redefine the US motor-cycle market but to remain leaders in that market. A distinctive capability is appropriable only if it exclusively, or principally, benefits the company which holds it. Often the benefits of a distinctive capability are appropriated instead by employees, by customers, or by competitors.

There are relatively few types of distinctive capability which meet these conditions of sustainability and appropriability. There are three which recur in analysis of the performance of successful companies. *Innovation* is an obvious source of distinctive capability, but it is less often a sustainable or appropriable source because successful innovation quickly attracts imitation. Maintaining an advantage is most easily possible for those few innovations for which patent protection is effective. There are others where process secrecy or other characteristics make it difficult for other firms to follow. More often, turning an innovation into a competitive advantage requires the development of a powerful range of supporting strategies.

What appears to be competitive advantage derived from innovation is frequently the return to a system of organization capable of producing a series of innovations. This is an example of a second distinctive capability which I call architecture. *Architecture* is a system of relationships within the firm, or between the firm and its suppliers and customers, or both. Generally, the system is a complex one and the content of the relationships implicit rather than explicit. The structure relies on continued mutual commitment to monitor and enforce its terms. A firm with distinctive architecture gains strength from the ability to transfer information which is specific to the firm, product or market within the organization and to its customers and suppliers. It can also respond quickly and flexibly to changing circumstances. It has often been through their greater ability to develop such architecture that Japanese firms have established competitive advantages over their American rivals.

A third distinctive capability is *reputation*. Reputation is, in a sense, a type of architecture but it is so widespread, and so important that it is best to treat it as a distinct source of competitive advantage. Easier to maintain than to create, reputation meets the essential conditions for sustainability. Indeed an important element of the strategy of many successful firms has been the transformation of an initial distinctive capability based on innovation or architecture to a more enduring one derived from reputation.

From capabilities to competitive advantages

A distinctive capability becomes a competitive advantage when it is *applied in an industry* and *brought to a market*. The market and the industry have both product and geographic dimensions. Sometimes the choice of market follows immediately from the nature of the distinctive capability. An innovation will usually suggest its own market. Pilkington discovered the float glass process, a system by which thin sheets of glass were formed on a bed of molten tin, which made the traditional grinding and polishing of plate glass unnecessary. Little need be said about the industry and markets where such an innovation is to be applied and it is other aspects of strategy that are critical. There are few geographical boundaries to innovation. While most innovating firms will begin in their home markets, successful innovation is rarely inhibited by national boundaries. The appropriate product market for an innovation is not always obvious, and identifying precisely what it is can be crucial. The demand for video cassette recorders turned out to be based on pre-recorded films rather than home movies. That required a playing time of three hours, not thirty minutes. JVC saw that small difference more quickly than Sony, and that was one key influence on success and failure in that particular market. The liquid crystal display, a scientific curiosity when it was introduced, was an innovation waiting decades for an application.

Other firms have distinctive capabilities based on their architecture, and the same architecture advantage can often be employed in a wide range of industries and markets. For BMW, the choice of industry and market segment was by no means obvious, but ultimately crucial. For Honda, the choice of market segment did seem obvious. In the wide open spaces of the United States, they anticipated little demand for the small machines which were popular in congested Japan. But this view was doubly wrong. The market for large bikes which they had chosen was one in which Honda had no initial competitive advantage. Success came only from a very different product positioning. The market segments these companies selected, high-performance saloons for BMW, light-weight, low-powered motor cycles for Honda, were both innovative but well suited to their underlying distinctive capabilities.

Reputations are created in specific markets. A reputation necessarily relates to a product or a group of products. It is bounded geographically, too. Many reputations are very local in nature. The good plumber or doctor neither has nor needs a reputation outside a tightly defined area. Retailing reputations are mostly national. But an increasing number of producers of manufactured goods, from Coca-Cola to Sony, have established reputations world-wide, and branding has enabled international reputations to be created and exploited for locally delivered services in industries as diverse as accountancy and car hire.

A firm can only enjoy a competitive advantage relative to another firm in the same industry. So BMW may enjoy a competitive advantage over Nissan, but be at a competitive disadvantage to Mercedes. As this example illustrates, a competitive advantage is a feature of a particular market. These three firms compete in several different markets, or market segments, and the pattern of relative competitive advantages and disadvantages is different in each one. The value of a competitive advantage will depend on the strength of the firm's distinctive capability, the size of the market, and the overall profitability of the industry.

It is easier to sustain a distinctive capability in a narrow market than a wide one, more profitable to hold it in a wide market than a narrow one. And the profitability of a firm depends both on the competitive advantage the firm holds relative to other firms in the industry and on the profitability of the industry itself. If there is excess capacity in the industry—as in automobiles—then even a large competitive advantage may not yield substantial profits.

But if entry to an industry is difficult, then a firm without any competitive advantage may nevertheless earn very large returns. There is little reason to think that the large monopolistic utilities which control many parts of the European energy, transport, and communications industries have strong distinctive capabilities of the kind that characterize BMW, or Honda, or IBM. Their market dominance has not been built on doing things that others could not do as well, but on doing things that others were not permitted to do at all. Yet many of these firms are very profitable. There can be no greater competitive advantage than the absence of competitors. Profits come not only from distinctive capabilities but from possession of *strategic assets*—competitive advantages which arise from the structure of the market rather than from the specific attributes of firms within that market.

Illustration 1.1. The Structure of Strategy

Identifying the firm's distinctive capabilities

Types of distinctive capability	Architecture	Chapter 5
	Reputation	Chapter 6
	Innovation	Chapter 7
	Strategic Assets	Chapter 8

Distinctive capability becomes competitive advantage when applied in appropriate markets

| Means of choosing markets | Markets | Chapter 9 |
| | Mergers and acquisitions | Chapter 10 |

A competitive advantage is valuable if sustainable and appropriable

Deriving value from competitive advantage	Sustainability	Chapter 11
	Appropriability	Chapter 12
	The value of competitive advantage	Chapter 13

Business strategy concerns the relationships between the firm and its competitors

| Maximizing the value of competitive advantage | Pricing and positioning | Chapters 14 and 15 |
| | Advertising and branding | Chapter 16 |

Business strategy concerns the relationships between the firm and its suppliers or distributors

| Defending the value of competitive advantage | Vertical relationships | Chapter 17 |

Glaxo and EMI

Corporate strategy is concerned with matching markets to distinctive capabilities. Business strategy looks at the relationship between the firm and its competitors, suppliers, and customers in the markets which it has chosen.

In the 1970s, two British firms, Glaxo and EMI, developed important innovations. Both depended critically on their sales in the US medical services market. Glaxo had found an effective anti-ulcer drug, Zantac. EMI's scanner was the most important advance in radiology since the discovery of X-rays. Glaxo transformed itself from a medium-ranking drug company with uncertain future to Europe's leading pharmaceutical producer. EMI, crippled by losses on its scanner business, ceased to exist as an independent company and is no longer involved in medical electronics.

EMI's capability was much the more distinctive. The scanner won the Nobel Prize for Physics for its inventor, Geoffrey Houndsfield. The market for anti-ulcerants has long been recognized as a potentially lucrative target—ulcers are common, persistent, and rarely fatal. An effective therapy emerged from the research of a British scientist, Sir James Black, but it was a US company, SmithKline, which developed Tagamet, the first commercial product based on it. Zantac was discovered after Glaxo refocused its research programme following the publication of Dr Black's results.

For both Glaxo and EMI, the choice of markets was not a difficult issue. Their markets were suggested by the nature of their innovation. (Although this was less obvious at an earlier stage of development in the scanner. EMI had a defence-based technology seeking an application, and it was a lateral leap by Houndsfield which took the company into medical electronics. For Glaxo, however, the innovation followed the market and the market the innovation.)

The key questions for both companies were issues of business strategy. The choice of market identified suppliers, customers, and competitors. Relationships with suppliers were not of special importance to either company, but relationships with customers and competitors most certainly were.

EMI attempted to create its own US distribution network and to price at a level designed to recoup development costs. President Carter, concerned about spiralling medical bills, imposed a 'certificate of need' requirement on publicly funded hospitals. This delayed sales while General Electric developed its own version of the scanner. Although EMI had little experience of any manufacturing in this field, far less overseas, the company established a US manufacturing plant, which ran into serious output and quality problems. When GE entered the market, EMI was rapidly swept away and the rump of the business was sold to its larger competitor.

Patent protection—which had not proved sufficiently effective either for SmithKline or EMI—served Glaxo well, and helped ensure that its competitive advantage was sustainable. It began to market its drugs in the US through Hoffmann–La Roche, whose sales of Librium and Valium had made the firm by far the most effective European pharmaceutical company in the US market. Glaxo entered Japan through a joint venture with a Japanese partner. In Britain and Italy, where Glaxo had a strong, established market reputation, the company went it alone. It skilfully exploited concern about possible Tagamet side-effects and priced Zantac at premia to Tagamet which reflected the company's own variable relative strength in different markets. By the mid-1980s, Zantac had become the world's best-selling drug, and over the decade, the company earned about £4 billion in profits from its sale. By any standards, Glaxo is an outstandingly successful European company.

Many large companies have sponsored or encouraged histories of themselves. Often they are self-congratulatory panegyrics, but the best are substantial works of scholarship. BMW has one of the finest of business histories (Mönnich, 1989—in English translation as Mönnich, 1991). There are probably more books about IBM than any other company; some examples are Sobel (1981), Rodgers (1986), Delamarter (1986), Mercer (1987). Marks & Spencer has also been the subject of several books, as in Rees (1973), Tse (1985), Goldenberg (1989), Sieff (1990). Saatchi & Saatchi is the subject of a well-written journalistic account in Fallon (1988), which despite its unfortunate subtitle gives insight into the origins of the company's failures as well as its successes. One measure of true success is that it attracts criticism as well as eulogy; IBM has achieved this and so has Glaxo (Lynn, 1991).

Business school cases, which are generally based on interviews with company management, provide both qualitative and quantitative information about company activities, especially for US corporations. They vary considerably in quality. Few contain much analysis, which the instructor or student is expected to provide, and they often reproduce the opinions and perceptions of the managers involved in an uncritical fashion. Honda and Komatsu are classic business school case studies. For Honda, the original case is HBS (1978), based on the BCG report (Boston Consulting Group, 1975); and the revisionist version is to be found in HBS (1983*a*) and HBS (1983*b*) based on Pascale (1984). The Komatsu story is found in HBS (1985) and (1990) with revisionism here in Kotler (1991, ch. 13). Emmott (1989) is a useful counter to the more paranoid views of Japanese achievement. The comparison of Glaxo and EMI is based on dell'Osso (1990*b*).

Newspaper and magazine reports—particularly from journals such as *Management Today* and *Fortune*—provide a constantly updated and replenished source of information and views on corporate performance. Text services now allow particularly easy access to these information sources. The accounts of company operations given in Chapter 1 and elsewhere in this book draw on all these three sources of information: histories, cases, and reports.

A further account of the evolution of thinking in business strategy is given in Chapter 21 and the references given therein. Gleick (1988) is an entertaining introduction to chaos theory.

2

Adding Value

What is corporate success, and how is it measured? In this chapter I explore the strengths and weaknesses of common performance measures by comparing six British supermarket chains. Some people judge success by size. They look at a firm's sales, its market share, and its value on the stock market. Sometimes performance is assessed by reference to rate of return. This can be measured as return on equity, on investment, or on sales. And sometimes success is measured by growth, reflected in increase in output, movements in earnings per share, or prospectively, the firm's price–earnings ratio.

All of these are aspects of successful performance. But I argue in this chapter that the key measure of corporate success is added value. Added value is the difference between the (comprehensively accounted) value of a firm's output and the (comprehensively accounted) cost of the firm's inputs. In this specific sense, adding value is both the proper motivation of corporate activity and the measure of its achievement.

This chapter defines and develops the objective of added value. It introduces the added value statement and the analysis of the value chain as means of making a quantitative appraisal of a firm's operating activities. This contrasts with the usual financial statements which concentrate, appropriate for their purpose, on returns to investors. In Chapter 13 I explore these issues in greater detail and describe how added value is the basis of all the more familiar measures of corporate performance. While this chapter identifies the various stakeholders in the business—employees, investors, customers, and suppliers—I postpone until Chapter 12 the issue of how added value is shared among these various stakeholders. In the final part of the chapter I use the added value criterion to identify the most successful European companies of the last decade.

Glaxo is not the largest public company in Europe. Depending on the criterion used—turnover, employment, net output—that title goes to Royal Dutch Shell, Europe's largest oil company, to Daimler–Benz, the German engineering conglomerate which owns Mercedes, or to British Telecom. Shell's sales are twenty times those of Glaxo, and Daimler–Benz, with nearly 400,000 employees, has a workforce ten times larger.

The difference in earnings is less marked, but BT's profits are twice those of Glaxo and Shell's twice those of BT. Glaxo's return on capital employed is exceptional—around 40 per cent. But there are many smaller companies which post higher rates of return. And pharmaceutical companies generally show a return on capital which is abnormally high since neither their principal investments (in research and development) nor their principal assets (the value of their drug portfolio) are recorded in their balance sheets.

Glaxo has done well for its shareholders. Money invested in the company in 1980 would have been worth thirty times as much in 1990. But the stock market provides the market's estimate of success. It is not itself the measure of success. You would have done better still to invest your money in Polly Peck over that same period but you would subsequently have learnt that the company's chief executive had been arrested on fraud charges and that your shares were, in fact, worthless. It is unwise to rely on market performance alone as a guide to corporate effectiveness.

So what defines a successful company? Success is intrinsically a relative concept. The best way to understand what it means is to compare the performance of different firms in the same line of business.

British supermarkets

Food retailing in Britain is dominated by six chains. The oldest and largest is Sainsbury's. John Sainsbury opened the company's first grocery store in south London over a century ago, and the family tradition and the philosophy of good quality products at competitive prices have remained central to the firm ever since. Conservatively managed, the company came to the stock market only in 1973 and since then has expanded steadily from its loyal, and mostly southern, customer base.

Tesco came into existence as an aggressive discounter and the slogan coined by its colourful founder Jack (eventually to be Lord) Cohen—'pile 'em high, sell 'em cheap'—still hangs around the company's neck. It is a slogan the company would like to forget because from 1977 the firm executed a bold strategic move. Tesco decided to shift market position and attract a different target customer. It offered higher price, higher quality products more like those of Sainsbury's and put a much greater emphasis on fresh foods and on own label goods. Today Tesco rivals Sainsbury's in both market position and market share.

Both Gateway and Argyll were created by amalgamations between weaker chains. Argyll's most important move was the purchase of the UK operations of the US Safeway corporation, and it has since focused its own shops around Safeway's business concept. Gateway was created by the acquisitive ambitions of Alec Monk, an aggressive chief executive whose star fell as rapidly as it had risen. His sprawling retail conglomerate was taken over in 1989 by a highly leveraged investor consortium, Isosceles, which has not found it easy to rationalize its operations into a profitable business.

Asda emerged from Associated Dairies, which distributed milk and dairy products in the north of England. The company pioneered large out-of-town superstores at a time when these were strongly resisted by established shopkeepers and planning authorities. Thereafter, the company began to lose its way. It diversified unsuccessfully into furniture retailing. It attempted to match Tesco's shift of position but its commitment to the change was signalled less clearly. Asda still has more non-food sales than any of the other stores, and this can be seen in its higher net margins. In 1991 Asda faced serious financial difficulties, embarked on a major fund-raising operation and appointed a new chief executive. With Asda's move up-market, the mantle of 'pile 'em high, sell 'em cheap' fell on Kwik Save, a chain of discount shops selling a limited range of branded goods at low prices from basic stores mostly in secondary locations.

The performance of these companies can be compared in many ways (Table 2.1). Sainsbury's has the largest market share, closely followed by Tesco. The profits of the companies, and their value on the stock market, follow broadly the order of their size. Kwik Save, although the smallest of the chains, is very profitable—its returns on investment and on equity are the highest in the sector. The firm does not do quite so well on either gross or net margin—gross margins are lower in a 'no frills' operation and its net margin is held back by its low-price, high-volume strategy. Asda, with a high proportion of more profitable non-food sales, comes out well here.

Sainsbury's and Tesco show lower returns on investment or equity than either Kwik Save or Argyll. Yet this is more a warning that these are unreliable indicators than a comment on the performance of the companies. Supermarkets have usually sold goods for cash at the checkout before they have paid their suppliers, and working capital for all these companies is actually negative. Little is needed in the way of fixed assets, beyond shop fittings and delivery vehicles, since the stores themselves may be leased. Kwik Save's return on capital is very high because there is very little capital employed in the Kwik Save business.

Sainsbury's and Tesco—the chains which have dominated the sector for many years—have chosen to reinvest heavily in building their own superstores. This would be a foolish thing for them to have done if they could have earned returns as high as those of Argyll and Kwik Save by developing the business in some other way. But they could not. The return on capital is simply a ratio of two numbers, not a guide to what you will earn by investing more in the business, and Tesco and Sainsbury's have been using their capital

Table 2.1. Performance of Supermarkets, 1989

	Asda	Gateway	Argyll	Tesco	Sainsbury's	Kwik Save
Size (Ecus m)						
Turnover	3,782	6,308	4,889	6,587	7,902	1,649
Profit	218	286	218	383	515	81
Market capitalization	2,678	2,378	2,319	3,281	4,699	1,184
Return (%)						
Gross margin	*9.3	5.0	5.4	7.3	8.2	6.5
Net margin	*6.2	3.5	3.6	3.9	4.4	4.1
ROI	18.9	NA	25.6	22.8	20.5	*40.5
ROE	18.0	17.0	24.0	18.0	21.0	*27.0
Shareholder return (1 year)	–10	3	–2	3	0	*24
Shareholder return (10 years)	45	293	*367	280	326	283
Growth						
Sales growth (%)	10	–12	8	15	18	*27
EPS growth (%)	14	16	23	17	23	*36
PE ratio	13	14	14	17	18	*23
Efficiency						
Sales/Ecus per square foot	759	NA	1,146	771	*1,323	NA
Stock turnover	13	NA	13	*24	20	19

NA Not available. * Italicized figures show best performer on each measure.
Source: Own calculations on data derived from Micro Extel and company annual reports.

as effectively as they can. It is worth their while to invest in stores so long as they can earn more from building stores than the 10 per cent or so return on capital they would have got from the bank. It mostly is worth their while, because the Sainsbury's or Tesco name adds value to a site (which a Kwik Save logo does not) and the stores needed for a Tesco or Sainsbury's style of operation are relatively specialist in nature. Ownership is a means by which Sainsbury's and Tesco can retain the whole of the added value their activities create. This reinvestment has the effect of driving down their return on capital but it makes them, taken as a whole, more profitable businesses not less.

What of return to shareholders? In 1989 only Kwik Save did well. This is not because the other businesses were doing badly but because the stock market (correctly) anticipated a recession which would favour Kwik Save's trading approach and damage the sales of other retailers. On a ten-year timescale, the outstanding performers are Argyll (which was a tiny company at the beginning of the decade) and Sainsbury's.

Kwik Save is the fastest growing of the chains—no surprise there, since it is also the smallest. Kwik Save also shows the most rapid growth in earnings per share. The price–earnings ratio is a measure of market analysts' evaluation of the quality of the company's earnings and their expectations of their security and growth. This measure divides the sector clearly into three groups. Kwik Save is on its own, with the highest PE ratio. Sainsbury's and Tesco each have similar ratings. Argyll, Asda, and Gateway have much lower market evaluations.

All these are financial measures of performance. What of the technical efficiency of these firms? Sainsbury's sells more goods per square foot than anyone else. Sainsbury's and Tesco turn over their stock most rapidly, but so they should, given their emphasis on fresh produce. In this light, Kwik Save, which relies heavily on packaged goods, comes out particularly well. All these measures tell us something about these companies. None, in itself, gives a complete picture.

The added value statement

What underpins the success of firms such as Glaxo, Sainsbury's, or Kwik Save is their ability to add value to the inputs they use. Table 2.2 sets this out for Glaxo. In 1990 the company bought materials worth 1,528m. Ecus. Its wage and salary bill was 901m. Ecus and the cost of the capital which the company used—premises, factories, machinery, and equipment—was 437m. Ecus. The resulting product was sold for 3,985m. Ecus, 1,120m. Ecus more than it cost.

That figure of 1,120m. Ecus is a measure of the added value which Glaxo created. It is the difference between the market value of its output and the cost of its inputs. It is a measure of the loss which would result, to national income and to the international economy, if Glaxo were to be broken up and the resources it uses deployed in other firms. Adding value, in this sense, is

Table 2.2. Added Value Statement: Glaxo 1990

Relationships with	Financial Flow	Value (m. Ecus)
Customers	Revenues	3,985
Labour	Wages and salaries	901
Investors	Capital costs	437
Suppliers	Materials	1,528
	Added value	1,120

Source: Glaxo plc annual report and accounts

the central purpose of business activity. A commercial organization which adds no value—whose output is worth no more than the value of its inputs in alternative uses—has no long-term rationale for its existence.

This assessment of added value is one which accounts comprehensively for the inputs which Glaxo used. It includes not only the depreciation of its capital assets but also provides for a reasonable return on the capital invested in them.[1] So added value is less than the *operating* profit of the firm—the difference between the value of output and the value of material and labour inputs (but not capital inputs). It is also less than the net output of the firm—the difference between the value of its sales and the cost of its inputs of materials (but not its inputs of labour or capital).

The strength of Glaxo's competitive advantage can be measured by looking at the ratio of added value to the firm's gross or net output. Each unit of Glaxo's sales costs only 0.72 units to produce. Glaxo's net output is the 2,457 Ecus difference between the cost of the materials it bought and the value of the output it sold. It achieved this with only 1,338m. Ecus of labour and capital, representing a cost of 0.54 Ecus per Ecu of net output.

Fig. 2.1 looks at the UK supermarket industry in the same way. The added value created by the industry as a whole is small at just over 1 per cent of gross output because some individual chains, like Asda and Gateway, are struggling, and partly because five-sixths of the output of the industry is accounted for by the cost of supplies. This is hardly surprising for self-service retailers, and Chapter 13 looks at firms at different stages of the chain of production. A comparison of added value and net output brings out the performance differences more clearly and this is done in Fig. 2.2.

There are two clearly outstanding performers in the sector—Sainsbury's and Kwik Save. The width of the sections in Fig. 2.2 reflects the size of the company. Sainsbury's adds most value overall, Kwik Save the most per unit of

---

1 The most appropriate means of charging for capital costs is a complex question which is discussed more fully in Ch. 13. The calculations in this chapter simply impose a rate of return on operating assets of 10%.

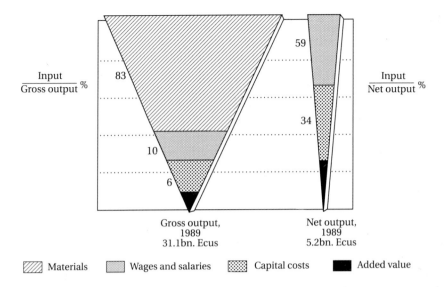

Fig 2.1. **Value Chains for UK Supermarket Sector, 1989**

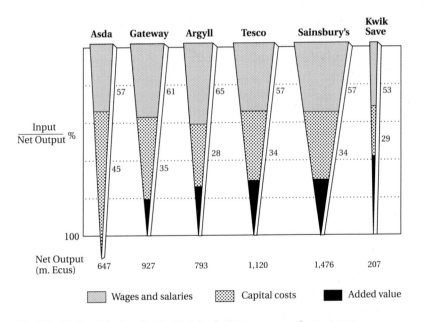

Fig 2.2. **Value Chains for Individual UK Supermarkets, 1989**

input. Each Ecu of Asda's output costs it 1.01 Ecus. Each Ecu of Kwik Save's, 0.82 Ecus. In a contestable market, characterized by rivalry and easy entry and exit, a firm with no competitive advantage will sell a unit of inputs for precisely one unit. So these ratios measure the strength of Kwik Save's competitive advantage. As Kwik Save grows—Fig. 2.3—it is likely, perhaps inevitable, that it will move into markets or market segments where its competitive advantage is less strong. But so long as it has some competitive advantage, the added value created by the business as a whole will continue to increase. For a more mature business—like Sainsbury's—overall competitive advantage is less but added value greater.

Glaxo's competitive advantage is stronger than that of any supermarket. By this criterion, Kwik Save's added value is 18 Ecus for each 100 Ecus of output, Glaxo's 46 Ecus per hundred. That results from the different market conditions the latter company faces. In its principal market—that for anti-ulcerant drugs—its main competitors are Tagamet and a more recent therapy with a different pharmacological approach, Losec, manufactured by the Swedish company Astra. But Zantac is widely thought to be superior to Tagamet. Losec must compete with Zantac's established record and reputation with doctors and their patients. The market is not very sensitive to price. Sufferers will readily pay a premium for what their doctors think is a better product and in many geographic markets much of the cost is in any case borne by the government or by insurers. Glaxo's competitive advantage in this market will diminish as other drugs become available and more familiar and as the end of patent protection allows more direct competition from generic versions of Zantac itself. But for the moment, Glaxo's competitive advantage remains strong.

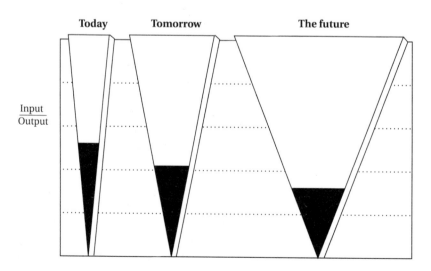

Fig 2.3. Growing the Business: How a Growing Firm Adds More Value

Not all firms succeed in adding value. Table 2.3 shows the added value statement for the Dutch electrical giant Philips. Each Ecu of Philips's output cost it 1.08 Ecus to produce. It was unable to cover the full costs of its activities in the competitive markets it faced. Philips is a striking case because it is a firm with enormous strengths and clear distinctive capabilities. Its record of innovation in consumer electronics is second to none—the company invented the compact cassette and pioneered the compact disc (CD) and video-cassette recorder (VCR). Yet it has repeatedly failed to translate these innovations into its own commercial success. The contrast between Glaxo and Philips, like that between Glaxo and EMI, is a measure of the importance of strategy in translating distinctive capability into competitive advantage.

Table 2.3. Added Value Statement: Philips, 1990 (m. Ecus)

Revenues	24,247
Wages and salaries	7,666
Capital costs	2,932
Materials	15,716
Added value	(2,067)

Source: Philips NV annual reports and accounts

European winners

By the criterion of added value, Glaxo is a success, and Philips a failure. Table 2.4 shows the European Community's 'top ten' firms of the 1980s measured by the ratio of added value to net output. Most of the companies in that list are household names. Benetton is famous for its knitwear, sold through franchised retail outlets around the world. Reuters began as a news service, providing syndicated material to newspapers, but its principal operations and profits are now derived from providing on-screen information in financial markets. Petrofina is Belgium's oil company with a range of upstream and downstream interests. LVMH is a French conglomerate focused on luxury goods. The company's title reflects three, Louis Vuitton luggage, Moët et Chandon champagne, and Hennessy cognac. Guinness produces not only the famous Irish stout, but also controls many leading brands of Scotch whisky—Johnnie Walker, Bell's—and other branded drinks such as Gordon's Gin.

Cable and Wireless is a British-based international telecommunications company. It holds the franchise for local telephone services in Hong Kong, owns Mercury, the second licensed public telecommunications operator in the UK, and provides international services around the world. BTR is an acquisitive, wide-ranging manufacturing conglomerate which has earned

Table 2.4. Europe's Most Successful Companies, 1981–1990

Position	Company	Activity	Country	Costs per unit of net output	Average sales (m. Ecus)
1	Glaxo	Pharmaceuticals	UK	.54	3,498
2	Benetton	Textile	Italy	.57	1,019
3	Reuters	Information	UK	.67	1,206
4	Petrofina	Oil	Belgium	.67	13,979
5	Kwik Save	Food Retailing	UK	.68	1,609
6	LVMH	Luxury Goods	France	.70	2,583
7	Guinness	Drinks	UK	.71	3,875
8	Cable and Wireless	Telecom	UK	.72	1,959
9	BTR	Conglomerate	UK	.74	7,404
10	Marks & Spencer	Retailing	UK	.74	7,678

Source: Own calculations based on Euroequities database. (Chosen from non-financial companies with sales in excess of 1 billion Ecus.)

large returns both by trading in businesses and by squeezing additional profits from the firms it has taken over. Marks & Spencer is a British retailer, now increasing its operations in continental Europe, most famous for its range of reliable clothing at value for money prices.

The list contains a disproportionate number of UK companies and Table 2.5 attempts to redress this balance by identifying the leading companies in each of the main regions of the European Community. Some common characteristics are clearly apparent among the companies represented in both the overall European list, and in these regional lists—brands and reputation, customer and supplier relationships, market dominance and control of strategic assets. These are key elements in successful strategies and they will be recurrent themes in this book.

Corporate success is not measured by size, or market dominance. Corporate success is not simply about the magnitude of profits. Shell and British Telecom earned much larger profits than any company in Table 2.4,

Table 2.5. European Companies by Region, 1981–1990

Position	Company	Activity	Costs per unit of net output	Average sales (m. Ecus)
UK/Ireland				
1	Glaxo	Pharmaceuticals	.54	3,498
2	Reuters	Information	.67	1,206
3	Kwik Save	Food Retailing	.68	1,609
Italy				
1	Benetton	Textiles	.57	1,019
2	Eridania	Food	.88	3,449
3	Mondadori	Printing	.90	1,092
Benelux				
1	Petrofina	Oil	.67	13,979
2	Hunter Douglas	Household Goods	.82	1,001
3	Unilever NV	Consumer Goods	.85	31,992
Spain/Portugal				
1	Tabacalera	Tobacco	.91	3,780
2	Cepsa	Oil	.92	4,235
Germany				
1	Wella	Toiletries	.83	1,091
2	BMW	Cars	.84	11,079
3	Porsche	Cars	.85	1,558
France				
1	LVMH	Luxury Goods	.70	2,583
2	Bongrain	Food	.83	1,065
3	Pernod Ricard	Drinks	.84	1,699

Source: Own calculations based on Euroequities database.

but they did so because they are very large companies. But nor is success just about the rate of return on capital. You can run a drug company with very little capital employed but not an oil business or a telephone network. Size, market share, and profitability are aspects of corporate success, but success is not any one of these alone. The reason I believe it is appropriate to describe Glaxo as the most successful European company of the 1980s is that, more than any other major company, Glaxo added value to the resources it used. It is that achievement in adding value which underpins the financial returns, provides the basis for its future development, and explains the remarkable returns which its shareholders have enjoyed. How these and other successful companies add value is the subject of the remainder of this book.

All jurisdictions require corporations to file annual financial statements. Stock market performance is widely tracked and the listing requirements of the principal stock exchanges impose further obligations to provide data. (US requirements are particularly stringent and many large European companies have now obtained US quotations for their shares.) European company legislation generally requires firms to disclose overall employee remuneration and other information about their workforce and employment practices. US and Japanese firms do not have similar obligations, and this restricts analysis of the structure of their added value using published information. Several commercial databases provide standardized company analyses, mainly directed at potential investors. The high-quality database maintained by Euroequities formed the basis of the analysis of Europe's most successful companies described in Tables 2.4 and 2.5; the analysis is described more fully in Davis, Flanders, and Star (1991).

Added value (called rent or super normal profit by economists) is a concept with a long intellectual history. The original analysis is that of Ricardo (1819). The notion that rent-seeking is the primary objective of industrial activity is due to Schumpeter (1943, 1961), and developed in a more recent tradition by authors such as Demsetz (1973, 1988) and Posner (1975). Explicit application to the field of business strategy can be found in the work of Stewart (1991), who uses the term 'economic value added'. The approach adopted here is developed more fully in Davis and Kay (1990), and described further in the Appendix to Chapter 13.

II

BUSINESS RELATIONSHIPS

The added value statement is not just a means of looking at the financial consequences of a firm's activities. It also describes the set of relationships which constitute the firm. These relationships include its suppliers, its customers, its employees, and its investors. The firm must have relationships with the governments of the countries in which it operates, and its performance is influenced by its relationship with its competitors. It is the totality of these relationships which defines the individual firm and creates its distinctive identity.

The first task of the management of any business organization is to ensure the consistency of its contractual relationships—to establish that the planned output can be achieved with the planned inputs of labour, capital, and materials. For each of these contractual relationships there is a corresponding financial flow. The firm receives sales revenues from its customers, makes payments to its suppliers, meets its wage bill and its tax bill, and pays a return to its investors. These are totalled and summarized in the added value statement, while the competitive environment—the relationship between the firm and its rivals—determines the degree to which added value can be created. The purpose of business activity is to put together a set of relationships which maximize that added value.

Commercial relationships are of many kinds. Some are contractual—specific and legally binding obligations which can be enforced in the courts. Others are informal, or implicit. Often contractual relationships will be supplemented, or effectively superseded, by implicit terms. Most formal agreements between firms and their competitors are illegal. These relationships are defined by the rules of the competitive game, which may be disciplined—an understanding that everyone will lose from a price war—or may be unstable, aggressive, and undisciplined. Interactions with the government are imposed through tax legislation, may be prescribed by regulation, or may involve the public sector as provider of services or user of output.

The simplest form of commercial relationship is a spot contract. Money exchanges for goods, and that both defines, and settles, the relationship. 'Sharp in by clear agreement; sharp out by clear performance' (Macneil, 1974: 738). That is how firms buy stationery, or make telephone calls.

A spot contract is a simple bilateral exchange. Each party knows what it wants, there is a shared interest in meeting these requirements, and the transaction is of a type sufficiently common and sufficiently frequent to be made on standard terms. No extensive negotiation is required. Many business relationships meet these conditions. Many do not. Consider the following examples:

- The quality of a component is vital to a firm, but it is impossible to monitor quality by inspection.
- Two firms with different standard specifications need to agree the basis of supply.
- A market opportunity is available to several firms. It is profitable if one firm enters but not if more than one does.

In the first example, the buyer cannot immediately determine what he has bought. 'Clear performance' cannot be established. In the second case, there are many agreements which might be reached, and it is not apparent which is to be preferred. In the third, there is no agreement which can be reached (and any formal agreement would probably be illegal).

There is the need for co-operation—to encourage individuals to pursue a common goal against the contrary pressures of their own self-interest. There is the problem of co-ordination. It is often important that everyone should do the same thing while precisely what it is that everyone does is hardly important at all. But there is also a need for differentiation. All different aspects of an activity need to be covered within an organization, while if all firms in a market adopt similar strategies the outcome is unlikely to be profitable for any of them.

Chapter 3 defines and describes the problems of co-operation, co-ordination, and differentiation. Chapter 4 explains how the variety of commercial contracts and relationships we observe has been developed in response to them. These two chapters are considerably more abstract than others in the book. Some readers may find that difficult, or uncongenial, or be sceptical of the relevance of such an approach. I would urge them to go on to Chapters 5 to 8; I hope they will find that the analysis there is relevant and comprehensible, but that it is also more fully illuminated by the ideas put forward in Chapters 3 and 4.

3

Co-operation and Co-ordination

This chapter is a theoretical interlude designed to introduce tools, arguments, and concepts which are used extensively in later analysis. The essence of the firm is a set of relationships among its stakeholders and between itself and other firms. This chapter is concerned to describe the principal functions of these interactions. The most important objectives of commercial relationships are co-operation (joint activity towards a shared goal), co-ordination (the need for mutually consistent responses), and differentiation (the avoidance of mutually incompatible activities).

I believe that game theory is a helpful way of describing the nature of these relationships. So while my discussion of co-operation begins from the familiar business problem of achieving success in a joint venture, I go on to explain how that issue can be described by the most famous of all games—the Prisoner's Dilemma. The objectives of co-ordination and of differentiation are represented by the Battle of the Sexes and the game of Chicken respectively. I also describe the paradox of commitment—how it is possible to gain by limiting one's own options.

One of the most important insights to be gained from this formal approach to these questions is an understanding of why it is that recognition of these management problems is such a small step on the road to their solution. Explanation of the undoubted benefits of co-operation is rarely enough to bring about co-operative behaviour. This response requires a more subtle reconciliation of the interests of the individual as individual and those of the individual as a member of a group. Achieving co-ordination and differentiation also depends on appropriate incentive structures. The discussion leads, in Chapter 4, to a description of how relationships can be structured to reduce or avoid problems of non-co-operation, disco-ordination, and inadequate differentiation.

The joint venture problem

In the last decade, many firms established joint ventures believing that the transfer of skills and expertise between them would be to their mutual advantage. In entering such an arrangement, a firm can co-operate wholeheartedly, or it can hold back. Wholehearted co-operation imposes significant costs on each firm. The firm must educate its rival. It may strengthen a potential competitor. But the potential benefits from exchange make full mutual co-operation clearly, and strongly, preferable to an outcome in which each holds back.

There is an important, and general, distinction here between perfunctory and consummate co-operation—a distinction familiar to anyone who has dealt with children or difficult employees. Perfunctory co-operation is that degree of co-operation which can be imposed, through legal agreement or the threat of sanctions. In consummate co-operation both parties work together to a mutual end, responding flexibly, sharing skills and information. The difference is the difference between a relationship with the local telephone company and a relationship with a marriage partner. Since consummate co-operation cannot be enforced by contract the question of how it is to be achieved is one of the most fundamental of management problems, and one which will recur throughout this book. Each firm will enter a joint venture uncertain about how the other will behave. If the other firm holds back, then it is clear that the best thing to do is also to hold back. But if the other firm co-operates wholeheartedly, then the best thing to do is again to hold back. Indeed, playing a cautious role oneself while receiving the full co-operation of one's partner is the most advantageous outcome. Holding back is a *dominant strategy*, which means that it is the best response whatever you expect the other party to do. But of course it is a dominant strategy for the other party also. So both partners will choose to hold back. And that is the outcome despite the evident benefits of consummate co-operation.

This paradox is known as the Prisoner's Dilemma after a story described below. It is particularly forceful because most people, on first exposure to it, fail to grasp its full nature. It seems obvious enough that without effective communication, and understanding of mutual benefits, the potential gains from co-operation will fail to be realized. What is needed is better communication and understanding. Yet the essence of the paradox is that communication and understanding do not help. The partners may fully appreciate the mutual benefits of co-operation, and recognize that the likely outcome is that they will both hold back. In discussion, they will agree that wholehearted co-operation would be best, and promise to provide it, but they will hold back nevertheless.

There are two ways in which it is possible to escape from this kind of difficulty. One is to change the structure of the pay-offs. Suppose there were to be some penalty to holding back. If the penalty were sufficiently large, it could turn consummate co-operation into a dominant strategy. If this were true for both parties, then the mutually advantageous outcome would be whole-hearted co-operation. Usually this is done by making legal contracts. The simplest transaction can have, in a trivial sense, a Prisoner's Dilemma structure—I would do better not to deliver the goods to you and you would do better not to pay for them—but we can avoid that result by making a binding agreement.

This does not work for the joint venture because a contract to co-operate fully is not one which the courts are able or willing to monitor. The alternative escape route is to establish a continuing relationship with the other party. These relational, or implicit, dimensions of business behaviour—ones which cannot be enforced through legal agreements—are of great practical importance and will recur throughout this book. In some less developed countries, where managers and individuals are unable to make binding commitments to each other, Prisoner's Dilemma outcomes are very widespread and a serious obstacle to doing business.

The Prisoner's Dilemma—the problem of co-operation

Problems such as the joint venture can be analysed in a more formal way using the language of game theory. This language is a means of giving precision to the intuitions which we all have about the outcomes of these situations. The games are best regarded as extended metaphors—never to be taken literally, or implemented directly, but capable of focusing attention on different aspects of why strategic interactions so often produce results that were no one's intention.

The metaphor that makes the Prisoner's Dilemma such a well-remembered game is based on the following story, due to Albert Tucker. Two prisoners are arrested and put in separate cells. The sheriff admits he has no real evidence but presents the following alternatives. If one confesses, he or she will go free, and the other can expect a ten-year goal sentence. If both confess, each will be convicted, but can expect a lighter sentence—seven years perhaps. If neither confesses, the likely outcome is a short one-year sentence for each on a trumped up charge.

Fig. 3.1 shows the possible outcomes of this game. Each partner has the choice of confessing, or not confessing, and the pay-off to each strategy depends on what the other party chooses to do. A structure such as Fig. 3.1—a *pay-off matrix*—is a simple way of describing this kind of interdependence. Since the pay-off is imprisonment, higher numbers are worse. Prisoner 1 is uncertain what his collaborator in crime will do, but notes that if she confesses, he will get seven-years by confessing and ten for remaining silent; if she does not confess, he will go free with a confession and otherwise serve a year in gaol. So whatever his conjecture about her actions, he does better to confess, and so does she. Both go to gaol for seven years.

Despite the fanciful nature of the example, the Prisoner's Dilemma is a real

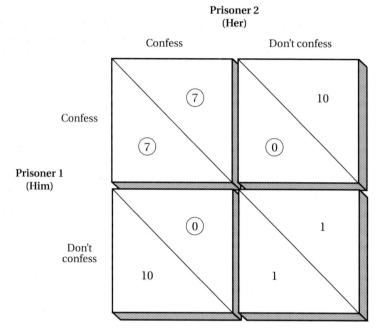

In each quadrant, the bottom left pay-off is for player 1 and the upper right for player 2. Circles indicate that a pay-off is the best outcome for that player given the strategy of the other.

Fig. 3.1. The Prisoner's Dilemma

problem with daily business application. Several instances will be developed at greater length in later chapters of this book. One—which is at the heart of the joint venture problem—is the problem of sharing information. That problem arises both within organizations, and between firms at different points of the supply chain. Typically, the best overall outcome both collectively and individually, is achieved by free and frank exchange of information; yet there are almost always strategic gains to be made by withholding part of the picture. The problem of signalling product quality where the buyer cannot immediately assess the product being purchased is another Prisoner's Dilemma. The danger is that the purchaser expects low quality and the seller's incentive is to meet these expectations. Price behaviour between competitors poses a Prisoner's Dilemma. All firms have a common interest in avoiding a price war; each firm has an individual interest in undercutting its rivals.

We experience the Prisoner's Dilemma in our social and economic lives as well as in our business experience. We drop litter in the street although we know it would be better for all of us if no one did, we demand wage increases in excess of inflation although we recognize that inflation can only fall if we

show restraint. Those politicians who bemoan the irrationality of the outcome have failed to understand the issue. The problem—and the paradox of
the Prisoner's Dilemma—is not that we fail to recognize where our best interests lie. The problem is that we do.

Repeating the game

The Prisoner's Dilemma may be resolved if the game is repeated. This is not
simply a question of learning by experience. Suppose we have both encountered the Prisoner's Dilemma, reached its inevitable outcome, and spent our
seven years in goal. Released, we commit the same crime again and are faced
with the same proposal. You might think that, chastened by our previous
experience, we might choose not to confess this time. But the same remorse-
less logic applies. If I believe you are likely to listen to the lessons of experience, and refrain from confessing, then I will confess. If I believe you will
confess, then the best strategy for me is to confess. Another seven years
imprisonment is in prospect for each of us.

So repetition does not, in itself, produce learning. But the prospect of repetition can modify behaviour, by allowing strategies to be developed in which
future behaviour is conditional on past performance. Suppose the two players
know that they will play the game twice. One prisoner makes the following
suggestion as they are taken to the police station. I will not confess this time. I
suggest you do the same. Whatever you do on this occasion, I will do on the
second. If you squeal, so will I, if you stay silent, so will I. The proposal makes
the prisoner's choice more complex. But the problem is that the offer is not
credible. A credible strategy is one which it pays to carry out, and the strategy
proposed here does not have this property. It pays to promise not to confess,
but once the promise is made, the rational action is to break the promise.

Theoretically, this would be true even if the game were to be played one
thousand times. Both players are sure to confess on the thousandth game, so
they might as well confess on the nine hundred and ninety-ninth, and so on.
But actually experimental evidence shows that people do not behave like that,
probably because a thousand times is so many that no one is certain how long
the game will really last. In repeated trials of the Prisoner's Dilemma, players
mostly reach co-operative solutions.

These experiments have identified some of the key features of successful
co-operative strategies in repeated games. They are nice—they begin by
expecting that the other player will co-operate, not that he or she will cheat.
But they respond to bad behaviour and punish it. Yet they are forgiving. Non-
co-operative behaviour should be punished, but not too severely. Tit for tat is
a strategy with these properties—I do what you did last time, I respond to
your deviant behaviour but allow you to correct it.

A repeated game strategy establishes a relationship between the two players. Each behaves in a way which is conditioned by previous experience of the

other player and by expectations as to how he or she will behave in future. The existence of a past and a future implies that it makes sense to behave in ways which are not the best for either player in the short run. It always pays to confess, but not doing so is to everyone's long-term benefit. Only the creation of a long-term relationship can achieve that outcome.

This is how the joint venture problem is generally resolved in practice. The decision must be turned into a reiterated game. So you seek to break the process down into a sequence of small steps. You use the early meetings to explore each other's attitudes. You offer wholehearted co-operation and await a response. If the other side fails to reciprocate, then the losses are not very great and you can hold back in future. If the other side does respond, then you continue to be wholehearted in your co-operation. In this piecemeal way, trust between the parties can develop, and you may succeed in establishing a co-operative relationship.

An important feature of this solution is that both parties expect the venture to continue. If it is likely to come to an end, each party begins to see the benefits of holding something back, of behaving strategically rather than of maximizing the joint gains from the venture. The relationship begins to fray at the edges. Indeed, the possibility that such an outcome will eventually emerge may poison the atmosphere between the parties from the outset. Joint ventures are much more likely to succeed if they are perceived as a preliminary to more intimate co-operation than as finite activities.

Changing the payoffs

There is another means of resolving the Prisoner's Dilemma, and games like it. That is to change the structure of pay-offs themselves. This is how criminals themselves deal with the issue. In Fig. 3.1 the prisoner who confesses while the other does not escapes scot-free. But suppose instead the likely consequence is a visit from the friends of the person who is serving ten years in goal, with consequences that could certainly be as bad as a five-year sentence. Then the new game is shown in Fig. 3.2.

What is the outcome in this revised structure? Here the best strategy for each player depends on what the other player chooses. If prisoner 2 confesses, prisoner 1 does better to confess also—a seven-year sentence rather than a ten-year sentence. If prisoner 1 does not confess, prisoner 2 is also better not confessing. A one-year goal term is preferable to a long period in hospital. This interdependence—in which not only is the outcome for me dependent on what others do, but the best strategy for me is dependent on what others do—is characteristic of most real business situations. The Prisoner's Dilemma is unusual in having a dominant strategy equilibrium— the best strategy is best regardless of the choice of the other player—and that is what lends force to the paradox.

In the absence of a dominant strategy, each player must estimate the

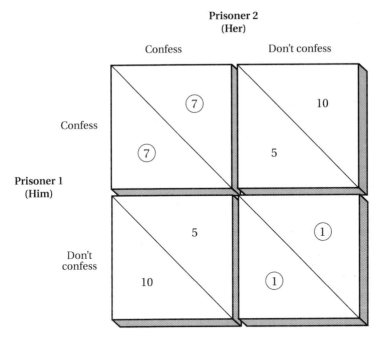

**Prisoner 2
(Her)**

Confess   Don't confess

Confess

Prisoner 1
(Him)

Don't
confess

7   7

10   5

5   10

1   1

Fig. 3.2. The Criminal's Revenge

other's likely response. If espionage is ruled out, the best approach is to put yourself in your rival's shoes. What would you choose if you were her? If *she* has a dominant strategy, that is easy, and you can simply choose the best outcome for yourself given her dominant strategy. But that is not true in this game, or in most; her action depends on her anticipation of your actions.

But of course you know what *you* plan to do, so you can find what would be her best response given that knowledge. And then you test your own strategy; is it a good one in the light of that response? If it is, then you have found what is known as a *Nash equilibrium*. The characteristic of a Nash equilibrium is that each player is making the best response given what the other player has chosen to do. And in the Criminal's Revenge, not confessing is a Nash equilibrium outcome. If player 1 does not confess, not confessing is the best strategy for player 2, and vice versa. Both go to gaol for a year.

Types of equilibrium

In the late 1980s, a British professional services firm was contemplating a merger or association with a German partner. Several potential German allies had made approaches, but the British firm was reluctant. It was a leader in its industry, and the English market for its services was more developed than the German one. It suspected that far more work would be referred from London to Frankfurt than from Frankfurt to London, and so it reckoned that a German firm had more to gain from an alliance with an English firm of comparable status than its English partner. In a German alliance, the English firm was likely to give more than it got. But its weaker English competitors were also being approached by German firms. If there had to be alliances, a strong partner was definitely better than a weaker one.

The pay-off matrix for this game, as the English firm saw it, is set out in Fig. 3.3. There were strong, and valid, arguments put to the English firm for staying clear of all German partners. But Fig. 3.3 demonstrates that that is not a viable approach. Forming an alliance—with someone—is a dominant strategy for the German firm. The game has one Nash equilibrium—the English firm takes the strong German firm as a partner—and that is what indeed transpired. Each firm decided to choose the best course available given the anticipated actions of the other players, and the English firm entered negotiations with its potential partner.

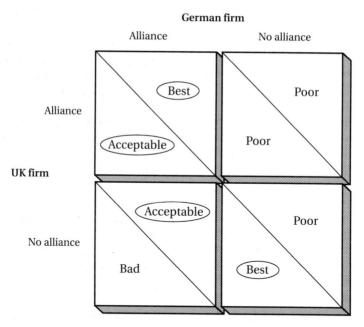

Fig. 3.3. Mergers and Alliances

Although the Nash equilibrium was the outcome in that case, there is nothing that guarantees either that a game will have a Nash equilibrium, or that it will have only one, or that if there is one the parties will reach it. A Nash equilibrium is a much less certain outcome than a dominant strategy equilibrium.

What if I am not confident that we both see the game in the same way—something which is often true of almost all the business games we play in real life? Then I may be uncertain that my opponent will adopt what I perceive as her best strategy, and she may have the same concerns about me. If so, we may fail to achieve a Nash equilibrium.

The problem of co-ordination

The Criminal's Revenge has two Nash equilibria. Confess–confess is a Nash equilibrium also, because if player 1 confesses, confessing is the best strategy for player 2, and vice versa. It is not certain that one Nash equilibrium will be reached rather than the other, even though it is obvious that one is better than the other, or even that any Nash equilibrium will be the solution. Perhaps the best that can be said is that games are less likely to reach outcomes which are not Nash equilibria, because players certainly have incentives to deviate from them. If the UK firm had opened discussions with a weaker German partner, it would have provoked an approach from the stronger German firm, since the top left-hand outcome is better for both than the top right.

So communication does help here. If we discuss the problem beforehand, we can both agree that not confess–not confess would be a better outcome than confess–confess. And if we believe from that discussion that the other is likely to act sensibly, then we have no incentive to depart from the not confess–not confess outcome. There is a fundamental difference here between the Criminal's Revenge and the Prisoner's Dilemma. In the Prisoner's Dilemma we can agree that not confess–not confess is the best outcome and yet it pays us, individually, to depart from it. In the Criminal's Revenge, the structure of individual self-interest now supports the outcome that is best for everyone.

But what if all the possible Nash equilibria are just about as good as each other? This is the common problem of co-ordination and it is characterized in the following way. There are several ways in which an activity which requires input from several individuals or groups can be performed, all of them more or less equally satisfactory. Each group can make decisions independently, yet the achievement of any workable outcome requires them to do much the same thing.

The metaphor that is used here is known as the Battle of the Sexes. A man and a woman are planning an evening out. He would prefer to go to the knitting demonstration, and she would rather go to the sumo wrestling, but each would rather be together than apart. The worst possible outcome, obviously, is that he ends up at the wrestling and she at the knitting demonstration. The pay-off matrix for this game is shown in Fig. 3.4.

This game, like the Criminal's Revenge, has two Nash equilibria: both end up at the sumo, or both end up at the knitting. But unlike the Criminal's

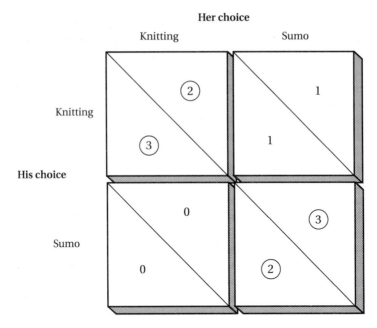

Fig. 3.4. The Battle of the Sexes

Revenge, there is no reason to think that one is better than the other. Which is the solution to the game? Take first the case where the two partners are unable to communicate with each other, and must make their own decisions, hoping to meet the other at the selected venue. Do you behave selfishly, hoping the other will not? Or do you go to your second choice, knowing that there is a real risk that you will both end up with a wasted evening?

Suppose the two partners do have an opportunity to discuss the matter. Communication may help to dispose of obviously bad outcomes—as with the Criminal's Revenge—but no more. It probably enables us to exclude the outcome in which he goes to the sumo and she to the knitting, but that is as far as it goes. Everyone can reproduce, both from business life and social life, the ineffectual discussion in which each group states its preferences and each group offers to give way. The Battle of the Sexes is a game with no apparent solution, which is no doubt how it got its name.

And yet it is a game with almost too many business applications to list; from the choice of the corporate logo and the determination of normal working hours to the relationships between the firm and its suppliers and subcontractors. Every one of these demands co-ordinated responses, and yet each poses a question on which there will be different views on the appropriate co-ordinated response.

There are two ways of escaping from the Battle of the Sexes: *commitment and hierarchy*. Prior commitment is another means of resolving battles of the sexes. What is needed is simply something to break the symmetry—to distinguish one Nash equilibrium from others. If we already have two tickets to the sumo, that settles it. If we always go to the knitting, that settles it too.

Hierarchy breaks the essential symmetry of the problem by putting one of the two partners in charge. He decides where the couple goes, or perhaps she does. The main contractor determines the specification and timetable. The chief executive makes the decision on the logo, the personnel director on the hours of work. There is an issue of some subtlety here. One-way communication—an order—is preferable to two-way communication—a discussion. Hierarchy is necessary as a means of resolving the problem of co-ordination, not because of the superior wisdom of the decision-maker or the greater significance of his (or her) preferences. The principal reason for giving authority to a chief executive is not to enable everyone in the organization to benefit from that person's unique insights, but because the most important requirement is simply that somebody should decide. Seniority systems—in which high positions are achieved by length of service rather than by merit—have the advantage that they make this very clear, both to those who wield authority and to those who are subject to it. So do systems of hereditary authority, which were once common in business as in politics. Business structures which emphasize seniority—as in Japan or Germany—often find problems of co-ordination easier to handle.

Commitment

Both the Prisoner's Dilemma and the Battle of the Sexes suggest that there are potential gains from commitment. Managers often emphasize the need for flexibility and the merits of keeping options open. They are often right. But there are also advantages in being able to make commitments. There are gains from being able to close your options as well as gains from keeping them open.

Look more carefully at how commitment resolves the Prisoner's Dilemma. At first sight, the best situation for me is one in which the other party commits herself, but I do not. Suppose I know that she is perfectly truthful and reliable, and that if she pledges herself not to confess, or to confess, I can rely on her word. For my part, I prefer to keep my freedom of manoeuvre.

In any preliminary discussion, we can quickly agree that we would both be better off if neither were to confess. I invite her to commit herself not to confess. She asks herself what I would be likely to do if she makes, and keeps, that commitment, and the answer is clear—I will confess. In that case, she will be better off confessing herself. So she chooses not to make the commitment in the first place. It is not only important to me that she should be able to commit herself. It is important to me that I should be able to commit myself.

The joint venture game can be seen in the same terms. Suppose one party has a reputation for wholehearted co-operation, while the other prefers to retain flexibility. The likely outcome is that although the first party could commit to the relationship, it chooses not to. The gains come not only from the ability to commit other people, but from being able to commit yourself. In the Prisoner's Dilemma game, if you too can offer a commitment not to confess, you will both reach the not confess–not confess outcome. If the commitment is available from one side but not the other, then the outcome is that both confess. The gains from flexibility are illusory. And the same is true in the joint venture. If you wait and see, the unavoidable outcome is that you will not like what you see.

The opportunity to make binding commitments is the central function of a system of contract law, and there do not seem to be any examples of industrial societies which have flourished without such a system. Yet the courts are not the only—or often the most important—means of enforcing commitments. In frontier societies, or even in parts of modern Italy, respect for central authority is weak. There, local codes, supported by social rather than legal sanctions, enable people to make effective commitments. And these mechanisms are important everywhere because there are many things which the courts cannot enforce. The law can force you to deliver goods, or try to make you deliver goods, but it cannot elicit your wholehearted co-operation, or insist that you respond flexibly to changes in conditions of demand and supply. And as modern economies evolve, the features of relationships which cannot be legally enforced come to matter more than the ones which can.

When William the Conqueror invaded England, he burnt his boats on landing.[1] There are two reasons why this made sense. One is that he wished to commit his soldiers—to deny them the option of fleeing. The second, and more interesting, is that it enabled him to commit himself. To see this, look at the series of decisions in Fig. 3.5. The first choice to be made is King Harold's— to submit to Norman rule or to fight William at Hastings. If the two armies fight, William may win or lose. If William wins, the English may submit or continue to resist. If William loses, he may quit, or attempt to fight on. This is known as an *extensive form* game, in which players move sequentially depending on the outcome of earlier moves. The best outcome from an English perspective is clearly that William should be defeated at Hastings and quit; the best from a Norman standpoint that the English should capitulate immediately, and failing that, they should submit after being defeated at Hastings. By cutting off the option of quitting, William rules out the best option for the English, and also increases the cost to the English of continuing to resist after an unsuccessful outcome at Hastings, since there is now no chance that such resistance will persuade him to withdraw. Win or lose, the outcome of Hastings is less attractive to the English. By burning his boats, William believes that he will increase the probability that the English will submit immediately, and, failing that, he also increases the probability that they will capitulate after a successful outcome at Hastings. The rest is history, of a sort.

1 Actually he didn't, but the story is a good one and widely repeated.

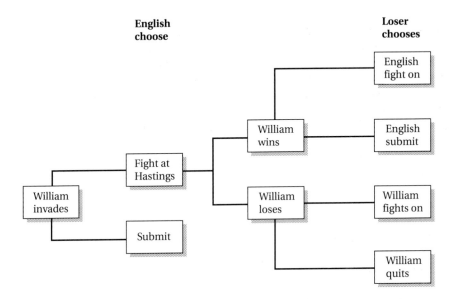

Fig. 3.5. The Norman Conquest

William was a successful entrant into a new market and the lessons of his success stand for anyone who would now essay market entry. William won, in part, because the strength of his commitment to the invasion of England was credible. The English lost, in part, because the strength of their commitment to fight on was not.

If commitment is a valuable tool, then inability to make commitments may prove costly. The Prisoner's Dilemma arises from the inability of the prisoners to make credible promises not to confess. Governments have often pledged themselves not to negotiate with terrorists who take hostages. The extensive form game of Fig. 3.6 makes clear why. If we rule out the option of negotiation, terrorists are worse off if they take a hostage than if they do not. So they do not take a hostage, the government has no choice to make, and it obtains its desired outcome. Unfortunately, the government's commitment is not *credible*. While it makes sense for it to say that it will not negotiate, once the hostage is actually taken the government will usually prefer to negotiate than to stand firm. That is what governments have mostly done, and, unfortunately, terrorists know this.

Voluntary commitment in business takes many forms. Firms often make a public commitment to a market. They incur expenditures which are of value only in relation to that particular market in order to persuade potential customers of their quality or their ability to provide service in the long run. Firms make gratuitous commitments to customers or to suppliers when they invest in a relationship in order to induce the customer or the supplier to make a tangible commitment, perhaps by investing in training or in assets. And there

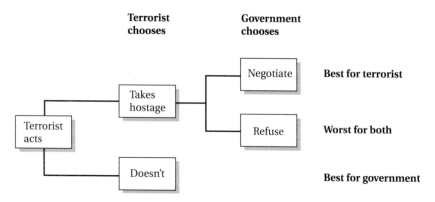

Fig. 3.6. Taking a Hostage

may also be opportunities to make commitments to competitors. Subsequent chapters will describe commitments of all these types.

Chicken: the problem of differentiation

In 1986, deregulation of London financial markets allowed any firm to offer its services as a market maker in government bonds. Twenty-eight firms—representing most of the major banks of the world—decided to do so. Taken as a whole, the London bond market is the largest of any financial centre and the market in British government securities is a key part of it. It was obvious to every participant that the market could not conceivably be profitable with twenty-eight firms in it. But not to enter would have been to cede an important and potentially lucrative market to rivals. Five years later, eighteen firms are still in business and the cumulative losses of them all have been put at around £1 billion.

The banks which participated—and those banks which decided not to, or subsequently quit—were engaged in a war of attrition. A war of attrition is one example of a class of games which I shall call Chicken games. The essence of these games is that a strategy is rewarding if used by one player but disastrous if employed by all. If the Battle of the Sexes is the archetypal game of coordination, Chicken is the archetypal game of differentiation.

Because of their dramatic structure, Chicken games have a fascination for movie-makers, and the classic war of attrition is found in the James Dean film of the 1950s, *Rebel Without a Cause*. The Dean version is particularly difficult to analyse and the game considered here is to be found in a more recent movie, *Stand by Me*. The rules are the following. Two vehicles drive towards each other, waiting for one to swerve. The winner is the player who sticks while the other swerves. If both swerve, they are poor players of Chicken. If neither does, they may not have an opportunity to play Chicken again. The pay-offs are shown in Fig. 3.7.

Chicken is another game with two Nash equilibria. In each, one player swerves and the other sticks. But that is not much help, because it does not identify which player is which. Nor does communication help, because what each player should do is proclaim absolute determination to stick. Here too, commitment may help; one suggestion is that one player should tear off the steering wheel and throw it out the window. If the other driver sees the commitment, then the result is clear. So might reputation, though it did not do enough for Dean's opponent.

But if this is not an available option (and it often is not—the list of firms which have announced they were committed to staying in a particular market is materially longer than the list of firms which have actually done it), what is the solution? A feature of Chicken is that it is a game with a solution in *mixed strategies*. That means that you should sometimes swerve and sometimes stick.

The idea that it may make sense to randomize behaviour is quite difficult to accept. Yet it seems to be central to the differentiation problem. One way to understand why differentiation benefits from randomization is to think of games in which the only solutions are in mixed strategies. The childhood game of stone-scissors-paper (in which both players choose an object simultaneously and paper covers stone, stone sharpens scissors, and scissors cut paper) is a good example. There random behaviour is the only possible way to play and any systematic strategy is a loser. The game of Chicken described in Fig. 3.7 has a very specific equilibrium in mixed strategies, with each player

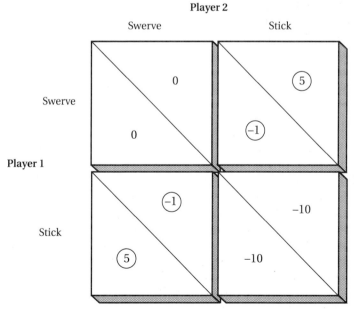

Fig. 3.7. Chicken

swerving nine times and sticking five times in fourteen tries. If they do this, the two players crash around one time in ten and win nearly one time in three and—most surprising of all—it actually pays to enter the game. If they were to repeat the game many times, the overall outcome would be positive. Yet that should not dispel the strong feeling that everyone has on encountering the game of Chicken—you should not be playing this game at all. You should be trying to change the pay-off structure, to improve the odds, or to transform the game into one which is repeated or has an extensive form.

Some lessons of game theory

The games described above are all, in an obvious sense, pathological. Although they describe social and business situations we all encounter, they all describe interactions which lead to perverse results. In the Prisoner's Dilemma, the players are driven to select an outcome that everyone recognizes as inferior. In the Battle of the Sexes, it is not clear that there is any outcome at all unless we change the structure of the game. And Chicken seems to have a solution but it is one in which no one can feel in control and the outcome is clearly unsatisfactory. Yet these issues of co-operation, co-ordination, and differentiation are fundamental to business life.

The precision of the game theoretic approach makes clear some fundamental problems in the strategic interactions between individuals, groups, and firms. The problems which arise in these games are not the result of any lack of goodwill or understanding on the part of the players, or of any failure to perceive the benefits of co-operative or co-ordinated action. Individuals can fully appreciate the benefits of co-ordinated action or co-operative behaviour and yet fail to realize them. Firms can recognize the dangers of insufficient differentiation and still fall victim. One of the tasks of management is to structure, and restructure, situations so that these problems are less likely to arise. Later chapters of this book describe practical applications of the various mechanisms—long-term relationships, reputation, and commitment—which have been developed to overcome the problems which are inherent in these pathological games.

Talk of relationships, reputations, and commitment has a slightly old-fashioned ring. It dates from an older business tradition which has been supplanted by a more aggressive individualism; a world in which, it is suggested, we can no longer afford these kinds of self-imposed restraints. The truth is that these are mechanisms which have evolved over centuries as means of dealing with problems in social and commercial relationships which have always been recognized, and these games do no more than formalize them. They are mechanisms we discard at our peril.

Chapters 3, 4, and 5 are concerned respectively with game theory, with the analysis of contracts, and with the value of a structure of relational contracts as a system of business organization. Each of these subjects has a major literature of its own, which is discussed under the appropriate headings. But the common theme throughout is that Contract structure, and therefore organizational form, must be adapted to the characteristics of the transactions which that structure and that form handle.

This general argument derives from *transaction cost economics*, a subject whose major proponent is Oliver Williamson; see, in particular, Williamson (1975, 1985, 1986). Williamson is the most important recent contributor to an organizational tradition in economics which, slightly apart from the mainstream of economic thought, can be traced through writers such as Coase (1937), Arrow (1974), Hirschman (1982), Milgrom and Roberts (1992). Williamson and Winter (1991) survey this tradition. Perrow (1986) is a standard critique of this approach.

The concept of the firm as a collection of contracts originates with Alchian and Demsetz (1972) and is extended by Klein (1983). This perspective is often contrasted with the transactions cost approach (as, for example, by Johanson and Mattson (1987)) but the presentation here illustrates the essential complementarity of the two approaches.

The theory of games originates with von Neumann and Morgenstern (1944). There are many good non-technical accounts of game theory. A recent, and outstanding, one is Dixit and Nalebuff (1991). As I have tried to do here, the authors use games to motivate structured thinking about general problems of interaction and interrelationship. Other textbooks (in ascending order of difficulty) are Luce and Raiffa (1957), Rasmusen (1989), and Tirole (1988). Vickers (1985) is a helpful introduction to business applications of game theory. Fudenberg and Tirole (1987) and Fisher (1989) offer divergent views of the value of game theory in these contexts.

The Nash equilibrium was defined in Nash (1950, 1953). A discussion of the variety of alternative solution concepts which have been proposed is found in Harsanyi and Selten (1988). Each of the principal games described here has a literature of its own. Axelrod (1984) explores experiments in the Prisoner's Dilemma and its applications across a wide range of disciplines. Cooper *et al.* (1989) describe experiments in the Battle of the Sexes. Commitment and its business applications are emphasized in Ghemawat (1991).

4

Relationships and Contracts

As in Chapter 3, my purpose here is to develop concepts which are applied in later chapters. Firms establish many different kinds of commercial relationships. The most common is the spot contract—an agreement for immediate exchange. But many important relationships are made as classical contracts—long-term, legal agreements which contain detailed provisions as to how dealings between the parties will evolve as events unfold. A relational contract is also a long-term relationship. But its provisions are often only partly specified and it is enforced, not by legal process, but by the need the parties have to go on doing business with each other.

  Sometimes one of these contract forms is appropriate, sometimes another. Long-term contracts are necessary when both parties must make specific commitments to the relationship. But there are many cases where such commitments are necessary but the critical terms of an agreement cannot be enforced by the courts. This is most often true when timely flows of honest information between the parties are essential or where flexible response is required in circumstances which cannot be fully anticipated. Here relational contracts come into their own. Marriage is a long-term contract, but best conducted as a relational one, and the same is often true in business dealings. Some business environments are conducive to relational contracting. Others allow or encourage opportunistic behaviour. These differences between firms, and between commercial cultures, are important to the nature of competitive advantage in firms and nations.

Most business relationships are made on the basis of spot contracts. I sell, you buy, and that is that. We might, or might not, engage in a similar transaction next week, or next year. Spot contracts are easy to make and cheap to transact. Spot contracts do not need lengthy negotiation. Nor are expensive lawyers called to draft their provisions. Spot contracts are based on standard terms and take place at market prices.

We make so many spot contracts that we often hardly think of them as contracts at all, and the law infers a contractual intention from our behaviour. When I buy a lettuce from a greengrocer, it is as if I say to the greengrocer's assistant, 'I offer to buy this lettuce at the price displayed' and he or she replies, 'As an authorized representative of the greengrocer, I accept your offer.' Even lawyers do not actually conduct these conversations. But if there is any subsequent dispute, the courts will act as though such an exchange took place. It is most unlikely that there will be a subsequent dispute. The transaction is complete, and there is not much left to have a dispute about. And the unit value of a lettuce is so low that it is not worth either party's while to engage in litigation. If I buy a rotten lettuce from my local greengrocer, then next time I shop elsewhere. If I buy a disappointing peach from a street market when on holiday, then I write my losses off to experience.

But although spot contracts form a majority—by number—of business relationships, the most important of commercial relationships are rarely spot contracts. Managers do not raise finance, rent property, hire senior employees, or deal with their principal suppliers through spot contracts. Although spot contracts predominate by number in business portfolios they rarely predominate by value. Spot contracts are effective when individually selfish behaviour works to the best joint interest of the parties. I have, you want, we exchange. We may need to haggle a little over terms but that is all. But many relationships require co-operation or co-ordination or differentiation, or benefit from commitment. Both parties do better if they pursue a recognized joint interest, or they need to agree to do the same thing, or different things. Such relationships run the danger of falling victim to the Prisoner's Dilemma, the Battle of the Sexes, or Chicken.

Chapter 3 showed how these problems can often be resolved by changing the pay-off structure or by engaging in a repeated game. In either case, the behaviour of each party is conditional on the earlier behaviour of the other. That means that the contract becomes *contingent*—it contains statements of the form 'if x then y'—and it acquires a time dimension and so becomes a long-term contract. These interrelated features distinguish *classical* and *relational* contracts from spot contracts. Classical contracts are *explicit*—they correspond to changes in the pay-off structure—and relational contracts are *implicit*—they are expressions of strategies for playing a repeated game.

The weakness of spot contracts

Why do firms make long-term classical contracts for their accommodation, but buy paper clips with a spot contract? Properties are very individual commodities. Most people bought their houses because they suited their own particular needs. The same is often true of business premises. If the firm were evicted tomorrow, it could find a substitute, but an imperfect one. And a property is a large purchase. The rent bill is the largest single payment which

Illustration 4.1. Three Spot Contracts

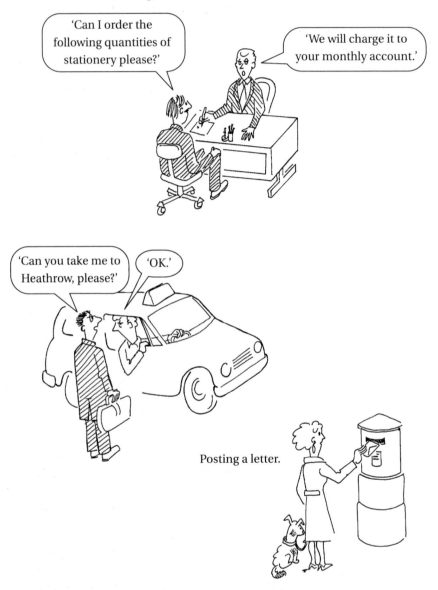

Posting a letter.

many firms make to any supplier. The contract is important, and if you have made a shrewd deal you would like to be sure you can get an equally good one tomorrow. And the same is true for the landlord. A vacant property may lead to significant loss of income. Both sides to the bargain value the certainty provided by a long-term relationship.

There is another reason for entering a long-term relationship. If a company moves into an office, it will print stationery with its address. It may buy furniture to fit. It will install a telephone and computer system. In all these ways it incurs substantial expenditures which are specific to that office and that address. Before a firm moves in, it probably has the choice of many equally good properties. But after it moves in, the property selected will be much preferred to any likely alternative. That gives the landlord a strong bargaining position. Under a system of spot contracts, the landlord could promise a low rent and then attempt to increase it after the tenant had made a commitment to the property. Knowing that this might happen, the tenant would be reluctant to move in at all. Whenever there are expenditures which are specific to the individual buyer or seller, then there is scope for such opportunistic behaviour. A long-term relationship protects the tenant against opportunism by the landlord.

Illustration 4.2. Two Classical Contracts

The property lease	British major works contract for highway construction
Typical length: 10,000–15,000 words	Standard form (excluding actual specification of works) is 76 pages.
Provides for:	Provides for:
• Period of tenure • Rent • Repair and maintenance obligations • Use of premises • Rights of assignment • Basis of adjustment to rent • Rights to regain occupancy • Basis of resolution of dispute	• Details of works to be performed (attached as schedule) • Quality of materials • Contract duration • Payment schedules • Anti-corruption measures • Rights to patents and royalties • Financial performance bonds

And the landlord may feel the same. The landlord will incur costs if the tenant moves out abruptly. Agents' fees will be incurred to find a new tenant and rent lost in the interim. By threatening to move out and impose these costs, the tenant might hope to renegotiate a lower rent. A long-term relationship protects the landlord against such opportunism by the tenant.

These business relationships require investment which is specific to the relationship. Sometimes such investment is tangible. Specialist sub-contractors manufacturing automobile components may need to dedicate tooling to the production of an item designed to the requirements of an individual assembler. A petrol retailer must brand the forecourt in the Shell or Esso style. Often the investment is intangible—the firm needs to learn its customers' systems or their specialist requirements. The McDonald's franchisee needs to learn the McDonald's manuals, the solicitor or accountant can advise effectively only after getting to know the client. The sharing of information may be important to making the best of the relationship, yet frankness may leave the parties to a spot contract exposed and in a weak position to negotiate good terms. It is obvious that banking and insurance will work to the best advantage of everyone in the long run if banks and insurance companies are well informed about the nature of the risks they assume. Yet in every spot contract with a bank or insurance company the borrower or the insured has an incentive to represent the position in the best possible light.

Asset specificity—the need to dedicate investment to a particular transaction or business relationship—is an important reason for making long-term contracts, but not the only one. If there are few buyers or sellers of a particular commodity, it is risky to rely on spot contracts. You cannot be sure—as you can be sure in a wider market—that there will be a continuing stream of sellers or buyers ready to supply, or to purchase your output, at a fair price. So standard commodities are bought on spot contracts, but managers look for longer-term arrangements for specialized components.

Illustration 4.3. Spot and Long-Term Contracts

Common spot contracts	Common long-term contracts
Standard components	Customized components
Capital goods purchase	Capital goods finance
Variable rate finance	Fixed rate finance

It is often supposed that long-term assets require the support of long-term contracts. In reality, the scope of spot contracts is surprisingly wide. A firm may buy business stationery every month and a shopper visit the local supermarket every week, but it is likely that they will make a separate spot contract with the stationer and the supermarket on each occasion. The stationery supplier will set up a distribution system and retailers will build their supermarket without any long-term contracts whatever for selling their output. Both parties are willing to make substantial capital expenditures which rely entirely on a succession of spot contracts for their viability. A good taxi-cab will last ten years, but all cab drivers make spot contracts with their passengers. Indeed, spot contracts are intrinsic to the service that taxi-cabs provide. Much business is conducted using long lived assets financed by revenues earned from spot contracts.

Long-term relationships are necessary to secure co-operative, or co-ordinated, behaviour. Mutual commitments are essential, or information flows are important, or flexible response is necessary, and the parties cannot achieve what they need by simple bilateral exchange. Long-term relationships with competitors are needed if Chicken games are to be avoided, or disastrous outcomes to them averted. Sometimes these long-term relationships are best established through classical contracts—formal, binding, legal arrangements. Sometimes they are better accomplished by relational contracts—tacit agreements between the parties which are enforced, not through legal processes, but through the shared needs of the parties to go on doing business with each other.

Relational contracts

What legal theorists call a relational contract is termed an implicit contract by economists and a trust relationship by sociologists. All these terms denote important aspects of these arrangements. The enforcement mechanism is between the parties themselves, not through the courts—the lawyer's formulation stresses this. The terms of the relationship are not written down, and often cannot be precisely articulated—hence the term implicit contract. And the relationship depends on trust between the parties and is—in the terms in which the word is commonly used—not a contract at all.

The most familiar of relational contracts is the marriage contract. The contract is intended to be long-term, and generally is. Most of its rights and duties are implicit. The remainder fall to be determined by agreement between the parties. The courts provide a means by which the parties to the contract can escape from it, but so long as it remains in force they will generally be uninterested in enforcing its terms.

To see why a relational contract is used here, it is only necessary to look at attempts to define marriage through a classical contract (Illustration 4.4). The Canadian contract is, no doubt, an effective contract; it just does not cover any important aspects of the relationship. The American contract does seek to do that, but anyone who reads it knows that such an agreement is not going to work. The attempt to define the arrangement in these terms denies its essence. It sacrifices the responsiveness and frankness which is at the heart of a successful personal relationship. There the parties trust each other not to abuse the opportunities which such openness creates and acknowledge that the disadvantages of a detailed specification of rights and mutual obligations would far outweigh the benefits of clarity about what these rights and obligations are. Most people enter marriage on the basis that it is far more important—even from their own selfish perspective—to maximize the joint welfare than to maximize their share of it through hard negotiation with their partner. They look for a larger cake rather than a larger slice.

Employment contracts are largely relational contracts. As with all business arrangements, there is a formal legal contract. But this is not the substantive agreement, and usually its provisions only become relevant when the relational contract is terminated by one party or the other. So important are the relational elements of an employment contract that 'working to rule'—strict observance of the terms of the legal contract—is often used as a form of industrial action, and can be seriously disruptive. Relational contracts will usually have a legal heart, but there is a relational contract when the

Illustration 4.4. Marriage Contracts

Extracts from a Canadian marriage contract

In consideration of the mutual love and affection of the husband and wife, they agree as follows:

1. The spouses acknowledge that, except as set out in this Marriage Contract, Part I of the Family Law Act, 1986, SO 1986, Chapter 4, as amended from time to time will apply to them . . .
2. The spouses acknowledge that this Marriage Contract is not to be construed as a bar now or at any time in the future to the spouses entering into other Marriage Contracts or other domestic contracts . . .
6. If there is any dispute as to the ownership of Property, title to any Property shall be conclusive proof of the separate ownership of the Property . . .

Extracts from an American marriage contract

Relationships with others, jealousy, and trust

The parties agree to discuss plans for activities that involve persons of the opposite sex when the other party is not involved, and where such activities are not directly a part of one's work.

They also agree to allow each other the power to veto such activities for a six month period . . .

Realising that trust is built by practical arrangements as well as by good intentions, the parties also agree to set aside one evening during the week and one evening each weekend to spend alone together . . . A calendar will be posted two months in advance.

Care and use of the home

The household work schedule now in effect, which assigns household tasks . . . will be attached as a modifiable amendment to this agreement . . .

The parties agree to continue their current practice of assigning one person the task of inspecting household work for cleanliness and neatness. Once a month, when Robert is inspector, we will conform to his standards. He will conform to the standards set by the other three inspectors in their weeks.

Source: The Law Society, *Maintenance and Capital Provision on Divorce*, London, 1991.

commercial reality is different. In a relational contract, the parties have expectations of each other which go beyond—perhaps far beyond—the terms of the contract.

Employment contracts are best made as relational contracts because they suffer rather than benefit from too precise a specification of obligations. Each party must be encouraged to respond to events. Both parties invest in teaching and learning which is specific to the particular business environment. Actions may often have consequences which only emerge much later. Each of these factors—response, information, learning—tends to become more important at higher levels of seniority in the organization. A firm may hire a

Illustration 4.5. An Employment Contract

> *Normally mentioned*
> Job title
> Sickness and pension arrangements
> Hours of work
> Holiday entitlement
> Grievance procedure
> Initial pay
> Termination arrangements
>
> *Normally not mentioned*
> Specific responsibilities
> Basis on which pay adjusted
> Promotion procedures
> Expected performance
>
> *Sometimes mentioned*
> Managers to whom responsible

cleaner on a spot contract—the job is well defined, the performance is easily monitored—but it needs a relational contract with its management. The range of jobs for which spot contracting is appropriate is steadily diminishing.

Relational or classical contracts?

Relational contracts work best when all parties recognize that they are bound into a repeated game. Lifetime employment, seniority-based promotion, generous pension schemes and other forms of deferred remuneration all serve this purpose. Many managers have come to see these as outmoded ways of doing business. This is often a serious error.

Relational contracts tend to be advantageous when the returns to the parties to the contract are more sensitive to the size of the cake than to its division. This is true also when the advantages of flexibility in the relationships between the parties, or a rapid flow of information between them, are important to the joint outcome. A classical contract is designed to eliminate flexibility. What each party must do is, as far as possible, precisely defined by the terms of the contract. A relational contract allows flexibility, and often encourages it. A classical contract inhibits the free flow of information: such information might be used against you. In a relational contract, information flows are the most natural thing in the world. That is why fashion businesses are generally characterized by relational contracts. Designers, manufacturers, and retailers have established associations. Legally, these take the form of a series of spot contracts. In practice, both sides assume that there are continuing affiliations. They expect to be provided with the latest designs and expect also to be willing to stock them.

Illustration 4.6. Classical versus Relational Contracts

Common classical contracts	Common relational contracts
Finance	Employment contracts with skilled workers
Property leases	Professional services
Long-term energy contracts	Relationships between fashion designers, manufacturers, and retailers

If the advantages of relational contracts are so clear, why is not all business done that way? Relational contracts have disadvantages. There is an inevitable conflict between our desire to get the best deal and the development of a relational contract. It is intrinsic to the relational contract that the parties to it do not obtain the best spot contract which they could achieve on all, or perhaps any, occasion. The Prisoner's Dilemma framework illustrates this very clearly. A good relational contract here leads to the 'nice–nice' outcome being achieved in each repetition of the game. Yet in every single trial, both parties know that they could do better by being nasty. In business contexts, there is never any shortage of tough bargainers who will point that out. A primary advantage of a relational contract is that it allows an easy flow of information. Yet every textbook on negotiation emphasizes the importance of maximizing information advantages. In the fashion business all parties benefit from a speedy flow of accurate data about the popularity of individual items. But the way to get the best price is to manage that flow of information strategically. As a manufacturer, I want to ensure that retailers take my slow-selling lines as well as my hot properties. As a retailer, I want to get adequate stocks of winners before they are generally recognized as winners. So both parties lie. The sales force tells retailers how well the dud lines are doing elsewhere; retailers express reluctance to stock goods for which they know customers are clamouring.

If I believe I am a good bargainer, or that I enjoy the stronger bargaining position, I may be reluctant to enter a relational contract. Relational contracts often rest on an even division of the gains from contracting between the parties to the contract. It is not impossible to have a relational contract between unequal parties but it is harder. It is harder still if the relative strength of the two parties varies over time and either, or both, wish to see this reflected in the terms of exchange. In such a context the tension between maximizing the value of the contract through free sharing of information and maximizing the firm's own share of it is particularly obvious. We have to care more about what we get than about who gets it. Often this is impossible (or wrong).

The problem of opportunism

Strategies for reiterated games, such as relational contracts, work so long as the game continues indefinitely. They break down if one or other party believes the game is likely to come to an end. Both prisoners confess on the last trial of the Prisoner's Dilemma and, worse still, if they believe the last occasion may be approaching they start to confess right away. Opportunistic behaviour occurs in relational contracts when one or other party believes— perhaps rightly, perhaps wrongly—that it pays to exploit the relationship even if that leads to its termination.

One purpose of a long-term contract—whether relational or classical—is to induce the parties to invest in the relationship. McDonald's franchisees have to learn the McDonald's system. They must then buy equipment and fittings that are not only specialized to hamburgers but specialised to that particular hamburger franchise. A car component supplier will have to tool up for an individual manufacturer. Professional advisers will expect to spend time getting to know their clients.

A relational contract allows scope for opportunism once these investments have been made. If McDonald's wishes to impose new and onerous demands on its franchisees, their ability to resist is much weaker after they have assumed the franchise than before. If franchisees had known what was proposed they might have preferred to join a different chain or stay out of the hamburger business altogether. They might therefore prefer the security of a classical contract. An automobile component supplier risks the possibility that the car manufacturer will seek to drive a harder bargain once the car is in production than might have been obtained before the supplier was committed to the manufacturer. Again, a classical contract, or an arrangement by which the manufacturers fund the capital investment, might be better. The professional firm will be reluctant to invest in a client relationship unless it is either paid for that investment or has a clear expectation of a continuing flow of business too.

How do the parties to a relational contract protect themselves against such opportunism? They are in a stronger position if the other party has been obliged to make contract specific expenditures also. Insisting on this may even be part of the contract—a process known as 'taking hostages'. Many franchise contracts are designed for this purpose—the franchisor imposes very particular requirements on the franchisee in order to increase the franchisee's commitment to the relationship. But the better insurance against opportunism is for the parties to be truly convinced that they are playing a repeated game.

Relational contracts and the business environment

There are generally short-term gains to be made from breaking relational contracts. This follows from the very nature of the relational contract itself. The contractor's freedom of action is not restricted by any legal requirement, but by concern for subsequent reputation. But since these short-term gains are available, breach of relational contract is a very usual way of generating immediate profits after acquisitions or buyouts. It follows that relational contracts are more difficult to make in business environments where such changes of control are common. The parties are less certain that the terms of the relational contract will be honoured.

In an environment in which relational contracts are unusual or unimportant, opportunism is not necessarily damaging to reputation. This may be cultural. The strongly individualistic values of the United States mean that the penalties for opportunism are often low. Taking maximum advantage of a strong bargaining position may be seen as good business rather than sharp practice. In countries like Switzerland, Italy, or Japan, social attitudes are different and opportunistic behaviour may prove personally and professionally damaging. Industries vary also in their capacity to develop relational contracts. Most of us deal with a particular real estate agent only once. We expect real estate agents to behave opportunistically. So they do little damage to their reputation when they do behave opportunistically. Most of all, it is easier to develop relational contracts if you already have many relational contracts. The value of a reputation for fair dealing is apparent to all. This creates networks and clusters of relational contracts. Some firms and industries trade extensively in this way; others hardly at all. Some economies are characterized by the widespread use of relational contracts; others use them little. The next chapter describes how architecture, a firm's network of relational contracts, can be used by firms to establish competitive advantage.

T his chapter draws on largely separate but largely parallel thinking in law, economics, and sociology. The concept of relational contracts in legal theory is principally due to Macneil (1974, 1978, 1980). Economists use the term implicit, or incomplete contracts, to refer to the same phenomenon. Olson (1965) is an early account. Grossman and Hart (1983, 1986) have made major contributions to this theory and Hart (1988) provides a survey. Within a sociological framework, MacAuley (1963) is a seminal discussion of the same issues. The concept of trust relationships is due to Fox (1974). The interaction between trust and social structures is spelled out in Granovetter (1985) and Zucker (1986). A valuable synthesis is provided by Bradach and Eccles (1989), abridged in Thompson *et al.* (1991). Schleifer and Summers (1988) provide an analysis of the take-over phenomenon in terms of opportunism.

The idea that the economic role of a firm is defined by its contracts originates with Coase (1937, 1988) but emerges clearly from Alchian and Demsetz (1972). Williamson has recently used the phrase 'a nexus of treaties' to describe this approach. I believe the term 'treaties' also has many inappropriate connotations and so have preferred to couch the discussion here in terms of contracts and relationships. Aoki, Gustaffson, and Williamson (1990) contains a number of contributions in this vein. Reve (1990) is a specific attempt to base a discussion of corporate strategy on a transaction cost view of the firm. The analysis of organization structure in terms of contract design is often called the principal-agent problem. Here see Jensen and Meckling (1976), Fama (1980), Fama and Jensen (1983), Pratt and Zeckhauser (1985), Hart and Moore (1990). Eisenhardt (1989) is a business-orientated survey.

III

DISTINCTIVE CAPABILITIES

The firm is defined by its contracts and relationships. Added value is created by its success in putting these contracts and relationships together, so it is the quality and distinctiveness of these contracts that promote added value. The distinctiveness is at least as important as the goodness. The reason is that in an efficient market there are few opportunities to make good contracts.

The term efficient market is most frequently used in financial markets.[1] An efficient market is simply one in which there are no bargains, because what is to be known about the item being sold is already reflected in its price. The advice, 'Buy Glaxo shares because Glaxo is a well-managed company with outstanding products', is worthless, even if it is a type of advice that is often given, because these facts about Glaxo are well known and fully incorporated in the value of its securities.

In broader business terms, the more general implications of market efficiency are much the same. Opportunities that are available to everyone will not be profitable for everyone or perhaps anyone; what other people can equally see and do is unlikely to be a sustained source of added value. So the question that every firm must ask of an apparently profitable opportunity is, 'Why will we be better at doing that than other people?' That is not a justification for the conservative executive we have all met who disparages every new proposal on the grounds that what is worth doing will already have been done. Often the question, 'Why will we be better at doing that than other people?' will have a clear and affirmative answer, and it is typically those firms that can give that answer and act on it that are successful.

The efficient market hypothesis denies that there is such a thing as an objectively attractive or unattractive industry, or more precisely denies

1 Fama (1970) is the principal survey of evidence on the efficient market hypothesis, which is described in any finance text, e.g. Brealey and Myers (1991, ch. 13). The June 1977 *Journal of Financial Economics* is a survey of anomalies in market behaviour.

that it will remain fundamentally attractive or unattractive for long. That means it directly conflicts with the portfolio planning approach to strategy, one of the most influential styles of thinking of the last two decades. This issue is considered more extensively in Chapter 11.

The implication of the efficient market hypothesis is that value cannot be added on a sustained basis simply by making better contracts than other people, since these opportunities are unlikely to remain available. Value is added by developing a set of relationships which others are unable to make. A firm can achieve added value only on the basis of some distinctive capability—some feature of its relationships which other firms lack, and cannot readily reproduce.

The firm may make a new contract or arrangement of contracts. This might be for a new type of good or service, as with ordinary product or process innovations. Or the innovation might lie in the form of the contract itself, as is often the case in financial services. The difficulty in establishing competitive advantage from this source is quickly apparent. Most innovation can be quickly replicated. Sustained competitive advantage depends on the ability to protect the innovation, through legal restriction (as for Glaxo and Zantac) or through strategy.

Added value can be achieved if customers or suppliers are systematically willing to undertake relationships on terms which they would not make available to other people. Most usually, this is the result of the supplier's reputation. International car hire firms offer the same models of car on the same terms as local firms but at higher prices. They attract customers not because the quality and reliability of their service is necessarily any better but because these customers believe the reputation of the franchisor provides them with an assurance of that quality and reliability. Reputation is often—as in this case—associated with a brand name.

The distinctiveness of a firm's relationships may rest in the group of contracts taken as a whole. While any part of it can be reproduced, the complexity of the set defies imitation. Typically, this requires that many contracts should have implicit, or relational, terms. If you can write a contract down, others can make the same contract. This architecture is a major part of what distinguishes Marks & Spencer, both in its internal architecture—its relationships with employees—and in its external architecture—its relationships with suppliers.

A firm with no distinctive capability may still achieve competitive advantage if it holds a strategic asset. A concession to exploit a resource, or an exclusive right to supply, is a strategic asset. In other markets, being first, or being the incumbent firm, may in itself confer advantages over any potential entrant. Some companies are no better—perhaps worse—

than other firms would be at the activities they perform—but they enjoy the strategic asset that they already perform them.

Illustration III.1. Sources of Competitive Advantage

Position	Company	Distinctive capability or strategic asset
1	Glaxo	Innovation (principally Zantac) with strong supporting strategies
2	Benetton	Architecture (subcontracting and franchise arrangements) and retail brand
3	Reuters	Incumbency advantages, reputation
4	Petrofina	Control of oil resources and dominant position in Belgian supply markets
5	Kwik Save	Market positioning
6	LVMH	Brands
7	Guinness	Brands
8	Cable and Wireless	Licences in regulated markets, incumbency advantages
9	BTR	Architecture (control systems between centre and operating business)
10	Marks & Spencer	Architecture (subcontracting and employee relationships), reputation

The European 'top ten' identified in Chapter 2 offers examples of all these sources of competitive advantage—innovation, reputation, architecture, and strategic assets (Illustration III.1). Glaxo's competitive position is built around innovation, principally Zantac. Benetton gains from its architecture—the distinctive structure of its subcontracting and franchising arrangements—and from its brand. Marks & Spencer enjoys similar strengths. Petrofina and Cable and Wireless hold strategic assets and may also gain competitive advantage from architecture. LVMH and Guinness exemplify competitive advantages built around brands. Reuters' position is based largely on strategic assets—incumbents have substantial advantages in information services although reputation also plays its part. BTR is a company with a powerful, and distinctive, architecture. Kwik Save does not fall easily into any of these categories; its competitive advantage seems to be in occupying a market position that its rivals have abandoned. Kwik Save is considered at greater length in Chapter 2, and the degree to which positioning can be a source of competitive advantage is discussed more fully in Chapter 11. Chapters 5 to 8, however, are concerned with these principal sources of competitive advantage—architecture, reputation, innovation, and strategic assets.

5

....

Architecture

Architecture is the first of the three primary sources of distinctive capability. It is a network of relational contracts within, or around, the firm. Firms may establish these relationships with and among their employees (internal architecture), with their suppliers or customers (external architecture), or among a group of firms engaged in related activities (networks).

The value of architecture rests in the capacity of organizations which establish it to create organizational knowledge and routines, to respond flexibly to changing circumstances, and to achieve easy and open exchanges of information. Each of these is capable of creating an asset for the firm—organizational knowledge which is more valuable than the sum of individual knowledge, flexibility, and responsiveness which extends to the institution as well as to its members.

So I introduce architecture through the experience of Liverpool Football Club, which has not only consistently performed well but which has consistently performed better than the abilities of its players would seem to allow. This distinction between the attributes of the firm and the attributes of its members is important in appreciating both the social and the commercial implications of architecture. But such structures can only be created, and protected from imitation, in a framework of relational contracts. What can be written down can be reproduced. Architecture therefore depends on the ability of the firm to build and sustain long-term relationships and to establish an environment that penalizes opportunistic behaviour. As with other distinctive capabilities, it is easier to sustain architecture than to set out to create it.

Some companies—like IBM or Marks & Spencer—have a powerful and identifiable corporate culture. The term culture has been widely used, and abused, in business over the last few years, often to refer to rather superficial aspects of corporate organization. But with these firms everyone knows what is meant. Although admiration for their products and their achievements in the market-place is virtually universal, their culture is not to everyone's taste. Employees are, in the main, fiercely loyal, and those who find the organization uncongenial leave.

The legacy of the architect of the modern company—Thomas Watson for IBM, Michael Marks in Marks & Spencer—is strong in both firms. But the myths which surround these figures draw attention away from central current reality: how little either organization depends on any individual or group of individuals. Each company has established a structure, a style, a set of routines, which operates to get the best out of relatively ordinary employees, and these routines have continued to produce exceptional corporate results over many years and through many changes in the economic environment.

Other styles of management are also distinctive and also successful. In the last twenty years, Japanese firms have dominated the consumer electronics industry and become market leaders in automobiles. Initially, their output was exported from Japan, but in the face of the rise in the value of the yen and protectionist reactions in both Europe and the United States, they have shifted production to the West. Nissan now builds cars in the north of England, and Akai makes video equipment in Normandy. In Western environments, these firms have pursued Japanese styles of relationships with subcontractors and employees and have achieved impressive levels of quality and productivity. They have succeeded in avoiding the alienation and abrasive labour relations seen in large-scale assembly activities in most Western countries, and have built demanding but productive associations with their suppliers.

These facts are well known, most of all to the Western competitors of these Japanese firms. But the successful implementation of these Japanese models in the West has been undertaken by Japanese companies. Those competitors which have responded most forcefully, such as Ford and Caterpillar, have done so by the more effective implementation of a traditional Western management style. It is only a slight exaggeration to suppose that, by the end of the century, Britain will again be a major locus in automobiles and Europe in consumer electronics, by virtue of largely closing down the indigenous industry and replacing it by greenfield operations, with new workers and new management systems, under Japanese ownership and control. Change has been effected, not incrementally, but by starting again. The structure of commercial relationships is fundamentally, and permanently, influenced by the past experience of these relationships.

The power of shared knowledge and established routines does not only benefit large companies. The Lumezzane valley in Brescia in northern Italy is not on many tourist itineraries. Although its natural scenery is attractive, its calm is shattered by the noise from hundreds of small metal-working establishments, which often continues late into the night. In parts of the valley it seems as though almost every house has a small factory attached. Casual tourists would probably be surprised that this style of economic organization had lasted so long. They might plan to revisit Lumezzane in a few years' time when these industries had finally been swept away by the forces of international competition, reinforced by global marketing and the research and development and quality control resources which only large firms can command.

That judgement could hardly be more wrong. Far from threatening Lumezzane, the opening of international markets has brought unparalleled prosperity. Most of the output of the valley is exported and the region is one of the richest in Italy. Nor does it rely simply on traditional craft skills. Lumezzane is a market leader in a range of sophisticated metal-manufacturing products including valves, taps, and the customized machine tools used in their production. The structure of relationships between the small firms of the Lumezzane valley, often specialized in a single component of the final product, which gives each access to the knowledge, abilities, and resources of the whole, has given Lumezzane a continuing competitive advantage in its markets. That competitive advantage has endured and grown.

There are strong common elements in these very different stories of organizational design and evolution—the corporate cultures of IBM and Marks & Spencer, the style of Japanese management, the networks of Lumezzane. In each, there is a pattern of relationships variously within firms, around firms, and between firms, which is complex, subtle, and hard to define precisely or to replicate. That pattern is the product of history, and is almost impossible to reproduce in the absence of that history. It is also a pattern of relationships which can yield substantial competitive advantage for those firms or groups of firms. Their competitive advantage typically arises through the acquisition of organizational knowledge, the establishment of organizational routines, and the development of a co-operative ethic. This allows flexible response, the sharing of information, and a process in which the monitoring of quality is such a natural characteristic of the organization that it is often barely necessary to make it explicit.

These patterns of relationships are the distinctive capability I call architecture. They rest on relational contracts, they rely on a strong sense that the participants are players in a repeated game, and by doing so they offer answers to the problems of co-operation, co-ordination, and commitment. Their distinctiveness comes partly from the implicit terms which are characteristic of the relational contract—what cannot easily be written down cannot

Illustration 5.1. Architecture

Types of architecture

Internal: Between the firm and its employees and among employees
External: Between the firm and its suppliers or customers
Networks: Between a group of collaborating firms

How architecture adds value to individual contributions

Through the creation of organizational knowledge
Through the establishment of a co-operative ethic
By the implementation of organizational routines

easily be reproduced—and partly from the overall complexity of structure, in which no individual sees, knows, or understands more than a small part of the whole. The remainder of this chapter elucidates these themes.

Architecture as a characteristic of the organization

In every field of human activity, and in every century of human history, there have been organizations whose structure others have tried, and failed, to replicate successfully—the democracies of classical Greece, the armies of ancient Rome, the city-states of medieval Italy, the administration of British India. In the twentieth century these exceptional organizations are often corporations. So *In Search of Excellence*, a survey of 'America's most admired corporations' became a best seller of the 1980s (Peters and Waterman, 1982). But excellence is not the same as architecture. Excellence is often founded on the abilities of individuals, while architecture is the achievement of an organization. The men who ran British India were, in the main, of mediocre talent. The achievement of the Raj was to create a system within which a small number of these undistinguished people could administer, tolerably well, one of the largest and most diverse nations of the world. Architecture does not create extraordinary organizations by collecting extraordinary people. It does so by enabling very ordinary people to perform in extraordinary ways.

Contrast this with a professional service firm or a university. The achievements of Price Waterhouse rest principally on the talents of its partners, and those of London University on its professors, and without the expertise of these partners or professors neither institution would have much to offer its customers. The organization may add value to these talents through a reputation which attracts other talented partners and professors as well as clients, customers, and students. And it may be that there are further gains to be realized through the pooling of the skills and knowledge which are to be found in the institution. But no one doubts that the excellence of the institution is based primarily on the excellence of its individual members.

This distinction between the attributes of the corporation itself and the attributes of the individuals within it has a commercial as well as a sociological significance. It is central to the distribution of the added value earned by the organization as a whole. If the exceptional performance of the organization rests solely on the exceptional talents of the individuals within it, then the rewards of that performance will accrue to these individual talents, rather than to the organization. We see this happening in professional or financial service firms where the high fees charged to clients are largely translated into the high earnings of members of the firm. An investment bank will be very profitable only if it can add value of its own to the abilities of its employees. Sometimes it can do this through reputation. Or the bank may dominate the channels by which these individuals can exploit their abilities. It can then demand a share of the value which they add. In these cases, the true competitive advantage arises from a reputation or a strategic asset.

But architecture is something different. An organization with distinctive architecture, like Marks & Spencer or IBM, will often emphasize its dependence on its people. But that dependence is to be interpreted in a particular way. The organization is dependent on them taken as a whole, because the product of the organization is the product of the collectivity. But it is not dependent on any particular one. Every individual with the organization is readily replaceable. It is only in these circumstances that added value can be appropriated for the organization itself.

Liverpool Football Club

Over the last two decades, Liverpool has been the most successful football club in England by a considerable margin and one of the most consistently successful clubs in Europe. What is particularly interesting about Liverpool's performance is not just that the club has done well; it has done better than could be expected from the quality of its players. That suggests that Liverpool is deriving competitive advantage from its architecture.

There are various ways of demonstrating that point. The most commercial of them is shown in Fig. 5.1. This measures club performance against expen-

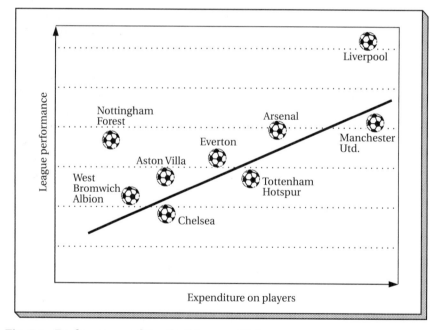

Fig. 5.1. Performance of Football League Clubs
Source: derived from dell'Osso and Szymanski (1991).

diture on playing staff—including both wages and transfer fees spent on acquiring players from other teams. Liverpool players rank more or less equally with those of Manchester United, but Liverpool's playing performance is decidedly better. For league clubs taken as a whole, there is a strong relationship between spending on players and competitive success, with a few outliers. Liverpool is the most marked of the outliers.

Much has been written about Liverpool's achievements, most of it not of a very scholarly nature. Two factors seem to be critical. Liverpool has built up a detailed intelligence on other clubs, other grounds, other players. The experience of each game is carefully reviewed and used to enhance that information base. Apparently, there are secret books in which that intelligence is inscribed, but there is more to this activity than is contained in the books—if Manchester United could overtake Liverpool by means of simple burglary, there would be no shortage of skilled volunteers to do the job. Rather, the books are a measure of Liverpool's commitment to the maintenance of its distinctive knowledge base.

If we were to build a model of the game of football, it would recognize that every time a player has the ball he faces the alternative of shooting for goal or passing it to a better placed player. If he passes to a player of similar calibre to himself, he will score fewer goals but the team will score more. If everyone in the team plays a passing game, every member of it can expect to score more goals than if their normal instinct is to shoot. That choice is repeated every few minutes in every match the team plays, and as in the Criminals' Revenge (p. 38) there are two equilibria—a passing game or a shooting game. Liverpool is well known for its passing game. Many of its opponents adopt a more individualistic style.

Liverpool illustrates the principal ways in which architecture can form the basis of a distinctive capability. The club has created an intangible asset—the organizational knowledge of the club—which, although it is derived from the contributions of individual members, belongs to the firm and not to the individual members, and cannot be appropriated by them. There are organizational routines—complex manœuvres, perfected through repeated trial, in which each player fulfils his own role without needing, or necessarily having, a picture of the whole. And there is the 'passing game', the co-operative ethic, in which the player's instinct is to maximise the number of goals the club scores rather than the number of goals he scores. Each of these sources of sporting success has its precise business analogies.

The co-operative ethic or the passing game

Most firms hope to establish a co-operative ethic. But the essential question here is how to establish consummate, rather than perfunctory, co-operation. While consummate co-operation is often achieved in small groups, it is rarely attainable across large organizations, where strategic bargaining between units is generally inevitable. Still less often is it accomplished between firms or within groups of firms. Perfunctory co-operation marks the limit of what can be prescribed in a spot or classical contract. Consummate co-operation demands a deeper relationship.

The sporting metaphor illustrates the distinction well. If football were a more predictable game than it is, the club manager could define a set of instructions which would describe when players should hold the ball, when they should pass, and when they should shoot. He could monitor the players' adherence to his instructions, and reward or punish them accordingly. This would be the analogue of running a business by a comprehensive system of classical contracts. It is how some football coaches—rarely the best—try to run their clubs and it is also how some managers—rarely the best—try to run their businesses.

The reasons such a structure would not work in football are clear enough. Football moves too fast and unpredictably for the instructions to be able to deal with the almost infinite variety of situations which might occur. This might not matter if the coach were always in a position to shout orders from the touch-line—another common characteristic of bad coaches and bad managers—but the coach is simply not in a position to obtain, or to assimilate sufficiently quickly, the range of information which is held by the eleven players on the field. The need for rapid response, and for quick absorption and exchange of information means that the passing game can only be implemented by the players themselves. It cannot be imposed. The maintenance of a co-operative ethic relies on the underlying structure of relational contracts—the unwritten rules, the tacit understandings, the common purpose which is sustained by the expectation of all parties that these will be part of continuing relationships.

These structures are of particular value—and here the football analogy is again helpful–where the nature of the business requires flexible responses

Illustration 5.2. The Cooperative Ethic

The military contract demands the total and almost unconditional subordination of the interests of the individual if the interests of the group should require it.

The military leader who views his oath of office as merely a contractual arrangement with his government sets the stage for a style of leadership critically different from the leader who views that oath as his pledge to contribute to the common good of his society. For the former, 'duty, honour, country' is a slogan adopted temporarily until the contract is completed; for the latter, 'duty, honour, country' is a way of life adopted for the good of all and accepted as a moral commitment not subject to contractual negotiations.

Source: van Fleet (1984).

and ready exchange of information. Fashion businesses, or film and television production, are striking cases. Sometimes the architecture is internal—the key co-operative ethic is that within the firm itself, as it is for Liverpool. Sometimes it is external—the passing game is played between the firm and its customers or suppliers, or among a group of co-operating firms in the same industry. Often both characteristics are found in combination.

Organizational knowledge

All firms possess organizational knowledge in the sense that an insurance company knows about insurance and an automobile manufacturer knows about automobiles. But what an insurance company knows about insurance is, as a rule, what its employees know about insurance, and is much the same as what other insurance companies know about insurance. Organizational knowledge, as I define it here, is distinctive to the firm, is more than the sum of the expertise of those who work in the firm, and is not available to other firms. If an insurance company builds up data and skills in the assessment of a particular category of risk, and if those data and skills are truly those of the company and not those of a small group of employees, then it has created organizational knowledge. That organizational knowledge gives it a distinctive capability and may yield a competitive advantage in the market for that risk category. The purest form of organizational knowledge is where each employee knows one digit of the code which opens the safe; such information is of value only when combined with the information held by all others. The analogy makes clear, too, why the issue is important; any individual who knows the whole code has access to the safe.

For some firms—professional service firms and many small companies in high-tech industries—technical knowledge *is* the business. But if the company is to add value, it needs to create organizational knowledge from the skills of its members. This is achieved when the combined skills of two experts increases the value of each. The problems the organization faces are, first, those of securing this exchange of knowledge and, secondly, those of preventing that knowledge, and the rewards associated with it, being captured by one or both of the individuals concerned. Both issues have been evident in the major accountancy firms where the supposed synergies between audit and consultancy have increasingly turned into tension for precisely these reasons.

Organizational knowledge is more easily captured by the firm when it results from the specific application of generally available technology. Most of an automobile company's knowledge base is derived from technical skills that are general to the industry, but the very large investment now involved in the development of individual models leads to the creation of organizational knowledge which is specific to that design. The application of information systems in a bank raises similar issues. The requirement here is to turn individual expertise into business knowhow. The problem of reappropriation

Illustration 5.3. Organizational or Individual Knowledge?

Cosworth provides a rare example of British commercial success and engineering excellence in one of the world's most competitive environments—motor racing. Since its foundation in 1958, Cosworth has become a hallmark company in high-performance engine design and construction.

Important as a complete understanding of technical detail has been to management decision-making, Cosworth is a company with the potential to create its own competition. This is because the company only survives by encouraging talented people to develop and exploit know-how that cannot be exclusively controlled by the company through patenting.

Because Duckworth, Costin, and Rood (the founders of the business) continued to work as a team, delegating neither authority nor responsibility for the engineering side of the company, an unusual structure developed at Northampton which, probably more by default rather than design, was highly conducive to ensuring that technical know-how was distributed as broadly as possible across the organization. As practising engineers, Duckworth, Costin, and Rood had a tendency not to recruit peers, but to recruit juniors who would make good all round deputies. Most of Cosworth's new generation of engineers thus came straight from university. As inexperienced graduates starting in an assisting and generalist role, Cosworth trained them as broadly as possible in a combined production/development engineering department before moving them into design work. Providing graduate engineers with general training at a single location has two effects:

1. it tends to inhibit the development of specialisms that encourage individuals to acquire exclusive knowledge; and
2. it promotes flexibility.

A structure enabling technical competence to be distributed as broadly as possible cannot prevent some know-how being transferred to competitors as experienced engineers simply move on to work for other companies. But it does prevent know-how from being permanently withdrawn from the company that originally fostered it through staff leaving.

Source: Aston (1991).

hardly arises in such a case. The difficulty is that of capturing the expertise in the first place. In passing on expertise, experts give up precisely what creates their value to the organization, and this can only be a rational strategy in the context of a relational contract and a repeated game. This is strikingly true of consultants, for whom the build-up of skills within the client organization is a threat to their continued role.

Organizational knowledge is often distinctive only at the price of being applicable to a narrowly defined market. Large competitive advantages come when the organizational knowledge is unique, appropriable to the firm, and relevant to a market which is large or a range of markets which is wide. This does not happen often. It was, perhaps, achieved by IBM, but eroded even

Illustration 5.4. Creating Organizational Knowledge

The Department of Social Security's Operational Strategy has had a chequered history. After the basic strategy was decided in 1982 there was a long planning process. Despite this, when the project began to escalate in 1987, the basic project control mechanisms were inadequate, technical skills were in short supply, and many of the system specifications later proved inaccurate.

At the beginning of the project the DSS needed consultants to provide expertise in project management and systems development. But external skill was employed in a piecemeal way when it could have been used to help generate the infrastructure necessary for its own staff to manage the project. In short, the department began its programme without a strategy for acquiring control over external staff. There were no early plans for skills transfer. The generation of technical expertise was further hampered when half the in-house programmers and business analysts were moved off the project in 1987 following strike action. System problems sometimes escaped notice because of the absence of skilled end-users. As one implementation manager commented during the pilot study:

> The user community . . . is not . . . skilled at doing the user testing or representing the user, because they don't have sufficient knowledge. We've lacked skilled users at times, and forceful users, who would insist the user spec. was met, who would insist that the design was as per user spec., and would then insist that completely independent testing was done.

Inland Revenue places considerable stress on the generation of in-house technical capability. In 1982 it opened a development centre at a greenfield site in Telford with the stated aim of building up expertise over the life of the PAYE project. Inland Revenue has successfully integrated technical skills and organization-specific, tacit knowledge, with the result that its systems were delivered on time and with computerization of the self-employed tax (Schedule D) added to the original programme.

Lacking a background in IT, the Inland Revenue initially needed consultants to help design and develop systems, review the implementation plan, set schedules and initiate multi-team management. Yet their effectiveness would have been limited had the Department not sought to capture some of these formal skills for itself. Several integrative mechanisms were significant in achieving this transfer of expertise. Consultants were brought in early to establish a project infrastructure which broke down the kind of committee system that the DSS struggled with for several years. Consultants were made full members of project teams, directly answerable to Inland Revenue project managers and were subject to the same schedules and assessment arrangements as internal staff. Working alongside the consultants provided opportunities for the Revenue's staff to increase their technical knowledge. 'Tasking' of this kind was specifically scheduled in to the programme. As the Development Centre's controller explained:

> We deliberately set out to have mixed teams of consultants and in-house staff working together. We do not put the consultants all in one place and ask them to deliver a part of the project and put our own staff in another place and ask them to deliver another part of the project. We put the two together with firm deadlines, integrated teams, and in that situation all our in-house staff will be learning from the special expertise of the consultants working with them. (PAC, 1987, paragraph 1783.)

Source: Dyerson and Roper (1991).

there as the knowledge base became diffused and the market more fragmented.

In other cases, organizational knowledge may take the form of organizational systems and routines. This is very much a key part of the effectiveness of strong retailers—and, indeed, it was the power of routines which lay behind the ability of British India to turn inexperienced youths into administrators of large tracts of territory. The transcription of individual expertise into organizational routine is a means by which some professional service firms—particularly management consultants such as McKinsey or Bain—seek to create added value which arises from, and adheres to, the organization and not just to the able individuals within it.

An internal control system is a different form of organizational routine. These tight financial reporting systems are most appropriate where uncer-

Illustration 5.5. Organizational Routines

Hanson Trust's capital approval controls are well known. Every capital expenditure above £500 in the UK and $1,000 in the United States must be submitted to the centre for authorization. Anthony Alexander, a group chairman at Hanson, explained: 'The accountants act as a counter or challenge to the enthusiasm of local management. Local management tend to win; having to meet the challenge of the accountants generates very strong commitment.'

In Tarmac, approval levels are substantially higher than Hanson's and differ between divisions. Above a certain level, capital investments must be approved by the centre. The centre's criteria are clear. They want to know who the sponsors are and what their credibility is. They ask whether the proposal fits the current business and supports the direction the business is going in. They seek assurance that the return on investment will enhance the profitability ratios. And they look at the level of commitment of the sponsoring management team.

The formal approval process is not analytical, nor is it intended to provide for wide discussion. The analysis and discussion will have already taken place informally. The approval process is almost a ritual for generating commitment: 'The system depends on Sir Eric looking the man in the eye and saying "Can you make that work", and the manager replying "Yes."'

In GEC the process is also designed to generate commitment. Lord Weinstock's naturally probing, occasionally cynical style ensures that managers propose only investments they fully support. The difference at GEC is that no formal approval is required from the centre or given by it. Certain types of investments, for example in buildings, do need approval. But there is no figure, such as £100,000, above which capital requests must be approved by the centre. One GEC manager told us: 'When I arrived, I started looking for the rule book. I wanted to make some capital expenditure that was different from the proposal in the budget. I wanted to know what the procedure was. People told me "There is none. If you think it is the right thing to do, then go ahead and do it."'

Source: Goold and Campbell (1987), 111, 122–3.

tainties are limited—so that the link from performance to outcome is tight—and in businesses which require little long-term investment—whose success cannot equally be monitored within the control framework. Within these limitations, increased margins and reduced costs have generally been achieved. The success of these companies, like BTR and Hanson, has spawned imitative 'mini-conglomerates', often managed by former employees of the original conglomerates. This replication of the systems has limited the competitive advantage of the originators and has forced the original proponents into ever larger acquisitions in order to maintain their distinctive capabilities.

The sources of architecture

Liverpool's achievements are the product of a structure of relational contracts. The relationships between players are rich and complex, but implicit. They rest on repetition and reciprocation. There is no room for team spirit in a world of spot or classical contracts. There are two reasons why distinctive capabilities in organizational design must rest on relational contracting. One is the essential Prisoner's Dilemma characteristic of the 'passing game', of the sharing of information, of flexibility in response. It is in everyone's collective interest to do these things, but in no one's individual interest. You can only benefit from a co-operative ethic, or the knowledge and expertise of others, in a context of reiteration and reciprocation.

This is apparent in organizations which have successfully established a strong architecture. There is an expectation of long-term relationships both within the firm and between its members, a commitment to a sharing of the rewards of collective achievement, and a high but structured degree of informality. This informality is sometimes mistaken for disorganization—in popular discussion of chaos, entrepreneurship, or adhocracy as conditions for innovation—but truly chaotic organizations rarely perform well, and a system of relational contracts substitutes an extensive set of unwritten rules and expectations of behaviour for the formal obligations of the classical contract.

If we look at the historical examples of immensely powerful organizational architecture—ancient Greece and Rome, medieval Italy, British India—we see all of them characterized by unwritten codes of behaviour, of great strength and considerable complexity. Indeed, many of the tragic heroes of literature are individuals who, for apparently good reasons, broke these codes and were destroyed by them.

But there is a closely related issue of imitability. If the structure of relationships which underpins corporate architecture could be formalized, it could also be imitated and would at that point cease to be a source of competitive advantage. Many books have been written which purport to describe IBM and Marks & Spencer. These books are available in any public library. They have been avidly read by would-be imitators of IBM and Marks & Spencer. Many employees have left Marks & Spencer and IBM and are available for other firms to hire. Their competitors have done that too. Yet attempts to replicate the architecture of these organizations have not been at all comparably successful. Clearly, there is more to the architecture than these books contain; more to the architecture than any individual employee, or group of employees, knows. Neither reading the book nor recruiting the employees is sufficient to allow reproduction of the IBM or Marks & Spencer architecture.

Internal architecture

Internal architecture is a structure of relational contracts between the firm and its employees, and among the members themselves. Some features of the formal structure of the firm follow immediately from that definition. There is a high degree of job security; if the labour contract is a spot contract it cannot be a relational one. This stability of employment needs to be mutual; it is not just that the firm rarely terminates the contract, but the employee rarely chooses to leave. There is a flat remuneration structure, or at least one in which differentials reflect seniority as well as merit, and performance is measured by reference to intangible as well as tangible criteria. If the labour contract is a classical contract it cannot be a relational one.

Relational contracting offers scope for opportunistic behaviour. In the main, the firm will be concerned for its own reputation in future relational contracts, and this is sufficient deterrent to its own opportunistic behaviour. But it needs to protect itself against such behaviour by its employees. Remuneration may be deferred, through seniority-related payment structures or generous pension arrangements. Opportunism among employees is inhibited by linking social and business life. Geographical concentration, or domination of a town by a single company, often helps. So does the recruitment of employees of similar background or homogeneous personality type.

Illustration 5.6. Structures of Relational Contracts

'IBM is not everyone's cup of tea, but it is a winner' (p. 153).

'There is a vibrant, intensely commercial personality at Sainsbury, which the potential recruit may react to warmly or positively dislike' (p. 305).

'P & G people have strong characters, but individual presence is tempered by the influence of the corporation' (p. 266).

Source: Reynolds (1989).

The objective is to stimulate collective rather than individualistic behaviour. The suppression of individuality is a serious objective of army training, for very necessary reasons. If soldiers thought of themselves as individuals, rather than as part of a collectivity, the irrationality of sacrificing the individual for the collectivity is immediately apparent. British India thrived on the limitations of those whom it recruited and, as E. M. Forster eloquently demonstrated, less limited people rendered the structure untenable.

All of this has disadvantages as well as benefits. For most people, working for the company is never quite such a powerful motivation as working for oneself. Since firms with strong internal architecture tend to restrict individuality and to recruit employees of characteristic, and familiar type, inflexibility is a potential weakness of such a structure. It is easier to keep a supertanker on course than a flotilla of small ships. And the supertanker is more effective at ploughing through choppy seas. But changing the course of the supertanker may be a more demanding process, and organizations with distinctive architecture, including successful ones like IBM and Marks & Spencer, have often proved monothematic or rigid.

Competitive advantages may accrue from structures that are so distinctive that others find them hard to reproduce—or, conceivably, may not wish to reproduce. Such cultures are powerful weapons, as the continued success of Procter and Gamble, IBM, or a number of Japanese corporations demonstrates; but like many powerful weapons, they are also dangerous ones. Dangerous to themselves—many of the most potent corporate cultures of the past are associated with organizations which no longer exist, or have been forced to abandon these cultures to survive—Krupps, the Great Western Railway, the shipyards of Clydebank, the Ford Motor Company. And such strong cultures have at times appeared more widely threatening.

While most organizations with strong internal architecture—whether Liverpool Football Club, Marks & Spencer, or IBM—would be described as firms with strong corporate cultures, architecture and corporate culture are not the same thing. Drexel Burnham Lambert had a strong, if deeply unattractive corporate culture built around highly individualistic behaviour (Illustration 5.7). The elaborate rituals which surround the marketing activities of life insurance companies may be classed as corporate culture, if culture is defined as patterns of collective behaviour, but are in no sense internal architecture. In these companies, strengthening individual motivation is all. Co-operative behaviour is not necessary or expected, organizational knowledge is minimal, and organizational routines are purely administrative.

If the passing game creates problems as well as solving them, then the same is true of organizational knowledge. We are all familiar with companies in which organizational knowledge is of the kind 'We don't do things that way here' or 'We tried that in 1970 and it didn't work.' Organizational routines may be pursued for their own sake long after their purpose has vanished. Such structures can have negative value—the whole is less than the sum of the parts, the organization produces less than the sum of the talents of individual members.

Illustration 5.7. Contracts Without Architecture

> Milken expounded on this point, saying, 'I would say there is no second in command. You could say on some days there's one hundred seventy people that are second in command, and other days, you know, there's ten. It depends on what's happening, what the situation is. People have responsibilities, rather than a formal organization chart.
>
> Indeed, someone once tried to draw an organization chart of Milken's group and it became a joke, a maze of crisscrossing lines, which was then screened onto T-shirts. Thenceforth, Milken's group was dubbed the 'T-shirt organization'.
>
> If the absence of clearly defined responsibilities caused some pushing and shoving among a highly aggressive and incentivized group of people, Milken probably did not mind. According to one former member of this group, Milken preferred that there be a certain amount of friction among his people, so that they would not develop alliances—and he could better maintain control.
>
> *Source*: Bruck (1989).

External architecture and networks

External architecture is found where firms share knowledge, or establish fast response times, on the basis of a series of relational contracts between or among them. Marks & Spencer pioneered a method of retailing, first for clothing and subsequently for a wider range of commodities—particularly food. The retailer was to engage in detailed product design. These products were then to be manufactured by a limited range of selected suppliers whose activities were closely monitored. These suppliers often commit a major portion of their output to Marks & Spencer and many of them have been suppliers to the company for decades, although there are no formal long-term agreements between them. These are very clear and very potent examples of relational contracts.

The merit of such relational contracts is that they facilitate the sharing of product knowledge and encourage flexibility of response. These advantages are important in business such as fashion retailing, where customer requirements may change rapidly and where there is strategic posturing by both parties. These arrangements again expose both sides to the risks of opportunistic behaviour. Typically, this is inhibited by the reputation of the firms involved in relational contracting and by the investment which both sides make in the relationship.

Networks are groups of firms which make relational contracts with each other. The metal-workers of Lumezzane were described earlier. Chapters 18 and 19 describe how similar structures are found in the Italian knitwear industry. Many other Italian products, from tiles to ties, are also manufactured by geographically concentrated groupings of small firms. Typically, these firms share, draw on, and contribute to a common knowledge and skill base, make spare capacity available to each other, and implicitly and explicitly monitor each other's quality while retaining a speed of response and a degree of motivation that large firms find difficult to emulate. Although Italy has developed this form of organization particularly far, analogous networks are to be found everywhere, from Silicon Valley to the diamond traders of Antwerp. Such networks are of particular importance in financial services, and explain the continued pre-eminence of traditional financial centres in New York and London even as economic power seems to have moved elsewhere. These networks create distinctive capabilities both for firms and for groups of firms.

Illustration 5.8. Architecture in Networks

. . . a nation's competitive industries are not spread evenly through the economy but are connected in what I term *clusters* consisting of industries related by links of various kinds.

Source: Porter (1990).

When an industry has thus chosen a locality for itself, it is likely to stay there long; so great are the advantages which people following the same skilled trade get from near neighbourhood to one another. The mysteries of the trade become no mysteries; but are as it were in the air, and children learn many of them unconsciously. Good work is rightly appreciated, inventions and improvements in machinery, in processes and the general organization of the business have their merits promptly discussed; if one man starts a new idea, it is taken up by others and combined with suggestions of their own; and thus it becomes the source of further new ideas.

Source: Marshall, (1890).

The 'pulling power' of stockbrokers Cazenove is based on the strength of its list of corporate and institutional clients and enabled that firm to emerge, independent, as one of the most successful in the City of London's Big Bang. Competitive advantage in broking generally, or in lead banking, rests on similar factors. The competitive strength of Lloyd's of London in the world insurance market is largely due to the ability of many underwriters gathered in a single room to exchange information relevant to risk assessment.

Some firms have obtained competitive advantage through the development of distinctive supply networks, often in areas of the world which others have found difficult to penetrate. Such architecture has been a traditional strength for many firms in Britain and in The Netherlands, Europe's two strongest trading nations. A section of the London Stock Exchange's official list was, until recently, headed 'Overseas Traders'. Multinational Unilever was formed by the unlikely conjunction of soap and margarine manufacturers in these two countries, bound together by the common requirements of sourcing raw material from West Africa. United States companies, such as United Brands, developed somewhat similar networks in Central and South America. The Japanese Sogo Shosha, trading companies at the centre of the Zaibatsu, were for long at the core of Japanese economic development. Lonrho has based a similar competitive advantage on its networks in Africa (based, in turn, on the distinctive capabilities of its dominant chief executive).

As with all other types of competitive advantage, the profitability of this type of architecture rests on the inability of others to replicate it. In advanced economies no company can expect to achieve the sort of position which a firm like United Brands enjoys in the countries in which it operates. Even so, in small countries a dominant local firm may develop a unique network of contacts and interrelationships. In Belgium, Société Générale has achieved that position, with interests across much of Belgian industry and finance. When the Italian Carlo de Benedetti saw a take-over of the somewhat sleepy Société as a means of enhancing his pan-European ambitions, the political strength of the company, on top of its economic interests, enabled it to survive his attack.

Architecture in Japan

It is Japanese industry which has been most successful in creating distinctive capabilities through architecture. In Japan we can identify the power of internal architecture, external architecture, and networks.

The 'three pillars' of the internal labour market in Japanese firms are lifetime employment, the seniority system, and enterprise unionism. The lifetime employment system emphasizes the long-term relationship between the employee and the company. Even Japanese companies, particularly small ones, cannot completely predict their labour requirements, and fluctuations are dealt with by employing part-time or irregular workers on spot contracts without detriment to the basic lifetime employment system. Although lifetime employment is particularly associated with Japanese companies, the reality of employment relationships in large continental European firms is not so different. The stark contrast is between Japan and the United States and, to a lesser degree, the United Kingdom.

The seniority system in wage determination and in promotion, heavy investment in on-the-job training which is company-specific, and an emphasis on enterprise unionism, are similarly designed to support relational contracting. The industrially based structure of Western unionism is designed to increase the union's negotiating power by diluting the common interests of firm and worker. The Japanese system is intended to reinforce that identity of interest. As in any relational contract, these concerns are reciprocated in the emphasis which Japanese managers place on employee interests over those of shareholders.

Illustration 5.9. Identity of Interest in Japan

'The major difference is that Hitachi union leaders share the managers' concern with the growth and prosperity of Hitachi as a corporation in competition with other corporations. Full-time British union officials may share with the Engineering Employers Federation a concern with the future of "the industry" in the abstract but have no special concern with the prosperity of particular concrete firms within it. Shop stewards are in fact likely to have such a concern, but the union ethos, as set by full-time officials, operates to discourage it' (Dore, 1973: 200).

Continuity and stability in supplier/assembler relationships are well-known features of Japanese business, and firms such as Toyota and NEC are surrounded by their keiretsu, or supplier group. Just in time inventory management, as developed by Toyota, is a striking example of a structure possible only under relational contracting. The urgent demand requires the urgent willing response of the partner in a long-term relationship, not the hard-nosed spot contract which can be achieved when the opposing party is most vulnerable. In the United States, customized components are generally manufactured in-house or by wholly owned subsidiaries of the assembler (Monteverde and Teece, 1982). In Japan these items are produced by independent members of the keiretsu, who are willing to take the risk of establishing dedicated production facilities and installing transaction-specific assets. The same supply processes are achieved through classical contracting in one country, through relational contracting in the other.

Japan has a long tradition of co-operative groupings of companies, originating in the zaibatsu which were dissolved by the Allies after the Second World War. Today's networks are looser associations of companies. Some of these kigyo-shudan, such as the Mitsui group, are descendants of the zaibatsu, while others, such as Dai-Ichi-Kangyo, are new formations. These groups typically include one company in each main industrial sector, including a bank and a trading company. There are commonly reciprocal shareholdings among members of the group.

Although there is some presumption in favour of inter-group trading among these networks, members of them also trade extensively with Japanese companies outside the group. The power of the network seems to rest partly in the exchange of information through it (hence the emphasis on 'one-set-ism', the requirement that the group contains precisely one company in each sector), and on the ready ability of the group to support transactions which benefit from relational contracting, such as financing, overseas distribution, and joint venture.

The social context of architecture

The Japanese experience, and the contrast between Japan and the United States, illustrates the degree to which relational contracting and architecture are the product of the broader commercial and social environment. Geographical proximity is important to networking, although the role it plays is not entirely obvious. Since transporting ties is neither slow nor expensive, why are most Italian ties produced in a single small region? At first sight it seems absurd that at a time when capital markets have become international and worldwide communication of data, funds, and information has become instantaneous, the financial institutions of the world should be concentrated in tiny and fabulously expensive areas of lower Manhattan and eastern London.

What lies behind this is the need to establish trust and penalize opportunism in a network of relational contracts, which is facilitated if business relationships are supported by a corresponding network of social relationships. We are all more inclined to trust people we know; a view which is partly based on instinct and emotion, partly on our capacity to make our own judgements (we are also inclined to mistrust some people we know), and partly on a rational calculation that people are less likely to cheat us if by doing so they sacrifice a social reputation as well as a commercial one.

It may be no accident that the City of London's pre-eminence rested on the homogeneity of background and values created by the English class system and the English school system. These factors may also explain why conscious attempts to emulate the competitive advantages of networking through replication are rarely successful. The extensive entertainment which is integral to Japanese business similarly serves to reinforce relational contracts.

It follows that some social environments are more conducive to the development of competitive advantage through architecture than others. Since the essence of architecture is that organizations or groups of organizations have values—social and economic—distinct from those of their members, there is a direct conflict between individualism and the creation of architecture. This conflict is reinforced by the absence of powerful sanctions against opportunistic behaviour in an individualistic environment. Competitive strengths based on these architectures are therefore relatively rare in those environments where the prevailing ethos is strongly individualistic. Where they exist—as in the financial sector, in networking activities in less developed countries, and in the performance of companies with a very distinctive corporate ethos—the activities concerned are commonly viewed by outsiders with a degree of hostility and suspicion. Nepotism is a term of abuse, contact networks are corrupt, and the organization man is regarded with uneasy laughter.

Our reaction is the same when we hear of Japanese workers gathering to sing the company song. But our incomprehension of this cultural divide applies also in countries where the difference is less apparent. We feel outraged, as apparently the Swiss do not, at the disgrace and imprisonment of Stanley Adams[1] for exposing improper and illegal behaviour by his employer, Hoffmann–La Roche. Networking within Italian communities resurfaced in the United States in the form of criminal conspiracies and political corruption (as it does in Italy also) and we feel relieved when it is stamped out; but we also observe it in Italy itself as a potent form of commercial organization. It would be wrong to make too much of the cultural origins of competitive advantage through architecture. There are many relational contracts made in the United States, and many classical contracts in Japan. But it would be equally wrong to ignore them. I return to these issues in Chapters 20 and 22.

The relationship between organizational structure and firm performance is a subject pursued in sociology, in economics, and in popular management literature. The most substantive tradition is in organizational behaviour—indeed, Weber's principal concern (1925) was with precisely these issues—but more recent literature begins with Burns and Stalker (1961), and Child and the Aston group (Child, 1974, 1975, 1984). Mintzberg (1979) is a managerially orientated synthesis. In economics see, for example, Simon (1961); Cyert and March (1963); Arrow (1974); Williamson (1975, 1985); and, for an empirical analysis, Steer and Cable (1978). Among management books, Peters and Waterman (1982) are the originators of 'excellence'; Morgan (1986) describes the style of organizations in terms of metaphors. O'Reilly (1989), Hampden-Turner (1990a, 1990b), and Kono (1990) review 'corporate culture'. Camerer and Vepsalainen (1991) assess culture in a manner closer in spirit to the arguments here. Although the style is very different, there are many similarities between my approach and that of Lloyd (1990).

On the more specific concerns of this chapter, the intermediate ground between markets and hierarchies has been delineated by writers from a variety of different perspectives. Thompson *et al.* (1991) is a valuable collection of articles which draw on these different disciplines. Richardson (1972) is an early contribution in economics, Pfeffer and Nowak (1976—interorganizational behaviour) and Miles and Snow (1986—networks) in sociological terms, while Johnston and Lawrence (1988) discuss 'the value adding partnership'. Other contributions on networks include Thorelli (1986), Jarillo (1988, 1990), Blois (1990). Joint ventures and strategic alliances are currently in fashion, and discussions include Ohmae (1989), Hamel, Doz, and Prahalad (1989), and Norburn and Schoenberg (1990).

The distribution of the product within which the whole exceeds the sum of individual contributions is described by the economic theory of teams (Marschak and Radner, 1972; Akerlof, 1976; Radner, 1985). Organizational routines are identified by Nelson and Winter (1982) as a source of competitive advantage. Organizational knowledge is developed as 'core competence' by Prahalad and Hamel (1990). The role of trust in exchange is emphasized in different ways by Arrow (1974), by Ouchi (1981), and by Hirschman (1982). Zucker (1986) provides a historical analysis of the way in which trust relationships are supported by organizational form and the social and cultural environment. Gambetta (1990) is a collection of related essays.

Italian networks have been widely studied. See Lorenzoni (1979), Piore and Sabel

---

1 Adams was imprisoned in Switzerland for disclosing information to the European Commission about illegal price-fixing.

(1984), Porter (1990). Lorenz (1991) describes analogous relationships within French industry. Gerlach (1987) and Odagiri (1991) emphasize the role of networks in Japanese management, while the operations of Japanese companies in the West are described in Dunning (1986) and Gordon (1988). See notes on Chapter 1 for the several histories of IBM and Marks & Spencer. The economics of Liverpool Football Club is developed at greater length in dell'Osso and Szymanski (1991).

6

....

Reputation

The second primary distinctive capability is reputation. Reputation is the most important commercial mechanism for conveying information to consumers. But reputation is not equally important in all markets. Customers find out about product characteristics and product quality in many ways. Sometimes they learn from search. Other attributes become apparent immediately a product is used. The importance of reputation can be seen in markets—from car hire to accountancy—where product quality is important but can only be identified through long-term experience. In these markets, reputations are difficult and costly to create but once established can yield substantial added value.

Most of the chapter is concerned with how reputations are built, maintained—and lost. The process of building up a reputation can be accelerated by staking a reputation which has been established in a related market, or by making a clear public demonstration of commitment to a market. But it does not always pay to maintain a reputation. The best strategy may be to milk it. In some markets this is so often true that few worthwhile reputations survive.

Reputation has been important to successful traders since pre-industrial society. Merchants were concerned to demonstrate the purity of their assays or the fullness of their measure. Craftsmen stressed the quality of their workmanship. But how were their ignorant customers to assess purity, fullness, or quality?

Sometimes they looked to the state to regulate the market for them. In other cases, traders banded together in guilds to monitor each other's work and established an honest reputation for the whole group. Some craftsmen relied on their own name, or that of their family. All these mechanisms are still important today.

Reputation is the market's method of dealing with attributes of product quality which customers cannot easily monitor for themselves. The composition of an apparently precious metal is such a characteristic. It is more costly to offer an assay of the declared specification. It is less profitable, in the short run, to provide full measure or good workmanship. The quality trader can only recover the higher costs of good quality if consumers know that the quality is good. If customers do not know this, then the firm will incur higher costs but obtain no higher price. This is both a problem and an opportunity.

In a market where consumers can easily ascertain the characteristics of the goods they buy, there is no reason why, in the long run, the price of any characteristic—including better quality—should exceed the cost of providing it. But if product quality cannot easily be established, then the firm which can provide its customers not only with higher quality but with the assurance of higher quality may be able to command a price premium which far exceeds the difference in costs.

Firms convey information about their products to their customers through advertising and branding, and the analysis of this chapter is closely related to that of Chapter 16. But firms also tell customers about their products in other ways—most notably through the product itself. Nor is providing information about product quality the only function which branding and advertising serve.

But reputation needs to have a name attached to it, whether that is the name of an individual, a profession, or a company. In some markets where quality standards are variable, names like Hertz or Avis, Price Waterhouse or Peat Marwick command large price premiums (Table 6.1). Car hire and international accountancy are both goods for which it is difficult for the customer to assess product quality in advance and major firms with strong brand names have come to dominate these markets. Yet in other markets—used car dealing or real estate broking—sellers generally are held in low regard. Car manufacturers have tried to remedy this by offering quality certification, but

Table 6.1. The Cost of a Car, an Accountant, and a Reputation

Renting a group A car in London, per week (July 1991) (£UK)		Hiring an accountant in Dublin, per hour (1990) (£IR)
Hertz	214	Partner, international firm £90
Avis	199	Manager, international firm £60
Budget	203	
Thrifty	157	Partner, local firm £40
Acton	147	Manager, local firm £30
Express	140	
East London	150	
Team Cars	150	

Source: Quotations by firms; Davis, Hanlon, and Kay (1992).

these efforts have not proved very successful. Clubs of estate agents, like ORPI in France, or franchise arrangements, like Century 21, have enjoyed only limited success, and in Britain the well-respected Prudential Assurance built up a large chain of estate agents only to conclude it could not manage it profitably and dispose of it at a loss of £300 million. This chapter defines the narrow class of markets in which building reputations can be a powerful source of competitive advantage, and describes how firms have achieved it.

Search and experience goods

Consumers find out about the quality of the goods they buy in many ways. They learn by search—inspecting the good or service and comparing it and its specification with alternatives. When a customer takes a train journey, or buys a lettuce or a camera, he or she establishes most of what needs to be known about the commodity before purchase.

You cannot learn much about the taste of the soup in a can, or the flavour of a beer, before you buy them. But you do discover these things almost as soon as you consume them. For some other commodities, knowledge of their quality builds up only slowly. It takes time to tell whether a baldness cure is actually promoting the regrowth of your hair. Perhaps experience is difficult to interpret. If you recover from an illness, you do not know whether you consulted a good doctor or whether you would have got better anyway. Often reliability is the key attribute. Reliability may be represented by the consistent flavour of a McDonald's hamburger, the frequency with which a machine breaks down, or the soundness of the opinions of a professional adviser. In each case it is only time and extensive experience that will tell.

Some goods are consumed on behalf of other people, and they may be slow to convey their experience of them to you. Few people will tell you whether your under-arm deodorant or breath freshener is working, or what they really think of the wine or whisky you serve them. You have to infer your cat's opinion of its food. Learning about the quality of these products is a slow process. Experience is less useful if commodities are purchased infrequently. Travellers may have a favourite hotel in Paris. Fewer have useful experience about which hotels in Bogotà are best.

There is a small category of goods for which neither search nor experience is of much value. Some goods cannot be inspected, and are consumed only once—like pension plans and funeral services. But there are less extreme instances. Search yields little information about the efficiency and reliability of a consumer durable—a washing machine or a car. Experience does, but by the time the consumer is ready to purchase again the range of models available may well be quite different. It is rare to buy the same dishwasher twice even if it is an excellent dishwasher. For these goods, neither search nor experience helps much, and consumers use other criteria in making their choices. They rely on their knowledge of the manufacturer (as distinct from their experience of the product), on the advice of the retailer, or on the recommendations of consumer magazines or trusted friends.

Most goods have many different characteristics. Some properties are revealed by search, others emerge immediately on consumption, and yet others through long-term experience. There are almost always some attributes which are never ascertained at all. But although no hard and fast distinctions can, or should, be made, the ways in which customers acquire information are important influences on market structure. Table 6.2 categorizes some goods by reference to the principal ways in which consumers learn about their salient characteristics. This classification largely determines the ways in which these goods are sold and influences the nature of competitive advantage in different markets and industries.

Table 6.2. How Buyers Learn about Product Characteristics

Search	Immediate experience	Long-term experience	In other ways
Office furniture	Beer	Medicines	Computers
Clothes	Canned food	Washing powders	Shares
Fresh fruit	Newspapers	Accountants	Pension plans
Electricity	Caterers	Managers	Dishwashers
Term loans	Production workers	Security services	

Signalling quality—a Prisoner's Dilemma

Many markets are characterized by the following problem. A commodity can be made to a high- or low-quality specification. Goods of known low-quality command much lower prices which reflect the trouble given and the necessary expenditure on repair, maintenance, and replacement. These costs far exceed the additional cost to the manufacturer of ensuring the high-quality specification. What if customers cannot tell, by inspection or by immediate experience, whether the good is of high- or low-quality? They can offer to pay the high price, or the low one; they might receive a high-quality item, or a poor-quality one.

This is a Prisoner's Dilemma (Figure 6.1). The consumer will offer a low price and receive a low-quality product. Both consumer and producer would be better off in the high-price–high-quality position. But even if both recognize that, they cannot bring it about, either unilaterally or by agreement. Chapter 3 described the two ways of escaping from the Prisoner's Dilemma. One is to change the payoff structure; the second is to engage in a repeated game. There are no others. If buyers and sellers are engaged in one-off transactions in which the buyer cannot monitor the quality of the product, then it is almost inevitable that buyer expectations will be low and that sellers will fulfil these expectations. This is what goes wrong in used car markets and real estate broking.

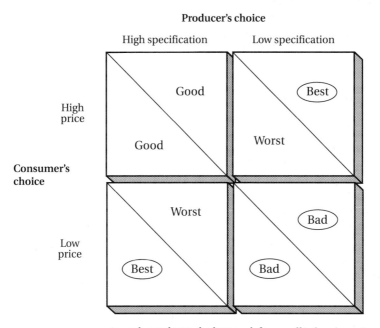

Producer's choice

In each quadrant, the bottom left pay-off is for player 1 and the upper right for player 2. Circles indicate that a pay-off is the best outcome for that player given the strategy of the other.

Fig. 6.1. The Product Quality Game

Japanese producers of automobiles and hi-fi equipment chose to change the payoff structure of Figure 6.1 when they entered. The manufacturers knew that their products were of high-quality. Their potential customers did not. Many of them believed that Japanese goods were shoddy imitations of Western products. Japanese manufacturers offered more extensive warranties than had been usual in the car and hi-fi markets. The effect of the extended warranty is twofold. It saves you expense if the product goes wrong. But the purchaser is typically looking not so much for insurance against fault when it occurs as assurance that fault will not occur. An extended warranty is an expensive thing to offer if your product is likely to go wrong. Offering it gives you an incentive to keep quality high, and is a credible demonstration of your faith in the product. A producer who offers an extended warranty is making a commitment which will prove expensive if—but only if—the product is unreliable.

The extended warranty serves the same function in the product quality game as the criminals who beat up the prisoner who confesses in the Prisoner's Dilemma. By unilaterally worsening the pay-offs to one strategy—the low-quality product—the manufacturer establishes a clear incentive to pursue a high-quality strategy. If consumers recognize this, customers and producers together can establish a high-price, high-quality equilibrium.

Such offers—money-back assurances, free trials, long-term warranties—are a familiar part of entry strategies in these markets. These devices are necessary because it is difficult to persuade consumers on the first trial that you are engaged with them in a repeated game, which is the alternative mechanism of resolving a Prisoner's Dilemma. Producers of long-term experience goods characteristically draw attention to the long-established nature of their enterprise. There is no clearer statement that the firm is playing a repeated game than 'founded in 1853', and it is banks and insurance companies, rather than the producers of search and short-term experience goods, which make these claims. A new entrant must signal long-term commitment to the market in other ways. Launch expenditures on advertising and promotion may play this role. Large initial expenditures are a demonstration of commitment to the market, and that is how consumers will interpret them.

Reputation is the name for a reiterated high-quality strategy in a market for long-term experience goods. How is such a reputation established? How is it sustained? When does it not pay to attempt to sustain it?

The profitability of reputation

All firms want to have a good reputation with their customers and the community at large, and it is difficult to imagine any situation in which a good reputation would not be of commercial benefit. But the class of markets in which reputation is a source of substantial and sustained competitive advantage is limited.

Reputation is rarely of critical importance where consumers learn about product quality through search. True, search is costly, and customers generally proceed by shortlisting only a few of the products which are available. A good reputation will help to put you on that list, a bad reputation will take you off it. But so will other mechanisms, such as advertising, widespread availability, or retailer recommendation. Branding is of least significance in markets where consumers learn about products through search (Chapter 16). Nor is reputation an important factor for immediate experience goods. If consumers can quickly learn about product quality for themselves, they need not rely much on reputation.

If customers cannot easily determine product quality through search or their own experience, they will be swayed by reputation. If product quality does emerge eventually, through long-term experience, then reputation will be hard to maintain unless quality is indeed high. It is these reputations that may command high prices.

International car-hire firms such as Hertz and Avis are predominantly franchise operations. They provide certification for local traders who would otherwise find it difficult to demonstrate the quality of their product to what—by the very nature of the product—is a transient clientele. Without this certification, these traders would gain nothing by providing quality since they would not expect to recover the above average costs of doing so in above average prices. In this market, the price advantage accruing to reputation is very large, as Table 6.1 showed. It is especially large in the business rental market, where reliability is of particular importance. The overall cost of a business trip is such that greater confidence that time will not be spent at the side of the road waiting for a breakdown truck is worth buying, even at a high price.

The accountancy market is increasingly segmented. The major international firms bring an international reputation to their services. They cater particularly for multinational clients who are often ignorant of the abilities of local practitioners. The reputations of local firms—if they exist at all—are valid only in a local market and in many countries the best local practitioners now trade under the brand names of the international firms.

To what extent are these returns the returns to being the best, and to what extent are they returns to being perceived (or supposed) to be the best? There is a distinction here in principle, and while in practice it becomes blurred, the answer is critical to the distribution of the added value which reputation creates. In most markets it is not too difficult for a potential concessionaire to meet Hertz standards, and the returns from the franchise accrue in large measure to the franchisor. In accountancy, there have often been several international firms chasing few outstanding local practitioners. This, together with the partnership structure characteristic of the accountancy industry, has ensured that the added value created through reputation largely remains in the country in which the service is provided.

Building reputation

In the long run, reputation can only be based on the provision of high-quality in repeated trials. Such a record will take longest to establish in precisely those markets for long-term experience goods where it is most valuable. There is no paradox here—it is precisely what market efficiency would predict. Only after much experience will consumers come to recognize that quality is high and only after further experience will they recognize that it is consistently high. The process of spreading reputation will be more rapid in markets where consumers are inclined to share their experience than those in which they are not. We talk to each other about shows we have seen, restaurants we have visited, and stores we patronize. Reputations are created and destroyed relatively quickly in these markets. We are less inclined to discuss condoms, lavatory cleaners, and sanitary products, and in Europe are often similarly embarrassed to discuss financial services. Established reputations in these markets tend to be both profitable and enduring, as Table 6.3 shows.

Table 6.3. The Profitability of Embarrassing Items

Returns on sales and investment in years preceding Monopolies and Mergers Commission Report.		(%)	
Condoms (MMC Report 1975)		*1970*	*1974*
LRC Products Ltd.	ROS	36	40
	ROI	76	79
Tampons (MMC Report 1980)		*1975*	*1979*
Tampax	ROS	38	30
	ROI	62	53
Southalls	ROS	26	17
	ROI	47	32
Pest Control Services (MMC Report 1988)		*1982*	*1986*
Rentokil	ROS	26	28
	ROI	90	92

Source: MMC Reports.

Reputations very frequently originate from another source of competitive advantage. This may be transformed into reputation with time or may be supplemented by it. Glaxo's current competitive advantage is based on innovation but, as Zantac patents expire, the company must hope that Zantac's reputation is sufficiently powerful to maintain its position against generic equivalents. Evidence from the pharmaceutical market generally suggests that it is very likely that it can. Over a twenty-year period, an innovation advantage will have been transformed into a reputation advantage.

The same process can be seen at work in many other cases. BMW's initial competitive advantage was based on its architecture, but this has been enhanced—and perhaps overshadowed—by the competitive strength of its reputation. It is firms with another source of competitive advantage which are best placed to develop reputation. The existence of another competitive advantage is itself an indication of continued commitment to the market, while the returns from that competitive advantage provide a base from which to invest in future reputation. It is obviously good strategy for Glaxo to build a reputation for quality in the market for anti-ulcer drugs. Not only is it easier and cheaper for them to build such a reputation than it would be for a generic competitor, but they have an opportunity to do so while still remaining extremely profitable.

But firms will always seek to accelerate the establishment of a reputation. The analysis of the Prisoner's Dilemma pointed to two methods of doing so—making credible promises which are costly if quality promises are not fulfilled, and public and credible demonstrations of long-term commitment to the market. Frequently, these two approaches are combined.

Mechanisms for achieving this include:

- introductory offers, warranties, money-back guarantees;
- substantial advertising and launch expenditures;
- staking a reputation derived from elsewhere.

The first of these strategies was described above. The second is explained more fully in Chapter 16. The third mechanism is the attempt to transfer reputation from one market to another.

Spreading reputation

Endorsement by famous personalities is a curious, but very clear, example of how reputation can be spread. Everyone knows that the celebrities give their endorsement, not because they have scoured the market for the best product, but because they have canvassed potential sponsors for the highest fee. So why are consumers influenced by the endorsement?

Purchasers of the endorsed product are not behaving entirely irrationally. The sportsman is, to some degree, putting his reputation at risk. If the product is of low-quality he damages his sporting reputation and his value to other sponsors, and he has therefore some incentive to ensure that it is not. For the manufacturer, payment of the endorsement fee is a demonstration of his commitment to the market. Willingness to pay the endorsement fee is therefore actually a measure of product quality. All parties are concerned to demonstrate their intention to participate in a reiterated game.

If the personality is truly putting his reputation on the line, there has to be some relationship between the area in which the reputation arises and the area in which it is pledged. It is credible for Seve Ballesteros to endorse a brand of golf shoe, and perhaps American Express cards. The connection can be weak. The cricketer Denis Compton's endorsement of Brylcreem was apparently effective. Compton, although not a hairstylist, was at least no worse qualified to know whether Brylcreem kept his hair in place than anyone else, and it is at least arguable that cricketers have more need than most people to maintain an immaculate appearance in trying conditions. However, neither Ballesteros nor Compton are useful endorsers of a management textbook, because the reader has no reason to think they are competent to judge management textbooks. If we are dissatisfied with the book, we will not think any less of them as golfer or cricketer. It is more effective to use a business school professor, and also cheaper.

Mlle. Pavlova the Incomparable, says;

"It is with pleasure that I state to you that O'Sullivan's Heels of new live rubber give me great comfort in walking. I have them on all my walking shoes and also a number of my dancing shoes. I recommend them to every member of the company."

O'Sullivan's Heels are made of new live rubber—rubber with all the spring in it—and are worn by successful people everywhere.

Ask your bootmaker to attach them. 50c. complete—or you can buy O'Sullivanized Boots and Slippers.

Fig. 6.2. Endorsements Then and Now

Guinness guzzler Rutger Hauer has revealed that his telly love affair with the creamy brew is nothing but froth. Rutger says he's a teetotaller—and allergic to the black stuff.

Gazza picked up £500,000 playing the Brut man of the Nineties. Then he revealed after-shave brings him out in a rash. He said, 'I can't stand the stuff. I might wear it for matches—but only to keep the opposition away.'

Wayne, who fills the cash machine in the glitzy Nat West ad, urges us to choose the bank for our hard-earned cash. But in real life actor Dean Gatiss closed his account because it didn't offer high enough interest.

Sun, 11 Nov. 1991, p. 9

Endorsement is, of course, simply the most explicit case of the most usual mechanism for developing a reputation in a new market quickly: staking a reputation which has been acquired in another market. BMW's reputation in cars reinforces its reputation in motor bikes, and vice versa. BMW also endorses a range of 'Active Line' sportswear. There is small reason to believe that the capabilities which distinguish BMW cars are applicable to the manufacture of sportswear. But since the revenue from the sale of sportswear is very small relative to the revenue from the sale of BMW cars, it would clearly be foolish for BMW to attach its name to poor-quality sportswear. The company is, however, pushing it a bit. If it were to endorse, say, garden furniture, it is not clear that its reputation would genuinely be at stake. If the garden furniture is disappointing, why should this lead me to think worse of BMW cars? The likely consequence is that the BMW marque is less likely to be effective in selling garden furniture, and indeed the attempt to do so may actually impinge negatively on the BMW reputation as a whole, by suggesting that the owner is careless of its value.

In 1988 Marks & Spencer launched a range of pooled investment products (known as unit trusts in the UK). It is not obvious why Marks & Spencer's capabilities in clothing and food retailing should be relevant to the management of unit trusts; thus, one might ask whether its reputation was truly at stake. The prospectus sought to answer this in explicit terms (Illustration 6.1).

Illustration 6.1. Marks & Spencer Financial Services

As with everything we do—fashion, furniture, food—Marks & Spencer takes the utmost care to select the best suppliers to give you both quality and value for money. Our approach to investment is no exception.

... the funds within the Investment Portfolio are invested by five carefully selected investment management companies. All of them have proven track records and have been chosen for their specialist skills after a rigorous selection process.

Naturally, we monitor the performance of each team very carefully.

Source: Promotional brochure for Marks & Spencer Investment Portfolio.

It put the Marks & Spencer reputation clearly on the line, and the association was successful. The launch attracted £56 million, an exceptional sum. But the risks involved were, and are, substantial. The charges levied were relatively high—in particular, the annual charge was 1½ per cent against an industry norm of 1 per cent. But this additional annual revenue—at £¼ million—is distinctly small beer when compared with an annual turnover of £6 billion and profits of £600 million on the mainstream business.

Marks & Spencer's incentive to ensure that its unit trusts provide a performance which matches the reputation it has earned in food and clothing is therefore very considerable. What must be in doubt is its ability to do this; not only because financial services are not its main business, but because the nature of investment activity is that it is difficult to guarantee outperformance simply by monitoring, however diligent. If the unit trusts do not do well, then the adverse impact on the value of its reputation taken as a whole need only be very slight to offset the gains it has made on selling unit trusts. By deliberately emphasizing its general reputation it has deliberately taken that risk. The key question for Marks & Spencer is whether the value of its reputation over the three businesses of clothing, food, and financial services exceeds its value over the two businesses of clothing and food. The answer to that question will only emerge as does the long-term performance of the trusts. In every attempt to spread reputation the firm must balance the added value gained in the new market against that potentially lost in the old.

Maintaining or devaluing reputation

Since reputations are difficult and costly to establish, traders with good reputations might be expected to work hard to sustain them. Mostly they do. But a reputation for good quality is valuable to those who provide poor quality as well as those who provide good quality. Sometimes, in fact, it may be more valuable to those whose quality is poor. Swindlers have been aware of this for millennia. On a more modest scale, spreading a reputation may ultimately stretch to milking it. Hilton began as a brand name for a premium hotel. But the Hilton hotel group devalued the product. It first sold its hotels outside the United States to an airline, TWA, which had limited skills in hotel management and a public reputation which, although not bad, did not compare with the original Hilton image. Within the United States, the Hilton Hotel Corporation expanded through franchising. In 1970, it owned three-quarters of the hotel rooms that bore its name; by the mid-1980s, that proportion was little more than one-third. The company moved into casinos, and suffered the humiliation of being refused a licence to operate in Atlantic City. Towards the end of the decade, the US group began to trade under a new brand name, Conrad Hotels, and joined with the new owners of the international hotels in a marketing campaign to restore the jaded image of the name.

Maintaining a reputation is most worthwhile if two conditions are met. The first is that the premium available for providing high quality—or, more precisely the premium for being known to provide high quality—is large relative to the cost of providing high quality. It is not much more costly to be a good doctor than a bad doctor and that makes a good reputation particularly valuable to a medical practitioner. It is cheaper for Toyota to ensure high standards in its cars than it is for some other producers and that makes Toyota's reputation for reliability particularly important to them.

The value of reputation also depends on the likelihood of repeat purchase. If you are unlikely to provide the service again, there is little reason to maintain a reputation. This is another recognizable characteristic of the Prisoner's Dilemma. If you are playing the game only once, or for the last time, then the right strategy is always to cheat. In markets where quality is not easy to determine and where buyers and sellers generally meet only once, quality is likely to be generally low unless consumers are willing to share their experiences with each other. Risqué night-clubs in foreign cities are generally disappointing.

Reputations can lose value for other reasons. The importance of quality certification to consumers may change. The introduction of standard quality grading in the supply of petrol in the United Kingdom led directly to a large reduction in brand advertising and was followed by extensive entry by smaller producers. 'You can be sure of Shell' did not have the same force if you could be equally sure of any brand of petrol that had the same British Standards Institution grading on the pump. In the law and accountancy markets, on the other hand, many customers are no longer willing to accept that any qualified practitioner can do the job and the increasing dominance of large firms reflects the need for additional quality certification. Official monitoring of quality can directly affect the value of reputation in an industry, and the incentives which producers have to maintain or enhance them. In petrol, the introduction of external regulation made reputations of wholesalers less valuable. In professional services, the weakness of the official system of regulation has strengthened the role of leading firms.

A reputation is only valuable, or worth maintaining, in a continuing market and its value disappears with that market. It is difficult to transfer such a reputation to a different product group. It is likely to be apparent to all that the reputation is of diminishing value in its existing market and consequently a less powerful asset to stake in a new one. The names of the great shipping and railroad companies have, in the main, simply fallen into decline. Where the market continues, however, the reputation may be transferred even if those who provide the service change. Why should lawyers continue to turn with confidence to *Halsbury's Laws of England* when they know that Lord Halsbury has been dead since 1921? The answer is that the current owners of that title (the publishers, Butterworths), perceiving that its reputation for reliability is an asset of considerable value and that the demand for legal reference books is an enduring one, have a powerful incentive to ensure that the current editors maintain high standards.

The analysis here, and that of Chapter 16, owes much to the insufficiently acknowledged arguments of Philip Nelson (1970, 1974, and 1975). Developments of this can be found in Kihlstrom and Riordan (1984), Grant (1986). The 'lemons' problem—why, in the absence of reputation mechanisms, markets for long-term experience goods rarely work well—is brilliantly expounded by Akerlof (1970).

A substantial economics literature is concerned with the modelling of reputation processes. Spence (1973) first emphasized the importance of signalling in market processes, a theme developed in Kihlstrom and Riordan (1984) and Heil and Robertson (1991). Schmalensee (1978) related this to advertising, while Schapiro (1982) and Milgrom and Roberts (1986) tie this in with reputation in an explicit way. See also Klein and Leffler (1981), Kreps and Wilson (1982), Rogerson (1983), Allen (1984). The role of brands and warranties is emphasized by Grossman (1981), Williamson (1983), Wernerfelt (1988), Weigelt and Camerer (1988), Lutz (1989).

Writers on marketing are mostly concerned with brands rather than the underlying reputation mechanism, although see Jones (1986), Jacobsen and Aaker (1987). On brand extension, see Tauber (1981), Buday (1989), Aaker and Keller (1990). Kaikati (1987) is a more earnest view of endorsement by celebrities than that taken here.

7

Innovation

Innovation is the third primary distinctive capability. Yet firms often fail to gain competitive advantage from innovation. In this chapter I explain why. I describe the costs and uncertainties associated with the process of innovation, and the difficulties firms encounter in securing the returns to innovation for themselves. What appear to be the rewards of innovation are often really the product of the firm's architecture. Some firms have established an architecture which stimulates a continuous process of innovations. Other firms have created an architecture which enables them to implement innovation particularly effectively.

The process of innovation often involves complex interactions between firms. Two common problems are those situations in which the innovator can often scoop the pool (patent races) and those in which success for all depends on the establishment of common technical standards (standards battles). This chapter introduces the problems of achieving competitive advantage which is sustainable and appropriable. I discuss these issues— which apply to all distinctive capabilities—more extensively in Chapters 11 and 12.

Business history is full of the stories of firms which innovated but failed to turn that innovation into sustainable competitive advantage. European business history seems to be particularly full of such stories. The British company EMI was one of the most effectively innovative companies there has ever been. It was a pioneer in television, a leader in computers, its music business was at the centre of a revolution in popular culture, and its scanner technology transformed radiology. Today only its music business survives.

Philips pioneered almost every major area of consumer electronics. The company invented the audio cassette and the compact disc and led in the development and manufacture of video-cassette recorders. Europe has often enjoyed an innovative lead in aircraft manufacture. Jet engines were invented here, and first put into commercial operation by de Havilland. Collaboration between Aérospatiale and the British Aircraft Corporation produced the world's only supersonic passenger aircraft. Sir Clive Sinclair created a reputation for innovation by bringing to market for the first time products as diverse as digital watches, personal computers, and battery-operated cars; and with it a reputation for commercial success that would ensure that most investors would flee from any project with which he was associated. But it is not only in Europe that innovation is no assured route to success. Bowmar pioneered the hand-held calculator, National Semiconductor and Texas Instruments once seemed to lead the world electronics industry, all only to see dominance go to Japan.

That catalogue itself demonstrates that there is no single cause of failure to derive commercial success from innovation. But the reasons why it is difficult to create competitive advantage through innovation fall into three broad categories. First, innovation is, by its very nature, costly and uncertain. It follows that even an innovation which is technically successful may not be profitable. Second, the process of innovation is hard to manage. The direction of innovative companies requires special skills, as does the control of innovation in firms whose market position does not principally rest on their technology. And third, the rewards of innovation are difficult to appropriate. Returns must be defended from competitors, from suppliers and customers, and may accrue to groups within the firm rather than to the organization itself. This chapter is concerned with these issues—the process of innovation, the management of innovation, and the appropriability of innovation. The problem of appropriability is a recurrent theme which runs through every aspect of innovation in business.

The process of innovation

Managing innovation is costly and risky. New products may fail because there is no demand, or insufficient demand. This is true of more fundamental innovations than the 'new' brands of confectionery or washing powder which fast-moving consumer goods markets attract. Battery-operated cars, three dimensional cameras, and holograms are more than the brainwaves of the mad inventor caricatures, but less than commercial products. Uncertainties go in both directions. Xerox succeeded brilliantly with photocopiers, but pioneered both fax machines and personal computers only to conclude, quite mistakenly, that these were not commercial products.

If innovation is costly and uncertain, it is nevertheless competitive. The attempt to innovate looks like the game of Fig. 7.1. This is a Chicken-type game. Perhaps there are no winners, because everyone holds back. Maybe electric cars would succeed if a major automobile producer devoted enough resources to the venture. The potential gains are very large. If several firms attempt to develop the same innovation, then the effect is to drive down returns for everyone, as has repeatedly happened in the aircraft market. The greatest prizes can come from developing a technology that others have

If innovation would succeed . . .

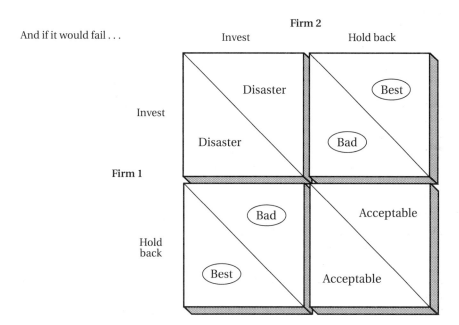

And if it would fail . . .

Fig. 7.1. The Innovation Game

rejected. Xerox developed electrostatic reproduction when potential competitors had concluded the market potential did not justify the investment.

Chicken structures can be seen most clearly when innovation is highly appropriable, so that the innovating firm is in a race in which the winner takes all. This is frequently the case in the pharmaceutical industry. In every Chicken game, potential participants need to consider carefully whether they wish to play at all. If there are many players, then it is quite possible that their combined expenditures will exceed the value of the prize for which they compete. If there are few entrants, then large prizes may be available for low stakes.

A variety of strategies are available to escape these difficulties. There is *commitment*—the tactic of pulling off the steering wheel and throwing it out of the window, so that rivals are in no doubt of your intention to stay in the game. The problem of commitment, as the extravagance of the example illustrates, lies in making the commitment credible. Pre-announcement of innovative products which have certainly not yet been put in marketable form and may not have even reached a prototype stage has been a regular feature of the recent evolution of the computer industry. It has been such a regular feature, in fact, that such announcements are no longer taken very seriously and so have lost their strategic value. It is difficult for firms to make commitments sufficiently credible, short of legally contracting to supply a product which has not yet been developed. This is a decidedly risky strategy, although it is one which is adopted in the aircraft industry, where there is little doubt that the product can be manufactured and uncertainties mostly relate to its cost.

The essence of Chicken is that someone needs to swerve, but there is nothing in the game to tell us who it should be. Often in real-life versions of the game, there *is* something to tell us who it should be. Costs may be lower or potential rewards higher for one of the participants. Inexperienced players are very unlikely to be the victor in a game of Chicken unless they bring some attribute that marks them out clearly from incumbents, and new entrants to the pharmaceutical industry have rarely been successful. Ventures by Guinness and Distillers proved disastrous and ICI became an effective competitor only after a very extended period of losses. Boeing and Airbus will minimize the risk of mutually destructive competition if they focus, as to a degree they have done, on aircraft better designed to meet the needs of American and European markets respectively; head-on competition is potentially enormously costly for both.

A reputation as a tough player is a powerful weapon in Chicken games, but it may be very costly to establish, since it militates against abandoning unprofitable lines of enquiry. It is not the strategy which successful long-term players have chosen to follow in markets where innovation is critical and research and development costs dominate total costs—Merck, IBM, Boeing. Failing all else, the best approach is the 'mixed strategy'—try some leads, do not follow all, keep your rivals guessing.

These competitive issues are much less critical where the process of innovation is specific to the individual firm. This is usually the case when technology is generally available but application in a particular context requires heavy expenditure. Implementation of information technology in the financial services industry provides a good example. General principles are well known and well established. But substantial investment is required in their development and implementation in the context of any particular firm or institution. The use of robotics in the automobile industry has similar characteristics.

Firm-specific innovation normally rests on the local application of generally available knowledge or technology. Success in this, although advantageous, is unlikely to create a sustainable competitive advantage unless the firm creates an architecture which enables it systematically to implement technology in advance of, or more cheaply than, its rivals. Halifax Building Society has been able to take advantage of its dominance in a West Yorkshire local labour market to build up a staff experienced in that organization and sensitive to user needs and so has been able to introduce information technology cheaply and rapidly in a way which other financial service firms have found hard to emulate.

Firm-specific investment is necessarily appropriable—the benefits of it accrue to the firm which undertakes it. If innovation is not firm specific, it may or may not be appropriable. Product innovations in fast-moving consumer goods industries are rarely appropriable. Once you have seen fromage frais in one supermarket many producers can make it and everyone can stock it. Innovative software, such as Lotus 1-2-3, is easier to protect. Such appropriability may, as in this case, be the result of legal protection through the copyright or patent system, or it may be the product of strategy.

Protecting and exploiting innovation

This issue of appropriability is fundamental. The central characteristic of a distinctive capability is that it cannot easily be replicated. A fundamental weakness of innovation as a source of competitive advantage is that mostly it *can* easily be replicated. The result is that the innovator may be exposed to the costs of innovation and the risks of development and introduction, only to see competitors share—or perhaps dominate—the fruits of success. Public policy has long recognized that there is a problem of appropriability. The results are potentially inefficient as well as unjust, since the prospect of replication reduces the incentive to innovate in the first place. Patent and copyright laws therefore protect innovators, and much innovation is publicly funded—including virtually all fundamental scientific research.

Patent law has been unable to keep pace with the range and complexity of modern innovation, and it is almost a matter of accident whether or not a specific innovation can achieve effective patent protection. Such protection works reasonably well in pharmaceuticals, although even here there is a well-known science of molecular manipulation, based on the attempt to invent round a patent by identifying a compound with essentially the same properties but distinct chemical composition. In other areas, patents may be used strategically. The innovation is surrounded with patents of doubtful value in the hope that legal costs will deter entrants. In many areas of innovation—such as product innovation in manufactured foodstuffs or in financial services—patents are generally useless. Most innovations—from calculus to junk bonds to flavoured yoghurt—are unpatentable.

If an innovation cannot be protected by law, it can sometimes be protected by commercial secrecy. This is almost never true of a product innovation. You cannot advertise new goods to your customers without at the same time advertising to your competitors. But for modest process innovations, secrecy may aid the innovator. Mostly, however, reverse engineering—working back from the final product to the initial design—gives the imitator an equivalent opportunity.

If neither law nor secrecy is sufficient to allow an innovation to be turned into competitive advantage, then strategy must be used instead. This is why appropriation is sometimes unexpectedly feasible. The Sony Walkman is an ingenious concept, but there is nothing about it that the innovator can protect. Any electronics manufacturer in the world who has seen it can make it. Yet Sony continues to be market leader. Marks & Spencer created a market for cook chill foods, offering prepared meals of higher quality and much higher price than had previously been available. The demonstration was immediately available to all food retailers and manufacturers; but Marks & Spencer continues to hold a prime position in the market.

The most effective way of turning innovation to competitive advantage is generally to deploy it in conjunction with another distinctive capability. Innovation and reputation, or innovation and architecture, are often potent combinations.

There are few innovations in the financial services sector that cannot be copied rapidly by competitors. But a reputation for innovation attracts customers, who can gain access to the latest products without having to shop around. Salomon Brothers has benefited from this and so have effective retailers like Sainsbury's. The reputation of the supplier may also induce customers to try innovations which they might otherwise view with reluctance. Coca-Cola did not sell a low sugar product until the availability of aspartame enabled the company to manufacture a good quality diet drink. Diet Coke then quickly gained an acceptability which drinks with other artificial sweeteners had not achieved, and established a new segment of the soft drink market in the process. Coke similarly established disposable cans in the market-place without themselves being the leader in this innovation.

It is firms with another distinctive capability which are generally best placed to derive competitive advantage from innovation. But even if this is not possible, innovation may yield competitive advantage with the aid of other strategic tools. The contrast between Glaxo and EMI, described in

Chapter 1, demonstrates the difference between success and failure in establishing complementary strategies for innovation. Distribution and manufacturing capabilities are generally important, and there is no necessary reason why the innovative firm should be the one to possess these particular attributes. If it does, then it is relatively well placed to appropriate the returns to the innovation. This was Glaxo's position in the UK market, but not in some of the other markets in which it also wished to compete.

If the innovative firm does not possess these complementary assets, it will need to acquire them. This can be attempted by building them up from scratch—as EMI attempted to do—or by establishing partnerships, as Glaxo did with Hoffmann–La Roche in the United States.

Standards

In some markets goods require the use of complementary equipment. An increasing number of new technologies associate hardware and software. Video-cassette recorders need video tapes, computers use software and operating systems, satellite television programmes require matching dishes. One of the most important standards issues of all will arise in the coming market for high-definition television, where there are three competing technologies, originating in Japan, Europe, and the United States. Yet standards also arise where no particularly advanced technology is involved—the use of a credit card requires both cardholder and acceptor, and the Visa and Mastercard networks define the two dominant world systems, putting increasing pressure on Amex's older but less widely accepted standard.

Fig. 7.2 illustrates a simple standards game. In reality there are many decision-makers, but two players are enough to illustrate the essential dilemma. If both customers choose either VHS or Betamax, there will be more software available to them than if they make different choices. Neither has any strong reason to choose one or the other. The important thing is that they should make the same choice.

This game is readily recognizable as a Battle of the Sexes—it is a problem of co-ordination. Like the Battle of the Sexes, it has no easy solution. More precisely, it has too many solutions, and so there is a real probability that no satisfactory outcome is reached. There are markets in which no standard evolves, as anyone who has bought a replacement windscreen wiper blade knows. For some time this seemed likely to be true of operating systems for small computers and it seems likely that it will be true of operating systems for large computers. The adoption of high-definition television is probably unstoppable but the existence of divergent standards will certainly delay it.

As in the Battle of the Sexes, it is not clear that prior discussion helps. There is no strong reason to choose one outcome rather than another—the important thing is to choose *some* outcome. Since all participants probably have slightly different preferences, discussion may well go on a long time. Attempts

A simple standards game

Customer 2

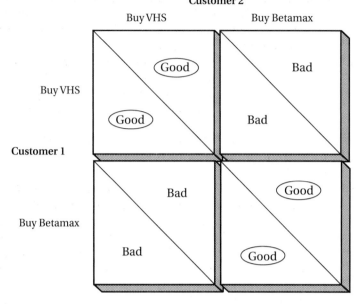

A worse standards game – where there are slight preferences

Customer 2

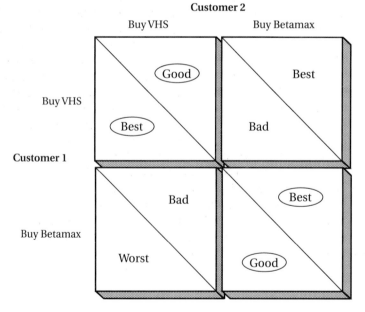

Fig. 7.2. Standards Games

to establish agreed standards are often protracted. The widespread use of EFTPOS—electronic payment systems in substitution for cash and cheque transactions—has been much delayed by precisely this type of difficulty. As with the issue of who goes through a door first, talking about it—after you, after you—does not necessarily resolve the dilemma.

Means of dealing with the Battle of the Sexes were described in Chapter 3. Hierarchy is one method. If someone has authority, a standard can be imposed. Sometimes governments, or standards institutions, may have this authority, but with the growing internationalization of the world economy the Battle of the Sexes often re-emerges as a game between different governments. Commitment helps, and a belief that one standard will win often ensures that it does win, regardless of the origin of that belief or the technical merit of the standard in question.

That means that it is rare for more than one standard to survive in the long run. More software will be developed for the leading standard and this in turn leads new purchasers to prefer the leading standard, creating a cumulative process. Technical quality plays little part in the choice. VHS is certainly no better than Sony's Betamax format. IBM's PC became the dominant standard although by common consent it offered little in the way of advanced or original design. Sky Television programmes have few critical admirers.

Two elements are critical in standards battles; the rapid achievement of an installed base and the credibility of the supplier. Sony mistakenly believed that its dominance of the professional video-cassette market would be translated into equal dominance of the consumer market. JVC instead pursued an open licensing policy which ensured that there were quickly more VHS than Betamax machines in operation. Although the denouement was to take a decade, its outcome was by then inevitable. British Satellite Broadcasting (BSB) was the approved satellite television broadcaster in the United Kingdom. The price of that official sponsorship was a variety of technical obligations, including the use of D-Mac, a new Community-sponsored standard (which would offer higher quality pictures to anyone who had the relevant equipment although almost no one did). These obligations contributed to a delay in reaching the air, with the result that the unofficial Sky Television had already established an installed base of subscribers. Sky emerged as clear victor in the resulting battle. Where authority seeks to determine the standard, the Battle of the Sexes is played, at length, in the offices of governments or the European Commission. In the television market, Rupert Murdoch's commitment to Sky was more credible than the fragmented and changing ownership of BSB. This credibility was the characteristic, above all, which IBM brought to the personal computer market.

Architecture in support of innovation

Often what appear to be competitive advantages based on innovation are in reality the product of distinctive capabilities based on architecture. There are two common types. One is the type of architecture that allows a firm to generate a continuing sequence of innovations. Even if the individual innovations themselves are inadequately appropriable, a stream of temporary competitive advantages, if repeated, becomes a sustainable and sustained advantage. The second is the architecture which enables a firm to adopt, quickly and effectively, generally available technology. The first is architecture directed to innovation itself; the second, architecture directed to the appropriation of innovation.

In many high-technology industries—particularly those associated with electronics, pharmaceuticals, or advanced transport equipment—technology is central to competitive advantage. That does not imply that innovation is the only source of competitive advantage—indeed even in these industries it is striking that the most successful firms are not necessarily the most innovative—but a flow of innovative activity, or a quick response to innovative pressure, is an essential requirement. Successful high technology companies are generally characterized by extensive networks of relational contracts. They reflect the requirements of architecture described in Chapter 5. Organization structures are informal, remuneration structures are flat and related to the performance of the organization rather than to that of individuals within it. The shape of the firm is built around requirements for speed of response and the free sharing of information—the characteristics which technological adaptation requires and which relational contracts facilitate.

The success of classically innovative firms like Hewlett-Packard rests less on any single innovation than on the architecture which has enabled them to develop a succession of innovative products. The continued lead enjoyed by Solid State Logic in the manufacture of synthesizers for recording studios rests not on the quality of its technology alone. It is combined with a set of customer relationships which enables it both to respond to customer needs and to secure product distribution.

Sony's architecture allows it to generate a seemingly endless series of innovations in consumer electronics. But Sony's reputation is also important. Customers will buy untried Sony products because of the strength of Sony's innovative record. Imitators have the near impossible job of replicating the architecture and the reputation rather than the relatively simple one of reproducing the innovations.

In other industries, innovation and technology are supportive of other competitive advantages rather than direct causes, and architecture may be a necessary complement to innovation-based advantages. Take a financial services firm, where lack of innovation can destroy competitive advantage but innovation cannot create it. You can be the worst bank in the world if your technology is bad enough but no amount of technical innovation will make you the best bank in the world; that is simply not the nature of competitive advantage in this market. In markets of this type, where technology is not *central*, it is almost inevitable that the contract between those who manage the firm and those who manage its technology is essentially classical in nature. It is credible that the value system of a small producer of high-performance engines revolves around success in technology, and that such innovation will be recognized and rewarded. You will not become chief executive of a bank by making its computer system work; nor should you. You will look for a more explicit reward structure, and the management of the bank, unable easily to monitor your performance, will focus on those indicators it can control. Inevitably, the contract becomes more classical in form.

As generally with the choice between contract structures, there are advantages and disadvantages to these different arrangements. Firms where technology is not central, which articulate the relationship between the innovator and the organization within a more conventional framework of hierarchical control, minimize the risk that technological enthusiasm will run away with corporate resources. The cost of this is a much more limited capacity to integrate technology into the rest of the organization.

The issue of integration of innovation technology into the organization is almost as critical as that of appropriability. In a sense, it is an aspect of appropriability—can the firm effectively 'own' the technology it deploys? In organizational terms, such ownership requires the effective integration of technology into the firm. In commercial terms, it requires that the added value created by innovation should accrue to the firm rather than to a subgroup within it, or outside it.

Innovation as competitive advantage

It is difficult to overstate the role of innovation in establishing competitive advantage, but it is easy to misunderstand what that role is. A common business mistake is to believe that innovation can compensate for competitive disadvantages in other areas. Such a strategy is almost never effective. Since innovations are rarely perfectly appropriable, a successful leap ahead is likely to be quickly imitated by stronger competitors. And since effective adoption of innovation is difficult, a successful outcome is less likely for the weak firm than for its competitors.

Midland Bank, the weakest of the four major UK clearing banks, was crippled by a disastrous US acquisition. It looked to technology to reduce the relatively high level of costs in its branch network and to achieve product innovation. But the deficiencies in management systems and competitive positioning, which lay behind its poor performance in the first place, equally prevented it from making a technical leap ahead of its competitors. These types of failure are widely repeated, and manufacturing companies, too, have often seen innovation as a quick fix solution to competitive weakness.

Technology is particularly often seen as a response to low-cost competition from lower-wage countries. In industries as diverse as the European cutlery industry and the US automobile industry, the belief that competitive disadvantages could be redressed through non-appropriable innovation has been shown to be false.

Innovation may be the distinctive capability which gives rise to competitive advantage, but that outcome is actually quite rare. More often what appears to be the return to innovation is in fact a return to a combination of competitive advantages. The most powerful of these are those deployed by firms such as Sony, which marshall all three distinctive capabilities—architecture, reputation, and innovation—and use each to reinforce the others. Firms less strongly placed may nevertheless give innovation a primary role in their competitive armoury; but unless they are favoured with regimes of high appropriability the translation of innovation to competitive advantage requires the strong support of associated elements of strategy.

This chapter owes an obvious debt to David Teece, whose ideas on the relationship between innovation, technology, and strategy are central. See Teece (1986, 1987). Also outstanding in a quite different style is McKinsey's man in Tokyo, Ken-ichi Ohmae; see, for example, Ohmae (1989), for lucid discussion of these issues in a Japanese context. The central issue of appropriation is developed in Levin *et al.* (1985).

The very large literature on the business applications of innovation and technology falls into several broad categories. One strand of thought is concerned to identify patterns of innovation and diffusion. Schumpeter (1961) is invariably cited as the originator of this. More recent analyses in this tradition are Abernathy and Utterback (1978), Griliches (1984), Landes (1969), Mathias and Davis (1991), while the Science Policy Research Unit at the University of Sussex has assembled very large empirical databases (Henwood and Thomas, 1984).

The relationship between organizational structure and technological capabilities is a second central theme, begun by Burns and Stalker (1961) and by Woodward (1982). See Willman (1986), Kay and Willman (1991), Abernathy and Hayes (1980), McCann (1991) for more recent contributions. The game theoretic issues relate principally to standards and to patent races. Discussion of standards is mostly empirical and case related. David (1986) deals with perhaps the most famous standards issue of all—the QWERTY typewriter keyboard; while Gabel (1987) is a useful collection of essays; and Grindley (1990), David and Greenstein (1990), Farrell (1990) a clear exposition of the issues. On patent races—the Chicken type problems—most contributions are theoretical—Harris and Vickers (1985) and Dasgupta (1988) are examples.

The economics of technology and innovation is surveyed in Geroski (1993) and Stoneman (1983), while broader surveys of its role in business are in Butler (1988) and Shaw (1990).

8

Strategic Assets

Some competitive advantages are based not on the distinctive capabilities of firms, but on their dominance or market position. These are strategic assets for the firm concerned. Strategic assets are of three main types. Some companies may benefit from a natural monopoly. They are established in a market which will not readily accommodate more than one firm. In some other markets, incumbent firms have already incurred many of the costs of supply, but entrants have not. In these the cost structure of firms may give them a competitive advantage. Still other firms benefit from market restrictions which are the product of licences and regulation. What distinguishes all these from true distinctive capabilities is that any other firm which had entered the industry, or had already made that expenditure or held that licence, would have enjoyed the same competitive advantage.

Firms which benefit from strategic assets are generally engaged in activities where government regulation is an important influence on business behaviour. Around 40 per cent of European business is in industries which are owned by government, extensively regulated by government, or which mostly sell to government. Sometimes the government creates, or reinforces, strategic assets; at other times, or at the same time, the state may limit the firm's ability to add value from them. The establishment and exploitation of strategic assets is often restricted by regulatory and antitrust policies. In the final section of the chapter I outline the main rules which govern European companies.

Distinctive capabilities enable companies to produce at lower cost than their competitors or to enhance the value of their products in ways that put them ahead of their rivals. Distinctive capabilities are the product of the organization or the firm itself—its architecture, its reputation, or its success in innovation. Yet some firms enjoy an advantage over their potential competitors even though there is nothing they can do which these other firms, if similarly placed, could not do equally well. These may be firms which have a licence which is not available to other firms, or they may be firms which are incumbent in a market which will not readily support more than one competitor. Their competitive advantage follows from the structure of the industry or the market, rather than from their own distinctive capabilities. These firms hold strategic assets.

Strategic assets, and the creation and exploitation of strategic advantages, raise issues about the proper conduct of business in ways which rarely arise when competitive advantage is based on architecture, reputation, or innovation. When distinctive capability gives rise to superior performance, the private gains made by the firm and its stakeholders will generally correspond to equivalent gains for society as a whole. Where strategic advantages are derived from legal privilege or market dominance, that equivalence of private profit and public good may not follow. The view taken in this chapter is that the firm may do what it is legally entitled to do, and what it is legally entitled to do is discussed in the concluding section which deals with anti-trust policy. But the subject raises wider questions of public policy and the ethics of business behaviour. These are considered further in Chapter 20.

Natural monopolies

Some markets are natural monopolies, and it is unlikely that more than one producer will serve such a market. There is a natural monopoly if there are economies of scale and the market is too small to support more than one producer of efficient size. In aircraft construction, and perhaps in mainframe computers, the world market is not big enough for more than a small number of producers to manufacture competitively. But even in industries in which there are substantial scale economies—such as the assembly of telecommunications switching equipment and automobiles—there will always be several firms. There are not many natural monopolies in manufactured goods industries in which there are few obstacles to trade and to global sourcing and production. Unless regulatory or other barriers to foreign sourcing prevent companies creating a truly international industry (as was true for many years in telecommunications switching), trade will destroy monopolies. Real monopoly is possible only if the market is defined very narrowly, as with certain kinds of specialist machinery, or in service or utility industries where the geographical boundaries of the market are limited.

The most striking examples of natural monopoly are to be found in the regional distribution networks of utilities. It would cost nearly twice as much to have two alternative supplies of gas, electricity, or water in residential areas as to have a single one, and this may also be true of road and rail networks. There may be natural monopoly, too, when the market is particularly local. Newsagents and bakers serve perishable products to customers in their immediate neighbourhood and often an individual market can accommodate only one. Sometimes there is natural monopoly when a firm fills a narrow market niche. The *Financial Times* and *Wall Street Journal* are profitable products but there is probably not room for more than one such paper in any geographical market and smaller countries do not have comparable daily dedicated financial papers. 'There is only one Harrods' is a well-chosen slogan because it is not clear that there could be more than one Harrods.

Standards can also create a natural monopoly if the market requires a compatibility standard and that standard is proprietary. Although compatibility standards exist in many markets, few of them belong to individual companies. The owner may have to adopt an open licensing policy in order to establish a dominant standard (as with the promotion of VHS recorders by JVC). Or anti-trust restrictions may prevent the owner from using the standard to establish a natural monopoly (as has happened repeatedly, explicitly or implicitly, to IBM). But within the computer industry, Microsoft and Lotus have succeeded in establishing particularly strong positions in their narrow market segments.

In some markets, customers are strongly attracted to the producer who already has the largest number of customers. At its simplest and starkest, the best computer dating agency is the one which has the largest number of dates on its books.[1] In telecommunications systems, the advantage of being number one is so great that competition in network provision is virtually impossible unless producers are obliged to offer access to each other's systems. Few people would trouble to use alternative networks such as Mercury or Sprint if they could only call customers who were themselves Mercury or Sprint subscribers, and then there would be even fewer Mercury or Sprint subscribers. Network operation advantages incumbents in many other industries, particularly in transport systems such as coaching or airlines. In financial services the 'thickest' market—the one with the highest volume of dealings—is the one most likely to have a willing counter-party, and this explains London's dominance in many commodity markets and Chicago's in many derivative securities. In pool betting, the most popular pool can offer the largest prizes, and that enhances the attraction of the pool—and in turn its value.

A natural monopoly is a game with Chicken characteristics—no more than one player can win, but two can lose, either through head-on competition or by mutual failure to recognize and exploit a market opportunity. In some natural monopoly markets, one player has ultimately decided to swerve. Lockheed has withdrawn from the civil aircraft market and McDonnell Douglas is now a minor player. Sony has abandoned the VCR standards war, and British Satellite Broadcasting finally quit its game of Chicken with Sky Channel. In other markets—like the London bond market—most players have been willing to stick. Four consortia were given licences to launch phonepoint services in the United Kingdom—a second-generation system designed to develop the large, and massively profitable, market for mobile telephones. None was willing to make the huge commitment to the market needed to

---

1 Although even here specialization allows many niche players to survive. Who matters as well as how many.

establish a large customer base and network of stations, and all failed—a Chicken game which proved to have four chickens.

Commitment is a key element in Chicken games, and it is the conspicuous nature of an incumbent firm's commitment which gives it a powerful advantage in a natural monopoly. In the original version, the newcomer, James Dean, was at a perceived disadvantage relative to an opponent who was an experienced player with a tough reputation. But, as in the movie, newcomers can displace incumbents if they have a competitive advantage, a stronger commitment, or a more effective strategy. Sony believed, wrongly, that its dominance of the professional video market would win the VCR battle. JVC came from behind, and won. Ryanair knocked British Airways off the route between London and Dublin.

The experience curve and sunk costs

Natural monopoly becomes a far more sustainable competitive advantage if it is combined with a strategic advantage based on sunk costs. The advantages of incumbency are often expressed by reference to the experience curve. This concept—popularized by the Boston Consulting Group—relates costs to cumulative output. It is claimed that costs fall by around 15 per cent with each doubling of overall output (Figure 8.1). This analysis conflates a large variety of different factors. The observed relationship reflects the influence of learning which is specific to the firm and learning which is general to the industry. It includes both costs which fall with the cumulative scale of output and costs which fall with the rate of output. It brings together the effects of technical progress in the economy at large with technical progress in particular firms and industries.

These distinctions matter a great deal in understanding what implications an experience curve might have. Figure 8.1 shows cited experience curves which are drawn from industries as varied as airframe manufacturers and broiler chickens. The apparent similarity is remarkable, but the causes and the implications are entirely different. The falling costs of the B-29 are truly the result of learning by experience—learning which is mostly specific to Boeing, and largely specific to that particular aircraft. This phenomenon underpins Boeing's position in the world aircraft market.

The only similarity between chickens and aircraft is that both have wings. The industry-wide adoption of battery rearing, supported by the use of antibiotics, turned chicken from a luxury product into a commodity staple. The market for chicken grew rapidly. While the causality in one case runs from output to costs, in the other it runs from costs to output. That difference is critical to the strategic implications. The world aircraft market is, and is likely to remain, dominated by Boeing. The market for broiler chickens is, and is likely to remain, both local and fragmented. Anyone induced by the

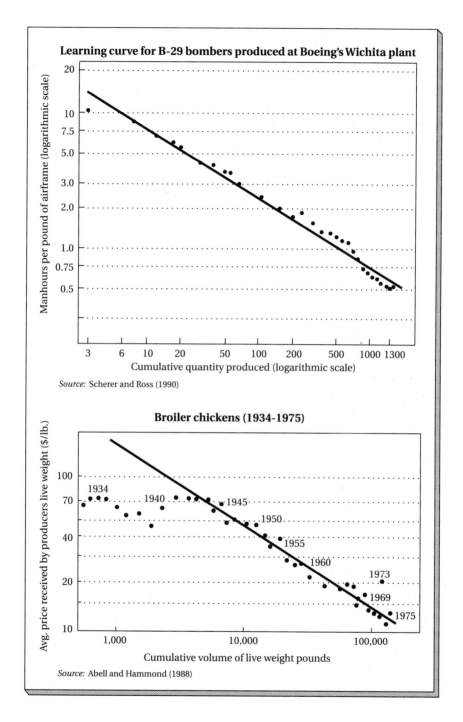

Learning curve for B-29 bombers produced at Boeing's Wichita plant

Source: Scherer and Ross (1990)

Broiler chickens (1934-1975)

Source: Abell and Hammond (1988)

Fig. 8.1. The Experience Curve

experience curve to aspire to be the Boeing of the broilers would be sadly mis-led. We need to look behind it at what drives costs in particular industries.

The degree to which incumbency—already being in the market—establishes a strategic asset depends on the structure of costs in particular industries. Boeing's experience is a good, and particular, example of a strategic asset which gives advantage to the incumbent firm. This strategic asset is the sunk cost of serving a market. An entrant aims to secure an established long-term position in a specific market. The costs incurred are of many kinds—building a plant, establishing a distribution network. Perhaps the market is one in which a credible supplier must build a reputation. Certainly, the firm will need to draw customers' attention to the qualities of its products. The measure of sunk costs is the proportion of the expected costs of supplying output which would still be incurred even if that output were not, in the end, to be sold.

The Channel Tunnel between England and France will have cost around £8.5 billion once completed. Its operating costs are estimated at around £200 million per year. Discounting these operating costs to the end of its franchise at 10 per cent, some 80 per cent of the total costs of the tunnel, in perpetuity, will have been incurred before it earns a penny of revenue. This is an extreme example of an industry in which a high proportion of costs are, literally and metaphorically, sunk. If no vehicle, no train, no passenger, ever passes through the tunnel, then over £8 billion will in any case have been spent. That is a sum that is frightening to Eurotunnel's bankers. If traffic is at expected levels, then 80 per cent of the costs of supplying a customer have been incurred before that customer arrives. That is a proportion which is frightening for Eurotunnel's competitors. And it is for this reason that the tunnel, like the Canary Wharf development in London Docklands, will eventually be fully utilized, even if that is for the benefit of the banks rather than the original owners.

Sunk costs are often confused with economies of scale, but may predominate in industries in which there are few economies of scale. An efficient modern electricity generating plant would be a combined cycle gas turbine plant with a capacity of 700 megawatts. This is roughly equal to the demand of a medium-sized town and its associated industry. About 500 such plants would be needed to satisfy European demand for electricity. However, at current gas prices, the construction costs of the plant would amount to about 30 per cent of the total costs of electricity generation over a twenty-year life of the plant. There are no economies of scale to speak of in electricity generation—or rather they are exhausted at a very low level—but sunk costs are very large. That gives incumbents an advantage over entrants.

Capital intensive industries are often industries in which sunk costs are important. But not always. Transport activities—such as airlines, shipping, and coaching—are also capital intensive. But there are active second-hand markets for aircraft, ships, and coaches, and it is easy to lease a ship or a bus for a fixed period. The sunk costs of entering these markets are relatively low.

Such industries differ from cement and electricity because, unlike cement plants or power stations, planes and ships do not have to be dedicated to particular markets. If market entry fails, you can fly your plane elsewhere, or sell it, and this is what unsuccessful firms in the airline business have regularly done. There is not much else you can do with your cement works or your generating plant except to produce cement or electricity, and to produce cement or electricity for a particular market. The critical point is not just that capital expenditure is important, but that capital expenditure is specific to a particular market. The cross-channel market provides a clear illustration of the distinction. A ferry operator has the option of using equipment on some different, and more rewarding, route. Eurotunnel plc can operate on one route only. That is a problem for Eurotunnel, but at the same time it makes the firm a very powerful competitor.

Where sunk costs are associated with capital investment, the value of sunk costs as a strategic asset will depreciate over time as the capital equipment itself does. An electricity generation set declines in efficiency, a cement works needs to be replaced, even a tunnel under the Channel ultimately requires refurbishment. In industries where there are several firms, sunk costs will almost always be larger for some firms than for others, depending on the stage of the investment and product life cycles that have been reached. The firms whose plants are oldest will always be those which are most vulnerable to entrants with competitive advantage. The combination of size and time dimension sets the upper limit to the size of the strategic asset which the incumbent firm can enjoy. But a strategic asset in the form of sunk costs enables the established firm to hold its own against a potential entrant so long as the entrant's competitive advantage is less than the sunk costs of the entrant.

The easiest sunk costs to identify are those associated with investment. Yet other, less tangible, sunk costs are often more important. Advertising expenditures are a sunk cost—they are specific to a market and they cannot be recovered if you leave that market. Other forms of expenditure on market recognition are also sunk costs—for an airline or a bus company, the cost of informing potential customers of your timetable is a substantial sunk cost, and public familiarity with your schedules and route network is a substantial strategic asset. The costs of establishing a reputation are largely market specific. These types of sunk cost do not depreciate in quite the same way that capital equipment does. So incumbents in these markets may hold even more powerful strategic assets than firms in capital intensive industries.

Strategic assets derived from sunk costs are valuable only if competitors must sink them too. Raising sunk costs in a market—as through advertising—may be an effective strategy for entry deterrence, but only if the resulting market structure is one which imposes similar obligations on competitors. Technological change may eliminate strategic advantages based on sunk costs, as when the position of established steel producers was undermined by the introduction of low-cost mini-mills.

Licensing and regulation as strategic assets

There are many markets in which firms gain strategic advantage through licensing and regulation. There are fewer such markets than there were, but there are still many.

Sometimes government has, through nationalization, created centralized and concentrated industries under its own control. Most European governments have determined the structure of communications, power, and transport industries in this way. All these industries are characterized by elements of natural monopoly, but the dominance of public firms was often extended into areas that were potentially competitive, and was, and frequently still is, supported by statutory monopoly. In other sectors, state monopolies were established as tax-gathering devices (the tobacco industries of France and Italy), or for regulatory purposes (the liquor monopolies of Norway and Sweden). Even where the firms involved have been privatized, or the markets concerned liberalized, the structure of the market has generally continued to be dominated by the history of statutory monopoly.

When governments own firms which operate in competitive markets, it may allow them to operate on an arms-length basis—as with the German government's holding in Volkswagen. Or it may use them as instruments of social and political policy. This has been true of most nationalized industry in Southern Europe and it poses special problems for private sector competitors. This is most strikingly true in the civil aircraft market, where the strategic assets and competitive advantages of Boeing are challenged by Airbus Industrie, a firm which exists for motives that are not primarily commercial.

A monopoly itself, government is often attracted to monopoly elsewhere. It was the Emperor Caligula who wished that the Roman people had only one neck. Government often finds it convenient to deal with a single supplier, or a small group, and may be willing to pay a price to do so. So government influence on structure has been important, and generally a concentrating influence, on industries where government is the principal purchaser. Power generation, telecommunications switching systems, and defence equipment are all industries where European governments have determined the structure of the industry. Mostly the results are fragmentation with local concentration, so that there are more firms, and less competition, than there would be in a freer market.

These attitudes are changing. Privatization has been widely discussed, although it is only in Britain and during a short interlude of Conservative government in France that much action has taken place in the principal European economies. More generally, public procurement has become more conscious of value for money and less nationalistic in attitude. The European Commission has adopted a variety of measures to require governments in member states to offer contracts on a European basis.

Nevertheless, a high proportion of European industry is either owned by government, has government as its principal supplier, or operates in a sector in which both entry and competition are substantially influenced by government action (Table 8.1). For firms in all these industries, the management of public affairs is a key component of corporate strategy.

Table 8.1. Government and Business in the European Community (Numbers employed in industries affected by government policies, estimates for 1986–1990)

Sector	Nos. employed (000)		
	UK	France	Germany
Rail travel	154.7	223.1	262.4
Air travel	43.9	52.1	58.1
Mining	162.9	32.0	172.0
Gas, electricity, water	297.0	210.0	250.0
Health service	1,301.4	1,059.2	1,236.3
Pharmaceuticals	70.0	66.0	87.0
Financial services	789.6	611.0	868.0
Professional services	1,257.5	894.4	868.0
Construction	1,020.0	1,200.0	1,468.0
Transport manufacturing, including aerospace	265.0	224.0	137.0
Telecommunication and postal services	438.7	470.7	499.8
Iron and steel	155.0	189.0	262.0
Computers and office machinery	83.0	59.1	78.4
Motor vehicles	238.0	348.0	734.0
Education	1,711.0	1,059.3	1,144.4
Total	7,987.7	6,697.9	8,125.4
No. employed in market priced business (all employed minus public administration)	19,617.0	16,026.0	20,542.0
% of employment influenced by government	40.7	41.8	39.6

Note: The degree of government involvement differs in different countries, ranging from a light regulatory regime, to complete ownership.

Sources: Eurostat: Employment and Unemployment, 1990; UN Industrial Statistics.

Anti-trust policies

Strategic assets may arise from natural monopoly, from licensing or regulation, or from action to establish market dominance and sustain incumbent advantages.

In two of these three categories—natural monopoly and regulatory monopoly—government plays a central role. And in the third—where strategy itself creates the strategic asset—government also frequently intervenes, through anti-trust policies, to correct real or imagined abuse. Where market power is found, or suspected, government and its agencies are rarely far away.

Government confers market power but also restricts its exercise. In the European Community, the most important provision is Article 86 of the

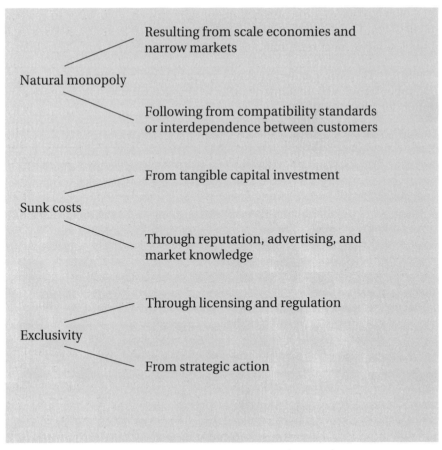

Illustration 8.1. Types of Strategic Asset

Treaty of Rome. This prohibits actions which constitute 'an abuse of a dominant position' within the Common Market, or a substantial part of it, and
which have an effect on trade between member states. The coverage of these
provisions is wide. Hugin, a manufacturer of cash registers with a modest
market share, was found to have a dominant position in the market for spare
parts for its cash registers; General Motors, a dominant position in the supply
of its own cars. The market for brass band instruments in the North of
England has been held to represent a substantial part of the Common Market.

Article 86 exemplifies a number of abuses: unfair selling conditions, limitations on production, undue discrimination, and tying restrictions. Practices
which have been found abusive include an incentive scheme for tyre retailers,
aggregated rebates in the supply of vitamins, and a variety of exclusive dealing arrangements. European firms are also subject to the provisions of Article
85, which makes illegal agreements between undertakings which restrict or
distort competition, and explicitly, but not exhaustively, rules out price-fixing
and market-sharing agreements as well as those abusive practices mentioned
in Article 86. A firm in breach of Article 85 or 86 may be fined—the Commission has levied substantial fines on companies found to be operating illegal
price-fixing arrangements and engaging in predatory behaviour—and may
also be liable for damages to aggrieved parties.

Most member states of the Community have some domestic anti-trust provisions. The most substantive are those in Germany and the United Kingdom,
which provide for administrative scrutiny of activities which are seen to have
anti-competitive consequences. Some specific practices, such as price-fixing,
are illegal under domestic as well as Community law in these and some other
jurisdictions. In the United States, the Sherman Act makes criminal any
attempt to monopolize trade or commerce and provides for punitive damages. The territorial scope of these provisions is wide and, in a celebrated
case, European carriers accused of predatory activities against Laker Airways
acceded to a substantial out-of-court settlement.

Any actions which firms might take, or contemplate, to use market power
or to deter entry are governed by these legal restraints. No firm would wish to
adopt strategies which break the law, and it is clear that actions such as price-
fixing agreements with competitors, or predatory pricing whose clear objective is to drive a competitor from the market, are illegal and may lead to
penalties or civil damages. More generally, however, what constitutes abuse
of a dominant position, or a restriction or distortion of competition, is a
matter of opinion, and one on which different lawyers and economists can
honestly disagree. Moreover, actions may often be simultaneously restrictive
of competition and of benefit to consumers—as when a manufacturer supplies only to retailers willing to conform to his high standards. Article 85
(although not 86) provides for a 'rule of reason' defence in such cases.

None the less, these legal provisions must always be in the minds of firms
managing strategic assets. Quite apart from obvious prudential considera-
tions, anti-trust enforcement is frequently complaint-led and strategies can

often be recast in ways that either take them clearly outside the scope of legal restriction or that are less likely to arouse the hostility of competitors or customers. It is often anti-trust proceedings themselves, rather than the ultimate consequences, which are damaging to the firms involved.

The creation and deployment of strategic assets centres around natural monopoly, sunk costs, and licensing and regulation. Most of what is written on these issues has been written by economists and their general perspective is that of public rather than business policy. Their interest is that of the concerned citizen rather than the business adviser. A fine overall treatment with that perspective and a wealth of (predominantly American) examples is Scherer and Ross (1990). Yao (1988) covers the issues of this chapter with a business policy orientation. The relationship between sunk costs and market structure is innovatively described by Sutton (1991).

Natural monopoly and concentrated market structures are based on entry barriers, scale economies, and the experience curve. Bain (1956) and von Weizsacker (1980) are classics on barriers to entry. See also Spence (1977), Salop (1979), Schmalensee (1981), Ghemawat and Nalebuff (1985). Emerson *et al.* (1988) and background papers provide a wide-ranging assessment of scale economies in European industries. Boston Consulting Group (1972) and Henderson (1973) describe the experience curve. See also Andrews (1980), Abernathy and Wayne (1974), Alberts (1989). Sharkey (1982) is a broader survey of issues in natural monopoly. First mover advantages are analysed by Lieberman and Montgomery (1988).

The emphasis in this chapter on sunk costs is closely associated with the theory of contestable markets, an approach which, if less revolutionary than sometimes suggested, has nevertheless influenced thinking on industrial structure considerably in the 1980s. Baumol (1982) and Baumol, Panzar, and Willig (1982) are the seminal contributions; a good critique is Shepherd (1984). For European experience of privatization and regulation, see Kay, Mayer, and Thompson (1986), Vickers and Yarrow (1988), Bishop and Kay (1988). Anti-trust policies internationally are annually reviewed by OECD (OECD, annual). European Community law in this area is definitively described by Bellamy and Child (1987). The intellectual background to anti-trust policy is described in Williamson (1987), while Bork (1978) is a critique which proved influential on US policies. Miller (1990) is an outstanding guide to how corporations should go about influencing policy. Although its perspective is British, lessons developed there have wider applications. Jordan and Richardson (1987), Calori and Lawrence (1991) are other sources on the relationship between business and public policy.

IV

FROM DISTINCTIVE CAPABILITIES TO COMPETITIVE ADVANTAGE

Part III of this book defined and identified the principal distinctive capabilities which distinguish successful firms—architecture, reputation, innovation—and explained how firms succeed in creating or exploiting strategic assets. The subject of Part IV is how these distinctive capabilities are applied in specific markets to create competitive advantage, and the problems which arise in ensuring that these competitive advantages can be sustained and appropriated.

This seems to leave a gap—or so it has appeared to some early readers of this book and to many of those with whom I have discussed its arguments. They recognize how corporate performance derives from distinctive capabilities. 'But how', they ask, 'are distinctive capabilities established?' Surely that must be the central question in determining strategy for the corporation?

How distinctive capabilities are created is a good question but it is not, I believe, the central question of corporate strategy. Distinctive capabilities of real commercial value are hard to create. That almost goes without saying, since if they were not hard to create they could not remain distinctive for long. What is even more important is to recognize that they are almost never created as the result of a conscious process of strategic choice. This is true for essentially the same reasons. Deciding what distinctive capabilities it would be good, and profitable, to have leads inescapably down the path of wish-driven strategy. The firm may formulate an objective in terms of a distinctive architecture, or reputation, or innovation. But in the absence of some unique attribute which enables that firm to achieve that objective ahead of others, and more comprehensively, whatever architecture, or reputation, or innovation is established can quickly be replicated. The search for distinctive capability is simply taken to a different level.

The question the firm should pose for itself is, 'What distinctive capability do we have?', not 'What distinctive capability would we like?'. Most large firms have some distinctive capability or capabilities—they could hardly have survived otherwise. Most small firms have some distinctive capability too—it is their founders' perception or possession of that which brought them into existence. The point is not that distinctive capabilities cannot be, and are not, created but that the deliberate act of creation is rarely achieved. If there is a single central fallacy in much modern strategic thinking it is the notion that the act of will is the most important element in corporate achievement.

It is not often rewarding to think about creating distinctive capabilities, but it is often useful to think about creating strategic assets. Strategic assets can be developed or acquired, and the process of doing so may well be both conscious and profitable. Large firms may enjoy market positions based on strategic assets even if they have no distinctive capability. Small firms may achieve modest profits from local strategic assets—the corner shop, the well-respected local trader. Many firms have successfully sustained strategic assets for long periods of time, as Chapter 11 explains. But firms may be very vulnerable if that strategic asset is eroded, as various privatized and deregulated firms have discovered. Strategic assets are often less secure sources of competitive advantage than distinctive capabilities.

The first part of the analysis of the firm's strategy is the description of its distinctive capabilities. The next requirement is to match these to appropriate markets. That matching is the subject of Chapter 9, which details the principles by which a firm should define the core business. One means—often the principal means—of securing markets is merger and acquisition, the subject of Chapter 10. Chapters 11 and 12 are concerned respectively with the sustainability and appropriability of competitive advantages, while Chapter 13 takes the analysis back to the criteria of success developed in Chapter 2, and describes how sustainable, appropriable competitive advantage may add value.

9

Markets

This chapter is concerned with how successful firms choose markets to make the most of their distinctive capabilities. It answers the question, 'What is the core business?', which has been a central strategic issue for many firms in the last decade.

I begin with the important distinctions between markets, industries, and strategic groups. Markets are bounded by the ability of consumers to substitute one product for another. Industries are determined by the way in which production is organized. Strategic groups are defined by the way in which firms compete against each other. So there may be—and often is—a global industry within which production is sourced on an international basis but many different local markets and several distinct strategic groups. The key issue for the firm is its choice of markets—in both product and geographic dimensions—and its membership of industry and strategic group follow from that.

A distinctive capability applied in a relevant market becomes a competitive advantage. For each distinctive capability there is a market, or group of markets, in which the firm which holds it may enjoy a competitive advantage. For some distinctive capabilities—as with those which are based on reputation or on some kinds of architecture—it is the nature of demand for the product which identifies the appropriate market. For other distinctive capabilities—as with most innovations—it is the technical characteristics of the product which define the markets in which they yield competitive advantage. Similar issues influence the choice of product position with a given market.

A distinctive capability, or a strategic asset, becomes a competitive advantage only when it is applied in a market or markets. Competitive advantage is intrinsically relative. A firm can enjoy a competitive advantage only by reference to other suppliers to the same market, other firms in the same industry, or other competitors in the same strategic group. Matching activities correctly to capabilities is perhaps the most important single element in the establishment of competitive advantage.

Most companies have recognized the importance of the issue in the last decade. 'What business are we in?' is a starting-point for every strategy discussion. Few chief executive's statements have not included some reference to focusing on 'the core business'. 'Sticking to the knitting' has become a catch-phrase.

But what is 'the knitting'? British Telecom, freed from state control which imposed restrictions on diversification, first concluded that its core business lay in the provision of telecommunications equipment to its established customer base and bought Mitel, a leading supplier of the hardware BT provided to its customers. A different senior management team reassessed the core business as the world-wide provision of telecommunication services, attempted to sell Mitel, and purchased McCaw, one of the leading providers of cellular phone services in the United States. What are the criteria by which managers should decide which, if either, of these concepts of the core business is correct?

'What business are we in?' is a badly formulated question because the term 'business' conflates three important and distinct concepts. Sometimes the word business describes the *market* a firm serves—the needs of its customers and its potential customers. More often it relates to the *industry* a firm is in—a group of products associated by common technology or supply or distribution channels. Sometimes the business refers to the *strategic group*—those firms the company identifies as its primary competitors.

Demand factors determine the market, while supply factors define the industry. P&O Ferries and Eurotunnel both plan to serve the same market, but they are in very different industries—one is a shipping company, the other is the manager of a construction project. European Ferries is part of the same industry as Hellenic Lines, but since one firm operates only around the English coast and the other only in the Aegean, they serve clearly distinct markets. From a technical point of view, both washing machines and refrigerators are white boxes with motors in them, and they are distributed through the same channels. But washing machines are useless at chilling food, and refrigerators do not clean clothes. The markets are for laundry services and food storage, and there is a domestic appliance industry but not a domestic appliance market.

The strategic group and the strategic market define the competitive battle-ground. The strategic group is determined by classifying together companies with similar strategies. Coke and Pepsi, with similar approaches to the market, form a strategic group; while Pschitt, a French soft drinks company whose aspirations to global branding must necessarily be limited, is differently placed, with a different competitive strategy. In France, Pschitt is in the same market but a different strategic group.

It is important for firms to identify all these—the relevant market, the relevant industry, and the relevant strategic group—but it is also important to

Illustration 9.1. Markets and Industries

The Market

    Defined by demand conditions
    Based on consumer needs
    Characterized by 'the law of one price'

The Industry

    Determined by supply conditions
    Based on production technology
    Defined by the markets chosen by firms

The Strategic Group

    Defined by the strategic choices of firms
    Based on distinctive capabilities and market positioning
    Subjective in determination

understand that they are not necessarily the same. Bass, Britain's largest brewer, saw beer as a market with unexciting growth prospects and redefined its core business as leisure. It bought Horizon Travel, a leading supplier of package holidays. Bass was right to observe that pubs and holidays were alternative ways of spending leisure time, and that they competed for the same share of consumer expenditure. But the skills involved in brewing beer and managing public houses were quite different from those required to package and market inclusive holidays. There is a leisure *market* but there is not a leisure *industry*. The acquisition was not a success, and Bass sold Horizon to another firm in the inclusive tour industry.

Stung by Theodore Levitt's charge of marketing myopia, and concerned by the future of the oil market after the 1973 Arab–Israeli war, several oil companies redefined their business as energy supply, and diversified into coal. But the management of coal-mines could hardly be more different from the management of oil exploration. Few of the diversifiers still retain their coal interests, although many more are still in gas, where the required capabilities are not so different.

The core business is the set of markets in which the firm's distinctive capability gives it competitive advantage. In the case of British Telecom, its competitive position rests on its strategic assets—its licences and the incumbent advantages it enjoys in supplying its established customer base. Since the company has no other evident distinctive capability, it has no competitive advantage in either the manufacture of telecommunications hardware or the provision of telephone service to customers in other countries. Here the core business rests on the supply of services to the existing customer base using the established network, and the diversifications, both unprofitable, seem to be the product of wish-driven strategy rather than the pursuit of competitive advantage.

The activities in which the firm's distinctive capability can give competitive advantage can be related to the markets, the industries, or the strategic groups in which the firm competes or might compete. The firm defining its core business should look at all of these, but its primary focus should be on identifying those *markets* in which it can effectively deploy its distinctive capability. The industry, and the strategic group, are defined by the choices which other firms have already made. Concern for the market focuses attention on customer needs, and competitive advantage often rests on using distinctive capabilities to meet these needs in new ways (as in British Telecom's more successful diversification into home security, which exploits the strategic asset of its captive domestic customer base).

The boundaries of the market

A market was once an event which occurred in a particular location at a particular time. Consumers would go there to meet suppliers and evaluate their alternative offers. For some commodities that is still true. Rungis, the successor to Les Halles, is still the food market of Paris and over 40 per cent of French fresh food is transported there and out again. The principal European market for refined petroleum products is in Rotterdam and even those who do not themselves trade there often do business by reference to prices determined in that market. But these commodity markets are now the exception rather than the rule. Even by the nineteenth century the term market had assumed a more abstract meaning. 'Originally a market was a public place in a town where provisions and other objects were exposed for sale; but the word has been generalized, so as to mean any body of persons who are in intimate business relations and carry on extensive transactions in any commodity' (Jevons, 1871, ch. 4). But like these historic markets, the modern market continues to have a product dimension and a geographic dimension—we talk of the London taxi market or the world oil market.

The definition of the product and the geographic dimensions of the market have received an unusual amount of attention because the issue arises in almost every case in which competition policy authorities are involved. The key question in determining the boundaries of the market is the opportunity which consumers have to substitute one product for another. They no longer walk between market stalls appraising one supplier's price and quality against another's. But if they still have that quality of information about alternative offers, and the opportunity to choose one source rather than another which the traditional market-place provided, there is a single market.

If the market is defined as the area within which consumers can readily substitute one good for another, then the market will often be a narrow one. There is no such thing as the European car market. An Opel Kadett in Germany is not in the same market as the Vauxhall Astra in the United

Kingdom, even though they are the same car, because buying the car in Germany is not a realistic option for most British consumers. Within Germany, an Opel Kadett is not in the same market as the BMW 535, because very few consumers see the cars as alternatives. The existence of a single market, rather than distinct markets, is suggested by relative price uniformity and demonstrated if movements in the price of one good have large effects on the sales of the other. Applying either of these tests confirms that the 'European car market' must be divided into many product segments and many geographic areas.

This 'law of one price' is a means of defining the boundaries of the market. 'The more nearly perfect a market is, the stronger is the tendency for the same price to be paid for the same thing at the same time in all parts of the market' (Marshall, 1890). This criterion is particularly useful in identifying the geographic boundaries of the market. Table 9.1 shows how the prices of some commonly traded commodities vary across the European Community. There may be a single European market for oil products but not for automobiles, pharmaceuticals, domestic appliances or life insurance. This is true even though for all these products, except life insurance, sourcing is done on a European-wide basis and the goods concerned are extensively traded across national borders. There is a European industry but that is not the same as a European market.

Table 9.1. Prices in European Markets (Belgium = 100)

	German cars	Pharmaceuticals	Life insurance	Domestic appliances
Belgium	100	100	100	100
France	115	78	75	130
West Germany	127	174	59	117
Italy	129	80	102	110
Netherlands	NA	164	51	105
UK	142	114	39	93

Sources: Commission of the European Communities (1988), 'The economics of 1992', *European Economy*, 35, March. Nicolaides & Baden Fuller (1987), dell'Osso (1990*a*).

One of the more common confusions of the last decade has been to mistake the globalization of industry for the globalization of markets. A multi-domestic market—one in which the same product is sold in many different markets around the world—is very different from a global market, in which customers are free to buy in any geographical location they like and prices are equalized world-wide. There are global markets for goods such as tin or aircraft, but rarely for manufactured consumer goods or for services. And the single European market which the European Community seeks to establish in 1993 is a legal rather than a commercial concept. European markets for many commodities will continue to be fragmented long after 1992. For other goods—as for most resources and many agricultural products—a single European market existed when the concept of a European Community was no more than a visionary ideal.

Strategic errors can be made by companies which define markets either too widely or too narrowly. EverReady was a market leader in the provision of dry batteries for small appliances in the UK. In 1975 the company decided to adopt a global branding strategy but was inhibited because it did not have the world-wide rights to its potent brand name. So it decided to change both brand and corporate identity to Berec. The strategy was not a success. The benefits of the EverReady name were large and those of global branding negligible. The company lost market share in its traditional geographic markets, but failed to make corresponding gains elsewhere.

At the same time, long-life alkaline batteries, until then mostly confined to specialist applications, were making inroads into the zinc-carbon segment in which EverReady specialized. They had already come to dominate the market in some of the overseas markets which EverReady had targeted. Duracell, EverReady's principal competitor, focused its marketing efforts on long-life batteries but in order to facilitate its global branding strategy, EverReady put back the launch of its own competitive products. EverReady had assessed the geographic dimensions of its market too broadly and the product dimension too narrowly. Profits fell substantially and the company was acquired by Hanson, which redressed these errors, restored the original brand identity, and has since made the battery business one of the most profitable elements in its corporate portfolio.

Matching markets to distinctive capabilities

The question 'What is our core business?' should be redefined as 'What markets are those which best enable us to translate our distinctive capability into competitive advantage?' The narrow market definition adopted here implies that most firms must expect to compete in many different markets, both product and geographic. The boundaries of the firm are determined by the markets it selects. The boundaries of the industry are determined by the markets which similar firms select. The basis of that selection should be the maximization of competitive advantage, and the key to that is the nature of the firm's distinctive capability itself.

Reputation is most obviously of value in the markets in which that reputation has been created. The *Oxford English Dictionary* has an immensely powerful reputation for comprehensiveness and accuracy. But not many people want twenty-volume dictionaries, so that in its own market the reputation is not worth what it costs to create. Revenues from sales of the dictionary do not defray the expenses of maintaining and updating the databases from which it is derived.

The profitability of the activity depends on exploiting the distinctive capability—the reputation of the *OED*—in other markets. The most obvious markets are those for other dictionaries. A single-volume Oxford dictionary is not much better than—or even very different from—several other single-volume dictionaries. The underlying lexicographical knowledge is generally available and fine nuances of scholarship matter little in a one-volume dictionary. But the reputation of Oxford books is very valuable in selling single-volume dictionaries. For this to be true, two conditions have to be fulfilled. The dictionary has to be a long-term experience good, which it is—accuracy and comprehensiveness are key features of a dictionary and it is not easy to assess these by browsing through it in a shop. And the Oxford reputation has to be credibly at stake on the one-volume dictionary, which it is—if the single-volume dictionary is found to be error ridden, then the standing of the principal dictionary will be damaged.

The reputation can be extended to English language teaching materials and helps to sell other works of reference, and these are successful Oxford businesses. But it is less valuable for classic novels, which are search rather than experience goods. (Although publishers seek to differentiate their products by adding introductions, notes, and bibliography.) You can tell in the shop that a book with *Pride and Prejudice* on the cover is indeed *Pride and Prejudice*; only experience will tell you whether you will like it but the publisher offers no warranty on that.

Reputation is of value in the market in which it is created, and in related markets for long-term experience goods. A well-managed reputation can gradually be spread to other products, and this makes it a particularly powerful form of competitive advantage, since its value increases over time.

The matching of *architecture* advantages to markets depends on the specific nature of the advantage. Hanson's competitive strength rests on a system of tight financial controls negotiated between its small corporate centre and the management of its individual operating business. Such a structure works best for dominant firms in mature and clearly defined markets. Bricks and batteries have been particular Hanson success stories; London Brick and EverReady were both weakly managed firms with strong market positions in which a combination of close cost control and more aggressive pricing strategies produced handsome increases in profitability. This management style is less appropriate where the industry requires substantial long-term expenditures in support of research and development, where the pay-off is delayed or uncertain, and management has only limited influence over time or outcome. Does tobacco—now the largest single Hanson operating business—meet the criteria of dull maturity? Or do the requirements of long-term brand development, emphasized by other successful players in the market such as Philip Morris, make this a less appropriate market in which to deploy the Hanson architecture?

The particular strength of Benetton's architecture is the rapid response time which its systems facilitate. This style is appropriate for a fashion business but not suitable for other types of franchise operation—such as fast food—where consumer tastes do not change rapidly and product standardization, rather than product differentiation, is important to consumers. Within the clothing sector itself, the nature of the competitive advantage implies a market positioning—neither down-market, where fashion is less important in selling goods, nor at the top, where tastes are more stable and volumes lower. Benetton's competitive advantage is best maximized in the cheerful and fairly cheap market segment with which it has become associated.

BMW in the 1950s was a distinctive capability in search of a market. The company finally found, or stumbled on, an appropriate product group. In the kitchen furniture market, several German firms such as Poggenpohl and Bulthaup have succeeded with a similar market positioning based on a similar distinctive capability, and dominate the high-quality mass production sector. Other firms outside Germany specialize in craftsman-built kitchens and in cheap mass-produced cabinets. The top end of the volume segment suits this distinctive German capability particularly well.

For innovation advantages, the market is generally indicated by the nature of the innovation itself. Often it is the identification of the market that prompts the innovation. It was obvious for many years that there was potentially a large market for an effective anti-ulcerant, and the problem for the pharmaceutical industry was not that of identifying the market but of devising the product to meet it. Less commonly the innovation is independent of the market, and the competitive advantage goes to the firm which identifies the application. It was never difficult to manufacture low-quality adhesives. 3M succeeded in finding a use for them in the Post-it note, in which the limited efficiency of the product was actually a virtue. Modern innovations are often applicable across a particular wide range of product markets. Enabling technologies—for example in electronics or in optics—have allowed firms like NEC or Canon to be strong competitors in apparently quite disparate lines of business.

Product positioning

The position of a product is a means of defining its relationship to other products in the same market. In the car market, a Fiat Panda is positioned differently from a 7 series BMW. In the dishwasher market, a Miele is positioned differently from a Zanussi. In newspapers, *The Times* occupies a market position different from the *Sun*. We might choose instead to say that the Panda and the BMW, the Miele and Zanussi, *The Times* and the *Sun*, are in different markets. The distinction has only semantic significance.

The term positioning is also widely used in a broader sense. Sometimes positioning describes not just the position of the product in its market, but the relationship of the whole of a firm's strategy to that of its competitors. Michael Pórter, in particular, has written extensively about positioning in this way, and has warned of the danger of being 'stuck in the middle'. Porter (1980) is right to warn of the dangers of a confused strategy, but those writers who have misinterpreted him as advising against adopting a mid-market *product* position have been led into serious error. Many of the world's most successful firms have adopted product positions which are firmly stuck in the middle. Carling lager is neither the strongest nor the weakest. Sony equipment is neither the cheapest nor the most sophisticated. American Airlines aims to cater for a broad range of passengers. For these firms, as for many others, a mid-market position has proved the most successful way of exploiting their competitive advantage. Since mid-market positions commonly offer the greatest density of customers, this is hardly surprising.

Newspapers such as *The Times* or *Le Monde* are described as quality newspapers. The phrase is a useful starting-point for thinking about precisely what it is that quality means. Here is a possible definition. One good is of better quality than another if more people would buy it if the prices of the two goods were the same. A fine bordeaux is of better quality than a bottle of vin de table. Many more people buy the vin de table, but they do so because it is cheaper. If both wines cost the same, most people would choose the bordeaux. If they would not, then it is hard to know how we could say that it was of higher quality, and it is much less likely that it would command a higher price.

Now this definition is not without its problems. It suggests that Coke is a higher quality product than Pepsi. But no one believes that Coke is made of better materials, or manufactured under more closely controlled conditions, and the evidence of blind tasting seems to be that, if anything, consumers prefer the Pepsi flavour. But in Europe the public drink more Coke and this concept of quality asserts that, taking the product, its history, and its marketing together, Coke is perceived as of higher quality.

The Times and *Le Monde* pose a similar difficulty. *Le Monde* is, by any standards, a fine newspaper but it is not a paper which more than a small minority of newspaper readers would wish to buy. Arthur Hailey is not as good a novelist as Jane Austen even though his books sell in larger numbers. For products like these, and to some extent for all commodities, there is an accepted standard of quality which is not necessarily reflected in the marketplace. But it is the market's assessment of quality that determines profitable and unprofitable positions. We might prefer to read Jane Austen but we would rather publish Arthur Hailey.

Underlying this are two distinct factors which determine the nature of the product space. Within the same market, buyers look for different products partly because they disagree about what they prefer (horizontal differentiation) and partly because, even though they agree about what they prefer, they differ in their capacity to afford it (vertical differentiation). Consumers have variable requirements partly because their tastes or needs differ, and partly because they differ in their willingness to pay.

The term down-market products refers both to goods bought by low-income households—discount retailing—and to products which although not of low quality cater to tastes which are not well regarded—tabloid newspapers. Many managers instinctively shy away from down-market positions, from a sense that price-based competition is unlikely to be profitable, or from an understandable reluctance to be associated with products which they would not themselves wish to buy.

There are many markets in which this has given scope for very successful down-market entry—the *Sun* newspaper, Amstrad hi-fi equipment and computers, Formule 1 hotels, the growth of fast food restaurants. Branded wines of low quality have been successfully sold in several countries where wine-drinking remains a minority pursuit. (Wine is one of the few markets where branded products are often inferior to unbranded ones.) Early Western buyers of Japanese cars were attracted by their price, rather than by their luxury, style, or prestige.

The view that 'quality is king' is so prevalent that many readers will have already found for themselves rationalizations which suggest that these successful products are really of high rather than low quality. Yet few people would have wished to buy them had they not been cheap. This is another example of confusion between the market position of the product and the strategy of the firm. The quality of goods and services is distinct from the quality of the strategy, management, or organization of the firm that manufactures it. Formule 1 hotels are not good hotels, but they are good hotels for 20 Ecus per night, and Formule 1 is a highly effective organization.

Down-market positions require particularly strong management discipline. To minimize costs while maintaining standards acceptable to consumers requires detailed control of product specification. This is characteristic of companies as different as Amstrad and McDonald's. Down-market positions carry the further danger that increasing incomes, or the evolution of more sophisticated tastes, will steadily erode the size of the segment. Woolworth developed down-market retailing with great success only to see its market move away from it.

Matching position to distinctive capability

Just as the choice of market reflects a firm's distinctive capability, so must its choice of market position be matched to competitive advantage (Illustration 9.2). Where the source of competitive advantage is innovation, then the innovation may itself dictate the product position. The quartz watch can only be positioned down-market because the important feature of the innovation is that it offers, more cheaply, a capability for accurate timekeeping which was already available at higher cost. Glaxo had limited influence over the positioning of its product, but there were still some important choices to be made. Was Zantac to be priced directly against Tagamet, or sold explicitly as a premium product? The choice was made differently in different geographical markets based on Glaxo's assessment of the drug's prospects. Where volume sales were a realistic expectation, price competitiveness was important. But where you expected only to be a niche player, a substantial price premium proved more remunerative.

Illustration 9.2. Markets, Market Positioning, and Distinctive Capability

Basis of distinctive capability	Basis of choosing market and market position
Reputation	Reputation is created in a specific market. Add related markets if consumers think you can transfer attributes, and you know you can. Usually implies up-market position (but need not).
Architecture	The nature of relationships—internal, external, network—or their result—flexible response, organizational knowledge—often dictates market and position. Otherwise, seek mid-market.
Innovation	Product innovations usually imply market and position. Process innovations often do— otherwise seek mid-market position.

Sometimes architecture may dictate a market position. This was true for BMW. In other cases, architecture may be of value anywhere—as with Sainsbury's skills in retailing systems—and the most attractive position is a mid-market location which attracts the largest number of customers. Sometimes the same competitive advantage may be best deployed in different positions in different markets. Marks & Spencer's external architecture is valuable in all positions in the clothing market (and so it has sensibly chosen the middle), while its close control of suppliers is most effective at the top of the food market.

Where competitive advantage is based on reputation, a price and quality position towards the top end of the market is usually appropriate. This is where the six major accounting firms, or the international car hire firms, are located. Yet a 'value for money' reputation may be achieved with a mid-market position—Sainsbury's food or Marks & Spencer's clothing—and reputation may even be achieved in down-market positions, where the supplier's reputation assures the customer that despite the low price the product is of acceptable quality. The latter is the concept behind Amstrad electronic equipment and Formule 1 hotels. More usually, however, reputation advantages are deployed towards the upper end of the spectrum of product quality— more so than for other primary distinctive capabilities. The addition of a reputation to a capability based on innovation or architecture may therefore imply a move to a more up-market position. This has been a repeated characteristic of Japanese entry strategies.

This discussion shows that distinctive capabilities are frequently, although not necessarily, deployed most effectively in mid- or up-market positions. This is reflected in the average returns earned (Fig. 9.1). That does not imply that any particular firm can expect to earn more profit by moving up-market, or that a down-market position may not be the best way of exploiting a particular competitive advantage. The choice of market position must always be a reflection of the firm's distinctive capabilities. Sometimes the distinctive capability is, like reputation or architecture, one which naturally suggests a position at the top of the market. Where it is not, a mid-market strategy should always be the first to be considered.

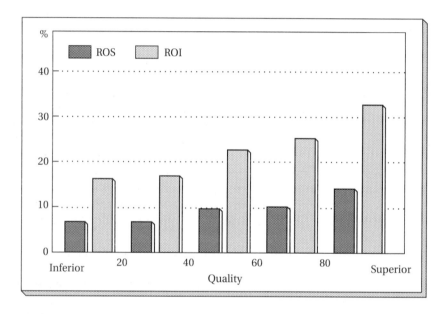

Fig. 9.1. Quality and Profitability
Source: Buzzell and Gale (1987), p. 107

Positioning when products have many attributes

Most products have multiple characteristics. This is strikingly true of both newspapers and supermarkets. A newspaper will contain many distinct news stories. It will probably have features, editorials, perhaps a crossword. It may list racing results, stock prices, weather forecasts, and radio and television schedules. When you buy a newspaper, you buy the package. You will only require a few of the thousands of items which a supermarket stocks. The attractiveness of the supermarket will depend on whether that product range is appropriate for your specific needs. You may also be influenced by the cleanliness and layout of the store, the attitude of the sales staff, and the speed of the checkout procedure, as well as by the price.

Any product can be defined as a bundle of characteristics, and each of these characteristics can be valued. Consumers look at the speed, acceleration, comfort, and reliability of a car. The price which each of these characteristics commands in the market establishes a 'going rate' for any particular specification. The profitability of any particular product position will then depend on its value relative to its cost and on the demand for the product at that price.

But often the value of one characteristic is very much dependent on all the others. Buyers of a Fiat Panda will not be willing to pay much extra for leather upholstery but purchasers of a Rolls Royce may regard it as essential. A *focused* product is one whose characteristics bundle is well targeted towards a particular market segment. Readers who are interested in gossip about radio and television personalities are probably not interested in analyses of the political situation in Latin America and vice versa. Newspapers which combine both risk being unfocused products. *Today* failed, in part, because the lack of clarity about its overall product position led to precisely this lack of definition in its editorial content. Customers who buy fresh fruit in a supermarket may also demand fresh bread, a variety of cheeses, and have high expectations of the quality of store layout. Customers for canned fruit may be more willing to buy pre-packaged bread and cheese and to pick products out of cardboard boxes. To satisfy some of these attributes without satisfying them all may lead to an unfocused market position. This means that the costs of the product will be too high relative to the value of the characteristics bundle that is offered.

The importance of focus depends on the number of products available in the market-place. An unfocused product is one which might be everyone's second or third choice but no one's first. This is viable, and may indeed be optimal, if few first choices are available. Henry Ford's unfocused model T was exactly right for an early stage of development of the car market but became steadily less successful as demand for automobiles grew and product choice expanded. Focused television channels which specialize in sport or music are sustainable only when the number of programmes available is relatively large; when few frequencies are available all channels are typically unfocused. Focused airlines—specializing in business travellers or backpackers—have not succeeded because the density of traffic on most routes is insufficient to support frequent, economic, focused services. Yet if the number of products in the market is very large, focus again becomes less critical, because there will be some customers for almost any bundle of characteristics. A restaurant which provides gourmet food on plastic tables with paper napkins may find a clientele for whom that is precisely the product they require. Such restaurants survive in London, Paris, and New York, although less frequently in smaller towns.

Matching competitive advantage to geographic market

A distinctive capability needs to be matched to a set of geographical markets as well as to a set of product markets. It is rarely possible to extend reputations outside the geographical market within which they are created—they have to be built afresh. Citibank's attempts to build retail banking networks in Europe have been repeatedly disappointing. The Citibank name, however well known in New York and in (global) wholesale money markets, has little significance to European retail customers. Citibank's most successful European venture, KKB in Germany, continues to trade under the name it held when it was acquired. (In September 1991, after eighteen years, it was changed to Deutsche Citibank.)

Reputation most frequently travels when customers do. Hotels, car hire, and professional services are all extensively bought by purchasers whose normal residence is elsewhere. International reputation is powerful in these markets and reputation is the driving force behind the internationalization of the industry.

A firm with competitive advantage in one market may find it advantageous to serve other markets even if it has little or no competitive advantage in them—no innovation to offer, no reputation to bring, architecture that is valuable only elsewhere. This will be true if there are economies of scale or economies of scope. *Scale economies* exist when the costs of providing a common product decrease with the volume of output; *scope economies* if the cost of providing two distinct goods and services from the same firm is less than the cost of providing both separately.

Scale economies dictate that many producers of manufactured goods serve a range of geographical markets. It is now impossible to be a viable automobile producer on the basis of one geographic market alone. So there is a European and increasingly a world car industry even though European cars are sold in a series of distinct national markets. There is a world market in aircraft—aircraft are particularly easy commodities to transport—and a viable producer of large aircraft must serve the whole of it. For these firms, the geographical boundaries of the market and the industry coincide. But, just as the car industry is one where the boundaries of the industry are wider than the boundaries of the market, so the boundaries of the industry may be narrower then those of the market. Although there is a world market in cut diamonds there are no scale economies in diamond-cutting and the industry is local and fragmented. In general, the greater the importance of scale economies the wider will be the dimensions of the industry relative to those of the market.

Scale economies will encourage firms to produce in different product markets if these have important common components. This is true of the automobile and aircraft industries, and it may be true of domestic appliances also. Even though refrigerators and washing machines are in different markets, if both are white boxes with motors, then there may be scale economies in combined production, and Fiat's strength in the manufacture of small motors for these appliances was a factor in Italy's dominance of the white goods industry. But the use of common distribution systems was a much more important common factor for these different types of appliance, and this is a characteristic instance of scope economies. The distribution of both refrigerators and washing machines together is cheaper and more effective than the distribution of either separately.

These scope economies arise because the products share the same retail outlets. Closely related scope economies arise if consumers wish to buy bundles of commodities. Rank Xerox's competitive advantages relate to the provision of photocopiers, are modest in relation to the supply of toner, and non-existent in the handling and distribution of paper. Yet consumers need all these things to make their copiers work and if they want to buy service packages there may be scope economies in serving all three product markets.

Scope economies are common where networks exist. The advantages of interlining and hub-and-spoke operations give benefits to airlines who operate multiple routes from a single airport over those who offer only one. For this reason it may pay airlines to operate routes which would not be profitable on a stand alone basis because they contribute to the value of a route network taken as a whole.

These extensions to other geographical or product markets are effective only if the firm enjoys a competitive advantage—from reputation, innovation, architecture, or possibly an exclusive franchise—in at least *some* market. Neither scope nor scale economies can compensate for an absence of competitive advantage since scale and scope are essentially replicable attributes. This issue is discussed in more detail in Chapter 11. Scope and scale are characteristics which can enhance competitive advantage, but they cannot substitute for it.

The industry, the strategic market, and the strategic group

The choice of market is the most important element of strategic choice. But industry matters to the company in several ways. The criteria which statisticians apply in determining industry boundaries and organization are very similar to those which firms themselves should employ in determining their strategic business units. The principles to be applied—common enabling technologies, relatedness of markets, extension of competitive advantage—are broadly the same.

The scope of the industry gives a guide as to how other firms perceive related markets. So it may suggest other ways in which a competitive advantage might be deployed. Often, of course, the competitive advantages of these different firms will not be the same and it is right to pursue a different set of markets. Coke and Pepsi have strengths in soft drinks which are quite different from those of the local companies against which they everywhere compete, and it would be a mistake for a local company to think it should seek to match either their range of products or their geographical scope.

European car manufacturers have been successful in creating a single European car industry—thus deriving the benefits of scale production and international sourcing—while at the same time they have not fallen victim to the emergence of a single European market—in which prices would have been driven down to the levels prevailing in low-price markets. The broad industry focus, and the narrow market focus, have allowed producers to win cost benefits without accepting price penalties. And the same is true of other industries listed in Table 9.1, such as pharmaceuticals and domestic appliances.

While it is important for a firm to identify its competitors, it is no less important to identify competitors with different strategies than those with related ones. Indeed, the concept of the strategic group risks diverting attention from the first task of competitive strategy—the identification of distinctive capability. 'How can we be different?' is ultimately, a far more critical question than 'Who are we like?' There are few number twos who do not aspire to be number one but setting out to imitate number one is only occasionally the way either to be number one or to make the best of being number two.

The strategic market is the minimum area within which a firm can viably compete. It is a combination of economic markets drawn together by economies of scale and scope. Sometimes the boundaries will be narrowly defined, associated with fragmented industries where innovation is rare or inappropriable—as in many service industries. Sometimes, as in aircraft manufacture, the imperatives of scale and scope are such that the strategic market is the world market. A successful firm will dominate at least one strategic market.

For any firm, the core markets are those in which its distinctive capabilities, or strategic assets, are directly relevant. Without some such markets, there is no prospect of adding value. But the added value of the firm can be leveraged by the addition of other markets in which, even if it has no direct competitive advantage, economies of scale and scope associated with its key markets allow it to serve that market more effectively or at lower cost. It is these factors taken together which answer the question 'What business are we in?' with which this chapter began. Firms with true distinctive capabilities will generally do so in a unique combination.

A history of markets, literal and metaphorical, is described by Agnew (1986). More recent analysis of the issue falls into two quite distinct groups. One is designed as a guide to marketing managers. The dominant figure here is Levitt, whose principal contributions are reproduced in Levitt (1986); see also Curran and Goodfellow (1990). A specialist literature is concerned with the definition of the market for the purposes of anti-trust policies. Major contributions here are Landes and Posner (1981), Stigler and Sherwin (1985); Scheffman and Spiller (1987). Kay (1990) is a further exposition of some of the concepts in this chapter. Focus on the 'core business', much emphasized in the 1980s (Abell, 1980), was popularized as 'sticking to the knitting' by Peters and Waterman (1982).

The European Community's 1992 programme, despite its many achievements, has been responsible for considerable conceptual confusion; as stressed in the chapter, the single market is essentially a legal concept, not a commercial one. The programme itself, and some implications, are well described in Emerson *et al.* (1988). See Davis *et al.* (1989) for an attempt to sort out some of these conceptual issues.

There is now a very large literature suggesting the strategic advantages of up-market positioning. Crosby (1979) was an influential early contribution; a more recent discussion is Dale and Plunkett (1990). Empirical support is drawn from PIMS; see Buzzell and Gale (1987). Davis (1990) is concerned with the analytic and empirical issues.

10

Mergers

Merger and acquisition is the most common means of entry into new markets, and plays a central role in all discussion and formulation of corporate strategy. In this chapter I argue that this role is frequently over-stated. Mergers can, and do, add value. They achieve this when they enable distinctive capabilities to be exploited more widely, or more effectively, and I describe how this can be achieved. Yet a review of studies of merger performance suggests that the effect on performance is more often negative than beneficial. Frequently this is because this corporate activity is not based on a clear view of the firm's distinctive capability and an identifica-tion of the markets in which that capability is most effectively applied but is the result of financial objectives—the pursuit of a balanced or diversified business portfolio—or simply the thrill of the chase.

In recent years, joint ventures, strategic alliances, divestment, and management buyouts have given companies many more tools for restruc-turing their activities. I explain some of the reasons why alliances, like mergers, so often fall short of the hopes of their promoters, but the evidence so far encourages a more hopeful assessment of buyouts and divestments. In 1990, the European Community adopted a merger control regulation, and some individual countries also have merger policies. I describe these developments in the last part of this chapter.

C hapter 9 presented a careful, analytical approach to matching the activ-ities and market position of the firm to its distinctive capabilities. Decisions are sometimes made that way, and perhaps should more often be made that way. But the most common means of entering new markets, or leaving old ones, is through acquisition and divestiture. Within the European Community merger is a rapidly growing phenomenon. An acquisition may be a means of entering a new market, but it has many wider effects. It also brings with it new production facilities, perhaps new distinctive capabilities, per-haps new strategic assets. And an acquisition is a package. You buy, or you decline to buy, what is on offer.

Yet the same principles apply. Mergers are justified by the extent to which they add value. Value is added, and only added, if distinctive capabilities or strategic assets are exploited more effectively. In assessing a merger, the first requirement is to define the distinctive capabilities of the firms concerned. A merger adds no value if all that is acquired is a distinctive capability which is already fully exploited since the price paid will reflect the competitive advantage held. Adding value requires some 'synergy', which may be obtained from matching distinctive capabilities or strategic assets, winning access to complementary assets, or deriving economies of scale or scope related to the core business.

Mergers and acquisitions may be a means of entry into a new market in which an established distinctive capability has not yet been deployed. Rowntree's brands were established and successful in the United Kingdom. Neither the brands, nor the company's success in repeatedly creating successful brands, had been effectively exploited in continental Europe. The acquisition of Rowntree by Nestlé, already established in these different geographical markets, provided a basis for this market entry. Imperial Tobacco identified the potato crisp market as one which could use the architecture—a pattern of distribution arrangements—which was the mainstay of its dominance of the UK cigarette market. The company bought a small manufacturer of snack foods, Golden Wonder, and within a short period displaced the long-established incumbent, Smith's Crisps, from its number one position.

Mergers may add value if the distinctive capabilities of the two firms are complementary. The integration of good local firms into the 'Big 6' international accounting firms achieves this. The national firm holds a local reputation but fails to maximize its value because it has difficulty conveying that reputation to international customers. The international firm is well known to its international customers but can only extract value from that reputation in the local market if it can attract the best local practitioners. The combination of the two reputations enhances the value of each.

Sometimes an acquisition can add value if one firm has assets which are complementary to the competitive advantage of the other. Consulta, a small German company, had patents on some innovative lubrication products but it lacked the reputation to sell them effectively in what is clearly a market for long-term experience goods. Its acquisition by Castrol enabled it to sell these on the strength of Castrol's strong reputation in the lubricants market. Sony has a strong position in the development of high-definition television. There are potentially alternative Japanese, American, and European systems. The evolution of this market will depend both on the actions of broadcasters—who are subject to extensive government regulation—and on the behaviour of suppliers of pre-recorded material. Sony's purchase of Columbia Pictures gave the company—at enormous cost—control of one of the largest film libraries available.

Or a merger may be justified by cost savings based on economies of scale or scope. If there are cost savings based on excess capacity then merger may take place in a competitive market. The introduction of greater competition into the Spanish retail banking sector left Spanish banks with many more branches than were needed and mergers have provided an efficient basis for rationalization. These outcomes are not strictly the result of economies of scale and, in particular, large banks will not necessarily be more successful in this process than small. But it is through this process, rather than by the replacement of two plants by a single plant of greater size and efficiency, that cost savings from merger are most often realized. Airlines gain scope economies from network operations, and mergers and acquisitions have been a primary mechanism for building up such networks in the United States.

Merger can create or enhance strategic assets as well as distinctive capabilities. The most familiar route is to reduce competition, increase market power, and raise prices through the acquisition of a direct competitor. There were once two evening newspapers in London—the *Evening Standard* and *Evening News*. The *Evening Standard* 'acquired the title' of the *Evening News*, which immediately disappeared from the streets, and within a few days the price of the *Evening Standard* rose from 15p to 20p.

Acquisitions can sustain exclusivity, or maintain the value of a competitive advantage, if they inhibit entry. Control of bars by brewers, both through direct ownership and by tying arrangements, inhibits entry into new geographical markets by foreign beers, since it denies entrants ready access to a distribution network and increases the sunk costs of entry. In practice, virtually all new entry occurs through joint venture, limiting the ability of entrants to undermine the added value accruing to incumbents.

Or merger may be a means of appropriating or defending competitive advantage or added value against the demands of suppliers or customers. British financial institutions were concerned that estate agents were likely to become increasingly important distributors of their retail products, especially mortgages, insurance, and other services associated with house purchase. In order to defend their own added value, they bought chains of estate agents. Lacking the right kind of management skills, they lost a great deal of money in the process, and might have done better simply to have given up some of their added value.

The success of mergers

Despite these many reasons for merger, and the important role which acquisition plays in most discussions of corporate strategy, evidence on the consequences of mergers points to one clear conclusion. Taken as a whole, merger activity adds very little value.

This evidence is mostly drawn from the United Kingdom, but there is little need to apologize for this. Merger is, overwhelmingly, an Anglo-Saxon phenomenon. Despite the rapid growth of acquisition activity in other European countries—particularly France—in 1988 UK firms were responsible for 85 per cent by number and almost 75 per cent by value of all acquisitions in the European Community (Geroski and Vlassopoulos, 1990). Among other major world economies only the United States has a comparable pace of merger activity.

The simplest means of assessing the effectiveness of merger and acquisition activity is to ask companies themselves whether they think mergers were successful. On this self-rated basis around half of mergers succeeded and around half failed. In this study the relative size of acquiror and acquiree was the single largest influence on the probability of success—happy partners were of similar size. An alternative way of ascertaining the opinions of companies themselves is to see what they subsequently do with the businesses they acquire. Over a twenty-five-year period, around half of acquisitions were subsequently divested.

But these methods are subjective, and do not address the issue of added value directly. An alternative is to compare pre- and post-merger profitability, normalizing by reference either to the experience of other firms in the same industry or matched non-merging firms. Their results are selectively summarized in Table 10.1, but the pattern of relative decline is clear enough. A similar picture has been established in the United States—substantial profit deterioration in those firms which were subsequently divested, more modest but still distinct deterioration in those which were retained. The most optimistic conclusion is that of Mueller (ed.) (1980), in the only major study to include mergers across the whole European Community. Their conclusion is that 'no consistent pattern of either improved or deteriorated profitability can therefore be claimed across the seven countries. Mergers would appear to result in a slight improvement here, a slight worsening there.'

Evidence from the stock market is rather more favourable to merger. Acquirors almost invariably pay a bid premium, so that merger announcements lead to an increase in the market value of the acquired firm. Sometimes the share price of the acquiror rises, sometimes it falls, but for a selection of merger stocks taken as a whole, these broadly balance out so that merger announcements are, on average, neutral in their effect on the acquiror's share price. The implication is that mergers do add value—the merged concern is, on average, valued more highly than the sum of the two merging companies. More or less the whole of that gain goes to the shareholders of the company which is acquired.

There are, however, some problems with this interpretation of the data. Acquired firms tend to have done worse than the stock market in general in the period before (though not immediately before) acquisition, and acquiring firms rather better. When the stock market performance of acquiring firms is measured over a longer period of time than that of the merger announcement, the average pattern is one of underperformance. A portfolio of newly merged companies can be expected to do worse than the market. The stock market's initial assessment (like, perhaps, that of the managers of the companies involved) seems to be unduly optimistic.

Table 10.1. The Performance of Mergers

Method of evaluation	Major studies	Conclusions
1. Subjective opinions of company personnel	Hunt *et al.* (1987)	Around half are successful
2. Whether acquired business is retained in the long term	Ravenscraft and Scherer (1987)	More are divested than retained
3. Comparison of overall profitability before and after merger	Meeks (1977) Mueller *et al.* (1980) Ravenscraft and Cosh *et al.* (1990) Scherer (1987)	Nil to negative effect
4. Effect on stock market valuation	Franks and Harris (1986) Franks, Harris, and Mayer (1988)	Positive initial impact

Note: Studies in group 2 are of US companies, others for UK.

The most likely explanation of these facts, and their reconciliation with accounting data, is that the timing of acquisitions tends to reflect valuation anomalies. Mergers tend to be consummated when the acquiror's share price is relatively strong and the acquiree's is relatively weak. The apparent gains from merger reflect the correction of these discrepancies rather than the added value from the merger as such.

Why do mergers perform poorly?

None of this evidence should be interpreted as indicating that no merger is ever successful. Clearly, some mergers, including many of those discussed in this chapter, are effective in adding value to the businesses which they bring together. But the implication that both managers and markets substantially overestimate the gains from merger is a very clear one.

One reason why mergers fail to live up to the expectations of their originators is that the expectations themselves are rather ill-formed. Few claims are as evidently vacuous as those of Wilkinson Match, the unsuccessful product of a merger between British Match and razor-blade manufacturer Wilkinson Sword. That merger, the Monopolies and Mergers Commission was told, would give both companies 'substance', a quality which they wisely suggested was 'easier to recognize than to define'. But the example does illustrate a more general problem. The submissions which firms make in support of merger proposals to anti-trust authorities are very characteristically reliant on vague clichés, such as 'critical mass' or 'global player', or start from the belief that the mere fact that two businesses have distinct but similar activities demonstrates benefits from the combination.

It is now conventional wisdom that related acquisitions outperform unrelated ones. Yet the Saatchi acquisition of Ted Bates (page 13) is an instructive counter-example of a merger in which relatedness was a problem, not an advantage. While US studies of merger performance have tended to support an emphasis on relatedness, British ones have suggested that, if anything, unrelated acquisitions do better, a result which is clearly helped by the outstandingly successful acquisition records of some UK conglomerates such as Hanson and BTR.

The underlying issue, of course, is what relatedness means. The relatedness which creates added value is not simply that the companies are engaged in broadly comparable business activities. Benefits are likely to accrue from the merger only if the acquiror can deploy its distinctive capability effectively in the acquired business. This is a criterion which would rule out—as in the Saatchi case—many acquisitions of like firms in the same industry. But it would include at least some purchases of apparently unrelated businesses. Batteries and bricks are quite distinct products, but they are related from the perspective of Hanson architecture, which is particularly effective at generating returns from dominant positions in mature, low-technology, markets.

The value created by an acquisition has to offset the costs of the acquisition itself. The fees associated with the purchase are evident enough, as is the bid premium—the amount which has to be paid either to secure management agreement or to persuade shareholders to sell over the heads of incumbent management. There are also tangible costs, and substantial opportunity costs to senior management, in integrating acquired businesses.

Where value is added through merger, its *appropriation* is an important issue. International accounting illustrates the problem. Value is certainly created by the merger of local firms into an international firm. However, the combination of a shortage of suitable local candidates and the partnership structure of such firms ensures that the major part of the added value which results is retained by the local partnership rather than accruing to the international firm.

When the acquiror is a corporation, the distribution of the added value is mostly reflected in the price paid for the acquired company. Nestlé's purchase of Rowntree did indeed add value to the merged concern. However, the price Nestlé paid—twice the market value of the company before bid speculation began—included a bid premium which was in excess of any reasonable estimate of that added value. Nestlé paid out more than the gains from the acquisition to Rowntree shareholders, and in consequence took value from its own shareholders even as it created it overall.

Financial issues in mergers and acquisitions

Corporate diversification is often sought as a means of reducing corporate risk. 'Diversification is therefore a necessary type of corporate insurance which sound management must achieve on the behalf of its stockholders, so that the risks of separate sectors are pooled' (Harold Geneen, for many years the dominant influence on US conglomerate ITT, in Lamb (ed.), 1984). Such diversification is not, however, a means of adding value. The reason is a simple one. Diversification is something shareholders can—and characteristically do—achieve for themselves. They do not need the corporation to do it for them.

In practice, there are two important reasons for thinking that the diversified corporation is likely to be a bad substitute for a diversified share portfolio. It is much more costly to buy whole companies than it is to buy stakes in companies, because of the bid premium which needs to be paid to persuade *all* shareholders to part with their holdings. When the tobacco company BAT bought Eagle Star Insurance in 1983, it paid around 10 Ecus per share. Before take-over speculation affected the price, Eagle Star shares were selling for 4 Ecus per share, and, allowing for all the transactions costs associated with the deal, any BAT shareholder who wanted to diversify his portfolio into insurance could have bought more or less as many shares as he wanted at half the price of having BAT management do it for him.

The comparison is even clearer for a BAT shareholder who did not want to buy Eagle Star shares (and, given the company's subsequent performance, this would have been a wise decision). Such a shareholder is now required to hold shares in insurance in order to own shares in a tobacco company. There is now no tobacco company with shares quoted on a European stock exchange which does not have a very wide spread of extraneous interests. By forcing the prospective purchaser of tobacco shares, or insurance shares, into a fixed proportions package of tobacco and insurance which he may not particularly want, the imposed combination may subtract rather than add value. There is an extremely competitive market, through collective investment funds, in offering pre-packaged diversified portfolios for those who are not able, or do not wish, to perform it for themselves.

Such diversification, although often incorrectly rationalized as serving shareholder interests, is principally in the interests of the management of diversifying companies. This is not a negligible or disreputable consideration. It is harder to motivate management in declining businesses, and difficult to sustain an architecture which entails lifetime commitment to the firm if the long-term prospects of the firm are uncertain. This is a particularly relevant consideration for Japanese companies, where lifetime employment underpins their architecture, and it supports the structure of diversified groups which has traditionally been characteristic of Japanese industry.

Markets often find conglomerate companies difficult to assess, especially since companies are not required, and are often unwilling, to break down their overall performance into that of the different operating entities. There is a tendency to attach the price–earnings ratio characteristic of the principal business to the company as a whole, so that a diversified tobacco and financial services firm may well attract the low stock market rating applied to a tobacco firm rather than the higher figure applied to financial services.

For BAT the overall outcome was that the company with its diversifications was valued at little more than the tobacco business above, an observation which prompted an audacious bid to break up the company. BAT itself responded by divesting many of its non-tobacco interests, although it retained its financial services business. In the last decade, Mercedes Benz has similarly used the cash flow derived from the strong competitive advantages of its core business to diversify its operations, with rather little recorded success. Mercedes is not currently subject to the kinds of external pressure which was brought to bear on BAT, but times may be changing.

Joint ventures, strategic alliances, and minority shareholdings

It is not just international merger and acquisition activity which has increased. Joint ventures and strategic alliances, particularly those with an international dimension, have also mushroomed. In 1989, for example, GEC announced European partnerships across all the major areas of its business, including a link-up with Alsthom in power generation and with Siemens in telecommunications.

Yet so far these joint ventures have often fallen short of their founders' expectations. In the early days of the Community, one of the first large European alliances of this kind—the Dunlop–Pirelli union between the then giants of the European tyre industry—was widely hailed as the prelude to an increasing series of European alliances. It was not. The union itself dissolved in acrimony. Its failure and the subsequent poor competitive performances of both companies individually proved a real deterrent to the formulation of similar proposals. GEC's joint ventures quickly encountered difficulties—it seems relations with Siemens barely advanced to the point of encountering difficulties. Some cynical observers suggested that the primary aim of the policy was to complicate GEC's corporate structure to a degree that made a hostile take-over of the company impossible. Yet joint ventures have a long and successful history—it was a joint venture which discovered America and a strategic alliance between fundamentally incompatible partners which ended the Third Reich—and joint venture remains the most common means of entering new geographical markets.

Some alliances are predicated on the belief that they represent an intermediate contract form between the classical and the relational contract which offers the best of both worlds—the security and protection against opportunism of the classical form with the flexibility and information sharing of the relational form. It is simply necessary to spell out that hope to see that it is unlikely to be realized. The two contract types differ by reference to their means of enforcement—classical contracts are upheld by reference to the terms of the contract, relational contracts, which are not spelt out in formal terms, by the continuing need of the two parties to do business with each other. Now you cannot have classical enforcement of a relational contract, and while you can have relational enforcement of a classical contract that is the worst, not the best, of the two worlds.

Joint ventures fall into two broad categories—'common objective' and 'mutually beneficial exchange'. The common objective venture is typically one in which one party's distinctive capability requires the other's complementary asset, or two distinctive capabilities complement each other. The defeat of Hitler was based on a combination of the technical and material resources of the United States, the manpower of the Soviet Union, and Britain's convenient island location. Columbus's discovery of the New World was the product of the complementary assets of Isabella's wealth and his navigational skills (although, since he was in search of the East Indies, the latter should not be overrated). Mutually beneficial exchange is where each partner has skill or information or expertise which is of value to the other.

While most joint ventures contain elements of each, the balance between the two varies considerably. Glaxo's partnership with Hoffmann–La Roche to market Zantac in the United States is a traditional example of the first type. Philips's collaboration with Sony on compact discs is a case of the second. A stylized view of the pay-offs in the corresponding games looks as follows. In the common objective game, the result—success or failure—is common to both parties and the pay-offs are symmetric. The example in Fig. 10.1, which develops the joint venture game of Chapter 3, assumes that the overall gains from full co-operation are 10 and from partial co-operation, 4. In the mutually advantageous exchange game, however, the outcome may be asymmetric. It is possible for one party to gain from the other—and that, of course, is a result which each may try to secure.

It is immediately clear that co-operate is a dominant strategy for both partners in the first game and that hold back is a dominant strategy for both partners in the second game. In the common objective venture, it pays both parties to put the maximum effort into the common objective (although the parties can, and do, argue heatedly about shares of the returns). In the information and skill exchange venture, it is always better to engage in strategic manœuvres to get as much as possible while giving as little as possible—and this is true despite the clear mutual benefits from full co-operation. Recall that the Second World War featured an effective alliance so long as the objective—the defeat of Hitler—was common, and despite the evident advantages of continued co-operation the alliance collapsed once that common objective had been secured.

This pessimistic view of the outcome of the Prisoner's Dilemma game could be modified if it were played repeatedly. But the key characteristic of that repeated game is that it must be infinite, or at least uncertain, in length. A

The common objective venture

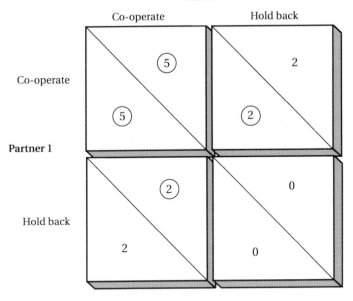

The information exchange venture

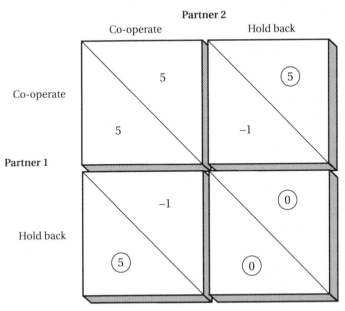

Fig. 10.1. Joint Venture Games

joint venture which is expected to last for a defined period will invite strategic behaviour towards the end of its life and once the parties realize that they will behave strategically now—this is the unravelling property which undermines many repeated game strategies. Joint ventures based on mutually beneficial exchange will be effective only if both parties believe them to be of indefinite duration—most probably because they are seen as the prelude to a full merger—and joint ventures with anticipated finite duration are unlikely to work. Few such ventures have not left at least one party unhappy with the outcome.

A minority shareholding arises when a firm takes a stake in another which is too small to give it control of, or direct influence on, the other firm concerned. In Britain and the United States, such a stake is most often seen as a preliminary to a full bid. In the United Kingdom, stakes over 3 per cent must be disclosed, the holder is expected to indicate his intentions, and a stake of 30 per cent obliges its holder to make a bid for all outstanding shares. There are proposals to extend the scope of rules of this kind across the whole European Community.

Yet in the business environments of continental Europe and, most of all, of Japan, minority shareholdings are common and their commercial function is rather different. Their purpose is to increase commitment to a relational contract. The holder has made an investment which is virtually useless to him in the absence of a continued trading relationship. (If shares are readily marketable then the sunk costs associated with such an investment are low but mostly they are not readily marketable.) For the company in which the stake is held, the collapse of the relationship leaves it with a significant fraction of its shares in what are no longer friendly hands. Thus for both parties the existence of such a minority stake establishes penalties to opportunistic behaviour. Like the exchange of gifts in almost all cultures, or the exchange of valuable tokens on engagement or marriage, minority shareholdings reinforce commitment in both a real and a symbolic sense.

Divestment and buyouts

While a vigorous pace of merger activity has been observed throughout the century, it was only in the 1980s that divestment and buyouts became almost as common as acquisitions. The corporate portfolio was restructured by sales as well as purchases.

The most important element was a reaction to the excesses of conglomerate acquisition in the 1950s and 1960s, and it was in the countries where that pace of acquisition had been most frantic—Britain and the United States— that divestment was most common. At a more intellectual level, the role of the corporate centre was increasingly called into question. In the vision of Sloan and Chandler (see Chapter 21), strategy was a corporate function, while tactical decisions were matters for operating businesses. But from the 1960s, strategy was increasingly a matter for the operating businesses themselves. What then was the corporate sector for? It was this that brought phrases like 'the core business' and 'sticking to the knitting' to the centre of public debate.

Divestment was often to another large firm which saw the unit concerned as part of *its* 'core business', but an increasing number of operating businesses were sold to the managers of the businesses themselves (the management buyout). Since these managers typically had little capital of their own to invest, such buyouts were frequently very highly geared. This led directly to detailed agreements between the company and its bankers and to extensive monitoring and supervision of the firm's business.

As with merger acquisition activity itself, such deals mostly happen in the United States or United Kingdom, although there is an increasing number in France. In the United States, buyouts were closely associated with the development of the 'junk bond' market. Attempts to establish such a market in Europe have been largely unsuccessful.

Some deals have been designed to 'go private'—to transform an existing public company into a privately owned one in which managers have a large stake without changing the basic operating activities of the business. There is a conflict of interest at the heart of such a transaction. If the business is the same, and the management is the same, what is the source of the added value which makes the business worth more owned by the management than owned by shareholders who employ the management? As a result of some notorious deals of this type—particularly the abortive management buyout of RJR Nabisco—and the failure of a number of other large, highly geared transactions—such as the purchase of Federated Department Stores by the absurd Campeau Corporation—such activities became discredited before they had spread far outside the United States.

While the performance record of mergers is generally disappointing, most assessments so far of the performance of buyouts have been neutral to favourable (Wright *et al.* (1993) provide a survey of the evidence). Stock market returns are markedly favourable, but data on operating performance are much more significant. There are two possible effects at work: the removal of the control of value-subtracting corporate centres, and the increased incentives of managers who own substantial equity stakes in their companies. The evidence cited suggests that both contribute to reported performance improvements.

Mergers, acquisitions, and corporate governance

Mergers occur in waves. The first great European merger boom took place in the 1920s when the development of mass-production techniques created the modern manufacturing corporation. Until then, the largest firms in European economies were frequently railways or banks. Many of the firms which still dominate the industrial landscape today date from that era. Imperial

Chemical Industries (ICI) was formed in 1926 by the amalgamation of Brunner Mond, Nobel Industries, United Alkali, and British Dyestuffs. Unilever was created from the merger of The Netherlands Margarine Unie, with the diversified British soap manufacturer, Lever Bros. Philips bought Mullard and put together its current business portfolio.

A second wave came in the 1960s. The United Kingdom clearly led this movement, and a belief that the internationalization of the world economy necessitated larger firms was an important motivation. Merger activity was also intense in the United States, while continental European economies distantly reflected the experience of their Anglo-Saxon competitors. The emphasis on economies of scale and size was common to the 1920s and 1960s merger waves, but there was also an important difference. In the 1920s, plants in many sectors of industry were clearly too small and rationalization was necessary to enable modern production methods to be applied in larger production units. The 1960s did not lead, overall, to any increase in plant size at all. Growth in that period was in the size of firms and it was accompanied by an increase in the extent of multi-plant operations and the development of multi-business corporations. And while the mergers of the 1920s were accelerating a process of industrial concentration which was evident in any event, the 1960s merger wave was itself the principal cause of increasing concentration. Without the effect of mergers, the balance between large and small firms would have remained broadly unchanged. In retrospect, that would have been a better outcome. The attempts to build an internationally competitive electrical industry around GEC, a volume car manufacturer in British Leyland, and a competitive full-range computer company in ICL, all fell far short of their promoters' hopes.

Similar arguments are used in the merger waves of the 1980s. Further internationalization of the world economy—as seen in the dismantling of trade barriers within Europe and the Japanese dominance of some manufactured goods sectors—provides the rationale for consolidation and large firms. In continental European economies—particularly France and Italy—there is a striking similarity between the arguments used today and those which were put forward in Britain in the 1960s. The growth in merger activity in these economies is the result.

A new feature of more recent mergers, particularly in Britain and the United States, is the degree to which they are justified by the acquiror's claim that he can make better use of the assets which he purchases. This issue is most clearly posed in hostile take-over bids. The acquiror appeals over the heads of incumbent management to the shareholders of the concern which it wishes to purchase. This is the operation of 'the market for corporate control'. Hostile bids in Europe are principally a British phenomenon—although de Benedetti's unsuccessful attack on Société Générale de Belgique may mark the start of a growing continental European trend—but the theme of better asset management is increasingly common in all mergers.

Ensuring that distinctive capabilities are fully translated into competitive advantage is the most critical of management tasks, and achieving that more effectively is a means of adding value. Philips is one of the largest and most respected of European corporations but adds little or no value and may even subtract it (p. 27). Does this mean that the European economy would be stronger if Philips did not exist? While a simple-minded answer to that question would be yes, the disappearance of Philips would mean the loss of many distinctive capabilities contained in its operating businesses. While the Philips management has been repeatedly unsuccessful in establishing sustainable competitive advantages from them, it is probable that a more effective management team could have done so. If Philips had been a British or American company, it would almost certainly have been the subject of a hostile bid, and the knowledge that this might happen would probably have led to much earlier management actions to restructure the company's operations.

Aggressive bids may therefore create value, or persuade incumbent management to create value, but sometimes they represent only an appropriation of value. It is hard to disentangle from published accounting data the extent to which much publicized corporate raiders have truly improved the performance of the business they bought although the examples of Hanson's brick and battery businesses, to which I have referred on several occasions, demonstrate that they can. Hanson recovered almost the whole of the purchase price of Imperial Group from the sale of its peripheral activities, retaining the cash-generating tobacco business more or less for free. The larger part of this came from the sale of Courage to the Australian company, Elders. If Elders brought a distinctive capability to its acquisition, then the release of Courage into the market-place genuinely added value. There is some argument for this— Elders's principal strength was in its Fosters brand and the Courage chain provided an outlet for this. But since the previous distributors of Fosters, Grand Metropolitan, had been remarkably effective in promoting the brand— turning a minor Australian beer into the best-selling lager in Britain—the argument is weak. If, as seems more likely, Elders simply paid too much for the business, then the rearrangement of assets is an appropriation of value in favour of Hanson rather than a creation of it. The source of the gain is irrelevant to Hanson shareholders but of considerable importance for public policy.

Merger policy

Acquisitions, mergers, or joint ventures in Europe are governed both by the mergers regulation of the European Community and by the laws of individual European countries. Where European companies have US subsidiaries, their actions will be subject to US anti-trust legislation and this has been an important issue in some major European mergers. The European regulation applies to mergers which meet two criteria. There is a size threshold—the two companies together must have a world-wide turnover of 5 billion Ecus (there are plans to reduce this to 2 billion Ecus by 1994). And the merger or 'concentration' must have a Community dimension. That requires that each company must have a turnover within the Community of 250 million Ecus of which no more than two-thirds are within a single merger state.

Mergers which are subject to Community control are, in most cases, exempt from scrutiny by national authorities—a 'one-stop shop'—and the Commission's decision is definitive. The criteria to be applied exhibit some ambiguity, reflecting the political compromises necessary to secure its passage. The regulation asserts specifically that 'a merger which does not restrict competition shall be approved' and that 'a merger which restricts competition shall not be approved'—implying an exclusive emphasis on competition policy. But the Commission is nevertheless required to have regard to 'the development of technical and economic progress within the Community', apparently opening the way to the presentation of much more general arguments in support of (or opposition to) a proposal. The merger regulation became effective only in September 1990, and experience of how this will be interpreted in practice can develop only slowly.

Smaller mergers, or those which do not have a Community dimension (as defined) are governed by the laws of individual countries. Although most European states have some form of merger control, only the procedures of Germany and the United Kingdom present a serious obstacle to merger in many cases. A merger involving German companies must be referred to the Cartel Office if it meets either a size criterion (turnover of 250 million Ecus or 10,000 employees) or a market share test (the market share of the combined enterprises exceeds 20 per cent). The Cartel Office must prevent a merger which it believes is restrictive of competition unless it (or the Federal Economics Minister) considers the damage to competition is offset by some wider economic interest.

The UK regime is similar. There is also a size criterion (40 million Ecus of assets) and a market share test (25 per cent of the relevant market) and a merger which meets either must be notified to the Office of Fair Trading, which recommends whether it should in turn be referred to the Monopolies and Mergers Commission, which is required to assess the public interest aspects of the proposal. In practice, mergers between large companies in the same industry are unlikely to be approved in either Germany or the United Kingdom. It is likely that the same will be true for European mergers if the geographical coverage of the two firms is similar, and the key issue in the implementation of the mergers regulation, on which evidence has yet to emerge, is how the Commission will view mergers between large companies in the same industry but whose principal operations are in different states, or groups of states.

For other mergers, involving smaller companies or vertical integration or conglomerate acquisition, anything goes. With proper preparation—and all three jurisdictions offer opportunities for early discussion of the authorities' likely view of a proposal—and skilled presentation of the arguments, public policy is unlikely to present an obstacle to commercially well-structured proposals. But there are many more merger propositions than there are well-structured proposals.

Many of the issues in this chapter are developed more fully in the essays in Bishop and Kay (1993). The historical role of mergers is described in Hannah (1976); recent European experience in Geroski and Vlassopoulos (1990). Hughes in Bishop and Kay (1993) provides a wide-ranging survey of evidence on the performance of mergers. Studies of self-rated performance are Hunt *et al.* (1987), Ravenscraft and Scherer (1987, 1989); case studies are found in Cowling *et al.* (1980); accounting performance is considered by Meeks (1977); and stock market outcomes in Franks and Harris (1989). For some particular cases mentioned, see Bevan (1974—Golden Wonder), Davis and Bannock (1991—Nestlé), Hill Samuel (1990—Consulta). On the relatedness versus unrelatedness issue, see Hughes (1993). On buyouts and divestments, see Wright *et al.* (1993), and Kaplan (1989).

The issues of portfolio versus corporate diversification are now covered in most finance texts, such as Brealey and Myers (1991, ch. 33). The performance of buyouts is reviewed by Wright *et al.* (1993). Joint ventures and strategic alliances are the subject of a burgeoning literature, see Harrigan (1986, 1988). Norburn and Schoenberg (1990), and a survey in Lyons (1991). For the strategic role of minority shareholdings, see Thompson and Meadowcroft (1987).

The 'market for corporate control' is a phrase due to Manne (1965) and the concept most fully elaborated by Jensen and Ruback (1983). Its operation arouses controversy at several levels; see Jensen (1984, 1986) for vigorous defences. Sceptics can find justification, and entertainment, in Burrough and Helyar (1990). These issues relate directly to concerns about 'short-termism' (Marsh, 1990) and systems of corporate governance (Davis and Kay, 1990; Bannock and Peacock, 1991). For a review of public policy issues in merger control, see Bishop and Kay (1993) and for its practical operation, Cooke (1986).

11

....

Sustainability

Distinctive capabilities continue to add value only if both the capability, and the distinctiveness, are sustainable. In this chapter I draw on case studies and statistical evidence to show that many companies are indeed successful in building sustainable competitive advantages from their distinctive capabilities. Of the primary distinctive capabilities, reputation is generally the easiest to sustain, innovation the most difficult, but each poses its own particular problems. Strategic assets can often be defended over very lengthy periods, but may be suddenly at risk when there are changes in regulation or market conditions. For a firm with strategic assets, skills in handling public policy may be as important as those of business management.

In the second part of the chapter I use the test of sustainability to explain why some factors which are often cited as sources of competitive advantage rarely yield substantial added value in the long run. I look at the role of scale, of market share, of business portfolio diversification, and of market positioning in achieving corporate success. Sometimes size or scale are themselves the product of distinctive capabilities. Sometimes diversification or positioning is the reflection of a distinctive capability. But if these factors are not based on distinctive capabilities, then competitive advantages derived from them rarely persist in the face of entry by firms which do enjoy true distinctive capabilities based on architecture, reputation, or innovation.

BMW, Honda, and Glaxo built effective strategies in support of their competitive advantages. BMW has added a powerful additional source of competitive advantage in branding and reputation to its initial distinctive capability. In the last few years, it has become possible for Japanese companies to attempt to match the BMW architecture. They have an equivalent network of suppliers, and a production-line labour force of comparable quality. At the same time the growth of sophisticated production control systems has reduced the number of workers required, and the complexity of relationships between them. The BMW brand remains powerful, both as reputation and as signal. It is possible that the first of these features of the brand can be replicated by Japanese competitors. The second may prove more elusive.

Honda has not only extended its distinctive capability into other markets but has added new distinctive capabilities. The company entered the automobile industry in 1967. Its first cars were the automotive equivalent of the supercub—simple, low-powered, functional urban transport. Subsequent models were positioned across other market segments. Most recently, the Honda NSX is intended to compete with Ferrari and Lamborghini. Honda has added reputation to its critical distinctive capability. By specializing in engine technology, it has achieved some success in innovation as well. The company has chosen a positioning somewhat up-market of its principal Japanese rivals, and supported its entry into most major geographical markets with a plant in the United States and an extensive relationship with Rover in Europe.

Glaxo's competitive advantage is more evidently vulnerable. Zantac faces increasing competition both from new drugs and, as patents expire, from generic substitutes. Glaxo has used the cash flow from Zantac to finance the largest research and development programme of any European pharmaceutical company. That programme has produced a variety of new drugs of which at least one—Imigran, a migraine therapy—has blockbusting potential. But expenditure in the pharmaceutical industry is no guarantee of success. The Swiss company Hoffmann–La Roche, whose tranquillizers Librium and Valium once gave that company a position equivalent to that Glaxo holds now, failed to sustain its market position. Glaxo's continued success requires the success of the portfolio of new drugs it has created.

All three of these companies appear to have sustainable competitive advantages. BMW's competitive advantage may be at, or past, its peak. That is not to say that the company will not continue to grow and prosper. But it is unlikely that its competitive advantage will again reach the levels attained in the 1980s. Glaxo's position is more knife-edged than at any time since the beginning of the decade, when its management had 'bet the company' on the success or failure of a single product. Whatever happens now, Glaxo will continue to be a major pharmaceutical company. But the range of possible outcomes is wide.

For twenty years, IBM enjoyed perhaps the greatest competitive advantage ever held by any corporation. Its distinctive capabilities, based on reputation and architecture, were not only strong but so well established relative to its competitors that it dominated the huge and fast-growing market for computers. These distinctive capabilities remain strong. Yet the market has evolved in ways that have substantially eroded the value of IBM's competitive advantage. The growth of personal computing—a development which, ironically, IBM pioneered—has given a large part of the total computer market to products which many firms can manufacture. These machines are largely undifferentiated and so IBM's ability to recover a price and market share premium for its name and its support is much more limited (although still real). The continuing fall in the price of computing of all kinds reduced these premiums more generally. IBM will remain a powerful company, with marked distinctive capabilities, but it will not enjoy such a competitive advantage again.

In other industries, the nature of competitive advantage has shifted backward and forward. After the creation of the European Community in 1957, the domestic appliance industry was one of the first to market consumer goods extensively across frontiers. The automatic washing machine was a new and widely sought product, and demand for it grew rapidly. Italian manufacturers, led by Indesit and Zanussi, came to dominate European markets. They achieved long production runs on individual models, common scale economies in sourcing components, and competed aggressively on price.

The market matured. As incomes rose and the cost of machines fell relative to other products, cheapness became a less powerful selling point. The development of flexible manufacturing processes reduced the advantages of large-scale operation. By the early 1980s, Indesit and Zanussi were effectively bankrupt. These names survive thanks to the Italian government, and the Swedish company Electrolux (which acquired Zanussi). The most profitable producers in this industry in the 1980s were not those with large multi-domestic marketing operations, but others—like Hotpoint in the United Kingdom and Bosch in Germany—which focused on machines designed for their own domestic market and sold through a distribution network over which they enjoyed substantial influence.

Some companies—like Honda—develop an increasingly powerful armoury of complementary competitive advantages. Others—like BMW and Glaxo—succeed in sustaining their competitive advantage by effective support for their distinctive capabilities. Some—like IBM—have competitive advantages which diminish in value as the structure of their markets changes. And others—Indesit—have competitive advantages which prove transient because the firm has no real distinctive capability. When can distinctive capabilities be turned into sustained competitive advantages and when do they erode?

Sustaining competitive advantage

Competitive advantages fade for one of two reasons. The distinctive capability may itself decline, and become less distinctive, or the markets in which that distinctive capability is applied may shrink, or otherwise become less valuable.

Innovation, as Chapter 7 showed, is always the most fragile of distinctive capabilities. Most innovation advantages are transitory because the successful innovation is quickly copied. In financial services markets there is neither copyright nor patent in innovation. Sometimes an innovation can be protected if proprietary knowledge can be kept secret—as with the documentation needed to establish a new financial instrument—but usually this becomes public or can—like most production innovations—be reverse engineered. Innovation yields a competitive advantage only for the length of time it takes for imitation to be effective.

This is true even if an innovation is protected by a system of tight appropriability. Patents expire, as they did for Hoffmann–La Roche. Xerox reaped handsome profits from its innovation when it could fully appropriate its benefits but has since faced intense competition from other suppliers. Even a patented innovation is vulnerable to a new technology.

Innovation advantages are most frequently sustainable where they are supported by other distinctive capabilities or protected by complementary assets, because then imitation of the innovation itself is no longer enough. It often happens that the competitive advantage from an innovation goes not to the innovator, but to the follower with the strongest set of supporting distinctive capabilities. This is how IBM has managed to maintain an innovative lead in several of its principal markets even though new developments have often been pioneered by smaller companies. Oxford Instruments has derived only limited added value from its strongly innovative record in magnets, because its distinctive capabilities are rapidly matched by companies such as GE and Siemens which have more powerful complementary assets.

Competitive advantages based on architecture can be sustained over long periods, but not easily. They require nurture. Organizational knowledge needs to be refreshed and replenished, and a co-operative ethic requires continual reinforcement. Yet firms with strong architecture—Marks & Spencer or Procter and Gamble—have sometimes maintained their advantages decade after decade, adapting their organizational knowledge and redeploying their relational skills in different market sectors.

But architecture is also easily destroyed. For many years retail banks derived competitive advantage from architecture. The quality of a loan portfolio emerges only over time. Successful banks built a structure of long-term relational employment contracts which protected their employees from the temptation to emphasize short-term performance. Customers are naturally inclined to give their bankers an optimistic account of their financial prospects. Successful banks overcame this by developing relational contracts with their customers.

In the 1970s and 1980s, several banks overrode these relationships, in pursuit—as they saw it—of a more performance-based internal culture and a more aggressive external marketing perspective. Spot and classical contracts were substituted for relational ones, internally and externally. 'Transactions banking' replaced 'relationship banking' and, in due course, the institutions concerned paid the price in bad loans and bad debts.

Organizational knowledge is typically market specific and may lose its value if the market changes. The depreciation of the value of the organizational knowledge accumulated over centuries in the Swiss watch-making industry is a remarkable, if extreme, case. Equally, organizational knowledge can often be conservative, and fail to see these market shifts occurring, or refuse to acknowledge their relevance when they have occurred. The craft skills of

European shipbuilders, or of Sheffield cutlers, were once the basis of strong competitive advantages but ultimately came to have negative value. The custodians of organizational knowledge knew a great deal about their industry that was no longer true.

More than any other distinctive capability, the sustainability of architecture rests on the skills of senior managers. Recognizing the nature of the company's architecture and the function it plays in the markets the firm serves is a necessary first step. Architecture is certainly not created by, and not much sustained by, the proliferation of identity and communication programmes of the last decade as chief executives and their consultants unveil the expensively orchestrated 'corporate culture'. These programmes often confuse the symbols of architecture with the substance, and fail to acknowledge the degree to which architecture must grow with, and from, the organization. It cannot be imposed, and if it could it would be replicated.

An alternative danger is that the company—or its new management—does not fully appreciate the elaborate structure of implicit contracts which establish its distinctive capability. It is always possible to establish immediate gains by imposing a better set of spot contracts, as Carl Icahn did when he acquired TWA. If you treat each game as if it were the last round of a repeated Prisoner's Dilemma, then you fail to derive the potential gains from repeated game strategies. Sometimes, of course, you *may* be playing the last round (and, in the end, it emerged that Icahn was).

Reputation advantages, although slow to build up, are often persistent and sustainable. Indeed, we use the phrase 'living on a reputation' to describe the process of sustaining competitive advantage with modest current input. Reputations can be eroded—the mismanagement of reputation by Hilton hotels was described in Chapter 6—and, occasionally, it may be best consciously to milk a reputation. Reputation advantages often fade as the market in which they are established declines. Yet because a reputation in a declining market is evidently a diminishing asset, it is correspondingly less powerful when applied in a new one. The transfer needs to be accomplished well in advance. Accountants, seeing their audit base under pressure, have wisely chosen to use their reputation to establish positions in related markets for other services.

The sustainability of strategic assets

Strategic assets fall into three broad categories. First, some companies enjoy natural monopoly. Second, a firm may have a licence, benefit from regulatory restriction on entry, or otherwise enjoy special access to scarce factors. Third, the cost structure of the industry, with a substantial component of sunk costs, may confer incumbent advantages. How well do these assets meet the test of sustainability?

Natural monopoly ensures that there is only one firm in a particular market, but does not tell us who it will be. A firm with a modest competitive advantage can easily knock out an incumbent whose only strategic advantage is natural monopoly. Even a natural monopoly may have no strategic advantage in a contestable market. So natural monopoly on its own may be difficult to sustain. This is, however, a result of more theoretical than practical interest, although the concept of contestability has been much discussed and widely cited in regulatory and anti-trust discussions. In reality almost all natural monopolies are also associated with sunk costs, and a natural monopoly in a market where costs are substantially sunk is quite readily sustainable, as is evidenced by the absence of competitive threat to local utilities and the substantial difficulties encountered by prospective entrants to telecommunications even in the face of regulatory support.

Sunk costs are a depreciating strategic asset if costs which are sunk today need to be sunk again, and again. There are substantial sunk costs in the automobile industry but these need to be replenished with each model cycle. So the entry fee to the world automobile industry, although large, is one which companies with strong competitive advantages have found it possible to pay. But in aircraft, where the model cycle is much longer and the benefits of learning by doing are enduring, entry has been feasible only with state support.

Sustaining strategic assets commonly requires the careful management of regulation and of anti-trust policies. France Télécom and Deutsche Bundespost have mainly been successful in persuading their governments of the advantages of an integrated telecommunications network under common ownership. British Telecom had to accept the licensing of a network competitor, the imposition of access obligations, and measures intended to disadvantage it in competition with new entrants. British firms, in particular, have suffered as a government committed to privatization and deregulation has attacked incumbent advantages. Some firms—such as British Gas and British Airports—have resisted market liberalization. Others—such as National Express Coaches and the electricity supply industry—were effective, at least for a time, in substituting strategic entry barriers for statutory ones. British Airways has seen considerable erosion of its strategic assets.

The management of a campaign against damaging market liberalization requires, in general, a combination of an effective political argument with an effective technical argument. European governments are less susceptible to the intensive Capitol Hill lobbying activities characteristic of US companies threatened by adverse public policy moves. The role of the legislature in Europe is typically more limited and the capacity of executive authorities to implement their judgements correspondingly greater. Purely political arguments are often unsuccessful because officials resist the implementation of what they see as wholly self-interested argument. Equally, compelling technical arguments often fail in the absence of a political rationale that brings them to government attention.

Companies vary widely in the sophistication with which they handle public policy issues, and this is particularly true in the changing environment created by the fashion for deregulation and the growth of powers in Brussels at the expense of traditional relationships in national capitals. Too often, issue management is perceived as a part of public relations, and corporate rewards go either for fire-fighting activities or for the preparation of self-congratulatory documents for which there is no external readership. Preventive action is often very much more effective than vigorous response to an issue which has become the subject of political controversy.

The persistence of profitability

Competitive advantages may increase or diminish. The evidence from Western economies is that competitive advantages do persist, but as they persist they erode. The best measure of the sustainability of competitive advantage is the extent to which a firm continues to enjoy above-average profitability year after year.

Table 11.1 brings together studies of the erosion of above-average profitability in a number of different countries. Its basic finding is that firms with high initial profitability at the beginning of the period studied (twenty-three years) can be expected to have higher than average profitability indefinitely, although the strength of the relationship varies considerably across countries, as does the dispersion of profitability. Above-average profitability is less sustainable in Germany and Japan, easiest to maintain in France and the United States. In all countries, initial profitability rankings were a good guide to longer-term profitability rankings.

Table 11.1. The Erosion of Above-Average Profitability

	Initial difference between most profitable* group of firms and the average of all (%)	Long-run difference between most profitable group of firms and the average of all (%)	Correlation between initial and long-run profitability (all firms)
France	8.5	6.4	0.36
Germany	4.6	0.5	0.24
Sweden	14.3	4.1	0.60
UK	9.1	1.9	0.34
US	5.5	4.7	0.58
Japan	3.4	0.7	0.31

* 'Most profitable' are those in the top sixth by initial profitability.
Source: Odagiri and Yamawaki (1990).

An analysis of around 250 British firms over an even longer period (Cubbin and Geroski, 1987) suggested that even over that period a minority of firms enjoyed excess profits that showed no sign of erosion. Such persistence was more likely for small firms than for large—indicating that sustained competitive advantage is more likely for focused businesses—and more likely for firms that did not engage in acquisition activity over the period than those which did—suggesting that acquisition served more often to dilute competitive advantage than to reinforce it.

Similar results are found in studying the evolution of market share. Market leadership positions decline, and the greater the extent of market leadership the greater the extent of decline (Table 11.2). Yet here too the rate of erosion is comparatively slow.

Table 11.2. Market Leadership: UK, 1979–1986 (average over 57 manufacturing markets)

Rank order	Share in 1979 (%)	Change in share 1979–86 (%)	Share in 1986* (%)
1	21.9	–2.1	20.1
2	12.2	–0.1	12.1
3	7.6	–0.1	7.4
4	5.3	–0.5	4.8
5	3.7	–0.2	3.5

* This is not equal to the sum of the first two columns because the identity of firms in each rank changes.

Source: Davies *et al.* (1991), tables 7, 13.

In the long term, corporate histories display a striking mixture of stability and mobility. Of the largest ten UK corporations of thirty years ago, there are several—ICI, Unilever—which are still in the equivalent list today and which would have been in the same list in every intervening period. There are also several which are no longer independent companies, or are now well below the list of leaders—Courtaulds, Imperial Tobacco. By contrast, Grand Metropolitan was an unknown company twenty-five years ago and Sainsbury's a medium-sized retailer. Similar patterns emerge for companies in Germany (Table 11.3).

Are competitive advantages more, or less, persistent today than in earlier periods? This is an impossible question to answer systematically but an intriguing insight is provided by Scherer and Ross (1990) (Fig. 11.1), who measure the stability of the list of the top 100 US corporations year by year over the century. From 1909 to 1940 the measure of turbulence showed a continuing downward trend, plateauing in the post-war period. Yet in the last decade, there has been a sharp reversal, and exits from what is now the *Fortune* list over the period 1977–87 matched the rates experienced at the

Table 11.3. The Ten Largest British and German Companies, 1962–1991*

Britain	Germany
Leaders in both years	
Shell	RWE
ICI	Siemens
BP	Hoechst
Unilever	Bayer
BAT	BASF
	Thyssen (ATH)
Leaders in 1962 but no longer leaders in 1991	
Courtaulds: Contracted and rationalized, demerged textiles	Rheinssche Stahlwerke: Acquired by Thyssen
Imperial Tobacco: Lost market share, acquired by Hanson	Mannesmann: Relative decline from steel and metal company
GKN: Engineering firm, contracted and rationalized	AEG: Poor financial performance, acquired by Daimler Benz
Esso UK: Slipped out of top ten	Gelsenkircher: Heavy industry conglomerate acquired by Veba in 1976, sold to Deutsche BP in 1979
P & O: Slight relative decline	
Not leaders in 1962 but leaders in 1991	
BT: Demerged from Post Office and privatized, rapid growth of market	Daimler–Benz: Successful core businesses and considerable acquisition activity
British Aerospace: Created by merger through nationalization	Volkswagen: The most effective automobile company in export marketing
British Gas: Expanded substantially when natural gas was discovered, privatized in 1986	Veba: Electricity, oil, and chemicals conglomerate partly privatized in 1965, made full public company in 1987
Grand Metropolitan: Small company in 1962, grew through merger	Bosch: Rapid organic growth in electrical sector
J. Sainsbury: Food retailer, rapid organic growth	

* Ranked by capital employed, 1972; ranked by sales, 1991.

Source: Times 1000 (or 300) in 1962.

beginning of the century. Over the century as a whole, the widely observed tendency for large firms to exert increasing control over the economic environment in which they found themselves does seem to have been a reality. But there are also clear indications that the greater internationalization of the world economy and a volatility of economic activity greater than that experienced over the previous fifty years have seriously challenged that control.

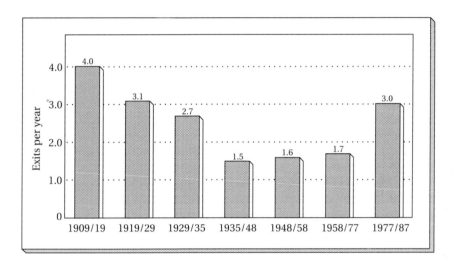

Fig. 11.1. Average Number of Exits from Top 100 US Corporations, per Year

Sources: Scherer and Ross (1990).

A variety of other indicators confirm this conclusion. The degree of industrial concentration measures the share of large firms in economic activity, and it is commonly measured both for whole economies and for individual economic markets. While through the twentieth century the clear trend has been one of increasing concentration, that is a trend which now seems to have been halted and reversed. The check seems to have occurred in the United States around 1960. In the United Kingdom, the merger boom of the 1960s increased concentration substantially and the peak was reached at the end of that decade. Since then, the average size of large firms and their share in total output have declined markedly. Between 1979 and 1986 the share of British manufacturing output held by firms with more than 1,000 employees fell from 67 per cent to 59 per cent and that of those with less than 100 employees rose from 14.6 per cent to 19.3 per cent (Advisory Committee on Science and Technology, 1990). In Germany and France, some increase in concentration seems to have continued into the 1970s.

Table 11.4 shows the international pattern of concentration. While individual European economies are more concentrated than those of the United States and Japan, they are also smaller. The picture for Europe as a whole is similar to that in the United States. The leading companies of both Europe and the United States are, on average, much larger than those of Japan although this picture must, to a degree, be modified by the extensive relationships between groups of companies in Japan. While industrial concentration is best documented, similar patterns seem to be evident in other sectors. The utility sector has been increasingly fragmented as measures to introduce competition and in some cases to force the break up or divestiture of established dominant firms come into force. In banking (Table 11.5) the leading

Table 11.4. The Size of Firms in Europe, Japan, and the US

	Average size of leading firm (no. of employees in 000)		Leading firm employment as % of all industrial employment	
	Top 10	Top 20	Top 10	Top 20
US	311	220	13.1	18.6
Japan	107	72	7.3	9.9
EC	311	233	8.9	13.3
France	116	81	23.2	32.5
Germany	177	115	20.1	26.0
UK	141	108	23.1	35.3

Sources: Scherer and Ross (1990); own calculations for EC.

banks of twenty years ago have steadily lost market share although the rise in the resources of Japanese banks means that overall concentration has risen not fallen.

Scale as a competitive advantage

In much casual discussion of strategic issues in Europe, size appears to be viewed as a principal source of competitive advantage. Sometimes the impression is given that size is the *only* source of competitive advantage. This increasing focus on a small number of companies in most industries may be the vision which many strategists have of the future. The verdict of the market-place does, however, seem to be different. Although large corporations will continue to dominate the international economy, the concentration of business activity in the hands of large firms, which was the most important feature of the industrial landscape in the first sixty years or so of this century, appears to have come to an end.

There is a tendency to confuse the indicators of success with the causes of success. The king may wear a crown, but it does not follow that you will become king by wearing a crown. In looking at Boeing or Toyota or IBM we

Table 11.5. The World's Largest Banks, 1970–1990 (by assets)

Rank	1970	1980	1990
1	Bank America	Citicorp	Dai-Ichi Kangyo
2	Citicorp	Bank America	Mitsubishi
3	Chase Manhattan	Crédit Agricole	Sumitomo
4	Barclays	Banque Nationale de Paris	Mitsui
5	National Westminster	Crédit Lyonnais	Sanwa
6	Manufacturers Hanover	Socété Générale	Fuji
7	Banca Nazionale del Lavoro	Barclays	Crédit Agricole
8	J. P. Morgan	Deutsche	Banque Nationale de Paris
9	Western Bankcorp	National Westminster	Industrial Bank of Japan
10	Royal Bank of Canada	Dai-Ichi Kangyo	Crédit Lyonnais
	Share of these in 1970: 24.3%	Share of these in 1980: 22.8%	Share of these in 1990: 27.7%
	Share of these in 1980: 16.6%	Share of these in 1990: 19.8%	Share of these in 1980: 19.2%

Source: The *Banker* magazine.

observe companies which are both large and successful. But the causation runs from their success to size, not from size to success, and it is quite mistaken to believe that by replicating their size one could replicate their organizational effectiveness.

Yet it is a mistake which is often made. In 1967–8 British Leyland was created by an amalgamation of the principal remaining indigenous British automobile producers, under government sponsorship and in pursuit of a strongly held view that the British industry lacked critical mass to compete effectively in increasing international automobile markets. Within seven years the company was effectively bankrupt and was nationalized. Despite continuing financial aid from the British government, the company's market position continued to deteriorate. A firm which, when established, held about 40 per cent of the UK car market, now, as Rover, has a 13 per cent market share. Its export sales, in real terms, are around half of what they were when the company was formed.

The company's partial revival in the 1980s rests on its collaboration with Honda. Honda produced its first motor car at almost precisely the same time as British Leyland was formed. It did so despite the opposition of the Japanese government, which took the view that the Japanese automobile industry was already sufficiently fragmented. Cars are now Honda's primary business and the company is now one of the largest and most successful manufacturers in the world. The difference, of course, is that Honda held, and holds, substantial competitive advantages while Leyland did not. Without competitive advantage, British Leyland's size did not help it at all; with competitive advantage, Honda's lack of size did not prove an enduring problem.

Economies of scale are a measure of the extent to which costs fall as output expands. In assessing how they influence the competitive position of different players, it is necessary to look at the very long run in which all costs can be varied. In this long term the type of plant and its scale of operation can be chosen freely and the form of corporate organization can also be changed. The mental exercise required to assess the magnitude of scale economies assumes that the industry could plan its output on a blank sheet of paper. To what extent would average costs then vary with the size and scope of output?

This is the exercise undertaken for Table 11.6, which provides estimates of the minimum efficient plant size for a range of European industries. For computers, cars, turbo generators, videos, and titanium oxides, such plants would have output which is large relative to the size of the European market. For crisps, bricks, and beer there is no advantage in organizing production on a European basis.

Yet these estimates exaggerate. I have yet to encounter a firm or an industry where managers did not initially overestimate the importance of scale economies. One reason is that most firms have many costs which are fixed in the short run and a variety of activities in which there is excess capacity. It is almost always possible to get more output out of the same inputs by working them more intensively for a short period of time. Many small businessmen have learnt that they are most profitable when they are overtrading. But most successful small businessmen have also learnt that they cannot overtrade indefinitely. Few costs are truly fixed in the long term. Even the Chairman's salary, the archetype of fixed costs, is ultimately something which varies with the level of output. The salary of the Chairman is systematically correlated with the size of the organization which he (usually) chairs (more systematically, incidentally, than with its profitability). Scale economies are not the product of the more intensive working of existing plant. Nor are they often derived from spreading corporate overheads more thinly over more output—the corporate overheads will grow again, for reasons as good or as bad as those reasons for which they were incurred in the first place.

Scale economies arise when there are real technical advantages to larger scale output. A telephone network can provide the same quality of service for twice the traffic with less than twice the number of lines, because the margin of spare capacity needed to assure service rises less than proportionately with volume. Or scale may allow greater specialization. It was Adam Smith who looked with wonderment at a pin factory, where early versions of mass production meant that one worker was no longer responsible for the manufacture of a single pin. The 'two-thirds' rule of process engineers arises because the material needed to form a container rises less than proportionately with the volume it will hold. Inventory and spare capacity required to support

Table 11.6. Potential Existence of Economies of Scale in European Industries

Industry	Minimum efficient scale of output per year	Minimum efficient scale as a % of total EC output
Integrated steel	9.6–12 m. tons	9.8
Bricks	25 m. bricks	0.2
Cement	1.3 m. tons	1.0
Glass bottles	133,000 tons	0.1
Petrochemicals	500,000 tons	2.8
Titanium oxides	130,000 tons	50.0
Detergents	70,000 tons	3.0
Turbo generators	6,000 MW	10.0
Public switches	400,000–500,000 lines	4.0
Videos	0.8–1 m. units	20.0
Potato crisps	30,000–35,000 tons	2.0
Beer	4.5 m. barrels	3.0
Cigarettes	36 bn. units	6.0
Tyres	16,500 per day	3.0
Motor cars	2 m. units	20.0
Mainframe computers	Large share of world output	Very large share

Source: Pratten (1988). Pratten estimates MES using the engineering approach. This tends to bias estimates upward—see Table 11.7.

unexpected demand or occasional breakdown rises less rapidly than the level of demand or capacity which is underwritten.

While economies of scale are mostly technical, tangible, and visible, diseconomies are mostly human, intangible, and invisible. As size increases, lines of communication are extended and distorted. Large plants provide a less satisfying work environment, and workers need to be paid higher wages and are more likely to engage in industrial disputes. Information flows are less immediate, flexibility of response is diminished. In an ideal world, these diseconomies of scale would be minimized while technical economies of scale would be fully realized. It is this ideal world that process engineers generally inhabit and into which general managers are frequently drawn. The idealization systematically biases judgement of efficient size.

Yet the relevant question is not what is possible in a perfect world but what is realistically achievable. At the level of national economies, arguments for central planning are always difficult to resist since it is clear that an ideal system of co-ordinated central planning will perform better than a chaotic market economy, but the practical issue is not the comparison of ideals but the level of performance which is actually likely to be realized. In the case of national economies it does not appear that those systems of planning which were actually implemented matched the effectiveness of market economies and the same issue applies to the management of large corporations.

Some firms do manage to achieve these things—to gain technical economies of scale while reducing, or at least minimizing the diseconomies associated with human factors. But that achievement (rather than scale as such) is their competitive advantage, and it is quite rare. The trend to smaller plants is more marked than the trend to smaller firms. Hughes (1990) estimates that the proportion of British workers in manufacturing industry in plants with less than 200 employees fell from 44 per cent in 1924 to 27 per cent in 1973 but by 1987 had risen to 39 per cent.

There are two primary methods of assessing the extent of scale economies. The engineering method is based, as described above, on the estimated production costs of hypothetical plants. The survivor method measures how the actual distribution of plant sizes evolves over time, in the belief that plant of inefficient size will lose market share to those of more appropriate scale. The survivor method therefore attempts to incorporate both diseconomies of scale from human resource management and market responsiveness. Table 11.7 compares estimates of minimum efficient size for a range of industries. The ranking given by the two approaches is similar—fertilizers, cement, and margarine production are at the top of all lists. But the minimum efficient size indicated by the engineering approach is in all cases massively larger than the survivor technique would suggest. In most of the industries listed, the technical economies of scale which the engineering approach identifies are wholly offset by the organizational diseconomies which the survivor method brings into account.

Table 11.7. Alternative Estimates of Scale Economies

Rank	Industry	Minimum efficient plant as share of UK market (%)		
		Pratten engineering estimate	Survivor estimate	
			Rees	Lyons (1980)
1	Fertilizers	23	1.4	0.9
2	Beer	12	0.9	0.05
3	Margarine	10	5.0	0.5
4	Cement	10	1.4	1.6
5	Bread	10	0.2	0.15
6	Bricks	1	0.3	0.1
7	Small tools	1	0.1	0.1

Sources: Lyons (1980); Pratten (1988); Rees (1973).

Mostly, there are some scale economies even in the long term. Some expenditures are truly fixed—such as those on advertising, product design, research and development. The significance of these costs, together with the degree of product differentiation in the market, determines the maximum number of viable producers. If the product is essentially homogeneous—as, for example, with utilities such as gas, electricity, and water—then the existence of quite moderate scale economies will make structures with more than one seller in a geographical market unviable and that is generally what happens in these industries. Product differentiation tends to increase the number of firms which any market will sustain. The car industry is one in which there are significant unrealized economies of scale. But there is also considerable variety of tastes. This ensures that the lowest cost producer does not scoop the entire market. So a variety of firms with different products and different market shares continue to coexist, and the market as a whole displays higher costs and higher prices than would be feasible if each market segment was concentrated on a particular model.

In this way, technology, time, and changes alter the cost structure associated with supplying any market. Changes in telecommunications technology have made what was once a powerful natural monopoly potentially competitive at almost all levels, from international calls to local service. The industry is far more fragmented than it was and this fragmentation is likely to continue. Airlines have seen opposite developments. The introduction of hub and spoke methods of operation and computerized reservation systems to make bookings have given major advantages to larger carriers and so promoted concentration. The way in which changing tastes and technology in the European domestic appliance market first swung competitive advantage towards size and then returned it to smaller producers was described on page 162.

There are not many European industries in which the European market or markets are unable to support several viable producers. But there are some; power generators, telecommunications switching equipment, automobiles. In these, a process of concentration and rationalization is likely to continue. But the rationalization is likely to be in favour not of the largest, but of those firms with the strongest competitive advantage.

If scale were a primary source of competitive advantage, then the greatest competitive advantage ever enjoyed by any firm was that held by General Motors in the 1950s. GM was the world's largest and most respected corporation, pre-eminent in an industry unquestionably characterized by substantial scale economies. Following the failure of Kaiser and Studebaker it was generally assumed that the automobile industry would concentrate around a smaller number of existing players. The notion that GM's dominance might be challenged by a new entrant to the industry then appeared inconceivable; yet that is precisely what has occurred, and Toyota, then a maker of sewing machines, became in 1988 the producers of the world's best selling car. In 1991, GM declared the largest loss incurred by any corporation. The lesson is that size cannot be a sustained source of competitive advantage. If size is its only source then size is something which a competitor with a true competitive advantage, based on a distinctive capability, can ultimately replicate.

Market share as competitive advantage

If size, as such, is not a competitive advantage, what of market share? The association of high market share and high profitability is one of the clearest empirical findings in business strategy. But as with the nexus between size and success, it is important not to confuse the manifestations of competitive advantage with the causes. Firms with competitive advantages are likely to have both high market share and high profitability, but it does not follow that a firm without a competitive advantage *will* increase its profitability by increasing its market share through price cutting, advertising and promotion, or market development. Nor, for that matter, does it follow that a firm which does have a competitive advantage will increase its profitability by increasing its market share. To use the analogy adopted by Buzzell and Gale (1987), height and weight are closely associated but you will not necessarily grow taller by eating more. You might (as an ill-nourished child) but you are unlikely to do so as a well-fed adult. The answer must depend, in all instances, on the specific circumstances of the case.

At the very least, however, the analysis suggests that building market share is likely to be part of the creation of competitive advantage and that a firm with low market share is unlikely to have a sustainable position. But there is less to this recommendation than it seems at first sight. BMW has little more than 1 per cent of the world car market, but if the market is redefined as the luxury car segment, its share is much higher. Glaxo has half the world market for anti-ulcer therapies, but a small share of the overall pharmaceutical market.

The underlying issue is that almost all successful firms enjoy a large market share relative to their perceived competition—it could hardly be otherwise. The PIMS database, appropriately for its purposes, asks firms to define their 'served market' by reference to these perceived competitors. For any firm with a competitive advantage there will be some market, suitably defined, in which it is dominant. If 'build market share' means 'build market share even if that is not the most effective way of developing your competitive advantage', then the prescription is a misleading one. If it means only 'build market share if that is the most effective way of developing your competitive advantage', then it adds little to our understanding of competitive strategy.

Attractive markets and market positions

Chapter 9 analysed a firm's choice of markets by reference to the application of distinctive capabilities. It did not consider whether the market was intrinsically attractive or unattractive. Yet it is rare to hear a strategy discussion which does not centre around that issue. The search for attractive markets was at the heart of the portfolio planning which was a dominant theme a decade ago, and still retains considerable influence on corporate behaviour.

The Boston Consulting Group's matrix, which originates this genre, is shown in Fig. 21.2. It assesses the quality of businesses by reference to two criteria: market share and market growth.

Here, too, the measurement of market share requires care in the definition of markets. Indeed, anyone who has used these portfolio planning structures will recognize how, if the firm perceives a business as successful, the market is always redefined in such a way as to give it a large market share. The particular contribution of this, and other portfolio planning techniques, is its emphasis on the objective attractiveness of the industry—here measured by market growth.

It is, at first sight, obvious that rapidly growing markets, such as those for financial services or electronics, are more attractive than declining markets, such as those for steel or tobacco. Yet it is the very obviousness of the proposition that is the problem. If these markets are objectively attractive, then they are attractive to everyone, and that will reduce industry profitability as quickly as entry can occur. To identify an industry as attractive is to say no more than to say that Glaxo is a good share or the Polish Zloty is a weak currency. It does not follow that a firm should enter an attractive market any more than investors should buy Glaxo or sell Zlotys. The issue is how much of that attractiveness, or lack of it, is already discounted.

Correctly perceiving the attractiveness of markets like financial services or electronics, many firms have entered, and many have lost money doing so. The largest money losers are often firms with no relevant competitive advantage, which see the appeal of a growing industry—observe Exxon's losses in the small computer market or BAT's in insurance. At the same time, firms like Hanson and BTR have built highly successful businesses by targeting acquisitions in industries which other firms saw as objectively unattractive.

PIMS shows some relationship between market growth and return on investment, but the effect is small. In Buzzell and Gale's analysis (1987), the difference between return on investment in fast-growing industries (averaging 11 per cent growth per annum) and those of shrinking industries (averaging 4 per cent decline per year) is about two points. This small effect actually overstates the impact of growth on profitability. Accounting profitability most frequently exaggerates true profitability when growth is rapid—the pharmaceutical industry, where true capital employed is much underrepresented because R & D expenditures are expensed, is an example of an industry where reported profitability overstates true rates of return. And faster growth *than expected* almost certainly has a positive outcome on profitability, and fast-growing markets inevitably include many in this category.

This is an aspect of a wider statistical problem. Industry profitability has strong cyclical elements—it is quite common for there to be good or bad years for all firms in the same industry. Once these cyclical effects are removed, very little of the difference in profitability between firms is explained by what industry they are in. For the sample of European firms from which the 'top ten' of Chapter 2 was selected, only around 10 per cent of the overall variance of added value was accounted for by industry factors—the balance relates to factors which are specific to firms themselves.

There is only one source of data which allows systematic decomposition of the variance of profitability not only by firm and industry but also by reference to the contribution of firm and business unit effects—the FTC line of business data compiled for a sample of US corporations in the 1970s. The evidence from these is striking (Table 11.8). Not only are industry effects small, but firm effects arise almost entirely at the business unit rather than the corporate level. Neither the choice of industry nor the choice of corporate parent adds materially to the profitability of US corporations. Value is added at the level at which competitive advantage is created—the individual business unit—not by portfolio planning.

Table 11.8. Contributions to the Variance of Profits across Business Units (%)

Corporate ownership	0.8
Industry effects	8.3
Cyclical effects	7.8
Business unit specific effects	46.4
Unexplained factors	36.7

Source: Rumelt (1991).

The efficiency of markets ensures that market selection is not a basis for competitive advantage, except when it provides a means of exploiting a distinctive capability which is specific to a particular firm. The same proposition must follow for positioning. Yet PIMS shows that high returns are associated with quality positions (p. 138). These are not simply returns to market position as such—if one position was more profitable than another and equally attainable, then others would adopt it and the returns from it would bid down. The high returns from quality positions reward the underlying competitive advantage—reputation in some cases, in others a distinctive capability in innovation or architecture—which allows that firm, but not others, to attain a high-quality position. For these firms, their competitive advantage is best exploited in a high-quality position. It does not follow that the same position would produce the same returns for other firms, and it cannot be expected that it would. The success of Mercedes does not mean that it is possible, or sensible, to recommend the same market position to Hyundai. Each should select a position which reflect its—quite different—sources of competitive advantage.

The confusion between good positioning and competitive advantage is a particularly common management error in markets for fast-moving consumer goods. Another British retailer—the Next Group—provides a chastening example. Next successfully identified an underdeveloped market for fashionable clothing of moderate quality for women aged 20–35, and sales and profits grew very rapidly. Mistakenly believing that its good fortune rested, not on its market position, but on competitive advantage in retailing systems, the company diversified into mail order, interior design, and financial services, with marked lack of success. At the same time, established retailers with strengths in retailing systems invaded its market niche, and brought the company to the verge of collapse.

Positioning is unlikely to provide sustained competitive advantage because positioning is rarely appropriable. Most market positions can be replicated, and if profitable they will be. Some market positions—as with that of Mercedes—are truly hard to emulate, but that demonstrates that the true competitive advantage lies in their quality of engineering, and in consumer recognition of it, rather than in the position as such. An exception to this general rule is found when a market niche is sufficiently small that it will support one profitable incumbent but not two. CNN is replicable but it is probably not profitable to replicate it. The conditions under which niche positions may create added value in the long run are discussed in Chapters 14 and 15.

Sources of competitive advantage

The final sections of this chapter examined factors which are often identified as sources of competitive advantage—size, market share, market selection, and market position. None of them is a *sustainable* source of competitive advantage because they are all characteristics which, given time and expenditure, other firms can replicate. In this they differ sharply from the primary distinctive capabilities—innovation, reputation, and architecture. Often, of course, a distinctive capability will enable a firm to achieve large size, take a dominant market share, or be best applied in a quality market position. But these factors are the outcome of that firm's competitive success, not the source of it. Confusion between manifestations of success and its causes is one of the most widespread errors in strategic thinking.

M any of the references in preceding chapters are relevant to the issues covered here. See, in particular, public policy management and the maintenance of strategic assets (Chapter 8), scale economies (Chapter 8), product positioning and product quality (Chapter 9). Ghemawat (1986) is a general discussion of sustainability.

Mueller (ed.) (1986) is a particularly useful overview on the persistence of profitability, as is Cubbin and Geroski (1987) and Jacobsen (1988). The performance of market leadership is covered by Davies, S., *et al.* (1991). The importance of market share, and the interpretation of empirical findings related to this issue, is widely discussed; see, in particular, Buzzell and Gale (1987). Early accounts of the portfolio planning approach are Day (1977), Hedley (1977), Hitchens *et al.* (1978). Critical surveys are Hapselagh (1982) and Coate (1983). See Oster (1990) for an 'efficient market' based critique of this approach. For the history of Next see Cronshaw and Kay (1991).

12

Appropriability

If a competitive advantage is to form the basis of corporate success it must also be appropriable. Appropriability is the capacity of the firm to retain the added value it creates for its own benefit. Adding value is an objective for a not-for-profit organization just as it is for a corporation. But while a tennis club or a university will wish to see that added value distributed to its members or though the community, the successful corporation must be concerned with appropriation.

If, and only if, the firm generates added value does it have something which it can distribute to its various stakeholders over and above the minimum necessary to persuade them to work for it, invest in it, supply it, or buy its products. When a firm successfully adds value, the government will generally seek to secure part of that added value through taxation (and, conversely, where companies are not successful in adding value there is no sustainable corporate tax base). Shareholders are the residual claimants on added value and, in the United States, are also the principal claimants on added value. This primacy of shareholders is less clearly true in other countries and other cultures.

Who benefits from the firm's success in adding value depends partly on the decisions of the firm, partly on the structure of the markets which it faces, and partly on the sources of the added value itself. To sustain distinctive capabilities based on architecture and reputation, it is generally necessary to share at least part of the returns among all the stakeholders in the business and to achieve their agreement, or at least acquiescence, in that distribution. The returns to strategic assets, in contrast, will generally be fought over by the different stakeholder groups.

The appropriability of added value

Adding value is not an objective only for profit-making institutions. The purpose of a university, or a tennis club, is to add value, just as the objective of IBM or Sony is to add value. They seek to create an output which is more valuable than the cost of its inputs. The test of the effectiveness of all these organizations is whether they have made better use of these resources than would have been the case if the same resources had been deployed elsewhere by another organization.

But it is easier to assert this objective for a corporation and it is easier to determine whether it has been achieved, because measuring the output of a corporation is a much simpler task. The output of a university is particularly difficult to assess, and is certainly not captured in any financial indicator. The product of the tennis club is the value its members attach to its facilities, which is not at all the same thing as the subscriptions they pay. If those who run universities or tennis clubs resist the imposition of financial measures of success it is in part because they correctly believe that the result will be to emphasize those aspects of output which are easy to measure at the expense of less tangible dimensions which are of equal or greater importance.

But it is not only the objective of adding value which is common to every activity which yields useful output—commercial or non-commercial. The structure of strategy is not so different for not-for-profit organizations. The university, and the tennis club, should define their distinctive capabilities, identify the markets in which these are most effectively applied, and review their positioning in relation to their competitive advantages and those of their competitors. The pitfalls of wish-driven strategy are as real, and as prevalent, for non-commercial organizations as they are for companies.

But there is a critical difference between the corporation and other organizations. For the successful company, the *appropriability* of the added value it creates is a key issue for management. The success of the corporation depends on its ability to retain a substantial part of the added value it creates, and to prevent it from being dissipated among its workers, suppliers, and customers. But the university or the tennis club have responsibilities to a very different group of stakeholders. The successful university is one which distributes its added value to its customers—its students—and if it is truly successful allows added value to spill over into the wider community. The appropriation of added value is wholly antithetical to its purpose. The tennis club similarly seeks to create added value for its members. The corporate chief executive correctly points to the profits of the company as a measure of its success. If the rector of a university or the captain of a tennis club were to do the same, we would conclude that they had fundamentally misunderstood the purposes of the organizations for which they were responsible.

In some organizations, the firm is no more than the aggregate of its members, the added value it creates is appropriated by the members, and when they depart so does the added value of the firm. This challenge of appropriation is particularly clear for the professional service firm. Drexel Burnham Lambert was briefly the most profitable firm on Wall Street. But the added value it generated was largely the creation of Michael Milken and associates. Milken and associates appropriated a large part of it, and when Milken was arrested and gaoled the firm collapsed. But Price Waterhouse and Linklaters and Paines earn more than they would do if each of their partners traded as individuals. The added value created is a product of the firm, although it is then distributed among the partners.

If appropriability against insiders is necessary for continued success, appropriability against outsiders is necessary too. Innovative firms can succeed only if they can appropriate the returns to their innovation. Often this is impossible; innovation is readily copied, or can only be exploited effectively with the co-operation of a dominant customer. The added value that has been created is real enough, but to prosper the corporation must create appropriable added value.

Appropriability is the ability to turn added value into profit. Yet it is possible to lay too much stress on the appropriability of added value relative to its creation, and this has been a feature of the past decade. Look at companies which would be towards the top of everyone's list of the world's most successful corporations. It might include IBM, Volkswagen, and Matsushita; Honda, Glaxo, Hewlett-Packard. Profits and profitability are certainly important to them all. Yet none of these companies is characterized by an exclusive preoccupation with profit maximization. All would acknowledge a wider set of responsibilities—to their customers and employees, to the communities within which they operate—and this is an important element in our perception of their success. Nor should this be a matter of surprise. The corporations envisaged by T. Boone Pickens and Professor Friedman are not the corporations for which many of us would like to work, and we would hesitate to buy the products of such businesses or lend them money unless we also had the services of a good attorney.

And yet firms with wider concerns, like those listed above, are successful against all criteria. IBM, Glaxo, and Hewlett-Packard have done well for their shareholders over the decades. The indifference of Japanese companies to the owners of their equity is notorious, most clearly reflected in their negligible dividends and high levels of retained earnings. Yet whoever is complaining about the performance of Japanese corporations, it has not been investors in Japanese securities. An appreciation of the importance of relational contracts in doing business, and of architecture in creating competitive advantage, makes these apparent paradoxes easy to reconcile.

The subject of this chapter is the degree to which firms can, do, and should appropriate the added value they create.

The government and the appropriability of added value

One constraint on the ability of firms to appropriate added value is the role of the government. The state is generally both a participant, and an influence, on the creation of added value.

Table 12.1 illustrates the issue for two state-owned companies—Électricité de France, and Statoil, Norway's national oil company. The government's objective for EDF is to ensure that any added value created within the organization benefits French consumers of electricity, and it is ready to allow this by accepting a modest return on its own investment. Customers are, by deliberate intention, allowed to secure added value at the expense of EDF. The objective of Statoil is quite the opposite. The enormous added value created by Statoil accrues almost entirely to the Norwegian government—indeed, it was for precisely that purpose that Statoil was established.

Table 12.1. Added Value Statements: State-Owned Companies (m. Ecus)

	Électricité de France (1989)	Statoil (1990)
Revenues	21,022	10,166
Wages and salaries	1,338	611
Capital costs	11,554	1,285
Materials	13,035	5,813
Added value	(4,935)	2,437

Sources: EDF and Statoil annual reports and accounts.

For Statoil and EDF, government influence arises directly through its shareholding. But private companies are also substantial taxpayers—creating or appropriating added value in order to make it available for public purposes. The position of British Petroleum—the largest operator on the UK side of the continental shelf—is not so different from that of Statoil, and the government has claimed a similarly large share of its added value. BAT's tobacco business appears in a rather different light if—as in Version B of Table 12.2—the value of its output is measured by the prices paid by its customers rather than the proceeds received by BAT. The difference—of over £5 billion—was collected by the company on behalf of the governments of the countries within which it operates. There are two alternative ways of viewing the relationship between the firm and the state, and Table 12.2 illustrates the contrast. In one (Version C) the government is another party with which the firm must contract, like its suppliers and its employees, in order to enable it to undertake its business, and taxation is the rent which it pays for that opportunity. In the other (Version B) added value accrues to the firm and the government appropriates a substantial part—in this case the larger part—of that added value. Both perspectives have their merits, but in either case the outcome is the same for BAT shareholders (Version A).

This point is particularly important for a firm like Gateway, which paid £57 million in taxes in 1989 although it only created £25 million of added value (p. 25). A firm cannot survive in the long run if the government appropriates more added value than the business generates, since it is then unable to meet the requirements of its suppliers and customers and the expectations of its

Table 12.2. Added Value Statements: BAT Tobacco, 1989 (m. Ecus)

Version A		Version B	
Revenues (sales at value to BAT)	12,988	Revenues (sales at market prices)	18,834
Wages and salaries	2,354	Wages and salaries	2,354
Capital costs	1,065	Capital costs	1,065
Materials	8,844	Materials	8,844
Added value	725	Added value	6,570

Version C		
Relationships with	Financial flow	Value
Customers	Revenues (sales at market prices)	18,834
Labour	Wages and salaries	2,354
Investors	Capital costs	1,065
Suppliers	Materials	8,844
Government	Taxes	5,846
	Added value	725

Source: BAT Industries annual report and accounts.

investors. Added value sets an upper limit to the range of tax demands which are feasible in the long run and the analysis of added value is a helpful approach to understanding the strengths and limitations of corporate tax structures. If a firm creates very large added value—as the activities of Statoil do—then the government can take a major share of that—as the Norwegian government does.

The government is an important stakeholder in almost all the businesses described in this book. Figure 8.1 is a reminder of the strength of government influence and involvement in European industry. And government is in a unique position in the appropriation of added value. Because it can legislate, it can demand and will receive. That exaggerates the difference. In a real sense, firms like Statoil, BP, and BAT negotiate with governments over what they pay. The tax structures they face are the subject of regular discussion. Governments are normally aware both that golden geese must occasionally be fed and that multinational companies have opportunities to create added value in other jurisdictions instead, either through tax planning or through substantive shifts of operations. If the government is not exactly another supplier, providing goods and services in return for a fair price, nor are these firms in the same position as small businesses which must take the tax system as they find it and may believe they receive nothing in return.

The relationship between the firm and the government is an issue for each company as is the relationship between the firm and customers, suppliers, employees, and investors. For Statoil and EDF, this is clear and explicit. The state is not only a stakeholder, but the principal investor and the only supplier of risk capital. But for BP and BAT, relations with government are of almost equal importance. BP depends on governments to license its exploration activities, it pays handsomely for these rights when the outcome is successful, and its operations are an important source of government revenue in many of the jurisdictions within which it operates. The effective management of public affairs is at the very heart of the business of BP or BAT, and the company's success is critically dependent on the competence with which they are handled.

Influences on appropriability

Mostly, however, the division of added value is a matter for agreement, not legislation. Two factors are critical in determining the way in which added value is divided between the various stakeholders. One is the degree to which any, or all of them, have contributed to the achievement of added value. The other is their negotiating power. How many and how concentrated are they? What alternatives do they have?

The profit-orientated firm will often want to share the added value it creates with other stakeholders, because doing so is good business. This is most clear where competitive advantage is based on architecture, or on reputation. Where competitive advantage derives from architecture, there are almost always short-term benefits to individualistic behaviour. The individual will always gain—for a time—by confessing, by shooting rather than passing, by holding back what they know. Sustaining co-operative behaviour depends on persuading him, or her, that the long-run gains outweigh the short-term benefits of opportunism. You cannot drive the hardest possible bargain in a relational contract. To do so is to destroy it.

The firm whose competitive advantage is derived from its reputation is often in a similar position. That reputation depends not only on the actions of the firm, but on the behaviour of many individual employees. This is most obviously true in service organizations, where the supplier's reputation will often be influenced by the customer's experience in dealing with relatively junior employees—the 'moment of truth', popularized by Jan Carlzon of SAS. (Although it is easy to overstress this. The moment of truth for most airline passengers is when the plane arrives safely and on time, and that is the product of routines and systems, not the smile on the face of the cabin attendant.) But sustaining the reputation of the firm requires that individual employees should feel that they, as well as the company, own the reputation. And ownership generally implies return.

But it is not only employees who can expect to benefit from architecture or reputation. Where firms have created external architecture, it is equally essential that suppliers or distributors share some of the gains that architecture creates. And reputations can easily turn sour if customers feel that too high a price is being extracted. The objective is to be seen as 'a good company to do business with'.

There is less reason for firms which benefit from innovation, or from strategic assets, to choose to share the added value which that innovation or those assets create. But often they will have to. The problems of effectively appropriating the returns from innovation were described in Chapter 7, and frequently undermine the effectiveness of innovation as a source of advantage. And a firm which enjoys the benefit of the strategic assets, incumbency and exclusivity, frequently finds that its position often confers equally powerful strategic assets on its suppliers, or its distributors, or its employees.

So while a firm will often, rationally, choose to share the added value it creates, it may also be forced to do so. The distinctive capability—innovation, reputation, architecture—is its own. Strategic assets may be under its control. But in turning that distinctive capability into competitive advantage in a market, the firm must deal with customers and suppliers. The structure of the markets it faces in doing so will determine its ability to retain added value for itself and its stakeholders.

If suppliers or customers have market power, they will be able to ask for some of the added value the firm has created, and they will generally succeed in getting it. Table 12.3, drawn from the PIMS database, shows how the influence of unions and the importance of purchases to customers are among the most significant of the variables affecting profitability. The growth of supermarket chains has enabled multiple retailers to appropriate some of the rents which previously accrued to the manufacturers of branded foods. This development both reduced the value of food brands and gave a further competitive advantage to the multiple retailers themselves.

Table 12.3. How Supply and Purchase Conditions Influence Profitability

	Impact of factor on return on investment relative to average (%)	
	Unattractive[a]	Attractive[a]
Market growth rate	−1.2	+1.1
% of purchases from top three suppliers	−0.8	+0.8
% unionization	−2.4	+2.9
Purchase importance[b]	−3.0	+1.8
Purchase amount[c]	−4.0	+5.2

[a] Unattractive means in the worst 20% by reference to this factor; attractive in the top 20%.
[b] Measured by proportion of customer's inputs from this supplier (high importance is unattractive, 75%).
[c] Measured by average order size.

Source: Based on Exhibit 4–10 of Buzzell and Gale (1987).

Strategic assets are often particularly vulnerable to appropriation by other stakeholders. There is no commonality of interest in sharing strategic assets—all players work for what they can get. That is often a lot. Some of the most striking demonstrations of this have occurred when the strategic asset is itself eroded. Pilots shared in the cartel profits which were earned by regulated airlines. Deregulation has been followed by acrimonious labour disputes and reductions in earnings—as at Continental Airlines and TWA, or in the protracted strike which surrounded liberalization in Australia. The establishment of new national newspapers in Britain was for long almost impossible, but the profits which resulted from limited competition rarely went to newspaper proprietors—many of whom were quite happy to lose money in order to sustain their own vanity—but were diverted to overmanning, overpayment of employees, and inefficiency. When new technology threatened to change market structure by allowing low-cost entry, dramatic moves were necessary. Rupert Murdoch shifted publication of his titles, over a single weekend, to a new greenfield site and dismissed his entire existing printing workforce. With the force of this example, other newspapers were able to follow suit—printing costs of the *Daily Telegraph* were reduced to little more than one third of their previous level.

In all these cases, added value is the subject of negotiation. The key to the outcome of negotiation is the best alternative that each party has to a negotiated agreement. The outcome of such a bargain will depend on the number of parties or possible parties, and the range of options which they have.

How numbers influence outcomes

Sometimes there is no other contractor, and the two parties must do business with each other, or not at all. Then the alternatives to an agreement are perilous. Sometimes there are strikes. Or there are interruptions to supply, or supplies are continued on an interim basis while a new contract is arrived at. Stores may delist products, or manufacturers decline to supply their usual outlets. Mostly these can only be temporary outcomes. Almost always, there is some agreement, and usually many feasible agreements, which would leave both parties better off. (These agreements form the *core* of the negotiation.) The breakdown of the relationship reflects a misjudgement by both parties of the firmness of the other's resolve. Or one party may see value in establishing a reputation in a repeated game.

In defence industries, there may only be a single likely buyer for a product innovation. The owners of global brands, such as Coca-Cola or McDonald's, will often need the approval of Third World governments before they can sell their products in these countries. In some parts of the world, business can only be done if it is done through local agents. In these cases, the other party involved may have contributed nothing to the added value in question. The international reputation of Coca-Cola owes nothing to the government of

Zaïre. In one-to-one negotiations over the distribution of added value, who created it may have very little influence on the final outcome.

This dependence on a single customer, supplier, or distributor may leave the firm involved in a vulnerable position. This is particularly true when a distinctive capability is developed in the context of a particular supplier relationship, and is of little use outside that relationship.

A subcontractor may develop an innovation which is specific to an individual product. Nissan UK was an independent distributor, awarded the franchise for Nissan cars when Japanese products were virtually unknown in Western markets. Nissan UK's founder, Octav Botnar, built up an extraordinarily committed network which made the United Kingdom the only important world market in which Nissan far outsold its Japanese competitors. But the value of Nissan UK's architecture was entirely dependent on the continued supply of Nissan cars. An acrimonious dispute over the distribution of the added value broke out into increasingly public warfare, leading to the termination of the franchise and a morass of litigation.

A more common situation is one in which a firm has a choice of exclusive relationships. The manufacturer of a consumer good must find a distributor in an overseas market. A retailer wishes to select a private label supplier. A specialist subcontractor is needed for a specific component. The availability of alternatives means that the firm is in a much stronger position than in one-to-one negotiations. Effectively, it can conduct an auction between alternative suppliers or distributors.

Often there are several potential parties on each side of a commercial relationship. The basic rule is that as the number of potential players increases, *the outcome depends less and less on market structure and the negotiating strength of the different parties, and more and more on the degree to which they can influence the total amount of added value created by their mutual relationship.* These issues, and the probable results of different types of negotiation, are considered more fully in Chapter 17.

The ability of a firm to defend its competitive advantage in the value chain depends on three principal factors—the alternatives available to buyers and sellers, the number of buyers and sellers involved at each stage in the supply system, and the extent to which the joint product of the relationship can be enhanced by the efforts of one or more of the parties. The ability of a firm to appropriate its added value depends critically on the structure of the supply and product markets it faces. It must try to influence that structure. That issue of business strategy is also considered further in Chapter 17.

Appropriation for shareholders

EDF adds value for its customers. Statoil adds value for the Norwegian government. Most successful firms add value for their employees and for the governments of the countries in which they work, through taxes, and for their investors. Along with the creation of added value runs the appropriation of added value among these various stakeholders. The degree to which added value is successfully appropriated by any or all of these groups is measured by the difference between what they earn, or pay, under the contract they have with the firm and what they would earn, or pay, under the best alternative contract open to them.

So for EDF we might measure the difference between what French consumers pay for their electricity and the cost of buying it from Germany or the United Kingdom or from new suppliers who contracted to provide electricity in France on a basis which would fully recover their costs in the long run. Or we look at what a prosperous firm pays its workers relative to the wages and benefits these workers could earn elsewhere. We might measure the taxes the firm pays. We assess what shareholders earn from the company relative to the minimum the company needed to offer to attract their capital into the business in the first place.

Once we begin to query the extent to which the prices recorded in a firm's accounts truly reflect costs or values, we open up a wide range of issues. Prices rarely reflect environmental costs, for example. This may lead to considerable understatement of the cost of electricity. If burning oil or coal contributes to global warming it may impose costs which are not reflected either in the price which EDF pays for its fuel or in what its customers pay for their electricity. Most of EDF's power is generated in nuclear powered stations and the risks associated with nuclear generation, which are not confined to France, should form part of an added value calculation. A firm which damages the environment appropriates added value rather than creates it. These issues are discussed more generally in Chapter 20.

But among the stakeholders in corporate activity, shareholders have a special place. They have a special place because they have the residual claim on the firm's added value and, in a free market, the firm's ability to generate added value for its shareholders is the usual test by which it is, or is not, able to go on operating in the long term. That is why profit—meaning return to shareholders—is often described as the 'bottom line' of the measurement of a company's operations.

Shareholders have that special place in the appropriation of added value in all capitalist economies. The degree to which that special place becomes primacy varies in different business environments. The shareholder interest is dominant in the United States and in Britain but less significant in Japan, while continental Europe is generally in an intermediate position. These issues raise fundamental questions of corporate governance and economic performance, and I return to them in Chapters 20 and 22. But the relationship between added value and other measures of financial performance is important everywhere. That is the subject of Chapter 13.

The subject of appropriability pulls together a range of otherwise apparently disparate issues. One important concern is the nature of the objectives of the corporation. This has both a normative side—what should be the objectives of firms?—and a positive side—how do firms in reality behave? The very notion that a firm can sensibly be viewed as a single entity with coherent objectives is challenged by, for example, Cyert and March (1963) and by Simon (1964); also by a variety of theories of the firm which start from objectives other than profit maximization—Baumol (1959), Marris (1966).

The normative issues are discussed further in Chapter 21, which addresses ethical issues in business more widely. In terms of the objectives of the firm, one extreme is taken by Milton Friedman, whose *New York Times* article 'The social responsibility of business is to increase its profits' is widely cited but this is an issue on which perspectives are particularly distorted by the ethnocentricity of US management writers; see Albert (1991) and Odagiri (1991) for offsetting views.

Management issues for non-profit organizations are considered in Connors (1980), Espy (1986). Drucker (1977) contrasts profit and not-for-profit management systems and Kay (1991*b*) develops the position of non-profit organizations within the overall framework developed here. Issues in business ethics and corporate social responsibility are covered in Chapter 21, and those concerning negotiating and bargaining in Chapter 17. For an environmental calculus in the electricity industry, see Lockwood (1992). Bruck (1989) is an entertaining discussion of appropriability within the corporation.

13

......

The Value of Competitive Advantage

In this chapter I explain how competitive advantage is quantified, how it is turned into added value, and how added value is reflected in conventional measures of financial performance, such as cash flow, profits, and returns to shareholders.

Competitive advantage is, necessarily, relative—a competitive advantage is something that one firm has over another. When I talk of competitive advantage without making a specific comparison, the implicit comparison is with a normal or representative firm—perhaps the weakest competitor, or a hypothetical entrant to the market in which the firm concerned holds its competitive advantage. The expected costs and revenues of that representative firm provide a benchmark against which the competitive advantages of other firms in the same market can be measured. In a contestable market, where it is easy for firms to enter or leave, the added value created by each firm will be exactly equal to the size of its competitive advantage. But if entry is costly, firms with little competitive advantage may nevertheless succeed in adding value, and if there is excess capacity in an industry there may be no added value even for firms which have competitive advantages. These relationships between the competitive advantages of different firms and the ability of any or all to add value are the subject of the first part of the chapter.

In the second part of the chapter, I explain how added value underpins all the principal measures of corporate performance, including cash generation, accounting profitability, and shareholder value. I demonstrate the fundamental equivalence between all these measures in the long run and show how each offers a valid but distinct perspective on corporate success.

The success of corporate strategy is generally measured by financial measures of corporate performance. There are many alternative financial measures. Some commentators emphasize profitability and earnings per share, others cash flow and returns to shareholders.

These different measures reflect a range of perspectives. The accountant stresses profitability and earnings per share, and looks to the strength of the balance sheet. This interests the banker, but so does the cash flow which the business is expected to generate. Economists have always regarded this as central, and urged that projects should be appraised on the basis of discounted cash flow techniques. Investors and stock market analysts are concerned with share prices, capital gains, and dividends. The corporate strategist emphasizes the strength of competitive advantage and so, in one way or another, do observers who attempt to assess the contribution a firm makes to the international economy.

Profits and earnings per share remain by far the most widely used measures of performance, and, despite challenges, accountants retain a dominant grip on the manner in which corporate financial statements are presented. There is a tradition in which advocates of alternative measures shower scorn on each other and, particularly, accountants. For some strategists, it is preoccupation with accounting numbers which is at the root of the decline of Western economies. For many economists, accounting information is meaningless mumbo-jumbo. One of the most popular movements of the 1980s has been the growth of interest in shareholder value. Its advocates argue that accounting profits are not related to returns to shareholders, and propose a return to a cash flow basis of assessment.

Much of this disagreement is exaggerated and unnecessary. Cash flow, profits, shareholder returns, competitive advantage are not different things, but different ways of measuring the same thing, and the different interest groups who are concerned with a company's performance are not pulling it in radically opposed directions, but adopting different perspectives on the same phenomenon. And the full exploitation of a firm's competitive advantage serves the interests of every observer and enhances every measure of corporate performance. The later part of this chapter explains this fundamental equivalence, and how the concept of added value underpins them all.

The measurement of competitive advantage

Competitive advantages are always relative. A firm has a competitive advantage—or not—over another firm which serves the same market, or over another firm in the same industry. In Fig. 13.1, drawn from Chapter 2, Sainsbury's has a very slight competitive advantage over Tesco. These firms serve similar markets, and they see themselves as members of the same strategic group. The battle for leadership in UK food retailing is fought between these two firms, and there is a skirmish in that battle at every new supermarket location. Does Kwik Save have a competitive advantage over Sainsbury's? There is a sense in which it does. 100 Ecus of output costs Sainsbury's 91 Ecus and Kwik Save only 82 Ecus. But Sainsbury's and Kwik Save are not really in the same market, or part of the same strategic group.

Each would see the other as a peripheral, rather than a direct competitor. Sainsbury's focuses its attention on Tesco, Kwik Save on new entrants such as Aldi and Food Giant. The comparison only makes any sort of sense because Sainsbury's and Kwik Save are part of the same industry—they are members of the same trade association, their performance is monitored by the same investment analysts, they are grouped together when official statistics are compiled.

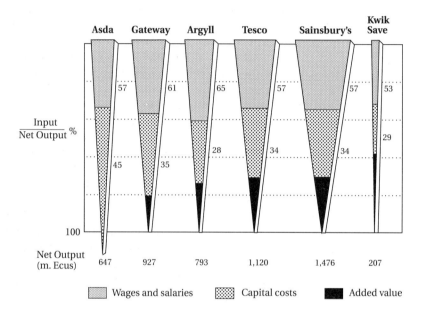

Fig. 13.1. Value Chains for Individual UK Supermarkets, 1989

If Kwik Save has a large competitive advantage, it is because its market niche is small and it has few rivals. Sainsbury's has a lesser competitive advantage in a broader, and more competitive, market segment. So although Kwik Save adds more value per unit of input, Sainsbury's adds more value overall. This is a trade-off which every firm faces. The markets where a company has the greatest competitive advantage are usually—and certainly ought to be—the markets which the firm is already in. As it expands into new product and geographical markets, its competitive advantage, relative to firms which are already serving these markets, is likely to be less. But so long as it has *some* competitive advantage over a firm which is profitably serving these markets, it should enter, even at the cost of reducing its overall competitive advantage. That is what has been happening, and will continue to happen, to Kwik Save. Initially, it chose the best stores, in the most suitable locations for its style of business—those situations in which it faced the least competition from its rivals. As its business grows, its overall competitive advantage diminishes but, so long as it handles that expansion correctly, the added value the company creates will nevertheless increase.

Sainsbury's enjoys a competitive advantage over Tesco, Tesco has a competitive advantage over Argyll. In any paired comparison, one firm, or the other, will have a competitive advantage. Certainly, any statement about competitive advantage should have, implicit in it, answers to the questions, 'In what market?' and 'Over whom?' Are there natural general benchmarks against which to measure competitive advantage?

Asda—as the weakest of the major firms in the food retailing industry, and the weakest in the mainline market segment—provides a possible baseline for the performance of the others. Asda is not a bad, or a badly managed, firm. Its stores are modern, clean, and well stocked with products that are good value for money. Asda has survived in a period when many weaker chains and very many independent grocers have failed. Asda has a competitive advantage over those firms, but that is no longer relevant since these firms no longer compete. In British food retailing, which is a competitive market and one in which overall standards are high, you need to be as good as Asda in order to survive. Strategy, and competitive advantage, are what distinguish the best companies from the ordinary, not what distinguishes the good from the bad.

A natural way to measure the competitive advantage of Sainsbury's and Tesco, of Kwik Save and Argyll, is in relation to Asda. Both Sainsbury's and Tesco are firms with competitive advantage, but Sainsbury's competitive advantage is greater than Tesco's. *Where no explicit comparator is stated, the relevant benchmark is the marginal firm in the industry. The weakest firm which still finds it worthwhile to serve the market provides the baseline against which the competitive advantage of all other firms can be set.* In this way, it is possible to measure the size of a competitive advantage. Sainsbury's competitive advantage over Asda is 10 per cent of net output and 1.7 per cent of gross output, implying that a unit of net output costs it only 90 per cent of what it costs Asda and that a unit of gross sales is achieved with 1.7 per cent fewer total inputs. The value of that competitive advantage over Asda is around 150 million Ecus per year, given that Sainsbury's has gross output of nearly 8 billion Ecus and net output of around 1.5 billion Ecus. That is a measure of the difference in the value created by a highly successful firm, with strong distinctive capabilities, over that achieved by the merely competent.

From competitive advantage to added value

The definition of that benchmark provides an immediate link from competitive advantage to added value. In a contestable industry—one in which entry and exit are relatively free and not very costly—marginal firms, the Asdas of their particular markets, will neither add value nor subtract it. They will not add value because, if they did, others would be attracted to enter the industry. Either returns to everyone would be bid down or the marginal firm would be joined by another, yet more marginal, firm over which the original firm had a competitive advantage. Nor in a contestable industry will the marginal firm continue to subtract value by earning less from its assets than it would if they were sold and the resources used elsewhere. If that were true, it should quit the industry. Some other firm would then become the marginal firm, and that would be the new baseline for competitive advantage.

Food retailing is close to being a contestable industry. Small-scale entry is not too difficult. Capital requirements are modest, and there are few regulatory restrictions. Stores can be used for other purposes, so that leaving the industry, or reducing capacity in it, is less costly than in many areas of business (although the growth of specialist superstores is changing this). No market is perfectly contestable, but this one is workably so, and several firms have entered and left. If others are discouraged from entry, it is from a perception of the strength of the competitive advantages of the incumbents. In a contestable market, as in food retailing, the added value earned by firms reflects the value of their competitive advantage.

Automobile markets are not at all contestable. Entry involves massive expenditures on plant and on model development. It requires the establishment of a distribution network. All of these are specific to particular products or groups of geographical markets. Governments are reluctant to let weaker automobile firms contract, so that the British, French, and Italian firms, which have generally been among the most marginal players in the world industry, have all received direct and indirect government support. In an industry with sunk costs and excess capacity, the marginal firm will earn less than the cost of capital, and this will drive downwards added value for all firms.

Treating PSA as the marginal producer in Fig. 13.2, Nissan holds a competitive advantage over them of 12.8 per cent. Although this competitive advantage is large, the firm over which it is held is so unprofitable that Nissan adds no value overall. Of Toyota's massive competitive advantage of 26 per cent, only around half is translated into added value. In the long term, PSA's position is not, on this data, a sustainable one. The company might improve its performance, so diminishing the competitive advantages enjoyed by Nissan and Toyota. These companies would then hold smaller competitive advantages, but the competitive advantages they did hold would be more fully reflected in added value. The world car industry taken as a whole might reduce its capacity, so that the profitability of the industry as a whole, and of each individual company, would increase. Or PSA might ultimately exit from the market, leaving a group of leaner and fitter firms among which Toyota's competitive advantage, although still real, would be smaller. Whichever of these outcomes occurs, in the long run competitive advantage is likely to be translated into added value.

The European banking industry displays, across its various markets, a range of outcomes (Fig. 13.3). In France and Germany, the major banks create small amounts of added value. The established banks do have a competitive advantage relative to entrants to the market, and perhaps also hold strategic assets.

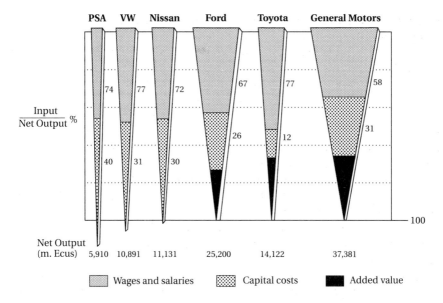

Fig. 13.2. Added Value Statements for Auto Producers, 1989

But no bank has a strong competitive advantage over another. In the English market, which is probably the most competitive, there is a wide dispersion of performance. Lloyds is outstanding, and Barclays has a competitive advantage over National Westminster, and particularly Midland, whose future is uncertain. In Spain, it does not seem that either of the major banks has a significant competitive advantage over the other, but both are extremely profitable. No one would describe the Spanish retail banking market as a contestable one. The added value Banco Santander and Banco Bilbao Vizcaya derive is not the result of their competitive advantages. It is the product of their strategic assets—established positions in a market in which competition is restricted and entry limited. As in the automobile industry but for opposite reasons, this is a situation which is unlikely to persist indefinitely. Entry is attractive even for banks which are at a competitive disadvantage relative to the incumbents, as foreign banks entering Spain mostly would be. However, the prospect of such entry is likely to create a more competitive Spanish banking industry, and there are many indications that this is already happening. Here too, added value is only likely to be sustainable in the long run if based on real competitive advantage and strategic assets which are impregnable, not merely transitory.

The measurement of capital costs

In order to measure either competitive advantage or added value, it is necessary to make a charge to the firm for the capital employed in the business.

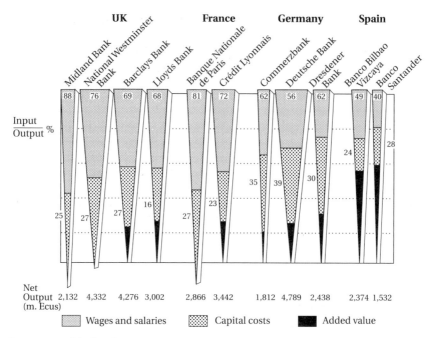

Fig. 13.3. Added Value in European Retail Banking, 1990
Source: Annual reports and accounts

That measure of capital costs links the value added statements of consecutive periods in the life of the business. There are several different ways of measuring capital costs, each corresponding to a different perspective on the operations of the firm.

Cash flow is the simplest basis. In this, capital expenditure is simply treated like any other expense of the firm, and charged against the value added statement as it is incurred. In assessing a stream of cash flows, no allowance is made for depreciation and no concept of capital value is necessary. In 1990, British Gas spent 2,873 million Ecus on new investment (Illustration 13.1), including fixed assets, replacement, and acquisitions. Each of the other methods of accounting for capital expenditure requires some continuing record of the capital invested in the business. The charge to the added value statement then falls into two components. There is a cost for the annual depreciation of these capital assets, and there is a capital charge, based on the value of the assets concerned—the amount the firm must pay itself (or pays its investors) for the capital equipment it uses or the funds which they have invested in it.

The most usual basis for assessing cost and depreciation begins from the most secure of historical facts—what the firm paid for the asset concerned. Historic cost accounting attempts to spread capital expenditures over the useful life of the asset concerned. Depreciation charges write off that historic cost. Under *straight line* depreciation (the most common European practice) an item which costs 10,000 Ecus and has an expected life of ten years will be

Illustration 13.1. Measuring Capital Costs for British Gas, 1990–1991 (m. Ecus)

Cash Flow Basis		Historic Cost Basis	
Expenditure on fixed assets less disposals	1,640	Total operating assets	14,859
Replacement expenditure	527	Capital charge at 10%	1,486
Acquisition expenditure	707	Depreciation	915
Capital costs	2,873	Capital costs	2,401
Market Value Basis		**Current Cost Basis**	
Market value at 1.4.90	14,102	Total operating assets	31,280
Historic cost depreciation	915		
Retained profit	947	Current cost depreciation	2,126
Decline in market value	2,109	Capital charge at 5%	1,564
Capital charge at 10%	1,410		
Capital costs	5,381	Capital costs	3,690

Source: British Gas annual report and accounts

depreciated at a rate of 1,000 Ecus per year. After three years, its historic cost book value—the amount which has not yet been depreciated and which remains to be written off—will be 7,000 Ecus.[1] Illustration 13.1 shows how these principles are used in estimating a capital cost for British Gas for 1990.

The historic cost of assets may bear no relationship to what they are currently worth. Inflation may have made historic costs meaningless. Some firms have land and buildings in their books at prices which they paid many generations ago. But prices do not only rise. Telecommunications has been transformed by fibre optic cables, digital switching equipment, and satellites, and the historic cost of copper wires, mechanical switches, and submarine cables is far above what it would cost to achieve the same results today using modern equipment.

Current cost valuations are based on the price of a 'modern equivalent asset'. That is a measure of what it would cost, in today's money and using today's technology, to undertake a comparable investment. Usually, the effects of inflation mean that the current cost value of assets will be higher than the historic cost, but in businesses related to information technology and electronics these values are often lower. Current cost valuations define what it would cost to get into the business now. Illustration 13.1 shows the cost of capital to British Gas on a current cost valuation basis.

1 Capital employed on a historic cost basis may be measured by reference to shareholders' funds rather than operating assets. These differ from the value of operating assets to the extent that the company finances its operating activities from borrowings rather than equity, on the one hand, and to the extent that the company invests its shareholders' funds in financial rather than operating assets on the other. One approach stresses the historic operating capacity of the business, the other looks at the amounts historically contributed by investors. The depreciation charge will be the same under both methods—financial assets and liabilities do not (or should not) depreciate, unlike operating assets—but the charge for the use of capital will differ in the two cases.

When prices were rising rapidly in the 1970s, many accountants favoured a shift from historic to current cost accounting, believing that the continued use of historic cost accounts misled investors and encouraged imprudent management decisions. Accounting standards based on current costs were promulgated in several countries, including Britain and the United States (Illustration 13.2). As inflation receded, however, interest in current cost accounts declined. British Gas is one of the few large firms still to publish current cost accounts (which is why its figures are used in this example). Historic cost measures are based on what was invested in the business in the past. Current cost valuations look at what would need to be invested to achieve the same result today. Both of these can, and do, differ from the market value of the firm. But this is, in a real sense, a measure of what today's shareholders have invested in the firm.

Another method for measuring capital cost, and capital returns, is by reference to current market value. The calculations required here are also shown

Illustration 13.2 Current Cost Accounting

Current cost accounting standards were adopted in Britain in 1980 (SSAP 16) and in the United States (FASB Statement 33) in 1979. The main elements of the British standard (the US standard was similar) were:

- Asset values to be measured by the replacement cost of a modern equivalent asset (or recoverable amount where lower).
- Depreciation to be based on these asset values.
- Inventory to be valued at the current cost of equivalent supplies.
- A gearing adjustment to reflect the decline in the real value of debt.

As inflation receded in the 1980s, interest in current cost accounting waned. Neither standard is now obligatory and few companies now issue current cost statements.

in Illustration 13.1. Again, it has two elements. There is an opportunity cost to the shareholders' funds invested in the business, measured here at their market value. There is also a depreciation charge. This begins from the historic cost figure (915 million Ecus) shown in the company's accounts. However, this account measure does not fully reflect the market's evaluation. The market value of the company fell by over 2 billion Ecus, despite retained profits in historic cost terms of 947 million Ecus. That implies a much larger overall depreciation charge, and an overall capital cost on a market value basis of over 5 billion Ecus. This figure will, of course, vary from year to year as the market's assessment of the company varies, just as cash flow-based measures of capital costs will vary with the company's own expenditure programme. Historic and current cost estimates of capital charges will be more stable.

The market value of a company's shares and its cost of capital together define the return which the firm must provide to satisfy its shareholders. That return in practice takes the form of dividends and capital gains (or losses). In any year, shareholder returns will be above, or below this. For British Gas in 1990, returns were below shareholder expectations. In earlier years, they had been above. The difference between the actual return to shareholders and the required return is the 'excess return'—the amount earned by them over and above what was needed to persuade them to invest their capital in the business.

These different bases for capital charges can be translated into different ways of assessing the added value generated by the firm. They correspond to:

- the net cash flow generated in the period;
- added value in historic cost terms;
- added value in current cost terms;
- excess return to shareholders.

Historic cost and current cost

Historic cost accounts are principally designed to report on managers' stewardship of the money which has been entrusted to their care. Although historic cost accounts are often criticized, mostly for not bearing interpretations which they are not intended to bear, this central purpose has caused them to remain at the centre of corporate reporting systems almost everywhere.

In using historic cost accounts, it is important to ensure, as the added value statement does, that the opportunity cost of capital employed is fully considered. Some of the more strident criticisms of the use of accounting profits or historic cost earnings per share to assess performance are made because firms can enhance these measures without adding value. The retention of earnings for reinvestment at rates of return which are below the cost of capital, or the exchange of equity for the shares of companies with a lower price–earnings ratio, will both increase earnings per share but are of no likely benefit to shareholders or other stakeholders.

Historic cost accounts provide one basis for the assessment of added value. And a firm which succeeds on this criterion has indeed added value. Historic cost is a measure of the resources which have been invested in the business, and capital charges based on historic costs are an accurate reflection of what could have been earned if these resources had been employed in alternative uses. If a firm earns more than this, that is truly a measure of its superior performance.

But historic cost accounts do not necessarily indicate the degree to which a firm enjoys competitive advantage today. If a firm adds value in historic cost terms but not a current cost basis, that is because it bought well in the past. It may have timed its asset purchases well, it may have conserved its capital equipment effectively, it may simply have benefited from inflation which it might or might not have anticipated. Its managers deserve credit for at least some of these things. But they are all history. They may be the result of competitive advantages which the firm once enjoyed. They are not a measure of its competitive advantage now. Current cost accounts look forward from the present, historic cost accounts backward from the present. Both have their distinct purposes. Competitive advantage is a description of today and tomorrow, not of yesterday.

The measurement of added value in historic cost terms is an appropriate means of assessing the quality of a management's past stewardship of corporate assets. It may be inadequate in its reflection of what they have built up for the future. It is also no guide to current, or future, strategic action. It is a mistake to think that a low historic cost of assets can ever be the basis of competitive advantage in a particular activity. It is relevant that a company owns a particular set of assets, but what they cost is irrelevant to how they should be used. There is almost no operating decision to which the historic cost of assets should be relevant. Historic costs are appropriate for financial reporting, not management accounting.

The marginal firm—Asda among supermarkets, PSA within the car industry—provides one benchmark for assessing competitive advantage. But on its present costs and revenues, PSA is not a viable producer in the long run. There is some consolation in holding a competitive advantage over a firm whose business future is uncertain, but not enough. In measuring competitive advantage and added value, there is a second benchmark which the firm should use. That benchmark is provided by a hypothetical company which is just earning enough to remain viable in the markets in which the firm is competing.

In a perfectly contestable market, these two benchmarks will always be the same. The marginal firm is, in these market conditions, the firm which is just earning enough to stay in business. If it earned more, there would be entry. If it earned less, it would immediately pack its bags and leave. In food retailing, there is little difference between the benchmark of the hypothetical viable firm and Asda. In the automobile industry, in which firms are reluctant to exit, or in the Spanish banking market, where firms are unable to enter, there is.

This hypothetical benchmark provides a clear answer to the measure of capital costs to be used in assessing competitive advantage and in determining the long-term viability and success of a firm's strategy. The level of capital costs which needs to be earned to remain viable is given by a current return on the replacement cost of assets. More than that is more than is required. Less implies that assets will not, ultimately, be replaced.

So although historic cost accounts are the measure of a management's stewardship of the company's assets, it is current cost accounts which are the key measure of its competitive position and its corporate strategy. Unless the firm enjoys a competitive advantage relative to the replacement cost of its assets, it enjoys no competitive advantage in the long run.

Shareholder value and cash flows

'Shareholder value' became a popular business term of the 1980s. By the end of the decade, few US companies failed to include a reference to the concept in their annual report. This new emphasis on generating returns for the company's stockholders had several origins. It became increasingly apparent that many of the conglomerate businesses which were put together in the 1960s and 1970s in pursuit of diversification or synergy diminished or concealed value rather than added it. The interest of managers was considerably heightened when the growth of new and creative forms of financing meant that no company, however large, was immune from the threat of take-over by raiders who promised to deliver more value for shareholders.

Shareholder value may be measured as the excess return to shareholders—the amount by which the total return they earn, taking dividends and capital gains together, exceeds the cost of capital. Excess returns calculated in this way are extremely volatile, and there is almost no apparent relationship between these excess returns and the underlying effectiveness of the companies concerned. Of the 'top ten' European companies described in Chapter 2, only four outperformed their local stock markets in 1990 and a portfolio of them would have moved in line with the market index. It is this that leads to talk of 'voodoo economics' and similarly extravagant phrases. The picture is different over a longer period of time. For the decade from 1980, nine out of ten of these companies beat the market, mostly by very large amounts. (The one which did not—Benetton—only achieved a quotation in 1986; this is discussed further in Chapter 19.) A portfolio invested in these companies offered a return more than 10 per cent per annum better than the market average. The longer the period of time taken, the closer is the relationship between shareholder returns and accounts-based measures of performance.

Table 13.1. 'European Winners': Share Price Performance (local index = 100)

	1980–90	1990
Glaxo	2,500	126
Benetton	80[a]	105
Reuters	350[b]	80
Petrofina	110	87
Kwik Save	500	97
LVMH	800	65
Guinness	400	129
Cable and Wireless	450	94
BTR	400	81
Marks & Spencer	300	133

[a] Since 1986.
[b] Since 1984.

Source: Datastream.

The reasons for this are clear enough. If historic cost figures are essentially backward looking, and current cost ones describe the present, market values look to the future. LVMH earns very substantial added value from its powerful brands but that is already reflected in the high price of its shares. Changes in the market value of the company today will reflect not its performance but its actual performance relative to its expected performance. Since expectations are high, it is difficult for it to outperform, and in the short term, such reassessments are as likely to be downward as upward, The stocks reported in today's newspaper as the fast-performing stocks of yesterday are not the best and worst companies in the market but the stocks about which new information became available. But as the period over which we look back becomes longer, those we recognize as excellent companies today are increasingly likely to have run ahead of yesterday's expectations and today's bad companies to have run behind them. In this way, value shows through in the long run.

Fig. 13.4 shows how Glaxo's share price responded to the discovery and marketing of Zantac. The first and most important lesson is that over a long period the performance of Glaxo's shares fully reflected the success of the company and Glaxo shares have been a wonderful investment. However, the year-on-year movements diverged considerably. When Zantac is discovered (1976), shareholders earn excess returns. They do so again when the drug completes its clinical trials (1981–2) and as it becomes clear that its marketing is proving successful (1983). Broadly, returns to shareholders anticipate— though not, it must be said, by much—the trading performance of Glaxo's business.

'Shareholder value' is particularly associated with cash flow methods of investment appraisal. It is impossible to quarrel with this approach, although it is also often impossible to quantify many of the elements of a strategic decision at all precisely. The effective manager has to steer a course between the spurious quantification of what are essentially matters for judgement, and a common unwillingness to attach even orders of magnitude to proposals which can only be justified by their financial returns. But the capacity to generate cash flow is a primary test of the company's ability to add value through its operations. And it is also the key to the firm's long-term financial health.

The equivalence of financial measures of performance

Current cost measures emphasise current performance; historic cost measures past achievement. Stock market values look forward; cash flows are the underlying product of profit and source of shareholder returns. These different measures differ essentially in timing rather than in nature.

Fig. 13.5 shows how the pattern of cash flows evolves for a typical activity. There is an initial period of investment, when the project requires expenditure but yields no revenues. As development ceases and output comes on

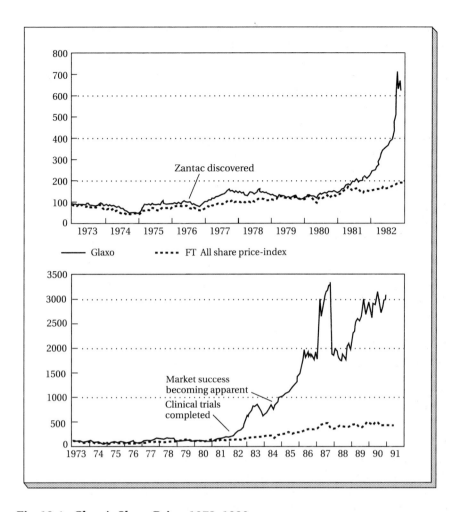

Fig. 13.4. Glaxo's Share Price, 1973–1990

stream, cash flows turn positive. Towards the end of the life of the activity, net cash flows may diminish as costs rise, revenues fall, or both. These may imply an economic life shorter than the actual physical life of the asset. These types of profile are familiar from activities as varied as product development and capital investment programmes.

The objective of historic cost accounting is to smooth the impact of these varying revenues and expenditures in a way that reflects the effect on the company's performance more realistically in the long term. The company is allowed to capitalize its initial expenditure, and then offsets that expenditure against the returns as they materialize. Typically, the cost of the assets concerned will have been written off before the end of the useful life of the asset, so that in the final stages profits fall less rapidly than revenues.

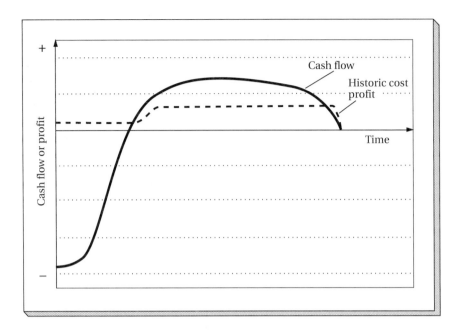

Fig. 13.5. From Cash Flow to Historic Cost Accounts

Current cost accounting came into existence principally because inflation made the use of the historic cost of assets misleading. Relative to historic cost accounts, current cost accounts tend to imply lower capital charges in the early years of a project or an activity and higher capital charges later in its life, when the replacement cost of assets will usually be above the historic cost. This effect is offset initially either by the holding gains which the firm earns or by the use of a real rate of return which is well below the nominal rate.

The stock market attempts to anticipate both cash flows and revenues. If the cash flow profile of Fig. 13.5 were completely and correctly anticipated, then the value of the company would rise by the whole of the prospective dis-counted value of the activity on the day it announced its intention. The stock market is neither as prescient nor as trusting as this implies, and it will look for evidence of successful completion of the development of an activity, and for the growth of revenues from sales. It is in these late phases of investment and early phases of realization that returns to shareholders are likely to be greatest (Fig. 13.6), as the experience of Glaxo (Figure 13.4) shows. Once an activity has reached its steady state, shareholders are unlikely to do better than in any alternative investment.

Historic and current cost profits both make allowance for depreciation of the capital invested in an activity, but not for the cost of capital itself. The same is true of calculation of shareholder return. This further adjustment is

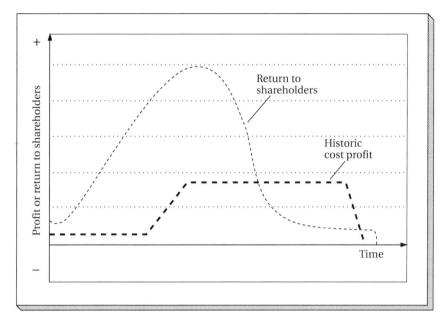

Fig. 13.6. From Historic Cost Profits to Market Values

necessary to derive added value from profits. Its impact is greatest in the first revenue-producing years, and tends to diminish as the capital invested in the activity is reduced.

The four ways of measuring the returns from the activity are shown in Fig. 13.7. The four profiles have different shapes, reflecting the different aspect of operations which each emphasizes. *However, the value of the areas under each of these curves is the same.* The approaches to performance assessment differ essentially in timing rather than in nature. Over the life of a firm, or an activity, the present value of all these things, discounted at the firm's cost of capital, are equal.

- Net cash flows from operations.
- Added value, measured in historic cost terms, plus gains from the sale of assets.
- Added value, measured in current cost terms, plus holding gains on assets.
- Excess returns to shareholders.

The returns which a firm makes rest on the added value which it generates from operations, and any gains it makes on the acquisition and disposal of assets. Fig. 13.8 illustrates the basic structure by which added value drives cash flow, accounting earnings, and shareholder returns.

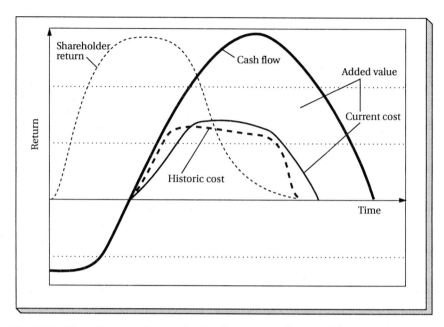

Fig. 13.7. Four Approaches to the Performance of an Activity

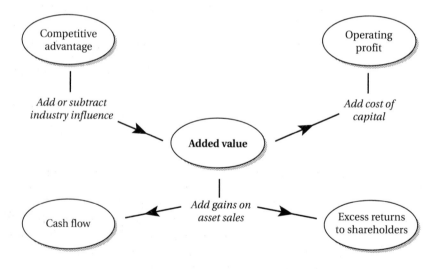

Fig. 13.8. The Equivalence of Measures of Financial Performance

Eurotunnel

Eurotunnel is an unusual company. It was formed to undertake a single activity—the building of a tunnel between England and France—and that activity is particularly well documented. The estimates of costs, revenues, and other operating data used here are drawn from the prospectus which was issued when the company was floated on the London Stock Exchange and the Paris Bourse in November 1987. Estimates of the market value of the company at various dates are based on estimates made contemporaneously by Warburg Securities. All these have subsequently been overtaken by events, but since updated information and estimates are not available in equally comprehensive form, these 1987 figures are used.

Table 13.2 shows the anticipated cash flow from the tunnel in various years. It follows broadly the pattern of Fig. 13.5. During the construction phase, cash flows are negative. Cash flow turns around when operating revenues begin. There are some subsequent capital expenditures but these are small and cash flow grows (in money terms) until the expiry of the firm's concession in 2042 when ownership of the tunnel is due to revert to the French and British governments.

Table 13.2. Cash Flows: Eurotunnel (m. Ecus)

	Operating revenue	Capital expenditure	Net cash flow
1990	0	1,017	−1,017
1995	897	0	897
2003	1,286	151	1,135
2020	3,629	0	3,629
2040	11,433	0	11,433

Source: Derived from Eurotunnel plc prospectus.

Table 13.3 looks at the added value created by Eurotunnel, in historic cost terms. As capital employed in the tunnel diminishes (because depreciation charges have repaid most of the initial construction costs), added value rises. What is the source of Eurotunnel's added value? Although the company did win its franchise against a number of competing bidders, there is little reason to think that Eurotunnel plc has much competitive advantage in building and operating tunnels (especially given what is now known about the outcome of its project management). But Eurotunnel enjoys large strategic assets. It faces little competition. Entry from competing tunnels is blocked by regulation (Eurotunnel has first option on any extension of services until 2020) and by the immense political difficulties and costs associated with entry.

Table 13.4 shows the evolution of shareholder returns. Excess returns to

Table 13.3. Added Value: Eurotunnel (m. Ecus)

	Operating revenue	Capital employed	Capital cost	Added value
1990	0	4,428	341	−341
1995	897	5,498	774	124
2003	1,286	3,849	613	659
2020	3,629	−691	258	3,371
2040	11,433	−6,299	−172	11,605

Source: Own calculations based on prospectus estimate.

Table 13.4. Shareholder Returns: Eurotunnel (m. Ecus)

	Market value	Capital gain	Net dividend	Excess return
1990	5,790	1,227	—	669
1995	11,364	1,133	177	173
2003	22,521	1,778	790	−163
2020	58,048	1,987	2,483	−1,197
2040	34,911	20,947	8,768	−12,179

Source: Own calculations based on prospectus and Warburg Securities' estimates.

shareholders are, in this projection, greatest as the Tunnel approaches completion and begins operations. Once the tunnel is established, it becomes a rather dull utility stock offering relatively poor shareholder returns, and there are large capital losses to shareholders as the concession expires. There is something paradoxical about the concept of predicted excess returns. These projections should be seen as a view of what shareholders would receive if certain events transpired—the tunnel is completed to time and budget, and the concession expires worthless. The tunnel will not have been completed to time and budget, and so shareholders are earning less than this projection allowed. This pattern of returns is, again, broadly that of Fig. 13.6.

Table 13.5 brings together the three measures of performance described above. Although the three columns display completely different patterns of returns, they each have the same present value. Cash flows, added value, and shareholder returns are all equivalent in the long term. Each provides a valid measure of the value, over time, of a firm's competitive advantages and strategic assets.

In Chapter 2, I proposed added value as the most appropriate measure of corporate performance. In Chapters 5 to 11, I described how corporate strategy creates added value. Only in Chapters 12 and 13, however, does the central role of added value become clear. It is the appropriation of added value—Chapter 12—which determines what the successful firm offers to its stakeholders. And it is the calculation of added value—Chapter 13—which determines the returns it offers to its shareholders.

Table 13.5. Eurotunnel's Performance

	Net cash flow	Added value	Excess shareholder return
1990	−1,017	−341	669
1995	897	124	173
2003	1,135	659	−163
2020	3,629	3,371	−1,197
2040	11,433	11,605	−12,178
Present value over life of concession	3,236	3,236	3,236

Appendix: Added Value Statements

This appendix considers some more technical problems which arise in constructing, and interpreting, added value statements.

Added value, materials cost, and net output

Glaxo's added value statement was presented in Table 2.2. As was emphasized there, added value is less than operating margin or profits because profits are constructed after subtracting interest on long-term debt from operating margin, and added value is calculated after subtracting a return on equity capital from profits. The range of relationships involved is shown in Fig. A13.1.

Value added is described as net output in Fig. A13.1, and in Chapter 2. My use of the term added value to describe rent, and in a sense clearly distinct from the economist's use of the concept of value added, may be confusing to some. But the economist's use of the word rent is quite unhelpful to non-economists—who immediately associate rent with property. And value added is widely used by non-economists when they mean, at least approximately, what an economist would prefer to describe as rent. When people say, 'A developing economy should move to higher value added activities', they do not mean that the degree of vertical integration should be increased. They advocate a shift to more highly differentiated products.

As Fig. A13.1 shows, the added value statement focuses on the operating activities of the firm, in contrast to usual financial statements which emphasize the returns to its investors. For this reason, the added value statement is best considered at the level of the operating business, rather than for the firm as a whole. Often it is not possible to assess this from published accounts, but Table A13.1 provides a breakdown of the activities of BAT Industries. BAT is a UK-based international tobacco company which has recently diversified into

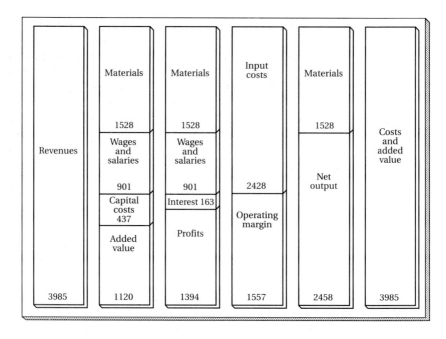

Fig. A13.1. Glaxo's Inputs and Outputs, 1990 (m. Ecus)
Source: Annual report and accounts

Table A13.1. Added Value Statement: BAT Industries, 1989 (m. Ecus)

	Tobacco	Financial services	Total
Revenues	12,988	6,734	19,722
Wages and salaries	2,354	842	3,194
Capital costs	1,065	469	1,535
Materials	8,844	5,647	14,491
Added value	725	(225)	500

Source: BAT Industries annual report and accounts.

financial services—principally in insurance. The aggregation conceals two differently structured businesses, with very different performances. All of the added value of the business is generated in the tobacco division, and the weaknesses of BAT's financial services activities dissipate some of the added value which is created elsewhere in the business.

The value chain

Different firms, in different industries, will perceive very different structures to their added value statements. Fig. A13.2 shows firms at various stages of the process of production. Statoil is a primary producer (although it is a partially integrated firm which also distributes refined products within Norway). As is usually the case with primary producers, net output is a large proportion of gross output. Added value is a high proportion of both. Most of this added value is appropriated by the Norwegian government in taxes and other levies on the company, as noted in Chapter 12. Honda, a manufacturing firm, is a stage further along the chain of production. Around two-thirds of the value of its output arises from bought-in components. Labour and capital are added to these and the company creates its own added value. Marks & Spencer, a retailer, has the lowest ratio of net to gross output—less than a quarter of its turnover is generated from its own activities. Within that, however, added value is a large part, reflecting the company's strong position even in highly

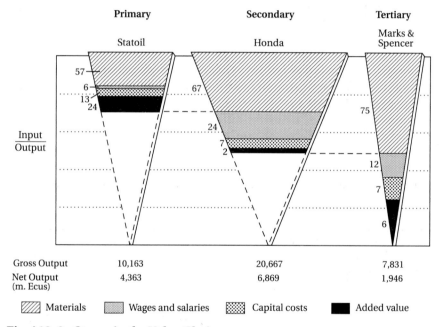

Fig. A13. 2. Stages in the Value Chain
Source: Annual report and accounts

competitive markets. In this way, net output and added value cumulate at each stage of production to make up the overall value chain, or business system, and to determine aggregate output.

Labour and capital intensity

Table A13.2 compares the added value statements of two starkly contrasted firms. Shandwick is an advertising and public relations company. For a professional services firm, bought-in materials are unimportant. Its sales are its own output, its costs are its own output. The ratio of net to gross output is higher even than for a traditional primary producer, such as Statoil. Return on capital is a meaningless concept for a firm such as Shandwick, and returns on capital for professional service firms appear very high. Capital is simply not an important input into the business, and if the firm has a competitive advantage—as Shandwick appears to—then the ratio of its added value to its capital employed may yield a very large number.

Table A13.2. Added Value Statements: Labour and Capital Intensive Companies (m. Ecus)

	Shandwick (1990)	EDF (1989) (accounts basis)	EDF (1989) (output revalued)
Revenues	144	21,022	24,500
Wages and salaries	75	1,338	1,338
Capital costs	5	11,554	11,554
Materials	30	13,035	13,035
Added value	33	(4,935)	(1,227)
Value added (net output)	114	7,957	11,665

Sources: Shandwick and EDF annual reports and accounts.

Électricité de France, with the largest nuclear generation programme of any company in the world, is capital intensive even by the standards of utilities generally. Capital costs account for more than half the value of its sales, and labour for little more than 5 per cent. For utilities, returns on capital employed can never be very high, because even if the company's added value is very large, the size of the capital base ensures that the ratio will be low. Mostly, in practice, the returns on capital to a utility depend on regulation or other government decision, since they occupy monopoly or near monopoly positions.

The striking feature of EDF's added value statement is the negative added value figure. In reality, this does not mean quite what it appears to say, since not much of EDF's output is sold in a competitive market, and the government of France is content to accept a low rate of return on its investment in the company to keep prices down for domestic consumers and for French industry. If output were valued at a price more in line with international electricity prices, EDF might be as shown in the final column of Table A13.2. Even with this adjustment, EDF's added value figure remains negative, if less dramatically so. This is not misleading. EDF's nuclear plant is not cost effective relative to modern conventional plant.

Added value and the cost of capital

The cost of capital is a central input to the added value statement.[1] Conventional calculations of the cost of capital frequently group two issues together—the cost of capital itself and the cost of risk-bearing but, as explained further below, it is clearer to keep these two issues apart.

There are two elements to a calculation of the cost of the capital to the business—the base (how the assets of the business should be valued) and the rate (what return on capital should be assumed). The issue of the base is discussed at some length in Chapter 13. For most issues of corporate strategy, the most relevant base is a current cost one. The underlying question is, 'What would it cost the firm now to lease assets to meet its current needs?' It is relative to that benchmark that the best measure of its competitive strength or weakness is obtained. In particular, a firm which on that basis has no competitive advantage relative to the marginal firm in its industry, or a hypothetical entrant, has no long-term future in that industry. A firm which has a competitive advantage on that basis, relative to you, has a potentially sustainable advantage over you.

Current cost is not the only relevant factor. Since published accounts are generally based on historic cost, this is the benchmark to use in understanding what firms are likely to report. And it is important to keep an eye on your cash flow, and that of your competitors. The shareholder value movement, and the threat of hostile take-over, have encouraged many companies to pay more attention to movements in market values as well. But for most companies, it is current cost measures that are most relevant for an added value statement.

Few companies now report current cost accounting data. Where the company is completing its own added value statements, its own management accounts will, or should, generate data on a current cost valuation or something close to it. For competitors, approximate current cost values can be constructed by using series for expenditure on fixed assets and indexing both these and the historic cost depreciation figures. This was the procedure adopted in compiling the list of successful European companies in Tables 2.4 and 2.5.

The yield curve describes how the cost of borrowing varies with the length of the debt incurred. Since the yield curve is rarely flat, the risk-free cost of capital will depend on the assumed maturity. The hypothetical question, 'What would it cost to lease the relevant assets?' answers this; the term of the borrowing should be matched to the economic life of the asset. For stocks and other short-term assets, a short-term interest rate is therefore appropriate.

---

1 This is a very incomplete discussion of the issues involved in determining the cost of capital, and should be read in conjunction with one of the many texts on the subject, such as Brealey and Myers (1991). It focuses on those issues which have particular application in relation to added value statements.

Risk in the added value statement

The purpose of business organization is to create added value, but that purpose is not always achieved. If that happens, then some stakeholder in the business will earn less than could have been achieved elsewhere. But which stakeholder?

Where a business operates as a corporation with shareholders with limited liability, its structure offers a clear answer to that question, and that is why the limited liability corporation has become the dominant form of economic organization throughout the world. Shareholders provide long-term finance for the company. The shareholders make a long-term contract with the corporation in which they are—implicitly—offered an expected yield above the going market rate for safe securities. In return, they accept the risks associated with the company's success or failure. If the venture is less successful than they hoped, they will earn less than a reasonable rate of return.

An organization without shareholders—a mutual financial institution, an agricultural co-operative, or a tennis club—has to deal with these potential problems in some other way. Most usually, this is through a combination of accumulated reserves and pledges from some stakeholders. These are often inadequate, and this frequently restricts the growth of these unincorporated forms of organization. But where there are other stakeholders who are bound into long-term contracts with the company—as with the customers of a life insurance company—then it is common for them to assume some of the risks that the firm runs.

Thus, there are two services being provided to the company—the provision of capital for the business and the bearing of the risks of the business—and in measuring added value each should be assessed, and charged, separately. Since the shareholders generally both bear the risk *and* provide some of the capital for operating the firm, these two costs are closely linked. But the proportions in which they are provided are not fixed. It is entirely possible to increase the capital employed in a business without increasing the uncertainty attached to the business, while other firms, such as a professional service business, may show very considerable volatility of returns without using much in the way of operating assets at all. In an industry which must maintain solvency reserves—such as a bank or insurance company—the distinction between risk capital and operating assets is particularly clear.[1] In an institution like the Lloyd's insurance market, which depends on risk capital but does not call on it until actually required, the distinction is clearer still.

Since the marginal firm to the industry is the benchmark for measuring competitive advantage, the relevant cost of risk-bearing is what it would cost that firm to obtain the risk capital it needs for its business. The price of risk may then be calculated as an addition to the cost of capital applied to the value of current cost assets.

1 Bank regulators distinguish 'free capital' and 'infrastructure assets'. See p. 295 in Ch. 18 for further discussion of this.

Where the risks of corporate activity are borne by the equity shareholders, the costs of risk-bearing are measured by the premium which they earn over the rate of return on safe securities. A series of studies of long-term rewards to shareholders in Britain and the United States have concluded that this averages around 8–9 per cent per year, after tax. This is an average figure for risk-bearing over the corporate sector as a whole.

The capital asset pricing model is a widely used technique for estimating the cost of risk-bearing for individual corporations. The basic idea underlying it is that the riskiness of corporate activity is measured by the volatility of a firm's share price relative to the market as a whole. A company whose shares moved in line with the market (a corporation with a ß of 1) would need to earn an additional 8 per cent on capital to reward its shareholders for the risks they had assumed. Companies with more volatile shares, relative to the market average, will need to pay more to their shareholders to bear these risks and those with stable share prices less.

One important implication of this approach to the cost of risk is that firms cannot expect to reduce that cost of risk by changing their capital structure. Higher levels of gearing will enable them to substitute cheaper debt for more expensive equity but, by increasing the volatility of the remaining equity, would increase costs by an amount which precisely matches the apparent savings.

If risk-bearing is bound up with the provision of capital to the business, it is also closely associated with its governance structure. It is equity shareholders who bear the largest part of the risks associated with corporate activity, and these equity shareholders also have a major influence on the management of the corporation. In Britain and the United States, such influence is exercised, theoretically, through the right to elect and re-elect directors and, more practically, through the opportunity to accept or reject offers for control from competing management groups. In Germany, France, or Japan the influence of shareholders is exercised more privately and less directly. And it is clearly efficient that responsibility for creating or increasing added value should be associated with those who benefit from it. That ensures that the pressure to add value is as great as possible. In the same way, the tennis club is controlled by its members, and the university should be accountable to the wider community.

The discussion in the first part of this chapter is closely related to the McKinsey 'business system' or the Porter value chain—see Porter (1985). The benchmarking process described here harks back to Marshall's (1890) 'representative firm'; yet it is hard to find the rank ordering of firms which serve the same market, key to the discussion here, pursued at either a theoretical or an empirical level. Benchmarking—direct comparison with competitors of both qualitative and quantitative kinds—is developed in Camp (1989) and Eccles (1991).

The shareholder value movement is closely associated with Rappaport. Rappaport (1986) is the clearest statement, but see Ball (1987) for the most outspoken attack on accounting concepts and Blyth *et al.* (1986) for a discussion of implementation; Reiman (1989) and Copeland *et al.* (1990) for the relationship of these concepts to corporate strategy. Shareholder value is closely bound up with LBOs and hostile bids; see the exchange between Jensen (1989) and Rappaport (1990). A long tradition in economics disparages the use of accounting rates of return. Harcourt (1965), Fisher and McGowan (1983) are classic references. Kay and Mayer (1986), Edwards, Kay, and Mayer (1987) explain some of the relationships which do exist and the analysis here draws on and extends that argument. Inflation accounting is well surveyed by Whittington (1983). Most empirical measurement of risk and the cost of capital in the face of risk is based on the capital asset pricing model, which underpins the discussion here; this is due to Sharpe (1964) and expounded in all finance texts. An extended illustration for a particular industry is Water Services Association and Water Companies Association (1991).

V

COMPETITIVE STRATEGIES

The issues with which the earlier parts of this book have been concerned are the traditional issues of corporate strategy. What is the core business? What markets should the firm be in? What are the objectives of the corporation? How should its success be measured and how is it reflected in financial performance?

This part considers issues of business, or competitive strategy. The answers to these earlier questions are taken as given. The firm finds itself in certain markets, facing certain competition, dealing with its distributors, suppliers, and customers. How should it manage these relationships?

Relationships with competitors focus particularly on pricing and market positioning. These are the subjects of Chapters 14 and 15. In some markets, competitors have reached a realistic modus vivendi, in which there are generally understood rules of the competitive game. I describe these as stable competitive environments. In others, there is no sense of a repeated game, and competition may be pursued to mutually destructive lengths. Sometimes technological change, or new entry, may shift an industry from stability to instability in its competitive process.

Positioning and pricing are relevant to relationships with customers as well as with competitors. Advertising and branding are mechanisms by which firms communicate with their customers, but are also strategic tools governed by competitive interactions. Chapter 17 is concerned with relationships along the value chain—backwards to suppliers and forwards to distributors.

CHAPTER

14

Pricing and Positioning, 1

*This is the first of four chapters concerned with issues of competitive
strategy—how successful firms manage their relationships with competitors, suppliers, and customers in their chosen markets. In this chapter, and
the following one, I consider issues of market position and product price.
Different types of competitive environment are found in different markets.
Some are stable. In these there are implicit rules of the competitive game,
understood by all parties. There is, in effect, a relational contract between
competitors. In other markets firms have neither desire nor opportunity to
establish long-term relationships with competitors and pursue price wars
or establish aggressive market positions indifferent to the future effect of
current behaviour. I describe these as unstable competitive environments.*

*The two key influences on market prices are the costs of firms and the
value offered to consumers. The less stable the competitive environment,
the greater is the degree to which prices will be determined by cost rather
than value. In the worst case, prices can be driven down to marginal or
incremental cost. Marginal and incremental costs are often thought to be
very low, but I explain how this is often a mistaken view and describe how
activity-based costing helps to bridge the gap between theoretical concepts
of marginal cost and accounting systems of cost allocation.*

*In other market environments there is more opportunity for prices to
reflect the value of products to customers. In these, market segmentation—
the identification of as many distinct product and geographical markets as
possible—is a principal means of securing as high a proportion as possible
of the value offered to consumers as added value for the firm. There are two
necessary conditions for effective market segmentation. There must be
economically relevant differences between the separated markets. These
may arise from differences in the incomes of customers, or in the ways they
use the product, or in competitive structure. And there must also be effective barriers to arbitrage at both wholesale and retail level.*

Television listings

The broadcasters of British television programmes hold copyright in the listings of their programmes. Although they allowed daily newspapers to tell their readers what would be shown on that day, a viewer who wanted advance programme information could obtain it only by buying one of the magazines produced by the broadcasters themselves. The *Radio Times* is published by the BBC, and the *TV Times* by Independent Television Publications (ITP). The *Radio Times* and the *TV Times* are similar publications, each glossy colour magazines which contain not only information about programmes themselves but features about television personalities, some general interest material, and much advertising. For all but brief periods, the two magazines cost the same.

In 1990, a new Broadcasting Act required television stations to license other publishers to carry their listings. (It is possible that by refusing to do so the stations had been in breach of European competition law.) New magazines appeared to compete with the *Radio Times* and the *TV Times*. The most important entrant was a German company, Bauer, with *TV Quick*. *TV Quick* contained fewer features, was less attractive in appearance and paper quality, and was introduced at a price of 10p per copy (against 50p for the *Radio Times* and the *TV Times*). ITP produced a similar magazine, called *What's On TV*, also at a very low price, and for a period reduced the price of the *TV Times*. The BBC made no competitive response. After some weeks, the price of *TV Quick* was raised to 30p. *What's On TV* followed. In March 1992 the *Radio Times* cost 55p, the *TV Times* 53p, *TV Quick* 40p, and *What's On TV* 30p.

Bauer, one of Europe's most successful magazine publishers, brought its competitive advantage to a market in which the strategic assets of ITP and BBC—their monopoly of listings—had suddenly been stripped away. The company had two groups of decisions to make. One was how to position its product. It could have chosen to go up-market of the *Radio Times* and the *TV Times*. There were other established market segments. *Time Out* is a general listings magazine, giving information about theatre, cinema, and club events as well as television programmes. *Hello* is a glossy general interest magazine which emphasizes television and entertainment, and both of these are more expensive than the *Radio Times* or the *TV Times*. Bauer decided instead to go down-market of all incumbents. In making this choice, it had to consider what the incumbents would themselves do, either by launching new products (which ITP did) or by repositioning their existing products (in the event, both ITP and BBC chose not to do this).

Bauer had to choose not only a position, but a price. In part, the price was dictated by its choice of position. It is unlikely that a magazine like *TV Quick* would have been successful if it had been more expensive than the *TV Times*. But how much cheaper did it need to be? As with its choice of position, Bauer's pricing strategy was necessarily contingent on its rivals' prices and its rivals' responses. While product position could not be changed rapidly (although it could be changed), price could be changed immediately, and was.

These issues—of positioning and of pricing—have to be considered by any firm entering a market, or reviewing its position in an existing market. They are among the key elements in the formulation of a business strategy.

The nature of the competitive environment

Bauer also had to consider the nature of the competitive environment it would encounter. The market it entered had been a stable one, with two principal competitors, each well accustomed to each other's behaviour. The *Radio Times* and the *TV Times* were in effective competition. Each monitored its rival closely, each hoped to gain readership from the other, and they competed in the quality of their production and their feature articles. But both BBC and ITP understood that a cover price war, or an advertising rate war, was likely to lead to losses for both, and they did not engage in either. The situation that followed the entry of *TV Quick* was very different, and the results were evident in market behaviour.

Competitive behaviour in industries with small numbers of firms is a classic case of a Prisoner's Dilemma. At its simplest, the payoffs have the form of Fig. 14.1. Each firm can choose to fight, or to accept, its rival's competitive strategy. As a rule, mutual acceptance is best for both—as it was for the *Radio*

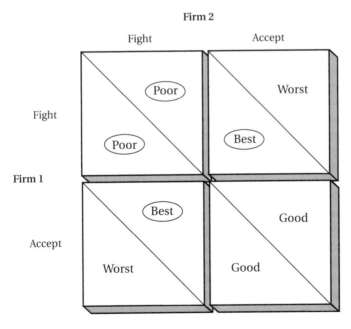

Fig. 14.1. Competitive Strategies

Times and the *TV Times*. Yet fighting is a dominant strategy for both parties. If the other accepts, you do better to fight. If the other fights, you must fight.

As in all Prisoners' Dilemmas, there are two available mechanisms of resolution—change the pay-offs, or repeat the game. Changing the pay-offs requires agreement between the players, and this is where competition policy intervenes to make such agreements illegal. Public policy does not want to make it too easy for potential rivals to avoid the 'fight–fight' outcome. So 'one-off' competitive environments are characterized by instability and bitter competition. This is what happens when there is tendering for a single contract, or in markets where technology is advancing so rapidly that there are rarely similar products, or the same competitors, in the market for any length of time. Price wars are an accustomed feature of the personal computer market.

The *Radio Times* and the *TV Times* chose not to fight each other because each had a clear perception that it was fighting a repeated game, and mutual acceptance of competitive strategies is likely only in markets which can be viewed as repeated games. It is not certain even in markets which *are* seen as repeated games. The co-operative solution is a possible outcome of a reiterated Prisoner's Dilemma but it is certainly not an inevitable one. Competitive environments may be stable, or unstable. Stable competitive environments are 'cold wars'—markets in which firms have adopted compatible repeated game strategies, as did the United States and the Soviet Union. Unstable competitive environments are 'hot wars'. Mutual accommodation has broken down. Or perhaps the nature of the competitive environment allows no room for accommodation. Competitors act to gain competitive advantage in every round of the battle, ignorant of, or unconcerned by, the consequences in subsequent rounds.

Table 14.1 shows the timetable for flights between Paris and London at February 1992. British Airways and Air France have evidently reached an accommodation. Their two schedules do not confront each other. Taken together, the two airlines offer passengers a flight more or less hourly through the day with a greater density of services at the morning and evening peaks. Their fare structures are virtually identical. Other airlines, in contrast, have positioned their flights directly against the most popular BA and Air France services, and have differently constructed and generally lower fares.

In this market, there is both a cold war and a hot war in progress. BA and Air France have each operated the route for many years, and can be expected to continue doing so. At one time, though no longer, they operated a cartel and shared revenues. So there has been plenty of opportunity to establish understood parameters of the competitive game. The other airlines are recent entrants. A year earlier, Air Europe would have been a principal operator, but Air Europe is no longer in business. Probably, in time, some of these newcomers will reach a *modus vivendi* with the incumbents and others will withdraw.

The example also illustrates how both types of competitive environment have advantages and disadvantages for consumers. The regular service

Table 14.1. BA and Air France Flights—Heathrow to Paris (February 1992)

	Departure times from London to Paris		
	British Airways	Air France	Other Airlines
0600–	0630		
		0725	0645 0730, 0730, 0750
	0740		
0800–			0830
	0900		
		0930	0940, 0955,
1000–			1000
		1025	
	1115		
			1125, 1130
		1140	
1200–	1230		
		1335	1325, 1330
1400–	1400		
		1530	1530, 1535, 1540
1600–	1630 1725		1720, 1730
		1750	
1800–	1845		1855
		1910 1940	1930, 1945
2000–		2040	
	2100		2100

Note: Excludes Air France flights from airports other than Heathrow, intercontinental carriers, London City Airport flights.

operated by the two national flag carriers is a convenient arrangement, and the easy exchange of tickets from one airline to the other enables passengers to arrive at the airport and take the first departing flight. Yet the level of fares is extremely high, and competitive pressure from entrants is the primary discipline on prices and service quality.

The difference between stability and instability in competition is of particularly great importance in competitive industries in which a high proportion of total costs is fixed, or sunk. In many businesses with these characteristics, the cost structure itself limits competition, as in electricity or water distribution systems. But in the record and book industries, extraordinary product variety brings about the conjunction of a highly competitive environment and a group of markets in which marginal production costs are far below average cost. For some branded consumer goods—consider perfume—advertising and promotional expenditures overwhelm production costs, and again the marginal cost of the product is low relative to its price, or the average costs of a unit. The same is true in industries like pharmaceuticals, where research and development costs are critical. Cement and electricity are industries with no significant scale economies but in which sunk costs form a major proportion of overall costs. These industries also suffer from cyclical demand and that increases the danger of extreme price competition.

The distinction between hot and cold wars simplifies reality. There is a full spectrum of competitive environments ranging from illegal collusive agreements at one end to battles so vitriolic that firms are prepared to damage themselves if they also damage competitors at the other. Neither extreme serves the firms involved, or their customers, well. The game theoretic perspective enables us to focus on the central issue. Do firms choose strategies appropriate to a repeated, or to a one-off, model of the competitive environment? This chapter is concerned with how prices are set in stable competitive environments. What factors determine prices in markets where the dominant influences on price are the level of suppliers' costs, and the value of goods to consumers? Chapter 15 looks at markets in which, in the heat of competitive battle, the prices charged by other firms become far more significant than either costs or values. It also considers what it is that makes one, or other, outcome more likely.

How costs influence prices

The creation of added value is governed by two factors—the value of the good or service to the customer and the cost of production to the firm. Added value is the difference between the two. The firm can never appropriate the whole of that added value. As the intensity of the competitive environment increases, prices will be bid down to the costs of other firms, and added value can only be the result of competitive advantages. In hot wars, price is driven by the marginal cost of production. In cold wars, firms are generally able to earn some of the value of the goods and services they provide.

The costs which are relevant in measuring the added value from a particular product, or activity, are the incremental costs associated with that product, or that activity. These are the additional costs which would be incurred in meeting greater demand for the product or the savings which would be made by discontinuing the activity. Although every elementary economics textbook stresses the importance of marginal costs, in reality marginal costs play very little role in business decisions. The cost estimates that form the background to pricing decisions are, as a rule, the result of allocations of accounting costs, in which virtually the whole of the expenses of the business are attributed to some product or another. And activities are monitored by reference to their contribution—the amount which they yield over and above the direct or variable costs associated with them.

There is a simple reason for this disregard of marginal cost. Marginal cost pricing is seen by most firms and accountants as a recipe for going broke. I noted in Chapter 11 that business people generally start from the presumption that a very high proportion of their costs are fixed. But very few costs are fixed in the long run. The majority are related to some specific business purpose and if they are not their rationale comes immediately under question. In the long run, every cost item can be varied—plant size, the Chairman's salary, the audit fee—and each of them can be varied in line with the scale of the business.

Modern systems of activity-based costing bridge this gap between the mechanical systems of cost allocation which have traditionally formed the basis of inventory valuation and the measurement of direct costs of particular outputs. In a capital intensive, multi-product organization these direct costs of individual products generally form a low proportion of the total cost, or value of output. The essence of this approach is an analysis of the causality behind a firm's expenditure. The Chairman is not employed to make one product or another, to serve one client or customer group or another, and the assignment or allocation of salary therefore appears an arbitrary process. But he does spend part of his time on activities related to finance and another part on activities related to sales, and the different outputs of the firm draw in turn on these activities. Building up the structure of costs in this way links the value chain of the firm, the overall added value statement, and the incremental costs associated with individual product.

If there are economies of scale and scope, or if the cost of new plant differs from the historic cost of old, then even when costs are fully attributed in this way incremental costs need not add up to the total cost of running the business.[1] If the difference is to be recovered on the basis of an accounting allocation of costs to products, then the competitive situation in some markets will

1 This result depends on understanding the 'envelope theorem' of cost analysis: if capacity is at the right level, neither too small nor too large for the scale of output, then marginal costs will be the same in the long run, when all costs are variable, as in the short run, when many costs are fixed.

support that price structure, but not in others. The costs which are not recovered in the latter will then be translated into increased prices in all markets, with further loss of business and added value. The better procedure is to see the cost structure as setting a pattern of minimum prices across all markets with additional recovery related to the value of products to consumers, and the state of competition, in the variety of markets.

How values influence prices

If costs matter to prices, so do values. Firms can appropriate value most effectively by identifying as many economic markets as they can, and pricing and positioning in each of them individually. To earn something approaching the value of its product, the firm must define the industry broadly, but define the market narrowly. Define the industry broadly, in the sense that the firm should pursue competitive advantage in every market in which its distinctive capability is relevant. Define the market narrowly, because the value of competitive advantage is maximized by tailoring pricing and marketing strategies to as many distinct markets as possible.

What marketing executives call market segmentation, economists call price discrimination. Curiously, the economic perspective tends to see it as a public evil and private good, while the marketing approach is the other way around. This difference in terminology reflects other differences in perspective. From a marketing standpoint, segmentation is almost a nuisance; consumers, regrettably and expensively, insist on being treated differently. In the economic view, segmentation is something for the firm to embrace enthusiastically—an opportunity to enhance profitability and increase sales by distinguishing economic markets and resisting the application of the law of one price. I prefer the marketing term, but the economic approach.

Market segmentation has several bases. It can be achieved through *individual pricing*. Shylock and Antonio negotiated a price for the use of Shylock's money which was specific to that transaction—a price which reflected the particular needs, aspirations, and alternative opportunities of the two parties. British Gas adopted a similar policy in respect of supplies of industrial gas until the Monopolies and Mergers Commission and Office of Gas Supply required them to sell by reference to a published tariff. Philanthropic doctors have always tailored their charges to the needs of their patients. The price at which branded foodstuffs are sold to individual supermarket chains is a keenly negotiated figure and a tightly guarded secret. No two customers will expect to visit a used car showroom and come out with the same car at the same price. In this extreme degree of market segmentation every single customer is, in a real sense, a different market.

For most transactions, the cost of negotiating individual prices is too high relative to the unit value of the sale for individual pricing to be feasible. Here *group pricing* is commonplace. Airlines do not negotiate prices individually but by offering a wide range of published tariffs, and by selling seats through a range of different wholesale outlets they achieve very similar effects. SNCF offers a carte jeune to students, a carte kiwi to children, and a carte vermeil to the elderly, each of which offers reduced fares in return for a fixed payment. Burberry raincoats are regularly available in London in January and July for little more than half their normal price, enabling price-sensitive buyers and local residents to buy at lower prices.

Product proliferation is another means of market segmentation. Here the firm offers similar, but distinct, products in different markets. This is a process which is profitable, and worth actively promoting, if the difference in price between the products is greater than the difference in the costs. First-class rail or air travel is a superior product but the premium greatly exceeds the additional cost. The price difference between hardback and paperback books is much larger than the cost of binding the volume in hard covers. Virtually identical domestic appliances can be found with different labels in different outlets at different prices.

These various examples of market segmentation display a number of common themes. Market segmentation is far more important, and far more extensive, in services than it is in manufactured goods. There are several reasons for this but the most important is that the essentially individual nature of most service provision makes it easy to prevent goods being transferred from one market to another. It is useless for Carrefour to offer reduced price groceries to students because it would quickly find that students were the only people at its checkouts even if they were not the only consumers of its products. But it is feasible for SNCF to do the same thing because SNCF is able to prevent a student reselling a seat on the train to another passenger. For market segmentation to be effective it is necessary that there should be relevant economic differences between the distinct markets and that it should be possible to restrict arbitrage between these markets. And the seller must also have a degree of market power. This need not be of the magnitude enjoyed by Shylock, or SNCF. It may simply be that the product is branded, or otherwise differentiated. But market segmentation cannot be imposed in an otherwise perfectly competitive market.

If prices can be determined individually, then every transaction is, in principle, undertaken in a distinct economic market; and if the unit value of transactions is sufficiently large there is a real sense in which this is true. Although it is generally true that the ability to segment markets enhances profits, enforced segmentation of this magnitude does not. In fact, PIMS evidence shows unit size of sale as one of the strongest negative influences of structure on profitability (Table 12.3). The advantage of distinguishing many distinct economic markets is mostly (although not necessarily) offset if the firm faces only a single monopsonistic customer in each one.

Discrimination between groups on bases other than geography generally encounters customer resistance and practical difficulties. A few service industries offer lower prices to the old, or to the young. In some industries, ingenious ways of achieving group discrimination are available—the airline requirement of a Saturday night stay is an elegant if not infallible means of distinguishing business from leisure travellers.

Others allow customers to group themselves. Non-linear price schedules, or commodity bundling, enable the same commodity or group of commodities to be sold at different prices to different customers. Rank Xerox was able to sell photocopiers at higher prices to large-volume users by requiring those who installed its machines to purchase consumables and service and support contracts from the company at relatively high prices. Most utilities offer a range of different price schedules targeted at different customer groups. British Telecom faces competition from Mercury on some services, such as high-volume business users, but is prevented by regulatory restriction from introducing explicitly discriminatory price schedules. The implementation of price packages—offering different service bundles to different customer groups—enables it to offer lower prices for additional services to these Mercury competitive customers while protecting revenue overall.

The more generally acceptable means of product market segmentation, however, is product proliferation—to fill the product space with a range of different goods each aimed at slightly different target markets. This can be used in both the geographical and product dimensions of the market. This is characteristic of the automobile industry, where not only are model specifications varied to suit different geographical markets but in all markets differences in specification bear no systematic relationship to the cost of these specification differences.

The two key elements in a strategy of market segmentation through product proliferation are the development of focused products and the identification of characteristics of special importance to individual markets with inelastic demand. The airline strategy of offering alternative classes of service developed almost accidentally. Airlines initially modelled their luxurious facilities on cruise liners and in due course came to offer economy seats to more budget-conscious passengers. By the 1970s, the division between economy and first-class service was insufficiently focused, and did not reflect the key distinction between the relatively inelastic demand for business travel and the much more price-conscious leisure market. Business travellers were making increasing use of the economy package. KLM pioneered the introduction of a third class of service, to increase the focus of the service packages offered. The innovation was quickly followed by most major international airlines. The creation of these different product categories divides the market more effectively, but at the same time stimulates substitution from more profitable segments. So business class draws customers both (profitably) from economy and (unprofitably) from first-class. Increased segmentation is not always remunerative, but more focused segmentation invariably is.

The most effective focus is the identification of a central user characteristic. Libraries combine more inelastic demand for books with more intensive usage, so that book durability is a far more valuable characteristic to libraries than to other users. This market distinction is exploited effectively by the paperback–hardback distinction. The same distinction can be used to discriminate by reference to the urgency of the purchase. Paperback editions are often published only after a lag so that the publisher segments committed and marginal users. Such temporal segmentation is also common in many consumer durable markets. Innovative products are sold first at high prices to enthusiasts, and then at steadily diminishing prices to increasingly price-sensitive users.

Geographical market segmentation

Table 9.1 (p. 131) showed effective geographical market segmentation in four European industries. In each, the principal firms have the required degree of market power. There are relatively few firms with differentiated products in automobiles and domestic appliances. Patents and branding confer market power in pharmaceuticals, and the life insurance industry is cartelized in most European markets. What is it that differentiates these markets in ways which make differential pricing remunerative? In the insurance industry it is the degree of competition, or its absence. Buyers of life insurance in Italy pay prices which reflect the concentrated and regulated structure of their insurance industry, while the United Kingdom, with much the most competitive insurance sector in Europe, also has the lowest prices. But what British consumers gain when they buy life insurance they lose when they buy cars. The United Kingdom has the highest car prices in Europe. This is the result of protection of high-cost domestic manufacturers through government policy and by the nationalistic policies of corporate buyers who dominate new car purchasing in Britain.

Nationalistic purchasing is also a factor behind the high level of domestic appliance prices in France. So too are the distinctive purchasing preferences of French buyers. France is the only European country where top-loading washing machines take a substantial share of the market. In pharmaceutical markets, governments exert considerable influence over pricing levels, since the dominant purchaser is either the state itself or the closely regulated private insurance sector. The governments of Germany and the United Kingdom, both countries with strong domestic pharmaceutical industries, believe that the interests of these industries are served by keeping prices relatively high. France and Italy, whose national manufacturers do not have equivalent shares either domestically or internationally, see their economies as better served by lower drug prices.

These market differences provide the rationale of segmentation, but they would not work unless producers were able to keep markets apart. In the automobile industry, the English Channel and the British attachment to driving on the left-hand side of the road effectively cut off the UK market from the continent of Europe. Further support has been provided by the imposition of different approval standards in different countries. Manufacturer influence over the dealer distribution network places obstacles in the way of individual buyers who wish to buy a car in one country and use it in another, except through the manufacturer's organized procedures.

In both life insurance and pharmaceuticals, regulatory barriers inhibit cross-border trade. Pharmaceutical firms, and many others, package their product differently for different markets. Simply varying the size or number of items in the pack makes arbitrage more difficult.

Only in domestic appliances is it not apparent what barriers there are to buying in a cheap market and using in a dear one. There is a real obstacle to personal arbitrage, since it is inconvenient to carry a washing machine on a cross-Channel ferry, but the inhibitions to commercial arbitrage lie more in manufacturer influence over the actions of distributors. In all cases, the relationships between manufacturer and distributor are an important influence on the sustainability of segmentation.

Differences between geographical markets

These examples illustrate the variety of differences between geographical markets which make market segmentation practicable. These include differences in the degree of market power which firms hold, individually or collectively, in the different geographical market. Life insurance buyers pay more in cartelized than in competitive markets. Cement prices are much higher in most northern European countries, where producers have more effective market control, than in more competitive Southern Europe markets. SAS charges higher prices for flights *from* Scandinavia—where it perceives the market as largely a captive one—than for flights *to* Scandinavia—where it believes customers are likely to consider alternative destinations.

There are also often differences in the nature and degree of government influence on the market. This is well illustrated in the pharmaceutical industry. Facsimile machines cost between 50 per cent and 100 per cent more in France, where approval regulations are used to protect French suppliers, than in the United Kingdom where they are not. The much tighter regulation of road haulage in Germany than in most other Community countries has kept trucking prices there relatively high.

Differences in consumer tastes and in product positioning may also make market segmentation attractive. The French pay a high price for their liking of top-loading machines, and their preference for suppositories helps segment the market for over-the-counter drugs as well as that for prescribed pharmaceuticals. It is very common to find products positioned as commodity products at home and as niche products abroad. This is particularly true of alcoholic drinks. Belgians and Germans visiting other European countries are often surprised to find Stella Artois and Löwenbrau positioned as premium products.

Illustration 14.1. Making Market Segmentation Effective

TECHNIQUES OF MARKET SEGMENTATION

Individual pricing

Negotiating each price

Group pricing

Dividing a market into customer classes

Product proliferation

Product ranges whose price differentials do not match cost differentials

CONDITIONS OF MARKET SEGMENTATION

Economically relevant differences between markets

The degree of competition
The availability of substitutes
Consumer attitudes to the product

Some degree of market power

Few sellers
Product differentiation

Barriers to arbitrage

Trade barriers
Private standards or tastes
Control over distribution

None of these differences is sustainable unless markets can be kept apart. Barriers to arbitrage between markets fall into three broad categories—legal rules, private standards, and control of the distribution network. The easiest way to sustain market segmentation is to rely on governments to use border controls to do the job for you, and this has been effective not only in cars and pharmaceuticals but in products as wide ranging as lawn mowers and chocolate. Since the famous Cassis de Dijon judgement (in which the European Court declared illegal the exclusion of the product, a blackcurrant liqueur, from the German market on the improbable ground that it was insufficiently alcoholic to meet German statutory requirements), regulatory barriers to arbitrage between markets have come under increasing pressure as a consequence of legal action and the Commission's 1992 programme. Member states are still entitled to impose entry restrictions, even on goods legally on sale elsewhere in the Community, if they believe they are necessary for purposes of consumer protection and safety. With time, these restrictions will inescapably be eroded, but it is already clear that in many industries (including life insurance, pharmaceuticals, and, probably, automobiles) barriers to arbitrage will persist long after 1992.

Even where legal standards do not encourage—or allow—markets to be effectively segmented, private standards may have an equivalent effect. There is no law that requires British motorists to use right-hand drive vehicles (it insists only that they drive on the left) and there is no specific barrier to the use or import of left-hand drive cars. But such vehicles are less convenient to have in the United Kingdom, and the low value which they command in the second-hand market more than eliminates any gains an importer might expect to make from dealing in continental cars. Plugs, sockets, and other compatibility standards also differ across geographical markets for many products. Although the cost of conversion may be low the need to do so, and the uncertainty in the consumer's mind that the final product will indeed meet his or her needs, restricts arbitrage.

The most important of these private standards is language. Labelling in a foreign language materially reduces the market value of many products, particularly those that require complex written instructions (pharmaceuticals) or advice and explanation (life insurance). The obligation to print a health warning on packets of cigarettes has proved helpful to tobacco companies in maintaining segmentation of European markets. Since the health warning has to be printed in a specific language it identifies each batch of product with a particular national destination and enables companies to keep better track of the progress of their product through the distribution chain.

This influence over distribution channels is an important element of all market segmentation strategies. Formally restricting the subsequent sale of a commodity to a particular area of the European Community is, in most cases, a violation of the Treaty of Rome and a series of cases has established the inadmissibility of such restraints. However, there are many devices which have equivalent effects. Informal pressure on dealers can generally be relied on to limit the extent of arbitrage especially where a legal selective distribution agreement is in operation.

Bibliographical notes for this chapter are included with those at the end of Chapter 15.

15

Pricing and Positioning, 2

In this chapter I consider further the issues of pricing and positioning discussed in Chapter 14. Successful companies must strive for stable competitive environments, and I describe the conditions that facilitate this, or make it impossible to achieve. Instability of competition does not necessarily mean that prices are bid down to costs unless there are very many firms in the market. Firms still have some discretion in their pricing behaviour but in unstable competitive environments that behaviour must not only reflect appreciation of the positioning of competitors but an analysis of the variety of their possible responses.

Positioning decisions are partly dictated by the firm's distinctive capability. Some firms are naturally suited to up- or down-market positions. This issue was discussed in Chapter 9. But positioning is also a matter of competitive dynamics. When there are few firms in a particular market, clustering behaviour—in which several firms jostle for the same market position—is a likely outcome. As the number of firms in the market increases, they are likely to spread themselves more evenly across the range of available positions.

Increasingly, a product can only be described by reference to a wide range of its characteristics. Many different features of a car are relevant to potential buyers, and a supermarket must decide which selection of many thousands of goods to hold in stock. For commodities like these, successful firms have to make a well-matched selection of product attributes. For these firms, focus—the consistency of attributes with each other—may be as important as position. Shifts of market position, which require changes in customer perception as well as product specification, need to anticipate competitor responses. They raise special difficulties for multiple-attribute products.

Stable or unstable competitive environments?

If firms are to maximize the added value they earn, they need to be able to price away from cost and towards value. Such strategies can always be undermined by competitors pricing towards cost. Value in use pricing will be sustainable only if at least one of three broad conditions is met:

- The product faces limited competition, either because of the firm's strategic assets or because it is strongly differentiated.
- Competing producers respect the firm's 'territory' (which may be defined in either geographic or product space).
- Competing producers recognize the integrity of the pricing structure, and apply it to their own products.

The examples given in Chapter 14 provide a variety of illustrations of each of these possibilities. The price discrimination practised by SNCF is possible because there is only one French railway system. If there were many (a world which is admittedly hard to imagine) then competitors would seek to attract lucrative business travellers away and the margins between different fares would be quickly eroded. If patent protection for pharmaceutical products were less effective, then prices would be generally lower and more uniform across different geographic markets. In both cases, it is the limits to competition which enable firms to charge prices which reflect the value of their goods to their customers.

European automobile markets illustrate both respect for territory and support for the integrity of the price structure. The high level of UK car prices would be reduced if distributors were ready to sell cars outside their designated territories, or if one or more major manufacturers were to sell at levels which reflected their costs rather than the established UK price structure. European insurance retailers and cement companies do not market aggressively across national boundaries. Airlines maintain broadly comparable price differentials between fare types and classes of customer.

Territorial divisions, or tacit acceptance by all firms of price structures which reflect value in use, depend on the existence of formal or informal agreements. Most formal arrangements fall foul of Article 85 of the Rome Treaty, which prohibits agreements between undertakings which restrict or distort competition. Article 85 (3) does provide for an exemption for agreements which enhance technical and economic progress. A number of arrangements have secured such exemption—such as selective distribution agreements in automobile markets. But cartels and collusive price-fixing, and most geographical or other market-sharing arrangements, are illegal if they affect trade within the European Community. These practices may also be prohibited by EC states' own national anti-trust legislation (as in Germany and the United Kingdom) and are generally illegal in the United States and Japan also. But the illegality of a formal agreement does not prevent firms operating within tacitly understood boundaries of the parameters of competition in particular markets. Without such understandings, much business would simply be impossible.

There are some academic studies of the problems of achieving co-operation without communication. In an original experiment by Thomas Schelling, Harvard students were instructed to try to meet someone the next day in New York City. There were no indications as to place or time, and no further information was available. A fair proportion of students given this brief would be found under the clock at Grand Central Station at noon, and therefore the chances of a successful meeting are quite high. The story demonstrates the importance of what Schelling called 'focal points' in non-verbal communication. These are outcomes which, for reasons that may be hard to define precisely, somehow have a natural 'feel' to them. Such focal points are often culturally specific. Harvard undergraduates might naturally gravitate to Grand Central Station. Few European visitors would succeed in locating it.

Focal points may be round numbers in prices, or fifty/fifty sharing agreements. Indeed, fifty/fifty sharing provides a striking example, since although there may be little difference in the amount received from an agreement to share something fifty/fifty and an agreement to split it in the proportions 49.9 per cent/50.1 per cent, it is often easy to reach consensus on the first and not at all easy to do so on the second.

If market conditions, and prices and costs, never changed, it would be relatively easy to establish rules of competition that avoided destructive price wars or mutually defeating encroachments into each other's markets. After a few plays of a common strategy, such as tit for tat, there is a good chance that the competitive environment might settle down. But demand conditions, costs, and individual market shares change. Firms then have to move prices, launch new products, invest in new capacity, accept gains and losses of customers. How are they to avoid these moves being misinterpreted?

Focal points are a particularly clear illustration of the importance of simple rule structures in non-verbal communication. Most markets in which competitors have coexisted for any length of time have well understood conventions of competitive behaviour. Price leadership is a common approach. One firm—usually the largest—initiates a round of price adjustments and, so long as the adjustment is reasonable, others will follow the lead. The car industry follows this pattern almost everywhere, with different price leaders in different markets. Or a price change may follow some external signal. Commercial banks usually move interest rates together in response to a change in the behaviour of the central bank. Indeed, this is such a well-entrenched convention that governments rely on it in conducting their monetary policies.

The timing of price changes is another standard convention. Many industries have a recognized cycle of price adjustment, in which prices are raised once a year at a regular date. Many fast-moving consumer goods markets have a tacit rule that price cutting takes the form of extra quantity for the same price, rather than lower prices for the same quantity. Promotions that take this form are understood to be temporary and induce no competitive reaction. In some of these markets there is a recognized cycle of whose turn it is to discount next.

If these conventions are to be effective, it is not only necessary that they be simple. It is necessary that breaches of them should be obvious. Some product-positioning moves that defy conventions are very obvious. Shifts into new geographical markets, or new product launches, are clear statements of aggressive competitive intention. Others may be very hard to identify. What of gradual upgradings of quality, or modest extensions of product lines? Certainly, the range of conventional signals seems much less in the *product* dimensions of competitive strategy than it is in the *pricing* dimension. But product complexity hinders the maintenance of competitive discipline, since the number of items to be monitored increases steadily. Yet even this can be overcome. Frustrated in attempts to reach an accommodation in any other way with its rival, Westinghouse, General Electric published a formula book which described exactly how it computed tender prices for electricity generation equipment. The effect was to make it easy for Westinghouse to follow its lead.

Successful Prisoner's Dilemma strategies are, it was suggested in Chapter 3, nice, but responsive, yet forgiving, and that is clearly true in the game of competitive behaviour. You do not assume that your competitor's intentions are all intrinsically hostile. You begin by offering the benefit of the doubt. If your rivals take advantage, your response is identifiable and proportionate to the threat. Yet you do not allow one aggressive action to plunge the industry into a price war for ever.

Despite these opportunities, while some industries establish a stable competitive environment on a sustained basis—retail banking—others are condemned to fight hot wars for ever—as in the personal computer market. There are factors which make stable competition almost impossible in some industries. Competition can rarely be stable if there are many sellers. Not only is it likely that some firm will break the conventions of the game, but even if they do not, the probability that someone will appear to be breaking them is high. And if there are many sellers, instability of individual market shares is almost impossible to avoid.

If it is better for the stability of competition that there should be few sellers, it is best that there should be many buyers. When buyers are fragmented—as in most consumer goods markets—then it is impossible to advertise price, or position, to customers without also advertising it to competitors. So conventions become easy to enforce. A small number of buyers can play sellers off against each other. They claim to be receiving discounts whether they are or not. Competitive discipline is impossible to maintain.

But while there are some industries where manufacturers sell directly to a diffuse public—petrol, or most services—most consumer goods are sold through retailers. Concentration in retailing implies that manufacturers face few buyers even though there are many final consumers for the goods concerned. It is then difficult to achieve stability in the competitive environment. This is a particular problem for firms producing branded foodstuffs.

Illustration 15.1. Factors Favouring a Stable Competitive Environment

- Stability of cost and demand conditions
- Well-established focal points in price and position
- Product homogeneity
- Few sellers
- Many buyers
- Similarity of cost structures

Stability in competition depends on similarity of background—as was shown by the Harvard students' choice of meeting-place. This may be the product of the common education, experience, and social position of senior executives. In many industries this is a very real factor promoting stability of competition—look at the insurance industry in most countries, the brewing industry world-wide, or the relatively comfortable competitive structures which characterize local industries in many small countries. The globalization of markets and industries is upsetting many of these competitive environments, as new entrants emerge who do not understand, or may not wish to understand, the implicit rules of the game of local competition. This has been particularly true of financial services. Diversity will also be a problem if some firms have markedly different cost structures. So attempts to maintain price discipline in retail petrol markets have repeatedly been thwarted by supermarkets and small importers who face supply conditions very different from those of the oil majors.

Pricing in unstable environments

In 1993 or 1994, the thirty-mile tunnel between Britain and France will open for service. As Britain has become more integrated in the European economy, roll-on/roll-off traffic—in which loaded trucks are carried by ferries between Dover and Felixstowe on one side and Calais or Zeebrugge on the other—has become a larger and larger proportion of total freight movements. Today, Dover is Britain's second largest port (the largest is Heathrow Airport).

While some of this traffic will shift to through rail services, most of it will continue to be carried in lorries. But in future lorries will have the option of boarding a shuttle train to be carried through the tunnel instead of a ferry. This is not an ideal service. Time will still be spend loading and unloading lorries at each end, and Dover–Calais, although short, is not a particularly convenient crossing. The reason the Felixstowe–Zeebrugge route is so popular is that if a direct road link could be built between the heart of England and the heart of Europe, it would almost certainly cross the sea between those two ports.

At present, it costs an average of around 200 Ecus to take a lorry between

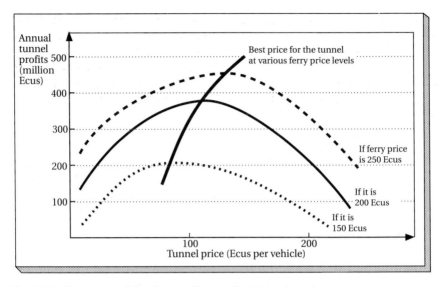

Fig. 15.1. Eurotunnel Profits at Alternative Price Levels

Britain and continental Europe. Ferries will go on providing this service after 1993. What should the tunnel charge? If the ferries were to continue to set current prices, then the choice Eurotunnel faces is described in Fig. 15.1. If price is too low, market share will be high but margins thin. If price is high then margins will be much greater but the result will be loss of market share. In fact, if the ferries do continue to charge 200 Ecus the tunnel will do best to set a much lower price—perhaps as low as 100 Ecus or so. The reason is that the tunnel's marginal costs of operation are very low. It costs it perhaps 15 Ecus to ship a lorry—until the point, still far distant, at which the tunnel is operating at full capacity.[1]

But would the ferries continue to stick with a price of 200 Ecus if the tunnel were to reduce its price to half of that? Fig. 15.1 shows how the choices open to the tunnel are changed if the ferry price is lower. The lower the price the ferry charges, the lower should be the price of tunnel services. In fact, it always pays the tunnel to undercut the ferries.

So does this mean that prices will tumble until channel crossings are practically given away? Not necessarily, because that outcome would be unprofitable for everyone. Fig. 15.1 enables us to find, for each ferry price, the best price for the tunnel. And in a precisely analogous way, we can find the best ferry price for each tunnel price. Both these relationships are shown in Fig. 15.2.

1 I have not ignored the warnings given at pp. 172 and 227 against thinking marginal costs are low because all costs are fixed—this is one instance in which they really are. This is a possible error, however, in thinking about ferry costs. It is true that once a ferry is on the point of departure, the costs of taking an additional vehicle on board are insignificant. But services do not have to be so frequent, and ferries can be sold or deployed on other routes. In the long run, there are almost no fixed costs of ferry operation. Tunnel costs, by contrast, are almost independent of traffic volumes.

What this describes is the Nash equilibrium, at B—the pair of strategies in which both the ferry and the tunnel are achieving the best outcome for themselves given the strategies of the other. In this Nash equilibrium, the tunnel price is 120 Ecus and the ferry price 225 Ecus. The ferries continue to do business, because there are still many users who prefer sea crossings which take them closer to their destination, but a large fraction of freight traffic uses the tunnel.

The nature of this Nash equilibrium illustrates that even in unstable environments competitors do not necessarily pursue each other to mutual destruction. The unstable environment is one in which each party takes no account of the *interests* of the other, but nevertheless considers the *responses* of the other, and that is the key difference. Not to consider other firms' responses would simply be irrational; but to take account of their interests requires a formal or a tacit agreement between the parties.

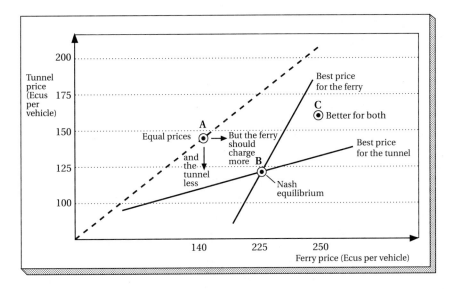

Fig. 15.2. Tunnel and Ferry Reactions

Is that Nash equilibrium the likely outcome to this competitive game? Certainly, there is nothing that guarantees it, but if anything other than a Nash equilibrium is achieved then it pays at least one player to do something different. For example, the instinct of both parties is probably that since they are offering very similar services they should charge very similar prices, as at A. But if they do, the tunnel will gain by lowering its price and the ferries by raising theirs, and presumably they will realize this.

At an outcome like C, however, both players might be making higher profits than they achieve in the Nash equilibrium. This might be the outcome of disciplined competition, rather than the unstable competition assumed in the model. The players are, after all, engaged in a repeated game. They will set new prices every season, and perhaps more often. Is it possible that they could achieve this outcome? The problem here is that because the cost structures of the players are so different, the temptation to depart from such a disciplined outcome is almost irresistible. The ferries have a tiny market share, at a very high price; surely they can gain a bit of the tunnel's volume by trimming it. And how would the tunnel react if they did? The Nash equilibrium really does seem the most likely outcome here.

A model of product positioning

It is common to talk of product positioning, and product location, and the geographical analogy is a helpful way of describing product strategies. Start by taking the locational model quite literally. Visualize a beach, uniformly lined with tanning bodies. In the course of the day, everyone on it will need an ice-cream, and will hasten to the nearest vendor. A boy and girl arrive, each with an ice-cream trolley. Where do they locate?

The answer to this problem is very clear, although most people find it surprising at first sight. They will stand together, in the middle of the beach. One—let it be the boy—will serve all the customers on the left. The other—the girl—will serve all the customers on the right. To see why this is so, consider, as in Fig. 15.3, what would happen if the girl were to move. All the customers to the left of A would now buy their ice-cream from the boy. The people at the far right of the beach have a shorter walk, but they were buying their ice-cream from the girl anyway. Indeed, if the girl were to stay where she is, it would pay the boy to move towards her, and capture the customers to the right of A as well. If instead of having mobile trolleys, they have to erect fixed stands, or even to rent their pitches from the local authority in advance, the Nash equilibrium outcome is still for both to choose sites in the middle of the beach. If customers are unwilling to walk all the way from the end of the beach, and would do without an ice-cream instead, it makes sense for them to move a little way apart. But unless this reluctance is very great, the distance between them will not be large.

This clustering behaviour is a phenomenon which is easy to recognize in the business environment. Look at any market which is dominated by two firms of comparable strength. See Hertz and Avis in car rental; distinguish, if you can, the Ford Taurus from the Opel Vectra. The leading firms in these industries pursue pricing and product strategies which can barely be distinguished from each other. At least one industry seemed designed to mimic the boy and girl on the beach. The Australian government decreed a two-airline policy for domestic aviation, and split the market initially between two carriers, one privately owned, one public, protecting both from new entry. Ansett and Australian Airlines not only charged identical fares and deployed virtually

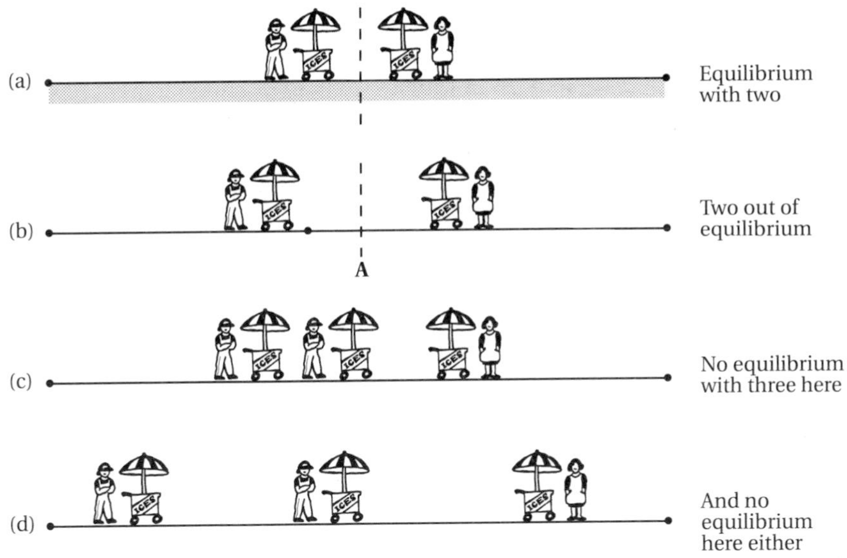
(a)
Equilibrium with two
(b)
Two out of equilibrium
A
(c)
No equilibrium with three here
(d)
And no equilibrium here either

Fig. 15.3. The Ice-Cream Sellers

identical fleets, but also came to operate virtually identical schedules. Two planes would depart almost simultaneously for a distant airport, followed by a gap until a further pair took off in the same direction.

The explanation of these outcomes is almost precisely that which underpins the behaviour of the ice-cream vendors. Two firms have broadly equal shares, and one modifies its product range or product formulation, or adopts a new marketing approach. A successful innovation of this kind would give it more than half the market, in which case it must pay to follow it. Or it fails, in which case it should be abandoned. In either case, the two firms will move in step.

But notice also that this story does not hold if there are three or more strong firms. A successful innovator will almost certainly make gains mainly at the expense of one competitor rather than the other. The loser may choose to follow the innovator, in which case it may well pay the third firm to move apart. Identity of strategies is a phenomenon of markets with two dominant competitors. It is much less likely if there are many players.

To see this most vividly, consider the outcome if a third ice-cream seller arrives at the beach. The best strategy for the newcomer is to locate immediately to the right or left of an existing supplier. But this leaves one supplier squeezed in the middle. In Fig. 15.3c, the boy in the middle must react, by jumping to one side or the other. And that provokes a further response. What if the new boy, less provocatively, distances himself a little to the left of the established suppliers, as in 15.3d? Then it always pays the two suppliers on the outside to edge towards the centre, until eventually they provoke a response. This is a game which has no Nash equilibria, and players of such games are condemned to endless, indecisive jockeying for position.

Certainly it is difficult to think of markets where three players of comparable strength have coexisted for long. The US instant coffee market has been dominated by three products—Nescafé, Maxwell House, Folgers—each with powerful backers—Nestlé, General Foods, Procter and Gamble, and has displayed comparable instability. There were three principal airlines operating between Europe and the United States—Pan American, TWA, and the relevant national carrier, and that was a competitive structure that did not last.

Perhaps the most striking demonstration of the instability of threesomes is to be found in political systems, especially in those countries whose first-past-the-post electoral systems resemble the operation of markets. Two-party structures endure, and generally show convergence of policies typical of two vendors on the beach. Sometimes, they move apart and if the gap is not narrowed a third seller appears. But if the third seller is to survive, he needs to eliminate one of the two others. Three-party systems are unstable and do not persist.[1]

Intriguingly, instability is particularly a problem of threesomes. As the number of players increases, so does the probability of a stable outcome. If there are many ice-cream vendors, they will spread themselves more or less evenly along the beach. There may still be some clustering and jostling for position at the ends. But convergence and instability are typically characteristic of small number competition.

The beach analogy, although very simple, illustrates some of the critical features of jockeying for position in markets (Illustration 15.2). In applying it, the distinction between horizontal and vertical product differentiation described in Chapter 9 must be borne in mind. Such differentiation is horizontal when the dimension along which producers array themselves is, like the beach, a neutral one. Clothes are manufactured in various sizes as well as in various qualities and some colours and some sizes suit particular individuals, some others. But everyone would agree that good tailoring is preferable to bad, and this is vertical differentiation. To apply the lessons of the beach more widely it is necessary to consider these various dimensions of product quality, and allow for the likelihood that products have multiple attributes. In the next section, this model is used to describe industries as different as national newspapers and food retailers.

Positioning in newspaper and food retailing

What are called quality and popular newspapers are differentiated primarily by the density and difficulty of the material they contain. The measurement of these factors is familiar to educational psychologists and enables us to iden-

---

1 This analysis depends on politics being unidimensional, as it is in many—especially Anglo-Saxon—countries. Where political preferences are arranged on more dimensions, as where a religious one is superimposed on a left–right spectrum, multi-party structures prove more enduring.

Illustration 15.2. Lessons in Product Positioning

- Mid-points suit consumers
- Small number competition may lead to clustering
- Small number competition may have no equilibrium
- End points may lead to clustering
- So niches may be uncomfortable unless truly differentiated
- Clustering is still possible with multiple dimensions
- But multiple dimensions may have more stable outcomes

tify in a particularly clear way the positioning of these different products. Table 15.1 illustrates the required reading age for Britain's principal national newspapers. Notice, however, that consumers are not uniformly arrayed along this beach. Interpreting where everyone is positioned on the newspaper beach is slightly tricky. We have information on the reading ages attained by the population of potential newspaper readers. But we do not know what kind of newspaper customers would like to read; we can only infer this from the pattern of what they do read. The ways in which newspapers are financed differ markedly along the quality spectrum. Despite higher fixed costs (they employ journalists), quality newspapers sell much more advertising revenue per copy and break even at considerably lower levels of circulation than popular newspapers whose revenue mostly comes from the cover price.

Table 15.1. The Reading Age of British National Newspapers

Newspaper	Required reading age (April 1988)
The *Independent*	17.4
The *Daily Telegraph*	17.2
The Times	16.9
The *Guardian*	16.6
Daily Mail	16.0
Daily Express	15.3
Today (Launch)	14.4
Today (April 1988)	13.4
Daily Star	13.1
The *Sun*	12.8
Daily Mirror	12.8

Four national newspapers have entered this market since 1969. The first (actually a relaunch of an existing title) was the *Sun*, which was initially positioned with a reading age below that of any existing title. The *Sun* rapidly became Britain's best-selling newspaper, and adjacent titles moved position towards it (reflecting the re-emergence of clustering behaviour at the end of the beach). This segment also attracted the second new entrant, the *Daily Star*, which was positioned to take advantage of excess printing capacity within Express Newspapers. *Today* was brought to market in 1985 by Eddie Shah, a proprietor who had enjoyed some success with free provincial newspapers and whose disputes with trades unions had won him considerable publicity. It is rather unclear what *Today*'s position was intended to be and the results of the launch were disappointing.

The fourth new entrant was the *Independent*. This paper was initially intended to fill the gap between the *Daily Express* and the *Daily Mail*, on the one hand, and the cluster of quality papers, on the other. As plans progressed, however, News International, owners of *The Times*, used an opportunity provided by a dispute with printing workers to dismiss the staff concerned and to print the paper at a different site using new technology (p. 188). This created some disaffection among *The Times* journalists and was associated with an increasingly right-wing tone in the paper's editorial content. The *Independent* chose instead to launch a paper directly into the market position which *The Times* was seen as having vacated, recruiting some of its staff in order to do so.

The positioning of newspapers reflects the range of tastes among newspaper readers, and so is an example of horizontal differentiation. The positioning of food retailers reflects whether they aim to provide high-quality products for high-income households, basic goods for low-income groups, or to strike a balance between the two. So food retailing is an instance of vertical differentiation. Chapter 2 described the positioning of the major British supermarket chains, and this is illustrated in Fig. 15.4. As was indicated there, these product positions have not always been the same. In the late 1970s Tesco made a very conscious decision to reposition from a down-market stance to one close to that of Sainsbury's, the market leader. Since then, others have followed, less successfully, leaving Kwik Save dominant in the down-market segment and eventually attracting new entrants there.

The failure of Woolworth to respond to shifting market conditions was very much in the mind of the management of Tesco. Yet changing the market position of a commodity (the services of a supermarket) which has multiple attributes raises special problems. An evolutionary change runs the risk of loss of focus. This was the fate of another British retailer, British Home Stores, which sought to upgrade its market position by introducing ranges of higher quality merchandise. But the existing customer base of Bhs did not want to buy these goods, and those who did were not customers of Bhs. The repositioning failed.

Tesco instead attempted to change the whole bundle of characteristics, bringing all aspects of its operations in line with its desired new position over a short period of time. It introduced a much wider range of fresh produce, and increased the proportion of private label goods. It raised the quality of merchandise generally and shifted the centre of gravity of its operations from

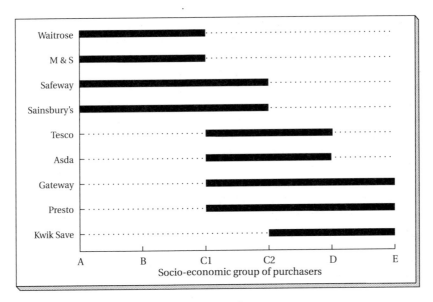

Fig. 15.4. Product Positioning of Supermarkets

city centres to out-of-town supermarkets. Its advertising emphasized the 'new' Tesco, and its logo and style of store layout changed. The overall objective was to attract a new customer group and accept that the repositioned stores would not be appropriate for many of its traditional shoppers. Taken as a whole, the operation was successful and Tesco now occupies a similar market position to Sainsbury's with similar market share.

It is apparent that such a strategy involves high risks. Coke's attempt to reposition its product with a new formula, preferred by customers in blind tastings, proved a fiasco, and Asda's emulation of Tesco was a failure. Tesco's success reflected the different basis of its competitive advantage. The company had established an internal and external architecture in its retailing systems—a distinctive capability which could be exploited in many different market positions. Its reputation (for cheapness) was of modest value. Such a reputation is easy to acquire. So Tesco sacrificed little of the company's existing distinctive capability, and exploited its new one more fully. Tesco's shift of product position was successful in the sense that it achieved its aims. Would it have been less profitable if it had remained in a more differentiated location? The answer to that question is not obvious.

Pricing and positioning

Decisions on pricing and positioning often have to be taken together. This was obviously true when Bauer entered the listings market. Even if they are separate decisions, as they will be if position is dictated by competitive advantage rather than competitive forces, they are interdependent.

What happens on the beach if boy and girl can charge different prices? Even if they can, they will not. They cannot charge different prices if they are standing together, since one vendor will win all the custom. No one should have been surprised that the *Radio Times* and *TV Times* were similar magazines and that each of them cost 50p. There is a general lesson here: that similar products command similar prices in competitive markets.

But what is meant by similar products requires careful interpretation. Consider the Coke/Pepsi game of Table 15.2. Coke and Pepsi are similar products but (in the precise sense defined on p. 135) Coke is of better quality; at equal prices, it takes a 70 per cent market share. Both Coke and Pepsi are heavily advertised.

Table 15.2. The Coke/Pepsi Game

	Coke		Pepsi
Parameters			
Marginal cost (Ecus)	0.24		0.24
Share at parity (%)	70		30
Price response elasticity		5.0	
Ad spend response elasticity		0.5	
Initial values			
Price (Ecus)	0.39		0.39
Ad spend (£000s)	630		630
Market share (%)	70		30
Profits (000 Ecus)	2,625		765
Nash equilibrium			
Price (Ecus)	0.40 (+0.01)		0.35 (−0.04)
Ad spend (£000s)	630 (+0)		430 (−200)
Market share (%)	58 (−12)		42 (+12)
Profits (000 Ecus)	2,350 (−275)		1,050 (+285)

At first sight, Coke and Pepsi might be expected to charge the same price, and advertise at similar levels, and indeed this is what they do in many markets. But this cannot be a Nash equilibrium. Coke should advertise more, and it would not be rational for Pepsi to follow them; Pepsi should reduce prices, and it does not pay Coke to follow. Since the products are close substitutes for each other, price cutting and advertising are equally effective for both players. But the costs of advertising are independent of the volume of sales, while the cost of price cutting is directly proportional to them. That makes advertising a relatively expensive promotional weapon for Pepsi, and price an expensive promotional tool for Coke. In the model described in Table 15.2, the Nash equilibrium outcome has Pepsi more than 10 per cent cheaper than Coke and Coke advertising 50 per cent more.

So why is this not what these two firms actually do? There are several explanations. One is that one, or both, players are making a mistake. Copycat strategy is a common resort of number two in a market. Number two wants to be number one, and believes that acting like number one will achieve that result. But in any market there is only room for one number one, and hence room only for one number one strategy. An alternative explanation is that equal prices offer a focal point. The observed outcome is not a Nash equilibrium in a one-off game, but might be an equilibrium for a repeated game. The competitive environment is, despite appearances, stable rather than unstable, and rules which would allow the two players to charge different prices are simply too hard to implement.

This chapter and the last have introduced several models of real business situations and problems. They are heavily over-simplified models. When firms use models of this kind, there is almost always pressure to make them more realistic. 'Introduce a smaller competitor.' 'Segment the market more.'

Sometimes these changes give greater insight, but more usually it is a mistake to complicate the model in this way. The demand for greater realism often reflects a misunderstanding of the role models play in the analysis of business behaviour. This misunderstanding is shared both by critics and naïve users of models. A model of this kind does not provide a forecasting tool. Nor can it tell a manager what to do. It is designed to focus attention on key issues—issues which may not have been obvious before analysis began. Shouldn't you be pricing to secure volume if you are the lowest cost producer? Can you compete effectively on advertising if you are number two? Models help to direct attention to questions like these in a more precise way. They exist to guide managerial judgement, not to replace it. I discuss this issue further in Chapter 21.

The best empirically orientated survey of the issues covered in these two chapters is Scherer and Ross (1990), but the orientation is strongly towards public policy. Scherer and Ross is particularly strong on the factors which make oligopolistic markets hot, or cold, wars. Porter (1980) covers similar ground in a business-orientated framework. On pricing generally, see Nagle (1988), Gabor (1977), Devinney (1988).

Tynan and Drayton (1987) is a survey of the marketing literature on market segmentation. The principles of price discrimination were established by Pigou (1920); more recently, see Phlips (1983), and a survey is Scherer and Ross (1990). Implications of geographical market segmentation within the European Community are in Emerson *et al.* (1988) and Davis *et al.* (1989). Focal points are due to Schelling (1960), while Axelrod (1984) is the classic empirical study of co-operative strategies with the Prisoner's Dilemma.

The original economic model of product positioning is Hotelling (1929) but this has been substantially extended and superseded in subsequent work. Eaton and Lipsey (1975); Phlips and Thisse (1982), who introduce the distinction between horizontal and vertical product differentiation; Ireland (1987); Pepall (1990). Positioning as a marketing problem is considered by Ries and Trout (1981), Davies and Brookes (1989). Positioning and focus are extensively discussed by Porter (1980) but the perspective here is rather different.

On the principal empirical examples discussed here: the British TV listings market was extensively documented in a case before the copyright tribunal. Today's position was described in McArthur (1988); for price discrimination by British Gas, see Monopolies & Mergers Commission (1988); the Eurotunnel problem is more extensively described in Kay, Manning, and Szymanski (1990). The GE/Westinghouse case is HBS (1980).

16

Advertising and Branding

Advertising and branding are important tools of competitive strategy. In this chapter I explain why they have been essential to some successful firms, while others have been equally successful while using advertising and branding little if at all. The main function of advertising and branding is to support competitive advantages which are based on the distinctive capability of supplier reputation. The information directly conveyed by advertising with this purpose is generally low. The value of such advertising rests principally on its demonstration of the supplier's continued commitment to the market. Producers of long-term experience goods—those commodities whose quality emerges only after repeated trial—use advertising as a signal of commitment. There are other kinds of advertising, and advertising can help in exploiting other types of competitive advantage, but this support of reputation is the most important way in which advertising contributes to corporate success.

While advertising creates brands, there are some differences between the functions of advertising and of branding. Brands are more often discussed than defined. A brand is established when an item sells for more than a functionally equivalent product. It is that characteristic which distinguishes a brand from the name of a product. The most usual reason for a price premium—and the most profitable reason—is that the customer is uncertain about the attributes of the product and is reassured by the supplier's reputation. But brands have other purposes. Some brands are little more than labels, although labels have their uses. Brands may be used by consumers to signal information about themselves to others—these are what is usually meant by brand images. Yet other brands may be attached to distinctive recipes or incumbent positions. The greatest corporate successes built around advertising and branding are those based on brands which have established several of these characteristics.

Advertising may seek to inform, or to persuade. The classified columns of a newspaper are full of what is intended to be informative advertising:

concise, compressed, and devoid of hyperbole. More expansive advertisements seek to persuade. Or do they?

Fig. 16.1 displays an advertisement for Bell's, which is Guinness's leading brand of Scotch whisky. There is no information in the advertisement. If you wish to learn whether Bell's whisky is a blend or single malt, whether its flavour is sharp or smooth, clean or peaty, what it costs, or where it is available for purchase, you will search the advertisement in vain. You do learn that the whisky is Scotch rather than Irish, Canadian, or Japanese, but that is all. Yet if the advertisement is not informative, nor does it attempt to be persuasive. It does not say that Bell's whisky is excellent or that it represents good value for money. It does not implore the reader to try Bell's whisky. Perhaps the advertisement is a bad advertisement. Its information content is so low that it is quite likely that a reader who was not already familiar with Bell's whisky would fail to understand what was being advertised. However, it comes from a programme which won several industry awards as the best advertising campaign of the year. This is not wholly convincing—just as economists mostly write for other economists, so copywriters often prepare material to appeal to other advertising professionals—but it is widely believed that such campaigns sell the advertised product and there is some evidence that this is so.

If the authors of the advertisement were asked to explain why they thought their work enhanced sales, their account would probably run something like this. The advertisement associates Bell's whisky with the atmosphere of a Scottish country house. Many people aspire to enjoyment of such an atmosphere. The advertisement encourages them to believe that by drinking Bell's whisky they come closer to realizing that aspiration. Set in cold print, this line of reasoning seems simply ridiculous.

This leads us to the conclusion that the effectiveness of modern advertising is fundamentally an irrational phenomenon. Indeed, this seems to be a conclusion on which both staunch defenders and fierce critics of advertising are agreed. Saatchi & Saatchi told us that:

Consumers describe the products that they call brands in terms that we would normally expect to be used to describe people. They tell us that brands can be warm or friendly; cold; modern; old fashioned; romantic; practical; sophisticated; stylish and so on.

. . . It follows that all brands, like all people, have a personality of one kind or another. But like the strongest individuals, the strongest brands have more than mere personality—they have 'character'—more depth, more integrity, they stand out from the crowd. (Saatchi & Saatchi, Annual Report, 1984.)

while John Kenneth Galbraith wrote that:

By art and reiteration people are persuaded to believe in the peculiar conviviality associated with a particular brand of beer, the specific health-protecting qualities of a given brand of cigarettes, the high social acceptability that is associated with the whiteness of shirt collars, the unique moral tone of a particular politician, the desirability or unwisdom of a specific political initiative. In all cases the effect is the same; the buyer is

Fig. 16.1. Advertisement for Bell's whisky

brought to a belief in the purposes of the seller. He or she surrenders to the will of the purveyor of the beer, cigarettes, detergent, or political purpose. (J. K. Galbraith, The Anatomy of Power, 1986, 29–30.)

Faced with this, many firms advertise in much the same spirit as those who spill salt throw it over their shoulder to ward off the evil eye; they do not know why they do it or how effective it is, but they are frightened of the consequences if they do not. Confronted with the kind of language employed in the Saatchi quotation above, many managers are relieved to pass responsibility for the firm's advertising to its marketing department.

But if advertising were truly irrational then we would expect it to be mainly aimed at ignorant and ill-educated people. It is not; it is directed to the affluent and well-educated. If it were irrational, we would expect all firms to use it equally. They do not; advertised commodities are generally consumer goods, not producer goods, and it is short- and long-term experience goods rather than search goods or those for which experience is of little value, which are advertised. Most goods, in fact, are hardly advertised at all (Table 16.1).

Table 16.1. What is Advertised?

Characteristics of the commodity	Advertising as % of value of output
Less than 100 users	0.08
10,000–99,999 customers	0.76
More than 1 million users	2.89
Consumer durables	1.11
Consumer non-durables	3.27
Raw/semi-finished materials	0.12
Components for finished products	0.18
Capital goods	0.31
Services	0.22
Retail distribution	0.35

Source: Davis, Kay, and Star (1991) based on PIMS data.

Not everything about advertising can easily be given an analytical explanation. Much advertising is aimed at a variety of psychological needs, some of which can be established by market research, many of which are still poorly understood. The process of advertising itself is one which involves skill and creativity, and computers are not yet good copywriters. But this chapter is not concerned with how to write good advertisements. It is concerned with the role of advertising and branding as strategic tools which can be efficiently, or inefficiently, deployed in support of a firm's competitive advantages. Most often, the competitive advantage which advertising and branding supports is reputation, although advertising may also be a way of announcing innovation, developing architecture, or sustaining incumbency. This does not explain everything about advertising. But it does enable us to focus on the role of advertising in competitive strategy.

Advertising as information

All producers need to convey information to prospective purchasers of their goods and services. This information may relate to the *availability* of the product. The simple fact of availability is often the essential content of the advertisement. This is what the classified advertisement that says, 'Bicycle, £10, ring 123456', is saying. It is aimed at consumers who already know they want a bicycle, and are well informed about the properties of a bicycle. The advertisement also indicates the means of availability. Often it is unnecessary to explain how you buy the product—consumers already know that branded food is on sale in supermarkets. But advertising may be necessary to bring that availability about in the first place. Supermarkets have limited shelf space and will only stock a new product if they believe that advertising will generate sufficient initial demand.

Illustration 16.1. What Consumers Need to Know about Products

Subject	What the producer tells them
Product availability	
Where, and how, you buy it.	The truth.
Product specification	
What it is, what it does, what it costs. Who is likely to buy it.	A generous interpretation of the truth.
Product quality	The producer's claims are not credible.

Manufacturers also need to convey information about *product specification*. Bell's is a clean, smooth, mid-price, blended Scotch whisky. Marlboro cigarettes are made from fine Virginia tobaccos. A Golf GT*i* has a top speed of 120 mph. Some Minolta cameras have an auto focus facility. Full specifications of cars or cameras may often be lengthy. An efficient method of briefly describing product specification is often to convey information about the characteristics of *potential buyers*. It is possible to say, 'These trousers are made from heavy gauge denim with a pleated front', but it may be easier and more effective to say, 'Jeans for the fashion conscious generation'. More concisely still, you can simply show a picture of the wearer. Producers will also wish to convey information about the *quality* of their goods. They will be more anxious to do so if the quality of their goods is high than if it is not.

All attempts to convey such information are governed by a fundamental principle. *Information is credible only if the provider has an incentive to tell the truth.* In general, producers will wish to be as accurate as possible about the availability of their product. It is not sensible to announce that a product is available if it is not (pre-emptive product announcements are an exception), and you will want to be as exact as possible about where it is available.

It is generally futile and frequently illegal to be inaccurate about verifiable aspects of product specification. There is no point in saying that a camera has auto focus if it does not. If I claim my product is manufactured from Virginia tobacco when it is made from the sweepings of Greek tobacco factories, I risk prosecution. The publishers of this book have a difficult task to perform in describing its potential readership. If they assert that 'Everyone should read this book', they run the risk that those for whom the book is truly intended will fail to distinguish it from the many other volumes in the bookshop. If, on the other hand, they define the category of potential readers too precisely, they may deter some potential purchasers. They therefore err on the generous side of accuracy. A real estate agent gains nothing by describing a garden shed as a mansion, since the purchaser will discover that the description is false. But some exaggeration may induce prospective purchasers to inspect the property. Other aspects of it may then appeal to them and lead them to buy it. So descriptions are flattering, but not absurd.

We typically buy high value items by assembling, from a variety of sources, a short-list of possible products and examining that short list more carefully. An important function of advertising is to encourage you to put the advertiser's product on your short-list. But it is simply time-wasting to be short-listed for jobs to which you will never be appointed. When we apply for a job, we describe our skills and experience generously, but we are foolish if we claim skills we do not have. The descriptions of specifications, and of potential buyers, conveyed in advertisements will contain some exaggeration, but not too much. We all recognize this and we discount accordingly.

Advertising and product quality

But what of performance characteristics that consumers cannot readily verify? Advertisers have an incentive to exaggerate, and they do. Consumers have an incentive to view advertisers' claims sceptically, and they do. The advertising game is shown in Fig. 16.2. We would usually be better off if advertisers told the truth and were believed, but this does not happen; there is a low-level Prisoner's Dilemma equilibrium. In consequence, advertisers have largely stopped making claims about product quality or do so in meaningless ways— washes whiter, goes better.

This is a Prisoner's Dilemma from which there is no escape. It is not possible to change the pay-off structure—there are bodies which seek to prevent advertisers from making factually misleading claims, but that is as far as it can go, and although individual advertisers occasionally make eccentric attempts at honest advertising, there is little they can do to change consumers' cynical

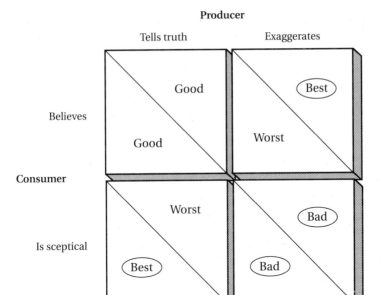

Fig. 16.2. Advertising as a Game

view of the industry as a whole. A curious paradox results. The only information which most advertisements contain is information which consumers could readily establish for themselves.

So how does the Bell's advertisement convey information about product quality? There is one, and virtually only one, important piece of information which the advertisement conveys. It is the fact that the advertiser has spent a great deal of money on advertising. And the advertisement conveys—indeed flaunts—this information; to such an extent, in fact, that the publishers of this book have been unwilling to incur the expense of reproducing it in a manner that does it any justice. The quality of the artwork is superb. The advertisement is in full colour, it is positioned on the back page of large circulation quality newspaper magazines, and it is one of a series of similar advertisements all of which have received equally wide exposure.

That expenditure is a very clear statement of *commitment* to the market. We have just spent 100,000 Ecus drawing your attention to the name Bell's, the advertiser implicitly says. If we intended to disappoint your expectations, to withdraw from the market, or produce a poor-quality product, that would be a foolish thing for us to have done. The advertisement assures the reader that the product is good, but not because it says the product is good. It doesn't say the product is good, and if it did the claim would be viewed with appropriate scepticism. The assurance that the product is good comes from the mere fact that the advertiser advertises. And the strength of this assurance is directly related to the amount the advertiser spends. It would be difficult to explain the prevalence of advertising otherwise. It is inconceivable that there are many people who are unaware that Persil is a washing powder or Coca-Cola a soft drink. The very ubiquity of the advertisements is a measure of the manufacturer's commitment to the market-place.

Of course, this chain of consumer reasoning is implicit rather than explicit. Consumer experience has confirmed that heavily advertised products tend to be of relatively good quality, and consumers react accordingly. Observing this reaction, producers have found that advertising is an effective means of signalling quality to the market-place.

This historical evolution can be seen in Fig. 16.3. The 1905 advertisement emphasizes the qualities of Coca-Cola—delightful, palatable, healthful, indispensable, the favourite drink of ladies. But why should the customer believe these assertions? Would not the Coca-Cola Corporation make them even if Coca-Cola was unpalatable, not healthful, and entirely dispensable? The 1990 advertisement gives no information whatever about the product. 'Coke is it.' 'Enjoy Coca-Cola.' It is difficult to think of valid grammatical constructions with less content. Over a shorter period, Philip Morris abandoned any reference to the 'clean fresh taste' or 'all-day smoking enjoyment'. One of the most successful marketing campaigns in history invites you only to 'Come to Marlboro country. Where the flavour is.' And cigarette advertising has continued despite restrictions in most countries which preclude advertisers from making any claims about the product at all. Advertising began from the belief that customers could be persuaded that quality was high by repeated assertion that it was high. It no longer tries to do that. The medium itself has now become the message. The persuasive quality arises from the fact, not the content, of advertising.

So the advertising we see and read falls into two broad categories. There is advertising which is designed to convey information about product category or product specification. Such advertising is relevant to all the product categories listed in Table 16.2—to search goods like jewellery, to short-term experience goods like paper tissues, to long-term experience goods like cat food, and evenly to goods like CD players for which experience is of little value.

But most advertising is in support of brands and such advertising is conspicuously expensive and generally uninformative. Such expenditure makes sense only if it supports a brand that can itself have substantial value. Table 16.2 shows how most advertising is aimed at experience goods, and especially at those of which experience is gained only slowly. For long-term experience goods, consumers also look to consumer magazines such as *Which*. These are most used where experience is of little value, and here advertising plays little role.

The value of a brand

A brand is established when a branded item sells for more than a functionally equivalent product. This enables the owners of the brand both to add value

Fig. 16.3.   How Advertising has Evolved

Table 16.2. How Consumers Obtain Product Information

Category of good	Average advertising/ Sales information	No. of products in *Which* reports, 1990
Search goods	1.79	4
Short-term experience goods	3.56	4
Long-term experience goods	5.04	17
Experience of little value	0.41	20

Examples	Average advertising/ sales ratio	Typical products
Search goods	curtains 1.17	socks
Short-term experience goods	paper tissues 3.14	pasta
Long-term experience goods	cat food 4.90	outdoor paint
Experience of little value	CD players 0.26	cordless phones

and to appropriate the value which they add. It is the characteristic which distinguishes between a brand and the name of a product.

This is a common confusion. A recent survey of great brands (Interbrand, 1990) cites the TGV as a successful brand. But TGV is the name of a product, not a brand. Passengers travel on the TGV because it goes from Paris to Lyon in two hours, not because it is the TGV. It is unlikely that travellers offered another service with identical characteristics would prefer to wait for the TGV, or that they would be persuaded to use a slow train by renaming it TGV. The TGV is not a brand any more than a refrigerator is a brand or Beethoven's First Symphony is a brand.

Most wine appellations are primarily labels; they describe the product rather than enhance its value. But some—particularly Champagne and Bordeaux—are brands. Many people who cannot readily tell them from wines of similar style without the appellation would nevertheless prefer to drink, or to offer their friends, these especially famous brands. And these examples illustrate that a brand need not be a proprietary product. (Brie, bank, and doctor are also brands. Their value is demonstrated by the jealous protection, and legal restriction, attached to their use.) Mostly, however, brands are proprietary because unless individuals or firms can appropriate the returns to the brand they will not be inclined to sustain its value. Unless access to the brand name is limited its value will be eroded.

What gives brands value? Why are consumers willing to pay more for branded products? First, and most importantly, there is the function of quality certification. I have already described the complex, but still potent, mechanism by which advertising expenditure supports quality certification. But advertising is only one way of creating a reputation and by no means the most important means of creating it.

Price Waterhouse developed a powerful brand in a period when advertising was prohibited on so-called 'ethical' grounds in many of the markets in which they operated. Marks & Spencer established a strong brand at a time when the policy of the company was not to engage in advertising at all. Brand names are potent in many industrial markets where advertising plays no role. How often have you seen an advertisement for ball bearings, or textile machinery, or original components for automobiles? Yet brand names—reflecting supplier reputations—are important in all these markets.

Quality certification is mainly necessary for long-term experience goods. But brands are also found in markets for short-term experience goods. Someone who buys a can of soup today and likes it may want to buy a can of similar tasting soup on the next visit to the supermarket. Branding provides this continuity. There is a need both for continuity and for consistency. Continuity enables consumers to relate their past experience to their future purchase. Consistency is achieved when regular purchase demonstrates that all cans of that brand of soup taste the same. Such consistency has some of the characteristics of a longer-term experience good.

Although this continuity function of brands is important, a brand which rests on continuity alone is not particularly valuable. The characteristic of continuity is one which can be quite easily replicated, and this seriously limits the premium which such a brand can command. There is also no need for more than a few continuity brands of any particular commodity. This can be easily verified in any supermarket. Where the central function of the brand is continuity—canned food, or bacon, or yoghurt—there will be no more than two or three brands available and the price premium between a nationally advertised brand and a secondary or supermarket brand will generally be low. Where branding provides quality certification for long-term experience goods—washing powder or shampoo—many more brands are usually to be found and price dispersion will be much greater.

Brands based on distinctive recipes are not strictly brands in the sense described, because there are no functionally equivalent products. The value of the 'brand' rests in the technology or the organizational knowledge which goes into it, not in the brand itself. To the extent that the attractiveness of Coke depends on that secret formula in the Atlanta safe, it is the formula, not the brand, that counts.

Most product innovations can be quickly replicated. Yet some firms continue to derive advantage from distinctive recipes which others find difficult to reproduce. This uniqueness is obviously exaggerated by advertisers, especially those who appeal to ill-informed consumers. But there is something to Coca-Cola's secret recipe, Colonel Sanders's distinctive blend of herbs and spices, and the characteristic texture of Pedigree Chum.

Or branding may be the statement of a competitive advantage which is based on incumbency. The brand name of an airline is not usually worth a lot, but the route network it comprises may well be. That is why airlines often buy each other, at premiums to asset value, but generally do not retain the name of the airline they buy. Incumbency, too, is the central competitive advantage of some long-established brands, like Mars or Kit Kat. There is nothing very difficult about broadly reproducing a Mars or Kit Kat bar. The obstacle to doing so is the sunk costs of achieving the same degree of wide distribution and consumer recognition in the face of a well-established incumbent.

The pharmaceutical industry illustrates these issues starkly because it displays markets with, and without, functionally equivalent competition. Patent protection ensures the uniqueness of a product specification. For the moment, therefore, the value of the name Zantac is based not on a brand but on the properties of the product which it describes—a distinctive recipe. But when patents expire, the profits Glaxo earns will have to rely on the brand value—on the willingness of doctors to continue prescribing Zantac in the face of competition from essentially identical generic substitutes. The issue, described in Chapter 6, is whether an innovation advantage derived from a distinctive product can be translated into a reputation advantage reflected in a brand.

Brands as signals

We use some products to give information about ourselves to other people, especially to strangers. Clothes often serve this purpose. A policeman wears a uniform so that everyone will know immediately that he is a policeman. Many of us wear more informal uniforms. Male bank managers normally wear suits, and public relations consultants wear different kinds of suits. The functions of a bank manager could be performed perfectly adequately by a man in jeans. But the wearing of a suit has become a conventional signal, and a bank manager who wore jeans would be seen by most people as signalling that he was an unusual bank manager. The rules for women differ from the rules for men. In Southern Europe, office-workers may dress more formally for leisure than for work and in Northern Europe it is the other way round. There is no obvious reason for these distinctions, but conventions are no less powerful for being arbitrary, and not to observe them is, in itself, a powerful statement.

Among consumer products, clothes are the most obvious of signals, but other products, especially those consumed in public places, may often have a signalling role. Cars, drinks, and cigarettes are common examples, and it is in these markets that brands play an important role as signals. Yet a signal works only if there is a cost to giving a misleading signal. Since it is often advantageous to be mistaken for a policeman, the law prohibits men who are not policemen from wearing police uniform. If there was no such law, we would be much more reluctant than we are to trust policemen. The police uniform would not serve its purpose and the intended signal would be ineffective.

However, no law prevents or can prevent people who are not investment bankers from driving BMW cars, or says that only handsome men may wear Levi jeans. For these signals to work, there has to be a cost to giving a misleading signal. Sometimes this is easy, because consumers do not want to give a misleading signal. Beer advertising is often designed with precisely this in view. However, people who are not investment bankers, but aspire to be, might wish to signal that they are investment bankers. Many men who are not handsome would like others to believe they are.

Price may be the cost of the signal. It is no accident that signals of high status are generally expensive, and this puts the producer of such a commodity in a particularly strong position. The high price of the product actually enhances the value of a Rolls Royce. Manufacturers of expensive clothes or luggage have the same opportunity. To ensure that the signal is immediately recognized, it may be reinforced by public display of the brand—the Burberry check or the Gucci logo.

Advertising on behalf of products which act as signals will not usually work unless the message is basically true. 'Bank managers wear Snoopy T-shirts' is unlikely to form the basis of a successful campaign. There is a remote possibility that enough bank managers might believe it for the signal to establish itself, but the possibility is remote indeed. But a small number of self-validating campaigns of this type—Giorgio perfume or Levi jeans—are the basis of marketing legend. Publishing seems to offer exceptional opportunities. 'Hype' is a term for this specific phenomenon. The assertion that everyone is reading a particular book encourages everyone to read it and makes the signal valid.

The signalling function of brands is easily exaggerated because the few successes are so outstanding. In the main, such signals are transient, and the enduring ones are almost all the signals of affluence—diamonds, Rolls Royce cars, Moët et Chandon champagne.

The role of branding

This chapter has identified a number of functions which brands serve. They are a means by which the producer can establish the *reputation* of a product. They provide *continuity*: assurance that an experience good will be the same today as it was yesterday. They may reflect a *distinctive recipe*. They may be a statement of competitive advantage won through *incumbency*. And consumption of a branded product may be a means by which consumers *signal* information about themselves to other people.

The most successful brands are those which combine several of these purposes. One of the strengths of Coca-Cola is that you know it will be both pleasant to drink and fit to drink in environments where you cannot be sure that local products have either characteristic. Indeed the world-wide reputation of Coca-Cola derives largely from its provision of precisely these quality certification characteristics for American GIs during the Second World War. Coca-Cola also provides continuity. Cola is an experience good and it is important to customers that every bottle is the same. There is a distinctive recipe. The strength of Coca-Cola's distribution network, and the universal

Illustration 16.2. The Functions of Brands

• Quality certification	Price Waterhouse, Persil
• Continuity	Campbell's soup, Danone yoghurt, Jacobs coffee
• Signalling	Gucci, Levis, Remy-Martin, Louis Vuitton
• Recipe	Kellogg's cornflakes, Pedigree Chum, Heinz beans
• Incumbency	Financial Times, Harrods, Mars bar

recognition of its name yield major incumbency advantages. And its very American associations give it a strong signalling function. Iranian mullahs do not drink Coca-Cola; aspirant teenagers in less developed countries do.

The Marlboro cowboy tells us that his cigarettes are a means of signalling identification with American culture. A brand strength based around signalling is reinforced by incumbency and continuity advantages. The Price Waterhouse brand is centred on quality certification, but gains strength from incumbency. It also benefits from signalling—many companies believe that having a prestigious adviser enhances their own reputation.

Branding works only for a limited range of commodities. But since branding can serve many different functions, these commodities are of several different types. There are unique purchases of experience goods—car hire and hotels in small foreign cities, automobiles. Brands are prevalent here, are supported by extensive advertising, and when successfully established they command large price premiums. There are goods whose quality is slow to reveal itself—professional services, baby food. Brands are important here too, but word of mouth reputation is often far more effective than advertising in sustaining the brand.

Contrast these with goods for which there is residual uncertainty about product quality—such as washing powder or deodorants. The problem here is not just that you have not learnt about the quality of the product even after using it. You fear you will never know for certain about the quality of the product, and you cannot rely on others to express true opinions. Branding is vital here and these are among the most heavily advertised of all commodities. Branding works also where there is a truly irreproducible recipe—for

Kellogg's cornflakes, or Diet Pepsi—and where the brand is the reflection of the advantages of incumbency—Mars, or Coke.

There are many commodities with none of these characteristics, for which branding is useless. The good is frequently purchased, its quality is easily monitored. The product is relatively standardized and its distribution is easy. In such markets, there are no powerful brands. Think of electricity or transport. Where advertising of these goods occurs, it is either informative—the timetable—or is a means of dissipating profits generated by regulated monopolies—corporate advertising by electricity utilities and international airlines. Few industrial products are subject to the branding which is familiar in consumer goods markets because purchasing is regular and quality is closely assessed by informed consumers. But ball bearings and aeroplanes—industrial products where quality monitoring is truly difficult even for sophisticated customers—are industrial markets with powerful brands.

Although brands serve many purposes, there is a broad spectrum (Illustration 16.3) from those brands where the brand primarily serves the labelling function—canned food—to those where reputation is the essence—accountancy services. As that spectrum is crossed, the number of brands increases. There need be few continuity brands; there can be many reputation brands. Continuity brands command low price premiums; reputation brands high price premiums. The value of continuity brands rests on their volume. The value of reputation brands relies on their price. There is no limit to the number of brands based on reputation which can exist in any market, but reputation drives down the rents to all. There can be few incumbency or continuity (labelling) brands in any market.

Illustration 16.3. The Brand Spectrum

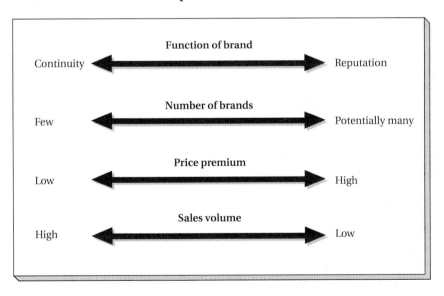

Most of what is written on advertising and branding is concerned with one or other of two subjects: whether advertising is a good thing and how to advertise. The first of these topics has produced some of the most readable critiques of modern business; see, for example, Veblen (1899), Packard (1957), Galbraith (1958). Literary style gives these writers a considerable advantage over the defenders of advertising. Some light on this issue is shed by empirical studies of the relationship between advertising and market structure: Comanor and Wilson (1979) for a survey and Benham (1972) for one of the more persuasive empirical defences of advertising.

There are many books on marketing strategy. Some of these are concerned with the strategy of marketing; the best introduction here is Kotler and Armstrong (1991). Others are simply general strategy books, as with Day (1990). The issues considered in this chapter such as what goods should be advertised, and what not, when do brands yield substantial price premiums, and when not, and how many brands can a market accommodate—issues central to the role of marketing in strategy—do not seem to be widely considered.

The analysis of this chapter draws heavily on the approach to advertising developed by Nelson (1974, 1975), the explanations of the mechanism of advertising of Ehrenberg and Goodhart (1980), and the view of brands put forward by Jones (1986).

The issue of brand valuation has attracted particular recent attention: see Murphy (1991) for a survey of the issues. Barwise *et al.* (1989) deal with the suggestion that brand values should be included in balance sheets. The analyses of Chapters 13 and 16 taken together bear directly on this latter issue.

CHAPTER

17

Vertical Relationships

Competitive advantage can be enhanced by the effective management of relationships with suppliers or distributors. Added value can be dissipated by the ineffective management of the same contracts. In this chapter, I describe the problems and opportunities created by these vertical relationships.

In any vertical relationship, whether with suppliers or distributors, the first, and central, issue is the contract price. This will partly be dependent on the style of the negotiation. Sometimes there is a formal or informal auction; sometimes there is a bargaining process which gives each party scope for obtaining information and revising offers. But the most important influence on the outcome is the range of alternatives available. The distribution of added value between the parties to a relationship depends on the number of alternative contractors to which each has access and the costs to each of a failure to reach agreement.

But contracts are not simply zero sum games, in which one party gains what the other loses. A contract is made to add value, and the design of the contract will influence the amount of value which it adds. The style of the contract is important, because it influences the ability and the willingness of the parties to exchange information and respond flexibly to changing circumstances. I define conditions under which firms should make spot contracts, and when they need long-term ones; when these should be classical, and when relational.

Other factors influence the total amount of added value created by a business relationship. Any contract implies an allocation of risks between the parties. While most negotiators attempt simply to impose as many risks as possible on the other side, this violates the fundamental principle that you can only take a profit on a contract once. So I consider how different risk allocations can influence added value by increasing or minimizing the costs of risk-bearing. And I review other influences on the value of a business relationship—how they can be framed to favour sales of one product over another, and how they may influence market structure. Anti-trust policies limit firms' abilities to use vertical relationships in this way and in the final part of the chapter I describe what these legal restrictions are.

Firms establish vertical relationships with their suppliers and their retailers or distributors. Only if they do so at keen prices will they be able to appropriate successfully the added value they create. But the price is not the only issue. Vertical relationships determine a *risk allocation* between the parties. A specialist subcontractor installs expensive equipment which is specific to a firm's requirements. Who bears the costs if demand is less than expected? Vertical relationships determine the *incentives* partners have to promote the firm's product. How do they allocate their resources, and their effort, between their contracts with the firm and their contracts with competitors? Does a supermarket display goods on the top shelf or in a gondola at the end of the aisles? Vertical relationships can be used to influence the *structure of the markets* in which the firm buys or sells. Retailers may deal exclusively with the products of a single manufacturer, as is common in the beer and petrol industries. Then the retail sector may remain fragmented and entry at manufacturing or wholesale level will be more difficult.

Vertical relationships are contracts, and the design of a contract is often as important as the contract price. You can get more cake either by increasing the size of the cake or by increasing your share. You may be able to increase its size by attention to the impact of the relationship on incentives, on risk allocation, and market structures. You may do best to work through spot, or classical, or relational contracts. These issues are relevant not only to contracts between the firm and its suppliers and distributors, but to contracts and relationships within the firm itself, such as employment contracts, or relationships between the corporate centre and its operating businesses.

The commercial relationships described in Chapter 4 are of many types. Where a manufacturer is only one of many suppliers to a retailer, and the retailer is only one of many outlets for that manufacturer's goods, trade normally takes place on the basis of spot contracts. If the product is somewhat differentiated, more complex issues of contract design may emerge. The producer may give incentives to promote his goods at the expense of others, by means that range from the payment of override commissions to the provision of promotional materials. Contract structure looks still more different, and considerably more complex, once the numbers of potential suppliers on each side of the relationship diminishes. Numbers determine contract price, and influence contract design.

A contract to buy energy is typically a long-term classical contract. Performance is easy to define and to monitor, and the detail of contract design will mostly be concerned with price escalation provisions. An employment contract is largely relational. Many of its terms are implicit. How long is it expected to last? The contract will usually specify a period of notice but that is something very different from the expectations of the parties. How will remuneration be adjusted in the light of inflation, individual performance, and the success of the company? What exactly will the worker be 'expected to do'? These are matters which are usually the subject of discussion before an individual joins a firm, to determine a mutually consistent set of expectations, but they rarely form part of the legal contract. If these expectations are not fulfilled, no one turns to the contract and the parties rarely litigate. The employee leaves the company. *Contract form* is always an issue in vertical relationships.

The quantity of beer sold in any particular bar will vary greatly according to the effort and ability of the publican. The bar staff can be friendly or rude to customers; hard working or idle; they can promote the sales of some drinks relative to others, or of food relative to drink. There are many ways of structuring the relationship between brewers and retailers. Some will attract good tenants and encourage them to win custom, others will appeal only to those for whom running a public house is a way to be paid for leaning on a bar. If the brewers limit the public houses they own to selling their beer, then that makes it harder for consumers to make price comparisons, more costly to switch to a cheaper or preferable brand—it is necessary to walk along the street, not just along the bar—and creates obstacles to entry by newcomers to the industry. This allows the brewers to earn higher profits, and to share these higher profits with the tenant. It will also induce the brewer to invest in providing more attractive facilities within the pubs that sell their beer. Contract incentives may create, or reduce, added value in all these ways.

Sometimes these practices may increase profitability but disadvantage the public, which is one reason why vertical relationships are often of interest to the competition policy authorities. Managers make contracts in these many different ways, although they rarely formalize the reasons. They make contracts in a particular style because experience has shown that particular contracts are appropriate in particular situations and others in different ones. The value of structuring that experience is that it teaches how to make new contracts, how to adapt established ones to changing circumstances, and may encourage managers to resist the notion that serious business should always be done on the basis of the most comprehensive of classical contracts drawn up by the finest and most expensive of attorneys.

The contract price

A contract is not a zero sum game, in which one party gains what the other loses. If that were so, contracts would be signed only if one party was making a mistake. Normally, both parties expect to gain. The contract adds value and price negotiations are negotiations over the division of that added value. Chapter 12, which analysed the effectiveness with which added value was appropriated, identified the factors which determine how added value will be split between the parties—the number of potential partners on each side of the relationship, the alternatives they have, and the contributions which each makes to the overall gains from the relationship.

In any relationship, there may be one, few, or many possible parties on each side. Table 17.1 defines the matrix of possibilities which this generates. In a one-to-one negotiation, any division of the added value from the transaction is possible: both parties would be better off agreeing to it than not. The range of feasible outcomes—the *core* of the negotiations—is wide. As the number of partners on each side increases, the range of outcomes narrows, because anyone who attempts to drive too hard a bargain will be disciplined by his partner's ability to seek other counter-parties. When the number of partners on each side becomes large enough, there is only one outcome in the core. That is the competitive outcome, in which each party is rewarded by reference to his incremental contribution to the added value created. If you are a good bargainer, try the bazaar or the used car showroom. If you have a good product, you may prefer the competitive market-place.

One-to-one negotiation in a situation of mutual dependence is sometimes described as the problem of splitting a pie. (The bakery seems to figure prominently in the analysis of vertical relationships.) If the two parties agree on how the pie is to be shared, they can have it. If they fail to agree, there is no pie. The pie represents the gains from the contract to the two parties taken together. If there is agreement on its distribution, the contract is effected. If there is no agreement, there is no contract. And since the parties each need each other if either is to compete effectively, there is no competitive advantage for anyone.

When the game of splitting a pie is played experimentally, the two players almost always agree within a few seconds that they will divide it equally. Certainly, that is what London Business School students mostly do, and they are probably more aggressive than most. Equal division in commercial life would suggest that innovators who depend on government or primary contractors must expect to give up about half the gains, or that the governments of less developed countries might look for half the returns which international firms will earn from operating in their countries.

Fifty/fifty sharing is a natural solution to the problem because it has an appearance of fairness. And a fifty/fifty division is an obvious focal point (Chapter 15, p. 237). Sometimes real negotiations have this fifty/fifty structure explicitly–as with royalties or with taxes. Most publishing contracts provide that the value of subsidiary rights which are not specifically dealt with will be divided equally between publishers and author. Often, however, the sharing of the gains from competitive advantage will be implicit rather than explicit, buried in the transfer price of a component or a supply rather than the subject of calculation. Here there will be no natural focal point, although a possible approach is to translate an agreed basis for sharing the benefit into a specific price, and this is common practice in subcontracting relationships.

Fifty/fifty sharing is a focal point if the parties see themselves as equals in other respects. If one party baked the pie (or believes so) then equality is a

Table 17.1. Types of Vertical Relationships

Number of buyers	Number of sellers		
	One	Few	Many
Examples of vertical relationships			
One	Some defence contracting	Specialist subcontracting, private label retailing	Franchising
Few	Branded packaged groceries	Heavy plant manufacture	Offshore oil supply
Many	Branded confectionery	Beer, petrol	Agricultural commodities and natural resources
Taxonomy of vertical relationships			
One	Bilateral monopoly	Auction	Controlled competition
Few	Negotiation	Oligopoly	Negotiation
Many	Controlled competition	Negotiation	Competition
Outcomes of vertical relationships			
One	'Splitting a pie'	Second highest bid wins	One takes all
Few	Depends principally on negotiation	Depends on negotiation and relative contribution	Depends on relative contribution and negotiation
Many	One takes all	Depends on relative contribution and negotiation	Determined by relative contribution

much less plausible outcome. Equality may also break down if one or other party wishes to acquire a reputation as a tough negotiator. Mostly, the prospect of a repeated game makes it easier to reach co-operative solutions, but here it can make things worse. Players may not mind losing a pie or two if they will be able to extract a disproportionate share of pies thereafter. But there is a price to pay for a reputation as a tough negotiator. It is difficult to sustain architecture-based advantages in such a framework and other parties will be reluctant to enter one-to-one relationships in the first place.

As the number of possible counter-parties increases, there are two cases to be distinguished—that where the firm selects one partner for an exclusive relationship (the specialist subcontractor) and that which seeks to secure as many partners as possible (the manufacturer in search of retail outlets). The first of these cases is essentially an auction. The firm is looking for the best bid. In a saleroom auction when a picture or a piece of furniture is on sale, the ritual of knocking down lots to the highest bidder has a clear outcome. The object is sold for its value to the second highest bidder. So long as bidders are not swept off their feet by the excitement of the saleroom, the winner waits for all others to drop out and then collects the item for £1 (or £10,000 depending on the units of the auction) more than the highest of their offers. This is a sum still less, and possibly substantially less, than its value to him.

The saleroom analogy cannot be exactly applied to commercial negotiations. The saleroom is an open auction, in which all bids are made publicly, and each player can revise his bid in the light of the bids of the other participants. Business dealings are rarely like that. When there are formal auctions, these are mostly of the kind conducted by public bodies, in which sealed bids are invited, and the lowest accepted. Although at first sight it seems that a mechanism by which upward revisions are allowed would yield a better price, the sealed bid system forces initial bids to be realistic, while in a saleroom auction the first bids will usually bear no relationships to the value of the object. The average outcome is no better, or worse than the saleroom system. Most commercial negotiations are intermediate between open outcry and sealed bid. There is some information and some disinformation about competing offers. There is some scope for revision of bids, but that scope is limited.

So the 'second price' rule is a realistic guide to what happens in analogous commercial negotiations. The price you get, or receive, is governed by what the next best supplier, or customer, can achieve. If all suppliers are equally capable, the buying firm can retain the whole of the added value created by the relationship. If one supplier is best, then that supplier will earn a share which is limited to the amount by which it is best. In a real sense, other firms can only appropriate what they themselves contribute to the relationship.

The choice of counter-party may be afflicted by 'the winner's curse'. In a saleroom auction all agree on what the object is; the bidders differ only in how much they value it. Some commercial negotiations are like that. The specification of the task to be performed is clear, and different firms differ only in their capacity, or their anxiety, to perform it. Other negotiations have a 'common value' property. When oil companies bid for offshore oil blocks, if they all agreed on how much oil was there they would all bid the same. Their bids differ because they have made different—and inevitably erroneous—assessments of the attractiveness of the territory. The winner's curse, which was first identified in the offshore oil industry, arises because the blocks you get are inevitably the ones in which your geologists have grossly overestimated the prospects.

The winner's curse is a particularly serious problem for the rather mechanical tendering procedures often carried out by public authorities. It may afflict both bidders and the authorities themselves. Business relationships typically have elements of both common and private value auctions. Firms differ both in their abilities to do the job and in their assessment of what is needed to do it. In choosing partners, it is necessary to look behind apparent differences in prices to their underlying rationale.

As the number of potential parties on each side of the relationship increases (Table 17.1), numbers and bargaining power matter less and contribution to the joint creation of added value matters more. What contribution means here is the amount which each party can add, or subtract, from the jointly established added value. This may not be at all the same as a measure of the effort which either party has put in. The value of a brand is created by its owner. But a supermarket can add to it, or subtract substantially from it, by its decisions both as to whether to stock it at all and on how to display it. The result is that each supermarket—and supermarkets at large—can extract a significant fraction of the value of a brand, and can do so even in a competitive outcome in which there are many supermarkets and many brands. Competitive markets do not solve all problems of appropriability, and competitive prices are not necessarily 'fair' prices; they are simply the outcomes of the market.

Spot contracts or long-term contracts?

Spot contracts are appropriate for goods of which there are many buyers and sellers, or for goods which are not important to either buyers or sellers. Spot contracts can be used when a party need not incur much in the way of expenditure which is specific to the particular buyer or seller concerned. If all these conditions hold, then the best strategy is simply to buy on spot terms from the most convenient supplier as and when the goods concerned are required. It is probably not worthwhile devoting much effort to searching for the keenest price, since competition is likely to have ensured that there is little variation between firms, and the unimportance of the transaction implies that the savings will not be large relative to the cost of search. For similar reasons, the contract will probably be made on standard terms. The costs of individual contract negotiation are too high. Manufacturers make contracts on that basis with retailers whose outlet or group of outlets are not critical to the success of the product, and when the commodity in question is not a major proportion of the turnover of the shop. That is how firms deal with minor subcontractors of standard parts.

If there are few buyers and sellers of a particular commodity, it makes sense to invest more in discriminating between them. The firm cannot be so confident that the operation of the market will have ensured the quality of the various suppliers. It may be more difficult to gain experience by trying different suppliers. If search is difficult, or costly, the firm will be anxious to lock in its preferred supplier to a longer-term relationship. And if there are few buyers and sellers, the firm will be more at risk if one or other party decides not to continue the relationship.

Illustration 17.1. A Spot Contract or a Long-Term Contract?

Advantages of the Spot Contract

Flexibility to changing needs
Pressure on both parties to perform
Low transactions costs through standard contracts

But a Long-Term Contract is Needed

If there are few buyers or sellers of equivalent products
Where the contract is particularly important to buyers or sellers
Where it is necessary to incur expenditures or acquire knowledge that are specific to particular contracts

In these circumstances, supply contracts are often made for agreed, finite periods of time, which will vary from a few months to a few years depending on specific characteristics of the commodity concerned. Alternatively, they may be indefinite but contain a fixed period of notice—as is common for employment contracts. Where there is a fixed term, both parties are likely to search the market again at the end of that period. Since they know that there is a fixed date of potential termination, both parties protect themselves by looking for alternatives, or for renewals, in advance of that date. This is how firms frequently make contracts for important but relatively homogeneous supplies for purchases as different as energy and labour.

Long-term contracts are essential if one or other party is to incur expenditures which are specific to that particular relationship. Such expenditures may be of several kinds. Customized components will require design activity which is specific to the purchaser, and often the installation of customer-specific equipment. There may be a large investment on one side, or on both, in knowledge which is specific to the customer–supplier relationship. This is often true in professional and financial services. There may be investment in training to handle the supplier's products. This is a requirement in industries as varied as Rolls Royce cars, McDonald's hamburgers, and life insurance. In all these cases, one party or both will seek the security of a long-term contract, which may be classical, relational, or combine elements of each.

Risk allocation in contracts

Any long-term contract, classical or relational, must cope with uncertainties about future events. The profitability of any relationship will be influenced by the movement of prices, general economic developments, and specific market trends. A contract that looks good today may not look good tomorrow. So the contract must assign risks between the parties. The likelihood that prices will change is one which is easy to identify. It is even possible to assign probabilities to alternative outcomes. These are risks. The nature of the exposure is well defined, although the outcome is unknown. Long-term contracts must also cope with uncertainties—events which will affect contract profitability but whose nature cannot now be anticipated. Insurers writing casualty and workers' compensation business knew, and used, statistical data on the incidence of workplace accidents but they did not know that they would one day be faced with asbestosis claims running into billions of dollars. Nor did those who write professional indemnity insurance expect that the collapse of the US savings and loan industry might prove immensely expensive to them. Thoughtful insurers know that these uncertainties exist, and must try to prepare for them, but cannot tell where the next might arise. Everyday commercial contracts must equally be prepared to handle these unknowable uncertainties—oil shocks, new pollution regulations, a Gulf war.

Most companies entering negotiation attempt to impose as many risks as possible on the other side. Although it is easy to understand why they do this, it threatens the basic principle that *you can only take a profit on a contract once.* If both parties to the negotiation are skilful and well informed, then the best outcome for both will be achieved if the contract maximizes the added value from the agreement and both parties drive the hardest bargain possible over their share. Generally some risk allocations are better than others at maximizing these *joint* gains, and a good contract will achieve that risk allocation.

Some risks can be reduced or eliminated. Financial markets enable firms to reduce the risks associated with fluctuations in interest rates, currencies, and commodity prices. Insurance allows a firm to pass on a variety of risks and uncertainties, particularly those that relate to events outside the control of the contracting parties themselves. Often a risk can effectively be hedged by the other party to the contract. If the contract price is fixed in money terms, the risks associated with price inflation will work to the advantage of the buyer and the disadvantage of the seller. So a price indexation clause reduces the risks faced by both buyer and seller. Hedging is a clear, and simple, way of adding value through contract design.

But many risks are unavoidable, and one firm or other must bear them.

There are various reasons why one risk allocation may be better than another. Often it is cheaper for one of the parties to bear a particular risk. The reasons why an international oil company can take the risk of fluctuating oil prices more easily than the proprietor of the local service station are almost too many to enumerate. The oil company can hedge the risk of price variation through its ownership of oil assets. It can raise capital more cheaply. It is better informed about developments in the world oil market. So the oil company accepts a contract in which it absorbs these risks. Often the oil company remains owner of the oil until the moment at which the customer puts it in his tank. This is not because the oil company is philanthropic, or unable to drive a good bargain. It is because the company finds it better to use its strength to negotiate aggressively on other things.

The risk that customers will not choose to use that particular service station is another matter. Local retailers may often be better informed than the company about the factors that influence customers' choice. Many of them are under their control—the cleanliness of the facilities, the hours for which the station is open, the friendliness of the staff. The contract will seek to leave the retailer exposed to this kind of uncertainty, and it usually does.

There are two basic principles of risk-sharing in contracts. Assign each risk to the party which has more control over it. If both have equal control—or, more commonly, if neither do—then assign it to whichever party can bear it more cheaply. Usually, but not always, this will be the larger of the two parties to the contract. With size comes greater opportunity to diversify. Illustration 17.2 shows the various risks associated with the property lease described in Chapter 4, and illustrates how, in broad terms, they follow these principles.

Illustration 17.2. Risk Allocation between Landlord and Tenant in a Commercial Property Lease

Nature of the risk	Who has more control over it?	Who bears it?
External damage to property	Neither	Insurer
General inflation	Neither	Shared
Landlord's needs change	Landlord	Landlord
Movements in rents of comparable property	Neither	Shared
Poor maintenance of building	Tenant	Tenant
Tenant's needs change	Tenant	Tenant

In a classical contract, the legal documentation defines the allocation of risks. In a relational contract, the terms of the relationship will be modified as events unfold. If the relational contract is to be sustained, the modifications have to be on the basis of tacit understanding, and mutual acceptance, of an underlying contract structure. In good relational contracting, the two principles described above are commonly implicit in that contract. Both parties bear the risks over which they have more control, and risks which neither can control are shared according to the abilities of the different parties to bear them. When Japanese automobile manufacturers establish relationships with subcontractors, the assembler typically takes most of the risk associated with uncertainty of demand, and the subcontractor most of the risk associated with specific input costs. General economic uncertainties, which neither party can influence, are shared between them in proportions which vary according to the current negotiating strength of the parties.

Incentive structures in contracts

Contract design is concerned with incentives as well as with risk allocation. Every firm is dependent on the quality and quantity of the work done on its behalf by its suppliers and its customers. Building contracts will normally prescribe the composition of the principal materials to be used, and a surveyor may be employed to check that the specification has been met. But often critical inputs like quality or effort cannot be measured directly. This is another problem with a Prisoner's Dilemma structure. The danger is that the supplier's or retailer's interest is, undetected, to skimp; the firm's to pay only for low quality, knowing that that is what it is likely to get. As with all Prisoners' Dilemmas, there are two routes of escape. One is to try to change the pay-off structure so as to reward performance. The other is to play a repeated game and attempt to establish a relational contract.

The difficulty with changing the pay-off structure is that pay-offs have to be related to measurable variables. A bank can set the targets for the volume of lending through a particular branch, for example, and banks do. But the volume of lending is an imperfect measure of the objectives of the bank. The quality of lending is equally important. Any fool can lend a lot if they are not very concerned about who they lend to, and many fools did. Lending quality is a long-term experience characteristic. And the bank manager has only limited influence on the demand for good loans. This depends as much, or more, on local and national economic conditions, on the level of interest rates, and on other variables over which the branch manager cannot possibly have control. Ideally, the bank would like to reward the manager's skilled sales effort, but it has no means of measuring this.

One approach is to design more complex forms of contract, in which performance is related to some base period, or to the performance of other branches. A weakness of such complex schemes is that increasingly effort goes into influencing the parameters of the scheme, rather than in performing well within it. After all, both are equally profitable. Another technique is to allow the individuals concerned to design their own contracts, relying on the insight that there is a joint interest in maximizing the added value from the relationship. Several petrol companies enter negotiations with their retailers with a sum in mind for the maximum they are willing to provide, or expect to receive from the outlet, and a willingness to contemplate any combination of fixed and output-related payments, which meets their intended objectives. Companies like Hanson and BTR operate on the basis of targets which they negotiate with their subsidiary companies. But in all these relationships, which have strong elements of the classical contract form, both parties have an incentive to engage in strategic management of the flows of information which form the basis of the contract.

Classical or relational contracts?

This emphasis on the management of information brings out the essential nature of the difficulty. There is a difference in the objectives of the two parties, and also a difference in the information which they hold. The problem of contract design arises from the interaction of these two differences. If the objectives of the two were identical, then the information difference would not matter. If both parties held the same information, they could design a contract best suited to their joint objectives. The interaction implies that each party, taken individually, stands to gain from strategic behaviour not only in implementation but in contract design. This dilemma is fundamental to a very wide range of management issues.

The relational contract is a means of attempting to avoid these difficulties. An alternative approach—and that which banks traditionally employed—was to engage in relational contracting in which both players play the high effort–high reward strategy in repeated trials. The viability of this procedure depends on a recognition by both players that they are engaged in an indefinite game. This implies a willingness to look at periods sufficiently long for characteristics which cannot be directly monitored to emerge, and requires penalties for opportunistic behaviour (through reliance on seniority and pension rights acquired through long service). It is at least not obvious that these methods worked less well for banks than the more aggressive classical contracting techniques they began to adopt in the 1970s.

The advantages of pursuing the relational route are greatest where there are major benefits from high levels of trust and co-operation, most commonly through the exchange of information and flexibility of response. That is why there are major relational elements in employment contracts. A classical employment contract can take the form either of a detailed job description or of 'Do what X says.' Neither works well. Almost any job description will be insufficiently complex fully to describe the requirements of the position. Anything that comes close to so doing will be too complex to permit flexibility. Relational contracts with suppliers and customers offer the same advantages, for the same reasons. But the firm will have to look for the protection of a classical contract if the relationship seems likely to be of a clearly finite term. This may be because the need exists only for a limited period (a build-

Illustration 17.3. Should a Long-Term Contract be Classical or Relational?

Advantages of the Classical Contract

You can establish a bargaining advantage
You can protect more fully against opportunism
You may reduce uncertainty

Advantages of the Relational Contract

Better information flows
Better transfer of firm or contract specific knowledge
Flexibility of response

ing contract, for example), or because the pace of technological development means that the very nature of future requirements is uncertain.

The firm should also be unwilling to depend on a relational contract if the costs, or the profitability, of opportunistic behaviour by the other party is very high. Here there are two alternatives. One is to tie down the counter-party in a classical contract. Another is to try to make a relational framework effective by increasing the level of the other party's sunk cost in the relationship. This is done extensively in employment contracts through devices as varied as stock options, pension plans, and seniority-based promotional structures. In supplier or customer relationships, the same results may be achieved by increasing the level of involvement between the two parties, by methods ranging from conferences to bonus structures. All of these convince the parties involved that they are engaged in a repeated game and remove or reduce incentives to short-term opportunistic behaviour.

If these devices are not available, then a long-term classical contract, which defines as far as possible the rights and obligations of the parties over an extended period, is the best solution. Classical contracts are also the best way of driving a hard bargain. It is also possible to construct asymmetric contracts, where the terms are largely relational on one side and classical on the other.

The difference in reputation dictates the structure of many contracts with relational elements. Insurance companies routinely impose unrealistic standards of care and of disclosure. Small firms accept bank finance which is notionally repayable on demand even though they know they could not repay if the demand were made. Managers accept these apparently onerous conditions because they know that in practice they will rarely be enforced. They rely on the reputation of the insurance company or the bank to ensure that it cannot behave capriciously.

Such apparently unequal contracts are not framed the way they are because, as is often thought, there is inequality of bargaining power. In most countries there is ample competition in insurance and banking markets. Even if there is not it is foolish to take the gains from a strong bargaining position by imposing conditions one does not intend to enforce. Since you can only take a profit on a contract once, it is better to raise the price. Banking and insurance contracts share a common feature. There is a need for major relational elements in the contract since the flow of information between the parties is crucial. But there is far more scope for opportunistic behaviour by the insured, or the borrower, than by the insurer or the lender. The one-sided relational contract is therefore matched by a one-sided classical contract.

Vertical relationships and market structure

Vertical relationships can often be used to influence market structure. Exclusive supply arrangements are common means for firms to achieve greater security of market share. They give managers greater control over the distribution system and tend to reduce the attractions of aggressive pricing or marketing strategies. A firm adopting a price-cutting strategy can expect to increase its share of outlets only relatively slowly, as existing contracts come up for renewal. Consumers will have to shift outlet, as well as brand, in order to gain the benefits of the lower price.

Exclusive supply arrangements are most common in specialist retailing where it is feasible for a single manufacturer to supply the greater part of the retailer's product range. Petrol, beer, and automobile distribution are industries where exclusive supply arrangements are common practice. This tends to encourage competition on service quality rather than on price and to increase the resources put into retailing overall. If a wide range of product choice is essential to consumers, exclusive supply arrangements do not work. Although several companies such as EMI and Virgin own record stores, it is not feasible for them to limit these stores to EMI or Virgin records. The damage done to the attractiveness of the store would exceed the gains from promoting the owner's records. Exclusive dealing arrangements are most effective where choice matters a little to consumers, but not too much.

For other products, it is more common to give incentives to concentrate purchasing than to require exclusive terms. Quantity-related discounts make diversification of supply more expensive, since the cost of a marginal unit of output will be less than the average. Companies are frequently forced to give such terms anyway by the bargaining capability of larger outlets for their product.

Both exclusive supply arrangements and aggregated rebates can be used to make entry on a limited scale more costly. Hoffmann–La Roche's practice of giving discounts related to total purchases of all vitamins from them was found to have discouraged entry by effectively requiring a new entrant to produce the full range of vitamins in order to sell any at all. In the United Kingdom, exclusive supply agreements seem to have been ineffective in discouraging entry to the automobile or petrol distribution markets, where excess supply in retailing has enabled newcomers to acquire capacity (although rarely the best). But they do seem to have succeeded in beer, where new entrants have introduced products only in joint venture with established producers.

Anti-trust investigation is often concerned with the use of vertical relationships to restrict competition, either by diverting established suppliers away from price-based competition or by inhibiting or raising costs for new entrants. But it is rare for vertical relationships to be structured solely for anti-competitive purposes. Exclusive supply arrangements are often a means of raising the quality of retail outlets when the supplier invests his capital and expertise in the business. Quantity discounts are often demanded by large consumers and conceded reluctantly by their suppliers. Increasingly, through franchising, the growth of private label retailing (in which the retailer rather than the manufacturer or wholesaler brands the product), and the decline of traditional wholesaling practices, the distinction between manufacturing and retailing has become blurred.

Observing this complex balance of factors, public policy-makers have often been equivocal in their attitude to vertical relationships. In the United States, the courts were traditionally unsympathetic to any restraints which appeared to have anti-competitive form but in the 1980s the attitude of the Federal Trade Commission and the judiciary has been generally benign. In Europe a vertical restraint is a prima-facie breach of Article 85. Any territorial restriction is likely to be challenged but several important exclusive supply arrangements–such as those in petrol, beer, and automobile distribution—have secured exemption under the terms of Article 85 (3). The variety of decision and interpretation in Europe is such that most practices which are commercially justifiable, with the general exception of territorial exclusivity, can be plausibly defended.

T he analytics of bargaining begin with Nash (1953) and have been developed by Schelling (1956), Weintraub (1975). Binmore and Dasgupta (eds.) (1987) is a more recent survey of the economics of negotiation and Smith (1987) of the psychology. There are many practical texts on negotiation; while many are banal, some are the result of more sophisticated analysis, such as Fisher and Ury (1982). Wall and Blum (1991) is a remarkably wide-ranging survey of all aspects of the subject.

A classic study of auctions and auction behaviour is Vickrey (1961). Engelbrecht-Wiggins, Shubik, and Stark (1983) is an extensive account, and Engelbrecht-Wiggins (1980) and McAfee and McMillan (1987) are surveys; a more recent major contribution is Bulow and Roberts (1989).

Issues in forming vertical relationships are discussed in Rey and Tirole (1986) and Tirole (1988). On vertical integration, see Alchian, Crawford, and Klein (1978), Buzzell (1983), Harrigan (1983), and Carney and Gedajlovic (1991). On the competitive issues, see White (1981), Comanor and French (1985), Hart and Tirole (1990).

VI

THE STRATEGIC AUDIT

Successful strategy requires the firm to choose the markets in which its distinctive capabilities yield competitive advantage. But the adaptive, incremental nature of strategy means that the starting-point is where the firm is now. Every firm is part of an industry, a member of a strategic group, and serves a variety of product and geographic markets. The strategic audit of the firm begins (in Chapter 18) with the analysis of that industry, that strategic group, these markets. Chapter 19 goes on to consider the firm's own distinctive capabilities and strategic assets, the markets in which they are, and might be, deployed, and the extent to which they yield appropriable and sustainable competitive advantages. The strategic audit of the firm determines the extent to which these competitive advantages are maximized, and realized.

In this way, Chapters 18 and 19 bring together the analysis contained in earlier chapters of the book and display their practical application. There are dangers in describing a process of strategy formation. The determination of strategy is not a checklist which can be handed over to the planning department, or to a firm of consultants. It emerges from the firm's analysis of its own capabilities, and is part of its everyday decision-making. Nor are there recipes for strategy, or a menu of generic strategies. Effective strategy, based on distinctive capabilities, is unique to the firm that pursues it.

Chapter 20 asks what light the structure of strategy throws on the competitive advantage, not of firms, but of nations. This issue falls into two distinct, though related, parts. To what extent does the competitive advantage of individual firms represent the creation of wealth for the national, or international, economy? And when is it simply an appropriation of wealth to the stakeholders of the firm? I go on to consider more directly how the competitive advantage of nations, or groups of nations, rests on their own distinctive capabilities.

18

The Industry

The strategic audit of an industry begins from the identification of cus-tomer needs. What are the characteristics of the products that serve these needs? Are they simple commodity items or do they have many attributes? What are the dimensions of these attributes? How do consumers learn about them—by search, by experience? Is that experience immediate, or long-term? What markets are served? What are their geographical and their product dimensions? Which are growing, and which contracting? Distinguish, at this stage, as many distinct economic markets as possible.

Costs, returns, and supply are equally important. What are the primary strategic groups that serve these markets? Describe the value chain. What determines costs? To what extent are these costs sunk, or current? Which firms in the industry succeed in adding value? Which are marginal? The next step is to bring these demand and supply issues together. What are the distinctive capabilities and strategic assets of firms in this industry? How sustainable are they, and how appropriable? To what extent have they been effectively translated into competitive advantages?

The answers to these questions enable the firm to identify its principal external relationships (with suppliers, customers, and competitors), to see how competitive advantages are established in the markets in which it competes, and to assess how these factors are likely to evolve. This chapter undertakes that exercise for four European industries—Italian knitwear, airlines, retail banking, and champagne. Taken together, these industries show several of the main problems, and challenges, confronting European business today. Some see changes in the geographical boundaries of markets, introducing new competitors, offering new opportunities. Some face challenges to established patterns of trading relationships. Others experience important changes in the regulatory environment. In the face of these challenges some incumbent firms are faltering, others are moving from strength to strength.

Illustration 18.1. The Strategic Audit of the Industry

The Industry Background

What is the industry?
Which are the major strategic groups? Who are their members?
What are the principal trends in industry and market?
Is there a relevant regulatory environment?

Demand and Markets

What markets are served? Define as many distinct markets as possible, in product and geographic terms.
What are the key product characteristics (in terms of consumer needs, not producer technology)?
How do consumers learn about these characteristics?

Costs and Supply

Define the value chain. Include previous and subsequent stages of production.
What are the main influences on costs at each stage?
Which firms in the industry add value? Construct added value statements and identify marginal players

Distinctive Capabilities and Strategic Assets

Is innovation important? Can it be protected?
Do firms have internal or external architecture and what specific benefits—information flows, flexibility of response, organizational knowledge—do they gain from them?
Are there long-term experience characteristics for which reputation matters? Do such reputations exist?
Are there strategic assets? What is their origin—incumbency, cost structure, regulation? Are they durable?

Competitive Advantage

Define the range of distinctive capabilities which appear in these markets. Which firms enjoy them?
How effectively are they translated into competitive advantages?
Are these competitive advantages sustainable, appropriable?
What is the profitability of the marginal firm?
Is competitive advantage reflected in added value?

Four European industries

In the last two decades, most European textile manufacturers have experienced intense competitive pressure. Low-cost imports, especially from the Far East, have challenged their markets, and although protectionist measures such as the international multi-fibre agreement have brought some respite, the overall picture is one of falling output, employment, and returns. Yet while France, Germany, and the United Kingdom have all seen their share of world textile production and exports decline, the opposite has been true of Italy. The Italian *knitwear* industry is particularly successful. Its output has mainly been directed towards the rest of the Community and Italy now accounts for over half of EC knitwear production. But there are also substantial exports to Japan and North America. Most people would identify Italian knitwear with Benetton and its smaller rival, Stefanel, whose market strategy and positioning follow it closely. But Benetton accounts for only about 8 per cent of Italian knitwear output. Much of Italian production is concentrated in a region around the district of Carpi, north-west of Bologna in the province of Emilia-Romagna. Most of the enterprises in that region are extremely small. Over half of the output of Emilia-Romagna is produced by firms with less than 20 employees and 75 per cent of enterprises have a turnover of less than 5 million Ecus.

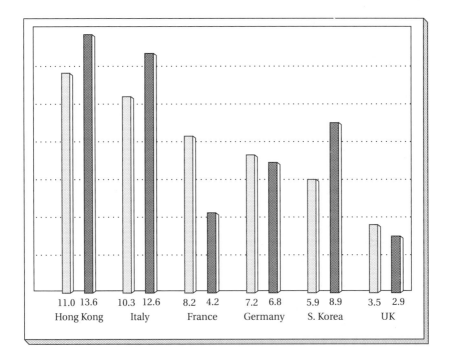

| 11.0 | 13.6 | 10.3 | 12.6 | 8.2 | 4.2 | 7.2 | 6.8 | 5.9 | 8.9 | 3.5 | 2.9 |
| Hong Kong | | Italy | | France | | Germany | | S. Korea | | UK | |

Fig. 18.1. Shares of World Textile Exports, 1973–1986

The European *airline* industry has been tightly regulated by a system of bilateral relationships between governments and a structure of cartel agreements between airlines themselves. These arrangements have limited the number of carriers on any route and fixed the fares and capacity which they offered. Each European state has its national airline, except for the three Nordic countries which have stakes in the Copenhagen-based SAS. From the smaller European countries, flag carriers such as Aer Lingus and Sabena operate both European and intercontinental services. Charter airlines fly passengers to holiday destinations, mostly from the Northern European states to Spain and to Greece. The largest scheduled airline—British Airways—and the largest charter airline—Britannia—are both based in the United Kingdom.

Over a decade has passed since US airlines were deregulated and pressure for liberalization within Europe has grown steadily. A number of 'liberal bilaterals' have been signed—mostly involving the United Kingdom—which have removed many restrictions on market entry and allowed free pricing on major European routes such as those from London to Dublin, Brussels, and Amsterdam. Airline agreements were thought to be exempt from European competition law but the Commission has been able to use its powers to insist on reform. A first set of liberalization measures became effective in 1988 and successive rounds will follow.

Europe looks to US experience to judge the likely consequences. Some well-established carriers—American, Delta—prospered on deregulation. Others—Eastern—did not. Some new airlines expanded successfully, others grew rapidly only to collapse. Concentration in the industry first decreased, then rose again as bankruptcy or merger took firms out of the industry. Some fares fell substantially, especially those on dense point-to-point routes, as in the north-eastern corridor or between the east and California, but others rose. Route structures focused on a hub-and-spoke operation with centres like Chicago, Dallas, and Atlanta acting as distributors for passengers with many different origins and destinations.

Retail banking in Europe also shows a heavy, but diminishing, influence of regulation. In most European countries, retail banking became concentrated much earlier this century. There are three dominant banks in Germany—Deutsche Bank, Commerzbank, and Dresdener Bank—and four in Britain—Barclays, National Westminster, Lloyds, and Midland. The largest retail bank in Europe is the French Crédit Agricole, a confederation of regional co-operative banks, with origins in the supply of finance to French rural communities. Although all these banks operate internationally in wholesale markets, their retail activities are mostly domestic.

In several countries, the conservatively managed banks have seen their markets challenged by savings institutions, such as Bausparkassen in Germany and building societies in the United Kingdom. Otherwise, new entrants to mainstream banking have been few and far between. Citibank is the largest bank in New York, where federal legislation has prohibited banks from conducting branch banking in more than one state, and has made the most determined attempts of any outsider to establish a European retail presence.

Supervision and regulation of the banking system is a primary responsibility of central banks in all countries. The Basle agreements have brought a degree of common practice into the standards applied internationally, but considerable differences of style and substance remain. The European Community's single market programme will not fundamentally alter this position, and banks operating outside their home country will still be subject to the rules and jurisdiction of the host state. The prospect of a single currency and a central European monetary institution raises the possibility of more radical reform.

Illustration 18.2. The Industry Background

	Strategic groups	General market trends	Regulatory environment
Italian Knitwear	International brands with retail outlets—Benetton, Stefanel. Small producers with some common marketing.	Overall demand growing. Shift to higher value products. Strong import competition.	Not important
European Airlines	National flag carriers. Second line scheduled airlines. Point-to-point (charter) carriers.	Overall demand growing.	Price fixing condoned. Entry limited. Both types of restriction under pressure.
European Retail Banking	National full service banks. Local banks. Savings institutions.	Overall demand growing. Shifting (but slowly) from paper-based to electronic media.	Supports cartelization. Restricts foreign entry. Latter under pressure.
Champagne	Traditional champagne houses with grandes marques. Independent growers.	Sluggish demand. Good quality substitutes are increasingly available.	Restricts use of marques. champagne appellation. Tighter regulation within EC.

The *Champagne* region is located around Reims in north-east France. Within the Community, and in some other countries, the appellation champagne can be applied only to wine produced from grapes grown in that area and subjected to the process of secondary fermentation in the bottle which gives champagne its characteristic sparkle. There are many growers within the Champagne area, and traditionally they have sold their output to the Reims-based houses—Moët et Chandon, Dom Perignon, Veuve Cliquot. The names of these houses are associated with champagne around the world, and their marketing efforts over many decades have established the particular position and prestige of champagne.

Champagne is a special occasion drink almost everywhere. The largest geographic market is France itself, followed by the United Kingdom. Sekt, generally inexpensive wine carbonated by gas injection, dominates in Germany. Everywhere champagne faces competition from other sparkling wines, mostly, although not necessarily, of inferior quality. In the United States, indigenous producers are free to describe their wines as champagnes and French champagne has a modest market share.

The long-established patterns of marketing and distributing champagne have begun to change. The once independent champagne houses have been increasingly integrated into the international drinks business. LVMH (Louis Vuitton Moët Hennessy) in alliance with Guinness, owns Moët et Chandon and Mercier. Remy Cointreau owns the Heidsieck labels. Growers have seen opportunities to gain some of the profits of the houses for themselves by direct sales, and minor brands have gained a share. The best-selling champagne in the United Kingdom is now Sainsbury's. These developments culminated in a confrontation between growers and houses at the end of the 1980s. The growers demanded increased revenues. The houses reluctantly conceded and attempted to push their additional costs through in higher prices. Sales volumes declined sharply.

Four European industries—several products—many markets. Each is subject to competitive pressures, and rapid change. The structure of all these industries will be significantly different ten years from now. But who will gain and lose from that process of change?

Demand and markets

Customers buying a sweater look for three principal characteristics—fit, durability, and style. Fit is a search quality. You can find the size on the label, you can try the garment on. Durability has to wait for long-term experience. But what of style? Many consumers can pick style with confidence. They know what is fashionable. Or they know what they like and care little for general opinion. Others are less sure of themselves. Search leaves them confused, and experience is long-term. Your friends will not often tell you that the colours are last season's and the styling suits neither you nor the prevailing fashion.

In France and Italy, where consumers spend a relatively high proportion of their budget on clothes, they continue to rely on independent skilled retailers to advise them on the experience qualities of the goods they buy. In Germany and the United Kingdom, it seems that only customers at the top end of the market are still willing to pay for this service. Where experience qualities cannot be reliably ascertained from the shop assistant they have to be vouched for by the reputation of either the retailer or the manufacturer.

The market for knitted outerwear is a European if not a global one, although there is some segmentation within this. A sweater is more a functional garment in Northern Europe, more a fashion item in Southern Europe, for reasons which are partly a function of local preferences and partly a function of local climate. Manufacturers classify the product market by the type of material used to knit the sweater, but the different uses matter more to consumers. Good-quality sweaters are fully fashioned, while cheaper ones are cut from large pieces of knitted fabric and sewn together. This distinction may not in itself be familiar to consumers, but the consequences for the appearance of the garment are.

If the knitwear market is defined broadly in both product and geographic terms, the airline market could hardly be defined more narrowly. A flight from Brussels to Hamburg is a poor substitute for a flight from London to Nice. Even a flight between the same destinations at a different time of day may be a substantially inferior product. The market is further segmented by the differing motivations for travel. Price discrimination based on this market segmentation is critical to airline economics.

Although most of the important qualities of a flight can be ascertained by search, the volume of relevant information is so large that search can be an expensive and costly process. Simply look at a World Airline Guide. The travel business is therefore one in which the role of the intermediary remains a crucial one. So crucial, indeed, that intermediaries are mainly paid by the airlines themselves. The development of computerized reservation systems (CRSs) which enable travel agents to obtain flight information, confirm booking, and issue tickets in a single operation has changed the balance of competitive advantage within the international airline industry.

But many characteristics of the airline product are assessed by customers themselves. Even for the same journey, airport may matter, so that there is an effective premium for Heathrow flights over other London airports. Airlines acquire reputations for quality of in-flight service, for reliability, and for punctuality, or the lack of these things. Flight safety is important, but is a quality which passengers are unable to monitor, and they look to public authorities to do it for them. Flight frequency and ticket flexibility are important attributes for some customers, but not for all.

A retail banking service is a multi-faceted product. It includes paper and electronic money transmission services, current and savings accounts, a range of interest rates and loan options, and may give access to a variety of other facilities—credit cards, insurance, stock and bond transactions. Yet a striking feature of the European retail banking market is that although the packages on offer in different countries differ considerably from each other, the packages available from different providers within one country are all very similar. This is partly the result of regulation, but also reflects the absence of much competition between banks. While in textiles and in airlines, consumers are free to choose a new provider every time they buy, inertia in banking habits is considerable and consumers perceive the costs of switching between alternative suppliers as high.

Most of the key characteristics of a banking product can be ascertained by search. But you cannot observe the solvency and security of the institution which provides them. All you can tell is that the bank has not yet failed, and sensibly banks have always stressed continuity and longevity in their advertising. But customers mostly rely on regulation to assure them of bank solvency, and look to the regulatory system to compensate them if it fails to achieve its objectives.

The geographic boundaries of the market in European retail banking are national. Many customers shop in a local market, valuing the facilities of a neighbourhood branch, but automatic teller machines (ATMs) and the postal service enable customers to bank anywhere within a country from any other location in the same country. But retail financial services cross borders only when their customers do. There is little cross-border purchasing of retail financial services. It is often suggested that 1992, financial market deregulation, and moves to create a single European currency will change this, and many retail financial institutions have adopted pan-European strategies with this in mind. Citibank, particularly, has made repeated, but not very successful, attempts to develop a presence across what it sees as a European market. But the lack of integration of European markets reflects less the multiplicity of European currencies than the incompatibility of national banking systems, which banks have slight incentive to change. And local knowledge is very important, especially in lending. There is still little pan-European retailing in any sector, and it is further away in financial services than in most.

Illustration 18.3. Demand and Markets

	The dimensions of the market	Key characteristics of the product	How consumers learn about them
Italian knitwear	European (global) market, segmented by price category.	Fit	Search
		Fashionability	Search/long-term experience
		Durability	Long-term experience
European Airlines	Narrowly defined; almost every trip is a distinct market.	Frequency and timing	Search
		Origin/interlining	Search
		Flexibility of ticket	Search
		Service quality	Short/long-term experience
		Safety	Not directly
		Punctuality and reliability	Long-term experience
European Retail Banking	National geographical boundaries. Well-segmented product categories.	Service quality	Short/long-term experience
		Product range	Search
		Solvency	Not directly
Champagne	Global market for commodity champagne. National markets for grandes marques.	Taste	Short term experience (but many customers cannot tell)
		Signal	Search

Champagne is a short-term experience good for a connoisseur, but it is also drunk by many who would find it difficult to tell one bottle of champagne from another, or to distinguish champagne from poor-quality fizzy wine. These customers need the reassurance of the label of champagne, or the marque of the champagne house. And champagne is a classic signalling good. The champagne drunk at a wedding reception is served for its symbolic function rather than to wash the dust of the church from the throats of the guests.

Costs, rents, and returns

The Italian knitwear industry divides clearly into two strategic groups. There are large international firms such as Benetton and Stefanel and the small and medium-sized enterprises of Carpi. A sweater can vary greatly in cost. A cheerful Benetton product may cost 75 Ecus but you can pay much more for a piece of designer knitwear. Fig. 18.2 shows characteristic value chains for these two items. Manufacturing costs are important at the lower end of the market, so that production efficiency can yield substantial competitive advantage here. But in the designer segment manufacturing costs are less significant relative to distribution and retailing costs. The appreciation that added value is more likely to be derived from efficiency and effectiveness in retailing and in earning premium prices by selling precisely what the consumer wants is at the heart of Italian success in the face of low-cost foreign competition. Indeed, part of the contribution of these firms has been to redefine the market by the promotion of Italian style to make that so.

Benetton *controls* the whole value chain, from manufacture to retail, but it subcontracts the larger part of its production and most of its shops are owned and operated by franchisees. Carpi output may be labelled by its producer or sold under the local labels of retailers or importers, particularly in Germany

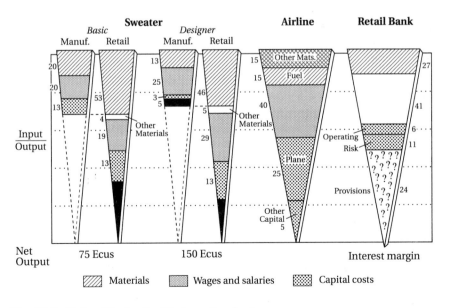

Fig. 18.2. Value Chains for Various Products

and the United Kingdom. Much of this output is designed in collaboration with the merchandiser, and it is also common for importers to visit Carpi or Bologna to select styles. Even though the average Carpi enterprise is small, an average producer will have more than 100 lines.

The *distribution* of added value created in the overall value chain—the shares of manufacturer, distributor and marketer, and retailer—is evidently an important issue. Benetton was one of the most successful of European companies in the 1980s, and this contrasts starkly with the performance of other European textile producers. Benetton illustrates that vertical integration through ownership is not necessary to the appropriation of most of the added value in the value chain. Because of the nature of Carpi activities, no overall financial information is available but the general impression of most observers is that returns were high from the late 1970s to mid-1980s but have since come under greater pressure.

In the European airline industry, costs are dominated by three principal factors—labour, fuel, and capital costs. (Capital costs are mostly those associated with aircraft ownership.) So operating costs are determined principally by the size of fleet and the number of flights operated. Substantial differences in costs per unit of output can result from differences in the rate of fleet utilization (the proportion of potential flying time for which a plane is actually in the air) and in the load factors achieved in passenger carriage, since a flight costs much the same to operate whether there are empty seats on it or not. While crew manning levels are influenced by regulatory requirements, the ratio of ground staff to aircrew varies substantially across airlines.

Cost levels associated with the provision of apparently similar services may therefore vary considerably, and such variations have often been observed. Some of these differences reflect differences in the mix of business, others differences in the efficiency of management. They persist because of the fragmented nature of the markets which the industry serves, so that there are few markets in which more than a small number of airlines compete directly, and because of regulatory intervention and state support of national flag carriers.

European airlines do not add much value (Fig. 18.3). Perhaps the most striking feature of Fig. 18.3, given that individual airlines have only limited control over their own revenues, is how close they all are to a break-even position. It suggests that costs follow revenues—that airlines spend what they are able to raise from their passengers. If traffic is buoyant, costs rise, if depressed, costs are more firmly controlled. This is a common feature of regulated industries and others with muted competition. One airline—British Airways—stands out and is considered more extensively in Chapter 19. So, to a lesser degree, does Swissair.

The analysis of added value for a bank is a matter of considerable difficulty.[1] The 'sales revenue' of a bank is the sum of its explicit charges and the interest margin which it achieves by lending at higher average rates than

1 That is why banks are exempt from value added tax; the complexity of fitting them into a common framework has defeated the tax authorities of most states.

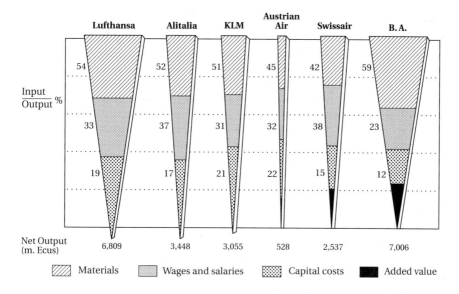

Fig. 18.3. European Airlines Added Value Statements, 1989

those at which it borrows. Against this have to be offset its operating costs, of which labour is by far the most substantial.

The capital of a bank is of two kinds. Like any other firm, a bank holds operating assets necessary for its day-to-day activities. It may own some or all of its branches, it will certainly have a computer system, and fitting out a bank branch is not cheap. These are its *infrastructure assets*—the tangible capital used in the business. But a bank must also have capital in order to protect its depositors against possible losses (this is its *free capital*). Regulators prescribe the capital backing required for each of its principal classes of lending and the degree to which different assets count for these purposes. Unsecured lending needs a higher reserve ratio than mortgages and there are limitations on the degree to which reserves can be held in property (although cash may be included in full). These are the two purposes of capital in any business. Capital is required both as a means of financing the operations of the business and as a reserve against the losses from unsuccessful trading. Banks are unusual only in that they are required to provide these reserves and make these distinctions in an unusually explicit way.

Fig. 13.3 (Chapter 13) compared added value statements for a number of European banks. Among the British banks, there is a relatively clear story. Success in adding value is directly related to the extent to which the firm concerned has chosen to serve the personal, rather than the corporate, sector, and the degree to which it has chosen to focus on domestic, rather than on international, business. The obvious implication, although this data does not permit direct verification, is that the profitability of these banks in these various markets varies considerably. Domestic banking is more profitable than international banking, personal lending more rewarding than corporate lending. This may, in turn, be a product of the different strengths of competition in these markets, or the strength of the competitive advantages which these firms enjoy. Barclay's distinctive capabilities—its reputation and the strategic asset of its established branch network—create competitive advantage in the UK personal retail banking market, but negligibly so in the international wholesale banking market. And for reasons which are connected, though not identical, it faces only a handful of competitors in the first and several hundred in the second.

There are many stages in the value chain for champagne (Fig. 18.4). Land within the geographical appellation of Champagne sells for many times the price of equivalent land immediately across the boundary, and in this way part of the added value of champagne is earned by the owners of land in the Champagne region. Added value is also appropriated by vigneron and champagne house, by governments which charge high taxes on sparkling wines, and by retailers who earn good margins on champagne. Overall, added value amounts to nearly half of selling price, divided between parties all along the value chain. The stakeholder who appropriates the largest part of that added value is the government.

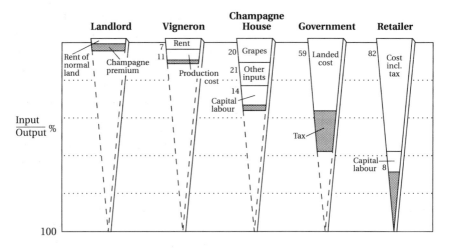

Fig. 18.4. The Value Chain for Champagne (UK)

The nature of competitive advantage

What distinctive capabilities have successful firms brought to these various markets? There are no strategic assets in the Italian knitwear industry. Entry is easy, and frequent. The only important regulatory restriction is the protection provided by the multi-fibre agreement, and the Italian industry has been successful largely because the firms involved have not chosen to rely on it. Innovation has played its role. The transformation of the sweater into a fashion garment was an important development. But this is a clear instance of an innovation which cannot be appropriated by any firm or group of firms. The 'total look' concept of Italian designers has also been widely imitated.

Competitive advantage in textiles rests on branding and on architecture. Almost all clothing is labelled but, as was emphasized in Chapter 16, a label is not a brand. It becomes one when it adds value to the product to which it is attached. Brands will add value to clothing when they convey some information which is not readily ascertainable. Branding may signify durability in market segments where these aspects of quality are important to customers, as for cashmere sweaters. It may also give an assurance that a garment is fashionable to customers who are themselves uncertain. And a brand may act as a signal. At the very top end of the market, designer labels add value, while other signals such as Levi, have been effective, mostly temporarily, in other market segments.

Architecture has proved an important source of competitive advantage in the fashion business. The strengths of architecture are demonstrated most clearly when rapid and honest flows of information are needed across a relationship and when flexible responses are required. The value of Benetton's distinctive architecture is in precisely this area. The same capabilities are to be found in the small, specialist subcontracting networks of Carpi. While other European textile producers invested in the 1970s in technologies designed to enable them to gain scale economies from long runs, and so to compete with low-cost production from outside the Community, the Italian industry exploited an architecture which did not make its firms the lowest-cost producers but which did make them the most responsive and the most flexible. And Italian distributors helped to develop the market in directions which maximized the competitive advantage which resulted from that distinctive capability.

In the airline industry, competitive advantages are largely based on strategic assets. Access to airports is important, and a good portfolio of slots at a major European airport is the best strategic asset an airline can have. Under regulation, certain route licences are of special value. Passengers attach importance to interlining—the ability to complete all legs of a journey with a single carrier. So an incumbent position at a major airport becomes a self-reinforcing advantage, and large carriers gain benefit from this. Computerized reservation systems give advantages to their sponsors, the major airlines. Large established airlines derive further benefit, since operators in travel agencies prefer to use those parts of the database with which they are familiar. CRSs also provide information to the airlines themselves.

A brand name is also a possible source of competitive advantage. Consumers see benefit from an assurance of safety and reliability, and from consistency in service quality. In an environment where the range of available products is so great that search is costly, the brand name is also a shortcut to information. You know that British Airways is likely to have a flight to London, or Lufthansa to Frankfurt, from any major destination. You do not have equivalent information about any other carrier.

Architecture does not seem to be of much importance in the airline business. Most relationships are the subject of toughly negotiated classical contracts. Nor are there substantial competitive advantages from innovation —technical innovation is mostly a matter for manufacturers rather than service providers and product innovations (such as KLM's creation of business class or British Caledonian's structure of discounted fares) are quickly replicated if successful.

Illustration 18.4. Distinctive Capabilities and Competitive Advantage

Industry	Distinctive capability	How it yields competitive advantage
Italian knitwear	Reputation	Fashion assurance
		Designer label
		Assures durability
	Architecture	Response to fashion
Airlines	Strategic assets	Airport hubs
		Route licences
		CRSs
	Reputation	Assures safety and reliability
Retail banking	Strategic assets	Branch network
		Customer base
	Reputation	Assures solvency
	Architecture	Customer relationships
		Employee commitment
Champagne	Strategic assets	Appellation contrôlée
	Reputation	The marque
		The name Champagne itself
		Signalling

The strategic asset of an established branch network seems to be important in retail banking. Possession of an established customer base is also a substantial strategic asset. The most important characteristic of a bank is that it is likely to give you your money back, and, less dramatically, that it will deal with your financial affairs in a responsible and prudent way. This is a classic long-term experience good, for which branding and reputation are vital. Architecture used to be an important asset in banking, and there is a strong need for information flows across a banking relationship which are honest rather than the subject of strategic manipulation. In recent years, however, banks have been ready to discard these ways of doing business in the interests of what they see as a more aggressive transaction-orientated style. The same is true of the internal architecture of banks, where the long time-scales involved in determining the quality of a loan or the value of establishing a relationship provided the rationale for equivalently long-term relationships between the bank and its officers (Chapter 17).

The champagne industry is all about strategic assets and reputation. The most important of strategic assets is the appellation contrôlée. This supports the brand, which in turn has two components, each of which adds value. There is the brand 'champagne' itself, and there is the marque of the champagne house itself, 'Moët et Chandon', 'Bollinger', etc. The function of the brand is partly quality certification. Most people drink champagne too infrequently for it truly to be, as it appears, a short-term experience good. And champagne is one of the strongest of signalling brands. Innovation, other than of the most incremental kind, is something the industry would do well to resist. There was once an architecture, of a sort, in the relationships between vignerons and champagne houses, but this has largely gone in the course of arguments over the distribution of added value.

The future of the industry

Carpi's distinctive capability, and part of that of Benetton, lay in the speed of response to changing fashion trends created by its architecture. The value of that distinctive capability has been diminishing. The development of computer-aided flexible manufacturing processes has meant that large knitwear producers are increasingly able to gain some of the benefits which Carpi producers had enjoyed. Abandoning the mistaken strategic choices of the 1970s, other European firms have attempted to reorganize production in ways which seek to imitate their subcontracting network. In Germany and the United Kingdom, the number of workers in knitwear has continued to decline but the number of enterprises has been increasing. Coats Viyella, for example, has adopted a 'Meritina Team Approach' in which a team of eight operates twenty-four machines with each operator having multiple skills. While a long way from a model of the Carpi network, it offers some of its advantages, in speed of response and mutual monitoring of quality. Carpi organization remains unique (although variants of it are to be found in other sectors of Italian industry), but the region's most successful years of operation are probably now behind it.

Within the European airline industry further liberalization will create a market environment in which only firms with enduring strategic assets, or other distinctive capabilities, can expect to thrive. Most of these are advantages enjoyed by the larger carriers, which have access to major hubs, substantial interlining traffic, and the benefits of computerized reservation systems. However, the costs of operating reservation systems, flexible ticketing arrangements, and providing service levels appropriate to international airlines serving predominantly business travellers are substantial. The strategic assets of the major carriers are of considerably less value in most leisure markets. Leisure travellers are mostly engaged in point-to-point journeys, so that interlining is of no importance, and they attach less value to choice of flight time or originating airport or to sophisticated reservation systems.

The outcome is that a clearer demarcation between strategic groups in the European airline industry will be evident in future. There will be a smaller number of larger scheduled carriers. There will also be a group of carriers serving routes primarily between northern and southern Europe, where leisure traffic dominates. These will be both large and small, since there are no scale advantages in this segment. The distinction between scheduled and charter services, already blurred, has no real function in a deregulated world. Within this structure, there is no obvious role for mid-rank scheduled airlines—either the national flag carriers of the smaller European states, or second line airlines in countries where there is already a dominant flag carrier. Such airlines incur the higher costs associated with serving a business market without fully benefiting from the higher revenues which it can generate. Although mergers and alliances are a likely exit route, it is unlikely that European governments will readily allow their national airlines to disappear. While in the past this protectionist instinct may have enhanced the profitability of efficient airlines by keeping fares high, in future it may depress profitability by sustaining unprofitable capacity through implicit subsidy or willingness to accept loss-making activities.

At first sight, retail banking and airlines appear to have many similarities. Both are service activities in which the emergence of a European industry has been frustrated by regulatory intervention which is now diminishing. The central difference, however, is that while the strategic assets of the airline industry are effective internationally, in banking the strategic assets—the branch network and the customer base—and the primary distinctive capability—reputation—work only at the national level. Retail banks moving into new geographical markets have distinctive capabilities of no real value in these markets and are at a disadvantage relative to incumbents who, in the main, do have such capabilities. To the extent that architecture advantages survive in the industry these too work in favour of incumbents—banking relationships are local as are information flows.

Against this, however, may be set the conspicuous inefficiency of the banking system in some European countries, especially in the south, and the uncompetitive environment which allows relatively high profits in spite of this. This makes entry tempting, but in the absence of a sustainable competitive advantage—and, in reality, in the presence of material competitive disadvantage—it is likely that the benefits of increased international competition will go mainly to bank customers, as a result of the improved performance of established local banks, rather than to the entrants themselves. Although there will be many forays abroad by European retail banks in the next decade, few will be profitable. At the end of the period structures will be rather similar to those that prevail now and changes in share and structure will mostly be within domestic markets rather than across them.

And what is the future of the champagne industry? At present, the industry is seeking to resolve its argument over who should get what share of the substantial added value it generates by attempting to extract more from the public. This is failing. The underlying problem is that the champagne brand, although immensely powerful, belongs to no one, and every grower has an incentive to exploit it rather than maintain it. It is an archetypal Prisoner's Dilemma, and while a sense of collective allegiance to the appellation may once have been strong enough to ensure a co-operative outcome, these days are gone. The reputation of champagne is almost certainly at its peak (and so, it would follow, is the price, in real terms). The grandes marques may well succeed in emphasizing their reputation, and so increasing the differential between theirs and purely generic champagne, but this will require well-considered strategy. But perhaps champagne is not like other commodities. Time, and market evolution, will tell.

Bibliographical notes for this chapter are included with those at the end of Chapter 19.

19

....

The Firm

*In this chapter, the strategic audit focuses on the firm itself. What are its
own distinctive capabilities and its strategic assets? Which are the markets
in which these might yield competitive advantage? Are there other markets
in which, although the firm may not have a competitive advantage as such,
it should nevertheless compete because there are economies of scale or
scope associated with its primary market?*

*What competitive advantages result, and relative to which competitors?
What are these competitive advantages worth? To what extent are they
realized in added value, and if they are not fully realized, what are the
factors which prevent full realization? When and to what degree have these
competitive advantages been reflected in the company's share price? What
steps is the company taking in order to secure the sustainability and
appropriability of its distinctive capabilities and strategic assets?*

*The answers to these questions define the firm's corporate strategy. They
describe the business, or businesses, the company should be in. The strategic audit must also tackle questions of business strategy. The analysis of
markets leads naturally to questions of market positioning and market
segmentation. Positioning will partly be dictated by the nature of the firm's
distinctive capabilities, and partly by an assessment of the positions of
competitors. In identifying its markets the company must distinguish as
many distinct economic markets as there are. What steps can it take to keep
these distinct economic markets apart? What pricing policies should it
adopt relative to its competitors? This latter is partly an issue of positioning, partly one of competitive dynamics. What is the role of advertising and
branding for the firm and in its industry? What is the nature of vertical
relationships with the firm's suppliers and towards its distributors—what
is their style, what is their effect on incentives and on actual and potential
competition? Can added value be effectively defended against them?*

*These are some of the principal issues for a strategic audit. This chapter
poses some of these questions for two companies—British Airways and
Benetton.*

Illustration 19.1. The Strategic Audit of the Firm

CORPORATE STRATEGY

Distinctive capabilities and strategic assets

What are the firm's distinctive capabilities? Consider innovation, reputation, architecture.

What strategic assets does it hold? Are there incumbent advantages, licences or other protection, access to scarce factors?

What are the relevant markets? Identify the product and geographic dimensions. What are the markets in which its distinctive capabilities and strategic assets are valuable?

Are there other markets, linked to these by scale or scope economies, which it pays to serve even if there is no direct competitive advantage?

The value of competitive advantage

What competitive advantages are derived from these distinctive capabilities? Over whom?

How do industry conditions affect the translation of competitive advantage into added value?

Relate added value to share-price/cash-flow performance.

Review the sustainability and appropriability of competitive advantage.

BUSINESS STRATEGY

Pricing and positioning

Does the firm's distinctive capability dictate its market positioning? If not, review positioning relative to competition.

Is the competitive environment stable or unstable? Can stability be increased?

In a stable environment, review industry pricing policies and rules.

In an unstable environment, review pricing strategies relative to competitors.

Are economic markets as fully segmented as possible?

Branding and advertising

How do customers obtain information in the principal markets?

Can reputation/brands be extended, and where?

What functions do brands serve in these markets?

Review sustainability of brands/reputations and evaluate relative to competitors.

Vertical relationships

Define principal relationships with suppliers/distributors.

What is the relationship to market structure?

Is added value defended from customers and suppliers?

How do vertical relationships divide risks, create incentives, and protect against opportunism?

What is the appropriate contract style—relational, classical, or spot?

Two successful European companies

British Airways' advertising slogan, 'The world's favourite airline' asserts its position as the largest of international airlines. United and American Airlines fly more passengers, but they do so mainly within the borders of the United States. British Airways was formed in 1972 through a merger of two state-owned airlines, the short-haul BEA and the long-distance operator, BOAC. Its early years were unhappy ones. The organization was notoriously overstaffed—it was the largest airline in the world judged by number of employees, but by no other criterion—and its efficiency compared poorly with that of other international carriers, which were in turn mostly below the standards of US airlines. When recession hit both the British and international economies at the end of the 1970s, British Airways ran into heavy losses.

After the election of a Conservative government in 1979, British Airways was one of the first state-owned concerns to be warned that it must face the future as a commercial organization. A new chairman was appointed, John King, a businessman with an abrasive reputation and a strong personal relationship with Mrs Thatcher. King recruited a chief executive who had experience, and considerable success, in marketing Avis car-hire activities in Europe. No less important than these appointments was the clear brief that the new management was expected to rationalize the airline's operations and could do so without political interference. The expectation was that a slimmed down airline would be floated as a private company.

The route network was cut back and manpower reduced substantially. With the assistance of economic recovery and substantial write-offs in the early years, financial performance improved considerably. Privatization was delayed by various factors, particularly litigation resulting from allegations that predatory activity by British Airways (and other airlines) had contributed to the collapse of Laker Airways, a cut-price competitor, in violation of US anti-trust law. After a substantial out-of-court settlement had disposed of this issue, the government sold British Airways to the public. British Airways is now easily the most successful of the major European airlines.

It was noted in Chapter 5 that many firms with strong architecture also have a mythology centred around the founders, and Benetton is no exception. It is alleged that the growth of what is perhaps Europe's best-known, and certainly its most ubiquitous, clothing company began the day Luciano sold his accordion and Carlo his bicycle in order to buy their sister, Giuliana Benetton, a knitting-machine. Carlo no longer travels by bicycle and Luciano could without difficulty hire La Scala.

Benetton is located in the second, and smaller, geographical centre of Italian knitwear production—the area around Treviso in the Veneto region. Benetton makes use of the network of small subcontractors that is characteristic of so much of Italian industry, but differentiated its strategy from that of most other Italian textile firms by an early move into retailing. The first

Benetton shop was opened in the university town of Padua in 1969. Today, there are franchised outlets for its products in over fifty countries, and Benetton's slogan—'The United Colours of Benetton'—captures its international appeal and its colourful, cheerful style. The stores are exclusive. They stock only Benetton clothing and Benetton clothing is sold only through them. Although knitwear is still its most important product line, Benetton stores—small and distinctive—now stock a wide range of outerwear.

Yet there are clouds in the Benetton sky. Its expansion into the United States has encountered both legal and marketing difficulties not experienced in Europe. The diversification strategy of the parent company has seemed erratic, and not very successful. Since the company gained a quotation on the Italian Bourse in 1986, its share price has drifted gently downward and its profits record has faltered.

Distinctive capabilities

British Airways' competitive strength is largely based on its strategic assets. The most important of these is its dominance of Heathrow Airport. Heathrow is the largest international airport in the world. London is not only a principal origin and destination point in itself, but also an attractive first point of call for travellers to Europe from other continents. Heathrow is the closest airport to central London (apart from a small City Airport which can accommodate only a limited range of aircraft), and the most readily accessible by car or taxi, although its public transport links are slower and of lower quality than those of London's other airports at Gatwick and Stansted. Heathrow is, therefore, substantially more attractive than other airports in the business travel market. Its advantages to leisure travellers, who are more likely to use public transport and who are unlikely to value the extensive interlining opportunities of Heathrow, are less clear.

Take-off and landing slots at Heathrow are valuable assets, and demand for them at peak times exceeds capacity. United and American Airlines between them paid over 500 million Ecus for the route licences of Pan American and TWA—a measure of the value of established rights to take-off and land. Forty-five per cent of flights from Heathrow are operated by British Airways, and these transactions suggest that the landing rights may be worth as much as the airline itself. Slots at Heathrow are controlled by a scheduling committee, chaired by a BA representative, which operates with a strong bias towards the preservation of established patterns of operation. Until 1991, this bias was reinforced by a Civil Aviation Authority ruling that no new airline could operate from Heathrow. This restriction has now been abandoned with the result that many more airlines, including United and American, but also Cathay Pacific, Delta, and Virgin Airways (a small, aggressive, cut-price British competitor), now have some landing slots.

British Airways holds licences to operate routes to which access is restricted. This is of diminishing value as entry limitations decline. Trans-Atlantic routes are now easy to come by and there is an increasing number of European air agreements, which allow more or less free access to routes between the signatories. Involvement in computerized reservation systems creates a further strategic asset and reinforces an existing one.

British Airways also has a distinctive capability based on its name and reputation—its 'brand'. This rests partly on customers' perception of the safety and reliability of its flights and of the consistency of the service standards it offers. And, as described on p. 298, customers and their agents know that if you want a flight to or from London, British Airways probably has one. These three capabilities—extensive access to Heathrow Airport, possession of route licences, and the British Airways 'brand'—appear to be BA's primary distinctive capabilities. Neither innovation nor architecture appear to be of much significance to BA.

Benetton's initial, and perhaps still primary, distinctive capability lies in its architecture. In one sense, Benetton is an integrated producer, controlling the value chain for the goods sold under its name through the stages of manufacture, distribution, and retail. In another sense, Benetton is simply the centre of a web of relationships between independent, but co-operating, organizations—its various manufacturing subcontractors, its many retailers.

Franchising is now common in many industries. The McDonald's franchise is a classical contract of the most elaborate kind. Not only does it impose extensive requirements on the franchisee, it reads in the McDonald's manual which defines how much beef is to be found in a bun and for how long french fries must be french fried. The result is an extraordinary uniformity in the McDonald's product around the world and from year to year.

The requirements of the fashion business are wholly different. Not only do customer preferences differ in Hong Kong, Madrid, and Chicago, but they also change from week to week. There is a high degree of similarity in Benetton outlets across the world, but also a necessary large element of diversity. Benetton products are the result of a constant process of iteration and adaptation between the company and its retailers, in which both qualitative and quantitative information flows back to Treviso.

The need for quick response in the fashion business is now widely recognized, and often equated with the use of advanced information technology. IT is important, and Benetton's systems are good, but advantages based on IT are not enough. Effective response to fashion requires not just information but analysis and interpretation of that information. It is important to know not just what sells but why it is selling; what reflects local variations or preferences and what national or international trends; and how customers react to products in qualitative as well as quantitative ways.

In this rapidly changing world, mistakes are inevitable, and lines and quantities are produced that fail to sell. In traditional retailing, manufacturer, wholesaler, and retailer each wish to ensure that another ends up with the unsold stock, and this leads directly to the strategic management of information flows. The manufacturer does not wish to correct the retailer's ordering errors, the retailer wants to gain a competitive edge in the availability of this season's best sellers. The exchange of frank and honest information is possible only under a structure of relational contracts.

In contrast to McDonald's, Benetton franchises are relatively informal and quickly terminable, although outside Italy the company typically takes an equity stake in the franchisee. There is a manual on store management and layout, but it is the basis of discussion between franchisor and franchisee in which the Benetton style and experience is implemented in a particular context. This forward integration is particularly distinctive to Benetton. The company's relationships with manufacturing subcontractors have the benefits obtained by Carpi firms described in Chapter 18.

For Benetton, these advantages are now supplemented by the strength of the Benetton brand. Branding in clothing is partly a matter of labelling—reducing search costs in a market in which the range of available products is bewilderingly large. It is also, as suggested in Chapter 18, a means of reassuring consumers who are uncertain of their own judgement that the goods they buy will achieve the look to which they aspire. The Benetton brand has achieved that effect.

Innovation has not been central to Benetton's success. The company did make new and extensive use of a technology by which sweaters were knitted first and then dyed to market requirements, and this was one of the methods initially used to achieve rapid response to fashion trends. But this technology is imitable. (It has not, in fact, been widely imitated and is now less important to Benetton itself.) Benetton's information technology is of high quality, but similar technology is available to many other retailers. Nor does the company have any important strategic assets. There are no economies of scale in its industry, few sunk costs other than those associated with its brand, and the fashion business and the retail business are both ones in which incumbents are quickly swept away if they fail to respond to the changing requirements of the market.

Matching markets to distinctive capabilities

The airline business serves more different markets than almost any other industry. Yet it is quickly apparent what defines the group of markets in which British Airways' distinctive capabilities yield competitive advantage. These are markets for business trips to, from, and through London. It is for these customers that access to Heathrow is valuable. It is in relation to these customers that route licences are valuable (in markets where leisure travel predominates, such as London to Palma or Malaga, fare fixing and route licensing effectively collapsed long ago). And it is these customers who are most likely to value the British Airways' brand.

Are there other markets which British Airways can serve efficiently even if it has little competitive advantage, because it benefits from economies of scale and scope? Although British Airways' competitive advantage in the leisure market is slight, it makes sense to make provision for it. It has often seemed attractive to airlines to focus exclusively on business travellers, observing the substantially higher fares they pay, but such airlines have generally failed (as is also true of other focused airlines such as those specializing in backpackers or budget travellers). The reason appears to be that airline economics (and passengers) do not favour small planes but business travellers do favour service frequency. So an airline which combines leisure and business travellers can offer better value for money to its business passengers than one which carries only business passengers. So British Airways is right to pursue a leisure market on business routes, although it should not seek a dedicated leisure market. It makes sense for it to take holiday-makers to Paris and Rome but not to Faro.

There may also be scope economies in offering routes which, although not profitable in themselves, yield returns through the generation of traffic elsewhere in the network. The route between London and Dublin poses this issue very clearly. Because of close commercial and personal ties between Britain and Ireland, this is one of the busiest air routes in Europe; one of the few on which there is both substantial business and substantial leisure traffic. In 1986 Ryanair and Virgin, low-cost operators offering point-to-point services without frills, entered this market and it is unlikely that the established carriers, Aer Lingus and BA, have made profits on it since. This route lies at the boundary between the leisure routes and business routes in European aviation. But can BA offer a full service to its business passengers without Dublin? In 1991, with profits under pressure, BA abandoned the route.

British Airways' aviation markets are:

- business travel to, from, and through Heathrow;
- leisure travel from Heathrow;
- interlining traffic related to Heathrow services.

It has a competitive advantage in the first of these markets, while the second and third buttress that primary competitive advantage through economies of scope.

Regulatory restrictions have so far excluded BA from US domestic operations, and from point-to-point services in continental Europe (except for the historical anomaly of Berlin flights). While BA has no competitive advantage in operating these services, it may gain interlining advantages from establishing relationships with airlines which do, and BA's (so far abortive) attempts to establish partnerships have a clear rationale.

Does BA's competitive advantage extend to markets outside aviation? Several airlines have seen themselves as participants 'in the travel business'. TWA linked with Hilton Hotels in the 1960s. An ambitious CEO of United Airlines created the Allegis Corporation, an attempt to offer passengers a 'total travel experience' in Westin Hotels, Hertz Cars, and United's friendly skies. The Allegis Corporation was dismantled by its board, under pressure from its bankers, shortly after its creation. Jan Carlzon, the publicity-conscious chief executive of SAS, has taken his company into a variety of air-line-related activities.

BA's strategic assets have no value except in the provision of flights. The only transferable asset is the brand. But the natural brand extensions carry more dangers than advantages. BA's recommendation of Hertz is safe, but of trivial value, since Hertz has little need of BA's endorsement. BA's recommendation of Rentawreck would be of real value to Rentawreck (and so potentially to BA) but BA has no ability to monitor the firm's abilities and so risks more than it gains. BA has no distinctive capability relevant to *running* hotels or *managing* car-hire firms. It is very clear that the 'knitting' for BA lies in the skies.

Benetton's distinctive capabilities are the result of its brand and its archi-tecture. In the product dimension of its market, the brand is most potent in knitwear. In the geographic dimension of its market, the power of the brand is greatest in Italy. As its use spreads beyond that product and these countries, its effects are like those of a stone thrown in a pond. It creates circular ripples, initially of a size comparable to the first, but gradually diminishing in magni-tude until, towards the edge of the pond, the effects are barely discernible.

Benetton has 48 outlets in London, 24 in Milan, and 22 in New York. Possibly all of these numbers are too large—the first two almost certainly are—but the relativities reflect demand as well as supply. Italian style is a mass-market product in Italy, and increasingly a niche item as the distance from Milan or Rome increases. Benetton does, indeed, have some claims to be one of the few European-originated global brands. Its common worldwide marketing activities are, to a degree, mutually self-supporting, but the value of the brand is not the same in all the markets in which it is deployed. And the same is true in the product dimension. The Benetton brand has continued, but diminished, potency the further removed the product is from knitwear.

Distinct from this, although related, are economies of scope derived from the 'total look' concept. It is not just that the brand sells the sweater and also sells the shirt; the sweater sells the shirt and vice versa. If co-ordination of this kind is of real value to consumers, it gives Benetton competitive advantage in related product markets even if its distinctive capability is of no value in them.

Benetton's architecture operates both forwards and backwards. Its relation-ships with subcontractors are principally effective in knitwear. The com-pany's information systems, and its relationships with franchisees, are potentially applicable to a much wider range of fashion items.

In many business areas, Benetton has probably exploited at least as many markets as it is profitable for it to exploit. Market saturation, evidenced by the number of its shops in many European cities, appears to be one reason for the company's diminishing profitability. There is further scope for geographic expansion in Eastern Europe, and in some of the markets outside Europe where the company's market penetration is relatively recent. It is often diffi-cult for a company to accept that its growth is constrained by limitations on the number of markets to which its distinctive capability is relevant. It may, nevertheless, be necessary.

As the company grew, executive authority extended beyond the founding family. A finance director was recruited from Citibank and in 1986 the company achieved a public quotation. A programme of diversification began. Financial services were given particular attention and in 1987 the finance director declared that within two years, the larger part of the company's income would come from financial services. Benetton did form an alliance with a Japanese insurance company; but it is not clear why Benetton's distinctive capabilities should be in the least relevant to financial services and, in the outcome, these ventures do not appear either to have been successful or to have had a material impact on the business of the company. Other moves out of the primary business were less extraordinary. The company now produces Nordica ski clothing and equipment and Asolo hiking boots, having bought established Italian companies with strong brands.

The value of competitive advantage

British Airways' strategic assets, and distinctive capabilities, are reflected more in its revenues than in its costs, so that analysis of the value which passengers attach to its services is the best means of valuing its competitive advantages. The assessment here is based on a survey of the fares paid by a sample of around 5,000 UK passengers travelling to or from overseas destinations.

British Airways' product sells for a substantial premium to superficially equivalent offerings from other airlines.

- The British Airways' brand is worth about 3 per cent of revenues—a British Airways ticket sells, on average, for 3 per cent more than a ticket from another carrier with the same origin and destination. This reflects the value of the search effect—the potential customer knows that British Airways goes—and appreciation of its product quality. This premium relates to London flights.
- British Airways currently operates those services where its brand is most valuable and it is unlikely that the company could command this, or any, premium on a flight between Washington and Chicago. United Airlines, however, might earn an analogous premium on that route for analogous reasons.
- Heathrow is worth, on average, 10 per cent of revenues on European flights—a ticket with Heathrow as an origin or destination commands a premium of 10 per cent over a ticket between Gatwick and the same overseas airport.
- Route licences are worth 8 per cent of revenues on markets to which they apply, i.e. fares are on average 8 per cent lower on European routes where liberalization has been agreed than on those where it has not.

Entry restrictions may be taken to have no impact on domestic services, which have been liberalized, or on Atlantic routes, where there is stiff competition, but still affect around half of European flights and most other international routes to Africa, Australasia, and the Middle and Far East.

Taken together, these factors suggest that British Airways might enjoy a competitive advantage of the order of 15 per cent. Any competitive advantage must, however, be measured by reference to a market, and a competitor. British Airways' added value can be compared with that of its European competitors (see Fig. 18.3, p. 295). BA can also be compared with its domestic competitors (Fig. 19.1). In both cases, British Airways stands out as adding value, but as realizing less than the full extent of its competitive advantage.

There are several reasons for this. One is that the comparison with European airlines cannot be a direct one. They trade in somewhat different markets, and some of the competitive advantages BA enjoys relative to the markets it serves are matched by competitive advantages enjoyed by Lufthansa, or KLM, relative to the markets which these firms serve. Frankfurt is a strategic asset for Lufthansa, and Schipol for KLM. The most relevant benchmark for BA is a London-based competitor, whose brand name is of no real value, which operates mainly from Gatwick and which has a very limited international and particularly inter-continental route network. This is the position British Caledonian and Air Europe held before they encountered financial difficulties, and which Dan-Air occupies now. As Fig. 19.1 shows, these airlines appear to have no competitive advantage and add no value—they are marginal firms within the European airline industry and in London-centred airline markets.

But around half of British Airways' potential competitive advantage appears to be absorbed in higher costs. Some of these costs are necessary to sustain its competitive advantages—in particular, the costs of international representation and complex ticketing and reservation systems—but, despite its well-publicized improvements in efficiency, BA is probably still unable to match the productivity level of these lean competitors. At the start of the decade, the whole of British Airways' potential competitive advantage over British Caledonian was dissipated in lower efficiency. It was the narrowing of the gap during the decade which led to the collapse of Caledonian and its acquisition by British Airways.

The valuation of Benetton's competitive advantage raises similar issues. The company's architecture gives it an advantage relative to other European outerwear distributors with strong brands, but conventional systems of manufacturing, marketing, and distribution. Its brand gives it an advantage relative to other outerwear producers which have access to efficient manufacturing systems, but which have no strong retail brand.

Fig. 19.2 compares Benetton with other European clothing firms which have neither comparable architecture nor strong brands. Marzotto is a large, conventional Italian textile manufacturer. SR Gent principally makes

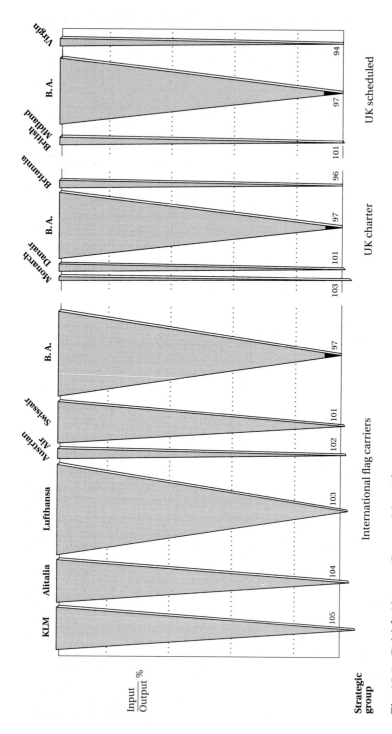

Fig. 19.1. British Airways Competitive Advantage

garments for Marks & Spencer, as does Courtaulds clothing, although Courtaulds also has some, relatively weak, brands. Burton is a UK retailer, mainly positioned somewhat down-market of Benetton, with little strength in branding. All of these companies are relatively marginal and Benetton's competitive advantage over them is of the order of 40 per cent. How does this figure divide between architecture and brand advantages? Fig. 19.2 also contrasts Benetton with other firms with well-regarded brand positions. Stefanel, the only other major company to share both these distinctive capabilities with Benetton, also has a comparable overall competitive advantage. Assessment of brand strength is inevitably subjective, and no other brand aims exactly to reproduce Benetton's market position. But Hugo Boss, Escada, and Dawson International (which manufactures high-quality, conservative knitwear under names such as Pringle and Ballantyne) have brand names as strong as (though up-market of) Benetton, with significantly lower ratios of added value to net output; if the Boss brand name is worth 30–35 per cent of net output, it is difficult to believe that the Benetton brand, in itself, could command more. As a first approximation, then, Benetton's overall competitive advantage might be evenly divided between brand and architecture.

Defending strategic assets and sustaining competitive advantage

British Airways has invested heavily in maintaining its strategic assets. Its management of public affairs is among the most effective of any European company.

Maintaining access to Heathrow and limiting access by its competitors are possibly the most important single strategic issues facing British Airways. The company has mostly been successful. The government and Civil Aviation Authority insisted that British Caledonian should be a Gatwick-based airline. But the attempt to develop a second hub there was rather ineffectual. Perhaps the most serious challenge came when British Midland (a small airline which had traditionally offered a few peripheral services from Heathrow) used the opportunity given by the combination of its established rights at Heathrow slots and deregulation of UK domestic services to build a competitive network of routes to Scotland and Northern Ireland.

The traditional US flag carriers—Pan Am and TWA—became less and less effective competitors. Yet they held the vital landing rights at Heathrow while carriers such as United, American, and Delta, which were increasingly assuming their markets, were forced to Gatwick. This anomaly became more and more difficult to defend. In 1991 the rule barring new airlines from Heathrow was abandoned and all airlines, including these, are now free to compete for slots. British Airways' dominance of Heathrow is by no means over, but it has suffered a serious setback. Lord King denounced the decision in intemperate terms and the company withheld its contribution to Conservative Party funds.

British Airways' attitude to route licensing is more complex. It generally

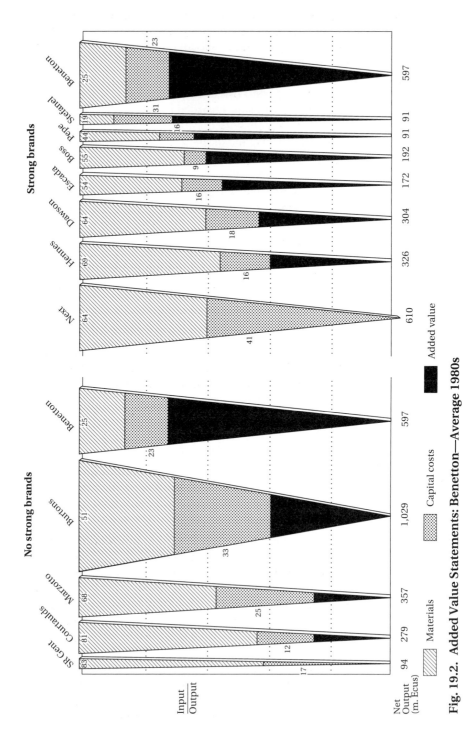

Fig. 19.2. Added Value Statements: Benetton—Average 1980s

supports deregulation, believing—probably correctly—that it has more to gain in market share from a more liberal European environment than to lose from lower fares and new (non-Heathrow-based) entry. Where there are limitations on the number of licences to be awarded, it naturally considers that it should receive them and its competitors should not. This was most forcefully represented in 1984, when BA fought off proposals for major transfers of route licences to British Caledonian, and again in 1987 when it persuaded the competition authorities that it should acquire the operations, and most of the route licences, of its troubled competitor. The European Commission did, however, impose more substantive restrictions on BA's assumption of British Caledonian's routes.

Sustaining Benetton's competitive advantages is not easy. Its architecture seems to have been quite robust to imitation—Stefanel is the most direct attempt at replication although within Italy, particularly, a number of franchise chains with similar features have gained strength. But the value of that advantage has diminished as industrialized producers have been able to achieve similarly rapid and flexible response through the use of technology both at retail and manufacturing level. Fig. 19.3 suggests that the gap between Benetton and Boss or Escada is one that has been narrowing, and the diminishing value of architecture-based advantages is confirmed by the increasing pressure on Carpi producers.

Fashion markets are notoriously fickle, and a brand which signifies fashionability is not easy to maintain. The most enduring brands in the fashion market have been those of the major couturiers—who themselves define fashion—or the classically conservative brands (like Boss) whose brand is partly a signal and partly a continued source of reassurance about style. Benetton was able to give its customers an assurance of fashionabilty in part because it had established what was fashionable. Can that assurance continue as fashion evolves?

Business strategy

British Airways occupies a mid-market position. It does not match the seat pitches or sleeper seats of some of its inter-continental rivals, and has left the provision of first-class seats on European flights to Lufthansa and Swissair. But it seeks, on average, a higher fare-paying customer than its domestic rivals, which are mainly focused on leisure travellers. This positioning is partly dictated by its competitive advantages—which point it firmly towards a business market—and partly result from a sensible pursuit of the widest market consistent with that.

Market segmentation is central to airline economics and British Airways is one of the more aggressive airlines in exploiting it. This involves a variety of fare packages—fully flexible tickets, fixed reservation fares, leisure fares with Saturday night stay requirements or flight restrictions—and the airline dis-

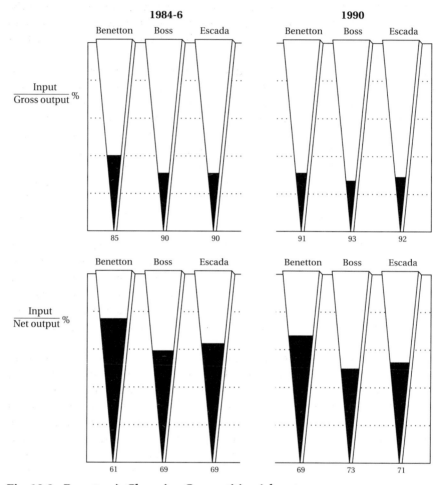

Fig. 19.3. Benetton's Changing Competitive Advantage

counts fares through wholesalers (consolidators) if flights seem likely to have too many vacant seats. Deregulation has brought greater pricing freedom, and BA has used this to widen greatly the business to leisure differentials on those routes where there is a captive business market. Despite competition, no other airline offers the service frequency provided by BA and its partners on the routes from London to Paris and Brussels, and at the beginning of 1992 a fully flexible return fare to Paris cost around 400 Ecus for a 200-mile trip, probably the most expensive major air route in the world and around four times the cost of a leisure fare with restrictive conditions.

Frequent flyer programmes have been widely developed in the United States. They serve two purposes. They reinforce incumbency advantages. A traveller who necessarily uses BA for many flights finds the incentive to use

BA for other flights reinforced. They also exploit the distinction between the business, which pays for the ticket, and the businessman, who may have freedom to chose his flight. BA is pioneering the introduction of frequent flyer programmes in Europe.

BA advertises heavily. Since its name is already well known and its commitment to its principal markets not in doubt, the purpose of this advertising, which mostly has little informational content, is not apparent. Its redesign of its livery and logo in 1984 was one of the most expensive in business history. Some well-publicized marketing operations, such as the 'relaunch' of economy as 'traveller' class and 'the world's biggest offer', in which BA ejected its business passengers for a day in favour of the lucky winners of a ballot, do not appear to have enjoyed much success. In these areas, BA—whose success is built on cold business logic of assets, revenues, and efficiencies rather than on anything mystical or intangible—may have fallen victim to its own rhetoric.

The vertical relationships that matter to BA are those upstream with airframe and aeroengine manufacturers and downstream with travel agents who retail its services. BA's principal suppliers are Boeing and Rolls Royce and although aircraft deals are among the most keenly negotiated of classical contracts, there are relational elements in the continuing exchange of information between manufacturer and customer. The company's frigid relations with Airbus Industrie are notorious.

Computerized reservation systems have had a complex, but profound effect on the world airline industry. A CRS allows a travel agent to search on screen for a suitable flight and then make a reservation and issue a ticket in a single operation. The order and method in which flights are displayed is critical. It is widely claimed that 50 per cent of reservations are made on the first flight shown. The developers of systems can gain by biasing the system in their favour and even if this is outlawed (as it now is under anti-trust rules in both Europe and the United States) operators are inclined to 'camp' in systems with which they are familiar. As a result, computerized reservation systems, which at first sight appear to offer opportunities to small airlines, have in fact strengthened the hands of large, incumbent airlines. BA has supplied CRS equipment cheaply to travel agents and has been closely involved in the development of systems. It first provided a UK package, Travicom, and more recently has been a partner in a European CRS, Galileo. BA has been particularly concerned to discourage adoption of the leading worldwide CRS, Sabre, developed by American Airlines.

Benetton's market position is mid- to slightly down-market. There seems no reason why its distinctive capabilities could not have been deployed in other market positions and Stefanel has chosen a slightly more up-market stance. Since distinctive capability does not dictate position, the rational stance is to look for a large market, or one which is not too heavily populated by competitors. The youth market provides the former, the young adult market offers the latter, as Next demonstrated, and Benetton's position is somewhere on that boundary.

Benetton's policy of exclusivity in its stores allows it considerable pricing freedom. In practice, it pursues a national pricing policy, expecting franchisees to maintain suggested prices (or encouraging them to do so in countries where competition policy prohibits restrictions on retail prices), and so ruling out competition between outlets (which are often located close to each other). The company could vary these prices across different national markets, reflecting different emphasis and market positioning. In some countries where Benetton representation is as yet undeveloped, it occupies a niche rather than a mass-market position. In practice, however, tax adjusted retail prices appear to be largely uniform. The US market—one in which the company might most naturally seek a price premium—is in any event a low-price market. Annual or more frequent sales are an important part of fashion retailing, and Benetton participates, although it does not discount particularly vigorously. Its competitive advantages should ensure that its stores are not overstocked with end-of-season lines.

Benetton also advertises heavily. The company's commitment to the brand is demonstrated by the universality of its retail outlets, but advertising reinforces this. Promotion was traditionally colourful, joyful, and emphasized 'the United Colours of Benetton'. In 1989 the company commenced an international advertising campaign which was designed to shock and offend, and did. It featured a nun and priest kissing, showed a newly born baby, and aroused controversy and created problems with advertising standards bodies in many countries. The objectives of this campaign remain unclear. The company noted that it had drawn widespread attention to the name Benetton. It had, but the approach seemed singularly ill-judged as a means of promoting a brand whose significance rests in reassuring uncertain consumers of the acceptability of their choice.

The way ahead

Both Benetton and British Airways are among the success stories of European business in the 1980s. Benetton has brought Italian flair and style to a mass market around the world and, while still pricing competitively, has achieved margins ahead of the strongest established names in the clothing market. The management of British Airways has transformed an overstaffed, inefficient public corporation into the most effective of major European airlines. Both achievements are the product of focused businesses which have developed around a clear recognition, and full exploitation, of their distinctive capabilities and strategic assets.

British Airways is clearly ahead of its immediate strategic groups—other European flag carriers and second line British scheduled airlines. The strategic assets which give BA that edge may be increasingly eroded, but in these comparisons the company holds competitive advantages as well. So

European deregulation is likely to benefit BA. The company does not have comparable advantages relative to the successful US carriers, United and American, or the successful UK-based, point-to-point carrier, Britannia. But it competes with these firms, and should compete with them, in only a limited number of markets. The message of, and for, BA is a simple one: you will add value by competing effectively in those markets in which your distinctive capabilities or strategic assets give you competitive advantage, and only in those markets.

It is a lesson reinforced by the experience of Benetton. Benetton is a successful company which has, to a degree, lost its way. It has lost its way because it has come close to exhausting the range of markets in which its distinctive capabilities are relevant. The result has been over-expansion in its traditional markets and diversifications which are at best irrelevant and at worst absurd. The urge to do something is strong in successful businessmen, and it is an urge which sometimes needs to be resisted. There is no way in which Benetton can sustain the growth rate it achieved in the 1970s and 1980s. It is difficult to recognize that and understand that in future the growth rate of the company will be conditioned by the growth of its markets rather than by the magnitude of its ambitions. But that is the experience of most companies which sustain their success.

S trategies in the aviation industry are discussed by Levine (1987). For British Airways, see Ashworth and Forsyth (1984), Campbell-Smith (1986). US deregulation is described in Bailey *et al.* (1985) and Kahn (1988), and the implications for Europe in Abbott and Thompson (1991).

The Italian textile industry is described in Bursi (1989), while Lorenzoni (1988) describes Benetton. On European banking, see Dermine (1990) and Piesse (1991). An economic analysis of the champagne industry can be found in Flanders and Thiry (1991).

20

....

The Nation

*While the larger part of this book is concerned with the implications of my
analysis for business policy, in this chapter I consider the relationship
between business and public policy. What are the connections between
competitive advantage in the firm and competitive advantage in the
national economy? The free market system succeeds when the pursuit of the
former secures the latter, but there is no identity between the two. I begin by
looking at the reasons why markets may fail to produce efficient outcomes.
I identify these as inequality of information, externalities, and the existence
of natural or strategic monopoly. When these conditions exist, firms may
add value for themselves but that added value may represent an appropriation of existing value rather than an increment to national wealth. I go on
to explore some implications for business ethics, suggesting that modern
corporations have both classical and relational contracts between themselves and the communities in which they operate, and that business
behaviour is governed by the terms of both types of contract.*

*In the second part of the chapter I look at the competitive advantages of
nations themselves. The basic sources are the same. The competitive
advantage of nations rests on the sustainable, appropriable distinctive
capabilities of architecture, reputation, and innovation, and on the
ownership of strategic assets. Sometimes the value of these distinction
capabilities is effectively appropriated by individual corporations, often it
accrues for the benefit of the population at large. But as with firms, the
pursuit of national competitive advantage relies on the identification of
distinctive capabilities, the choice of appropriate markets, and the maximization of the value of these capabilities. This has implications for the
industrial policies countries should pursue. Wish-driven strategies are as
unproductive for countries as for firms, and effective industrial policies are
directed to the reinforcement of strength rather than to compensation for
weaknesses.*

'It is not', wrote Adam Smith, 'from the benevolence of the butcher, the brewer, or the baker, that we expect our dinner, but from their regard to their interest. We address ourselves not to their humanity but to their self love.' (Smith, 1776: vol. i, bk. 1, ch. 2, p. 15.) Smith went on to describe the 'invisible hand', which drew men to achieve 'ends which were no part of their intention'. Smith drew attention, more clearly and eloquently than anyone before or since, to the greatest of paradoxes in economic institutions. A free market system based on the decentralized pursuit of uncoordinated objectives by individual firms not only works but appears to work better than any other form of economic organization yet implemented.

Smith's arguments have been restated in many different if less striking ways in the subsequent two centuries. Today, they are reflected in two principal strands of thought—two different attempts to account for the economic superiority of the free market system. The 'fundamental theorems of welfare economics' describe the conditions under which competitive markets will bring about efficient resource allocation. A competitive market equates prices to costs, with the result that resources are directed towards activities that reflect their value in alternative uses. A different school, often called neo-Austrian after influential proponents such as Hayek and Schumpeter, places emphasis on competition as a dynamic process. The business environment is endlessly innovative. Most innovations fail, but successful ones persist and form the basis of further development. Natural selection operates as between firms, activities and ideas as the biological process of natural selection works in nature.

The background is one which has produced more striking evidence on the origins of economic performance than any theory could have offered. Early critiques of modern totalitarianism were based on the threat they posed to individualism and personal liberty. The critics did not doubt that these regimes, with their capacity to centralize and co-ordinate resources, would be successful in economic terms. Experience seemed then to support that. Stalin's Russia had taken a pre-industrial society into the age of modern technology in two decades; Hitler's Germany had brought that economy more quickly than any other out of recession. But in reality it was the economic failure of the Eastern European regimes which brought about the collapse of their political systems. Whatever the superficial attractions of central direction and control, in practice it literally failed to deliver the goods. The immediate contrast between East and West Germany provided as close to a controlled experiment as social science is ever likely to see.

The results of that experiment, and its dramatic end, imply that for the foreseeable future the private value-maximizing corporation will be the principal engine of commercial activity in Europe. That makes it all the more important to understand the relationships between added value in the firm and added value in the nation. The first part of this chapter considers the degree to which value creation by the firm is, and is not, translated into wealth creation in the national, or international, economy. The second part is concerned with the competitive advantage of nations themselves, and how that is reflected in the performance of individual firms.

Both the welfare economics and the Schumpeterian perspectives are relevant to these questions. The welfare economics approach identifies the conditions under which the maximization of corporate added value makes the best use of available resources. In doing so, it also identifies the circumstances under which the maximization of added value at corporate level may be inconsistent with the best use of these resources. In the Austrian view, firms that succeed in adding value will prosper and grow, while those that fail wither and decline. From a social perspective, we might ask whether this process of natural selection does truly discriminate between desirable and undesirable characteristics—whether corporate added value is indeed created by forces of enterprise and innovation, or simply appropriated.

Added value and wealth creation

The clear and consistent perspective on the purpose of commercial activity adopted throughout this book is that the objective of the firm is to add value to the resources it uses. Its success in that is both the measure of its competitive advantage and the quantum of its achievement.

Yet adding value for shareholders, or other stakeholders, is not always the same as adding value for society. The issue here is once more the *appropriability* of added value. A firm may—most frequently through monopoly—add value although it has created none. It has merely appropriated it from consumers for the benefit of its shareholders or other stakeholders. Or a firm may create wealth it cannot effectively appropriate, as through innovation it cannot protect. So there is no necessary equivalence between the creation of added value by the corporation and wealth creation in the economy at large. There is a correlation, but it cannot be put more strongly than that.

The social benefits of corporate added value depend on its source. Where added value is the product of reputation, or architecture, there is a broad identity between the private and social value of corporate activity. The value of a company's reputation can very largely be appropriated by the firm which enjoys that reputation. With architecture, too, there is a basic equivalence of private and social interest. Yet when architecture depends on a network of relational contracts, within or outside the firm, the corporation jeopardizes that network if it emphasizes appropriability too strongly. Firms which are typified by strong architecture—Marks & Spencer, Sainsbury's, IBM—are also associated with an emphasis on good working conditions, high levels of employee benefits, and strong community involvement. These features are very evident in Japan, the home of architecture-based competitive advantage. And the returns from competitive advantage are shared more generally. More than averagely profitable firms pay above average wages. Contracts with profitable companies are sought after, and prized when obtained, and one of the common marks of the successful company is that consumers feel its products are good buys.

With innovation, the difficulties of appropriation are particularly real. Newton's invention of calculus may have been the most important scientific discovery of the millennium but very little of the benefit accrued to Newton or to his employer, Trinity College, Cambridge. Electricity was probably the most significant of product innovations ever but Rhein Westfälische Electrik earns more from it in a week than Benjamin Franklin in his lifetime. Much innovation takes place within corporations but is ineffectively appropriated, from EMI's scanner to AT&T's transistor, and the difficulties of appropriation imply that a good deal of economically important innovation requires public funding if it is to take place at all.

In contrast, there are three principal groups of circumstances under which firms may appropriate value they do not create.

- Externalities. Market prices do not adequately capture all the costs or benefits associated with particular activities.
- Information problems. Inadequate or divergent information on the part of buyers and sellers leads to market inefficiency.
- Monopoly, natural or strategic. There is insufficient competition to ensure that relative prices are aligned with relative costs.

Environmental factors are among the most important of externalities. The price of hardwood does not reflect the cost of renewing these resources or the costs of their non-renewal. The cost of electricity does not incorporate the damage from acid rain. In making calculations of profit and added value which are based only on the private costs of these commodities, firms may make choices which, from a wider perspective, use too much wood, or the wrong sort, or too much electricity, or generate it in undesirable ways. Added value may seem to be created at the corporate level, only to be destroyed at the national level.

The appropriability of returns to innovation comes under this heading too. The fruits of research or experiment can be obtained by those who have not borne the cost as well as by those who have. Indeed, there is a sense in which all externalities can be seen as problems of appropriability. If people owned the environment, they could, and no doubt would, stop us polluting it or make us pay for cleaning it up.

Markets may fail when information is deficient. Reputation is the market's own corrective to the problem of imperfect information. But there are markets where product quality is uncertain but there are few good reputations—estate agency and used car trading. There are others—medicine, airlines, and banking—where customers and politicians have insisted that reputation is supplemented by explicit regulation. They suspect that in these markets traders may exploit their superior information, as financial swindlers do, or simply behave complacently in the light of it. Concern for reputation may not give all airlines or all doctors sufficient incentive to maintain suitably high standards.

Differences in information often allow the creation of private added value through arbitrage. Knowing a stock is worth £2 when it is selling for £1 is as profitable as making it worth £2 when it was previously worth £1. Discovering value can be as privately rewarding as creating it. The information that the stock is worth more than previously thought is certainly valuable, but it is very unlikely that it is as valuable as it is remunerative. In this way, much of the added value created in the financial sector represents an appropriation of wealth, rather than an addition to it.

A firm is most often able to appropriate value it does not create when it holds a strategic asset. It is many years since the Earl of Lauderdale observed the potential addition to profits (Lauderdale, 1804, quoted by Stigler, 1966), and hence, he reasoned, to national wealth, from the creation of a water monopoly. But the profit represents an appropriation, not a creation, of wealth. The added value from plentiful water supplies was always there, and returns arise from the ability to lay claim to it.

Analogously, while British Telecom's profits do reflect the very large value of the telecommunications services it provides, that results from the public's need for communication, not the distinctive capability of the firm. If BT did not exist, other firms could, and would, provide analogous services at similar cost. The water monopolist does not create the value of the water supply, nor does the French cinema usherette who needs to be paid 2 francs not to obstruct your access to your seat add value to the film. A competitive advantage is, mostly, a public asset as well as a private one. A strategic asset is often held at the expense of the community.

Public policy and business ethics

The creation of added value at corporate and at national level cannot be assumed to be identical. That raises substantive questions about the ethics of business behaviour. When is it right for the corporation to appropriate wealth which it has not itself created?

Two extreme positions can be dismissed more or less immediately. It is not the job of the corporation to be arbiter or monitor of social welfare. Even if the company's managers were able sensibly to interpret such obligations, experience of state industries given imprecisely defined social objectives has shown that they are not, in the main, well-managed businesses. Simply from the point of view of operational effectiveness, it has been found desirable to set out narrower, more commercial targets.

But it is no more plausible to argue that the company may take any legal action which increases its profits. The supply of artificial limbs to British hospitals by subsidiaries of BTR, which together held around 75 per cent of the market, was the subject of an investigation by the Monopolies and Mergers Commission, which established that the company had regularly withheld supplies in order to secure price increases and had supplied misleading information as part of a process of what the company described as 'skilful negotia-tion'. Just as there are individual actions which are legal but wrong, so, too, there are corporate actions that are legal but wrong.

Managers often respond to these dilemmas by denying that they exist. Concern for the environment may be in the long-run interests of the corpora-tion even if damaging to its short-term profits. 'Good business is profitable business' is the theme of most of what is written on business ethics. Often this is true. The actions of the limb suppliers ultimately proved commercially fool-ish as well as morally dubious. The problem with the maxim that honesty is the best policy is not just that it is devoid of ethical content but that it gives no guidance as to what to do if, as is sometimes the case, honesty is not the best policy. A firm which imposes higher environmental standards on itself than its competitors are willing to adopt puts itself at a competitive disadvantage, may derive no long-run benefit that does not accrue equally to them, and can offset the costs it incurs only by gains, if any, to its reputation.

Often managers escape this difficulty by persuading themselves that corporate and public interests are identical. The executives of regulated industries routinely argue that increased competition would be damaging to the public interest. Sometimes this is true, sometimes it is not. No one should doubt that, in the main, they genuinely believe what they say. But what should they do if they know that preservation of their monopoly is not in the best interests of the public even though it is in the best interests of the firm?

To recognize these problems is only to begin to solve them. It is necessary to talk of business ethics, as of individual ethics. But the manager's position is yet more difficult because he is responsible not only to himself but to other stakeholders—shareholders, employees, customers—who have a legitimate concern for both the ethical behaviour and the financial performance of the firm. This pulls in many directions. It is more admirable to take a principled stance, or engage in philanthropic behaviour, with one's own money than with other people's. It is also more difficult to assess what that stand or that behaviour should be if one is responsible to a variety of groups with diverse values, expectations, and aspirations.

So what are the social obligations of business? The firm has both classical and relational contracts with government and the community. These classical contracts cover matters such as the tax the company must pay, or the prices which a regulated utility may charge. The government lays down the rules, the company must observe them, the state monitors compliance. There is not the smallest obligation on the firm to pay more tax than is legally required, or to keep prices below the level which the regulator will allow. If the govern-ment, or the regulator, or the public at large do not like the result then the rules can and should be changed. A new classical contract should be deter-mined.

But there are other matters which cannot be dealt with in this way. The community is entitled to expect that firms will show concern for the health and safety of employees, customers, and the public at large. It supports this expectation by laws which determine standards and impose civil and criminal penalties on those who fail to meet them. But the reality is that these matters are not dealt with well by regulations. In most contexts, safety is achieved by attitudes and behaviour rather than by close attention to rules.

In these areas—where there are social expectations of business behaviour which must be the subject of interpretation rather than precisely formulated obligations—there is an obvious Prisoner's Dilemma. The short-run commercial interest of every firm is to sail as close to the wind as the law will allow. But if they do so the result, and the necessary result, will be a detailed set of regulations for all firms which are not the best way of ensuring the common objective and which involve material and probably costly interference with ordinary business behaviour. The best outcome for everyone is for firms to see themselves engaged in a repeated game, to behave in a responsible manner, and for society to respond with a light regulatory rein—to achieve a win–win outcome to this Prisoner's Dilemma.

That is what is sensibly meant by the social responsibility of business. It is the establishment of standards of behaviour in areas where society has legitimate expectations of business but where these expectations cannot sensibly be given precise definition, quantification, and monitoring. Safety is an example; others would include the provision of training, the employment of disadvantaged groups, and the determination of transfer prices between divisions of international companies. All these are better handled through relational rather than classical contracts. Sometimes they can only be handled through relational contracts.

The content of these relational contracts—as with all relational contracts—is context and culture specific. A multinational company cannot lay down completely general rules, since being a good citizen means something different in the different jurisdictions within which it operates. The social responsibility of business is not the same in India as in the United States, not the same in Italy as in Britain. And the more extensive and demanding the range of classical contracts, the less the scope for the relational contract. Environments that encourage individualism, and tolerate opportunism, may take the same view of corporations. Local managers must be sensitive to these nuances within the overall framework of their corporate policy.

An important implication for public policy is that the less often managers are put in the position of being forced to choose between corporate advantage and social concerns the better. Capitalism works at its best when managers can single-mindedly pursue the interests of their own firm, knowing that in adding value at the corporate level they are also creating wealth for society. That means that environmental policies should ensure that the price of corporate inputs and outputs adequately reflects the costs imposed. It means anti-trust policies that ensure competitive advantage is achieved in competitive markets, and it means regulatory policies which clearly define the limits within which unavoidable monopoly power can legitimately be exercised. Although businessmen regularly excoriate these policies, the more thoughtful among them recognize that they are necessary if capitalism is to survive, or to deserve to survive.[1]

From the competitive advantage of nations to the competitive advantage of firms

Firms add value by competitive advantages established through innovation, reputation, and architecture, and by the management of strategic assets. In an international trading environment, we can look to the competitive advantage of nations within the world economy as we look to the competitive advantage of firms within their commercial environment.

The analogy holds only loosely. Just as large firms typically consist of many different operating businesses, which can maintain many distinct competitive advantages, so nations encompass many different varieties of economic activity. Yet the ways in which value is added and appropriated by countries are sufficiently similar to the ways in which value is added and appropriated by firms for the comparison to be worth pursuing.

Table 20.1 shows an assessment of added value for some nations of the world. The opportunity cost of factors to countries is less obvious than that for firms. Capital costs are set at 30 per cent of GDP and the cost of labour calculated such that added value in Portugal is zero. (Portugal is a country today marginal to the world's industrialized economies as Asda is marginal to British supermarket chains.) If competitive advantage is appropriately measured by reference to the performance of the marginal firm in its industry, the competitive advantage of nations is equally measured by reference to the performance of an economy which is marginal in relation to the industrialized world. This figure is not to be taken particularly seriously. It is a demonstration of a concept rather than a sober assessment of national competitive advantage. One consequence of this benchmark is that for most countries of the world, added value is negative. A majority of the world population lives in these countries. This may seem a harsh judgement, but not necessarily an inappropriate one. It is simply an assertion that most world economies are making ineffective use of their resources of capital and labour. National economic and social structures are more likely to be persistently value subtracting than corporate ones, because value subtracting companies eventually go broke. While there are some similar forces at work among nations, as the recent experience of Eastern Europe brings out, they are much slower and less effective.

1 In the United States, the excesses of capitalist behaviour have been controlled more effectively and for much longer than in Europe through anti-trust legislation since the 1890s and through securities laws since the 1930s. Fines, damages, and even imprisonment are imposed on businessmen who exceed the limits of permissible behaviour. Yet the rationale of capitalism itself is barely questioned and unions have never enjoyed the power achieved in Europe, nor has nationalization enjoyed popular support.

Table 20.1. Which Nations Add Value?

	GDP (bn. Ecus)	Nos. employed (m.)	Labour cost (bn. Ecus)	Capital cost (bn. Ecus)	Added value (bn. Ecus)	Input Output
Switzerland	1798	3.84	257	540	1,002	0.44
Germany	11,997	29.89	1,998	3,599	6,400	0.47
Norway	836	2.14	143	251	442	0.47
France	9,425	24.57	1,643	2,828	4,955	0.47
Japan	23,623	63.84	4,268	7,087	12,268	0.48
Italy	8,623	24.08	1,610	2,587	4,426	0.49
Kuwait	173	0.50	33	52	88	0.49
USA	40,446	123.87	8,282	12,134	20,031	0.50
UK	7,907	28.27	1,890	2,372	3,645	0.54
Portugal	476	4.99	333	143	0	1.00
Mexico	1,251	28.85	1,929	375	−1,053	1.84
Thailand	605	30.39	2,032	181	−1,609	3.66
Pakistan	294	32.81	2,193	88	−1,988	7.77
Nigeria	205	29.97	2,004	61	−1,861	10.08
Bangladesh	136	30.92	2,067	41	−1,972	15.49

Sources: International Financial Statistics; Yearbook of Labour Statistics.

The four factors of innovation, reputation, architecture, and strategic assets are instructive in explaining this list, but the balance among them is a rather different one. There are national reputations. The reputation for reliability established by many individual Japanese manufacturers may have attached itself to Japanese products as a generic category (and if, as is likely, the factors which make the achievement of high product quality possible for one Japanese manufacturer make the same achievement possible for all, this is a rational attitude for consumers to take). Swiss banks have a reputation for secrecy and security which appears to adhere to Swiss banks collectively rather than individually. American associations are important in the international success of Coke, Marlboro, and McDonald's (Marlboro advertising emphasizes this and Coke now seeks to play it down). But reputation is principally associated with the individual seller and returns to reputation accrue primarily at the level of the individual corporation.

Where innovation is very specific and appropriable then the value of the innovation is reaped by the innovator, and the contribution of innovation to national competitive advantage is broadly equal to the sum of the contributions of individual innovations to the competitive advantage of individual companies. The poor appropriability of much innovation, which works to the detriment of the creation of competitive advantage through innovation at the corporate level, often works to the advantage of the creation of competitive advantage through innovation at the national level. Although scientific knowledge observes no national boundaries as it observes no corporate boundaries, the transfer of expertise is always easier between those who work in geographical proximity to each other, meet each other regularly, share the same educational background, and speak the same language. In this way, the individual innovations which form part of the competitive advantage of individual firms in the United States, Germany, and the United Kingdom—countries with strong scientific capabilities and traditions—create a national competitive advantage which adds up to substantially more than the sum of its parts.

Often this creates an innovative *architecture*, and architecture is a competitive advantage which is of even greater importance for the nation than it is for the firm. The benefits of architecture are very clearly apparent in the mutually supporting networks of firms which can be observed in locations, and industries, as different as California's Silicon Valley, the Italian knitwear industry, the City of London's position in financial services, or the Keiretsu of Japan. Despite the diversity, the similarities between these structures are equally apparent. Each is a network of implicit contracts. Each achieves flexibility in response and the ready exchange of information which the existence of sustained informal relationships makes possible. Each links commercial and social activities in ways that raise sharply the penalties for opportunistic behaviour.

If architecture is often a prime source of national competitive advantage, the lack of it can also be a prime source of national competitive disadvantage.

The absence of a structure of trust relationships, the inability to enter effectively binding commitments, and an expectation that those who can behave opportunistically will, are all very recognizable features of the economic organization of poor countries. These nations are in a reiterated Prisoner's Dilemma in which cheat–cheat is the sustained equilibrium, and there are no straightforward mechanisms for moving to a co-operative outcome.

Strategic assets are an important source of national competitive advantage. It is relatively rare for a corporation to lay exclusive claim to scarce factors—whether a broadcasting licence or a natural resource—but common for a country to do so. A country like Kuwait derives its competitive position entirely from this source, and the experience of Kuwait raises questions of the appropriability of national competitive advantages.

Historically, patterns of industrial activity were very heavily influenced by access to scarce natural resources. The industrialized centre of the Ruhr developed in proximity to its coal and iron reserves. Trading and industrial activities developed around the great natural harbours of the world. In the textbook analysis of competitive advantage, it was climatic factors which gave England its strength in textile production and Portugal's in vinification. Today, these natural resource industries are much less significant proportions of overall industrial activity and many of the world's most successful economies are very poorly endowed with natural resources. The scarce factors that influence national competitive advantages today are more often the range and variety of skills to be found in the workforce.

One of Germany's identifiable distinctive capabilities is a labour force with much higher levels of general scientific education and attainment than are available in most other countries. Although this forms a central part of the competitive advantage of German companies and explains their strength in industries as different as high-performance automobiles and fitted kitchen manufacture, relatively little of that benefit appears as added value in the accounts of German corporations. The reason is that in each industry and across the German economy as a whole, there are many German firms competing for the opportunity to exploit that competitive advantage. Hence the returns to it go to the scarce resource—the German workers themselves—rather than to those who facilitate its exploitation. Because there are not so many German firms in any of these industries—Mercedes, BMW, Audi in automobile manufacture; Poggenpohl, Bulthaup in kitchens—some competitive advantage remains with them, but the wealth created by their activities is mostly in the pay packets of their employees.

An appreciation of the role of architecture and exclusivity helps in understanding the 'clustering' phenomenon which is correctly stressed in Porter's (1990) discussion of the competitive advantage of nations. This notes the tendency for powerful firms in the same industry to be found in the same country—whether it is the auctioneers of the United Kingdom, the tile-makers of Italy, the kitchen manufacturers of Germany, the optical firms of Japan, or the investment banks of Wall Street. Porter's discussion overemphasizes, however, the role of technical factors in this phenomenon. A supporting infrastructure certainly sustains these clusters. But their origins mostly lie in architecture, or in access to scarce factors. The competitive position of the City of London, for example, is based principally on its networking, and shared services have developed as a consequence of that. The competitive position of German kitchen manufacturers is developed because the national competitive advantage—the ability to recruit highly numerate production-line workers—which is a competitive advantage for one is a competitive advantage for others too. Often, as in Silicon Valley, these two forms of competitive advantage are combined.

Financial architecture

Architecture is of particular importance in financial services. Those who finance an activity need to monitor both the size and nature of the risks they assume and the honesty and competence of those who manage them. Those who are responsible for the activities have incentives to distort the flow of information, to understate the risk, and to overstate the performance. These issues have been raised at several points in the analysis of relational contracts and of architecture.

One common response is to impose extremely detailed classical contracts. Mostly this does not work well. The main consequence of the strict liability which attaches to statements directors make in company prospectuses is that these prospectuses contain little useful information. And classical contracts bind you only to the specifics of the contract, not to their objectives. Relational contracting is a better alternative, and that is why financial institutions often talk about relationships, even if they are rarely achieved.

In Britain, relational contracts work well within the financial sector itself, and form the basis of Britain's competitive advantage in financial services. However, there are few relational contracts between the financial sector and the industrial sector. Banks have traditionally lent principally on the security of assets rather than their knowledge of the business; equity investors hold small stakes and are positively reluctant to be made 'insiders', privy to information not available to the public at large.

Germany, by contrast, has no comparable strengths in its financial sector but does have a very different style of relationship between finance and industry, where both parties have no doubt that they are engaged in a repeated game. It is often suggested that this gives German firms a better system of corporate governance and a greater willingness to undertake, and to invest in, long-term activities. Japan has similar banking relationships and networks of cross holdings of shares between companies. Sweden has a particularly intricate structure of financial relationships between its banks and its industrial companies, centred around the Wallenberg group.

It would be naïve to engage in financial transactions on the basis of

relational contracts alone. There are many trusting paupers. Nor are all financial services, even successful ones, based on relational contracting. Michael
Lewis's description of Salomon Brothers (Lewis, 1989) is a caricature of an
organization with a strong culture but no architecture. It should be noted,
however, that such a style of operation is associated with activities, such as
bond trading, which are concerned with the appropriation of added value but
which create virtually none. But real financial architecture may contribute to
competitive advantage either, as in Britain, in the financial services sector
itself or, as in Germany, in the contribution the financial sector makes to economic activity more generally.

Industrial policy and corporate strategy

Successful corporate strategy begins with the identification of the distinctive
capabilities of the firm. But if wish-driven strategy and copycat strategy are
common mistakes of corporations, they are hardly less common mistakes of
governments.

Chapter 1 described how the principal European powers had each sponsored domestic computer manufacturers like ICL in the United Kingdom,
Siemens–Nixdorf in Germany, and, most of all, Groupe Bull in France.
Wanting to be IBM is not enough to make you be like IBM, and wanting a
national champion is not enough to guarantee success. No document epito-
mizes wish-driven strategy more clearly than the Ryder Report, prepared for
the British government in 1975 after British Leyland's financial collapse.
Starting from the premiss that it was essential for Britain to have a major volume car producer, it set out targets year by year for sales, revenues, and
investment towards that goal. None of this bore the slightest relationship to
reality either in prospect or in retrospect. Willing the objective is not enough.

The failures of wish-driven strategy are of two kinds. There is the hopeless
aspiration of Groupe Bull. And there is the Pyrrhic victory of Saatchi &
Saatchi, where the objective is achieved but at a cost that renders it futile. If
Leyland illustrates the first, exemplars of the second abound—most of all in
France, where magnificent but uneconomic projects are found in transport,
energy, and almost every industry in which the state has played a central role.

Copycat strategy fails to establish competitive advantage for the firm. It fails
partly because it is difficult to know which are the essential and which the
peripheral aspects of the success of the firm or group of firms to be emulated.
It fails partly because of the efficient market problem. If everyone can do it, it
ceases to offer competitive advantage, or profit, to anyone. Copycat strategy
fails for the nation for the same reasons. It would be foolish not to turn to
other countries and hope to learn from their success. But it is fatuous to look
to Japan, or another feared competitor, and believe that their achievements
can be replicated by adopting some fashionable selection of Japanese practices. Nor is it clear that if Western firms were to achieve Japanese cost and

output levels in markets like cars and consumer electronics, where leadership has already been lost and where Japanese distinctive capabilities are evidently particularly productive of competitive advantage, that there would be much profit in it for anyone. Learning from the experience of others must be a more sophisticated process.

The lesson for countries, as for firms, is that economic success comes not from doing what others do well but from doing what others cannot do, or cannot do as well. The competitive advantage of nations is equally built around distinctive capabilities, mostly on the exploitation of architecture and strategic assets. Europe, and European firms, have many. Europe has built up since the Renaissance an organizational knowledge which leads to continued dominance by European countries and European firms of almost every market in which fashion, design, and style are critical attributes, markets ranging from furniture to quality clothing. The high standard of mass education in most European economies—notably Germany—is a powerful strategic asset. Architecture is key to competitive advantage in financial services. This is particularly strong in Britain, although in some other European financial centres the complacency and exclusiveness which are often a disadvantage of powerful architecture have inhibited competitiveness. The intermediate time zone turns out to be an unexpected distinctive capability which gives competitive advantage in financial services. Britain holds title to one of the most potent of proprietary standards—the English language—and this is not only the basis of competitive advantage in entertainment and education but in related manufacturing industries as different as publishing and sound-mixing equipment.

These examples are taken to illustrate the key differences between an approach to industrial policy that stresses the exploitation of distinctive capabilities and the industrial policies which Europe has mostly pursued. The issue is whether to address weakness, or reinforce strength. The disappointing performance of many European volume manufacturing industries has led to state support of industries like steel, volume textiles, and automobiles, to no long-term effect. It has bred an emphasis on technology which is directed not at those industries, like pharmaceuticals, in which European companies have been successful in achieving commercial applications of their innovative capacities, but to those, like electronics, in which they have largely failed. Competitive advantage through technology requires the support of complementary assets, and you must concentrate your efforts in areas where you have these, not those where you do not. Industrial policy for nations, like competitive strategy for firms, begins from distinctive capabilities.

An industrial policy which reinforces strengths rather than compensates for weaknesses should not be confused with 'picking winners'—guessing which firms or sectors will succeed, and providing them with resources. Where firms have competitive advantages themselves, national competitive advantages will generally follow. The scope for industrial policy lies in the areas where that is not the case—where there are divergences between the competitive strengths of firms and the competitive strengths of countries. Sometimes firms find it difficult to appropriate the competitive advantages they create, or might create—as with pre-commercial research. Sometimes national competitive advantages exist which firms cannot fully appropriate, or appropriate at all—organizational knowledge or management, or the skills of German workers. It is in areas such as these—basic research, education, training—that industrial policy can help to secure competitive advantages both for firms and for countries.

The competitive advantage of nations is a subject founded by Smith (1776) but taken up by many subsequent authors: Olson (1982), Porter (1990), and Albert (1991) are recent examples. The fundamental theorems of welfare economics are due to Arrow (1952) and Debreu (1954); a more accessible account of these issues is to be found in the articles by Chipman and Bator in Townsend (1971). The neo-Austrian school is so called to reflect the contributions of Schumpeter (1934, 1961) and Von Hayek (1944, 1948, 1960). Kirzner (1973, 1989) gives a recent account. On business ethics Beauchamp and Bowie (1988) is a collection of readings; Reidenback and Robin (1989), and Barry (1992) are assessments of the ethical issues associated with profit maximization. The issues raised here by financial architecture are well discussed in Mayer (1987).

VII

THE FUTURE OF STRATEGY

The subject of business strategy is the management of the relationship between the firm and its external environment—its customers, its suppliers, its competitors, and the governments of the countries within which it operates. There is, of course, much more to management than strategy. But there is rarely a successful firm without an effective strategy, and strategy is usually the most public of management activities and the principal concern of the most senior executives. Strategy consultants are the most respected, and best rewarded, of business advisers.

Like Molière's M. Jourdain, who learnt that he had spoken prose all his life without knowing it, successful managers devised and implemented strategies long before business strategy was the explicit subject of books, courses, and public debate. That process began around 1960. Its origins were various. The development at Harvard Business School of a course in Business Policy, designed to integrate other aspects of management practice and to illustrate and to stress the strategic thinking demanded of senior executives, has exercised a continuing influence on business thinking and business education. Alfred Chandler's book, Strategy and Structure, published in 1962, is possibly the most influential published business history. Chandler studied the evolution of four US corporations (General Motors, du Pont, Exxon, and Sears Roebuck) and argued that their structure followed their strategy. Chandler explained that the development of multi-divisional organization was a response to the growing complexity of objectives of these large corporations, and the force of his argument derived from the way in which the strategic objectives of the firm dictated the way in which many other management issues were resolved. Chandler's analysis gained strength from what is certainly one of the most thoughtful, and probably the most quoted, accounts of a businessman's own experiences—My Years at General Motors by Alfred Sloan—which appeared at much the same time.

Activities and publications are seminal when they catch the mood of an age. Information technology was then beginning to create entirely new possibilities for data collection and management. Social sciences generally seemed ripe for the application of scientific methods, and such methods were certainly applied. Robert MacNamara was applauded for taking analytic skills tried in the Ford Motor Company to the Defense Department, with the hope that politics as well as business policy would be transformed by cold rationality. For a time, some believed that operations research and strategic planning could turn management into a subject like nuclear physics or electrical engineering. See, for example, Leavitt and Whisler (1958), Anschen (1960), Simon (1960), Ansoff (1965), Ruggles and Smalter (1966). These hopes are long gone—or at least sharply diminished—but the rationalist approach to strategy which they engendered has still dominated the subject for the last thirty years. (Ansoff, 1969, is a valuable collection of some of the major contributions of the previous decade.)

The rationalist framework is considerably influenced by the military analogy (James, 1985)—indeed, the very word 'strategy' has military origins (as in Liddell Hart, 1968). The model is based, at least loosely, on military practice (Evered, 1983). The first task of the strategist is to describe, understand, and analyse the environment. The second stage— the key task for the senior executives in the firm as it is for the senior generals of the army—is to determine strategy in the light of that analysis. The third phase is that of implementation. It is difficult to quarrel with this approach. Appraise, determine, act is the necessary structure of any process of logical decision-making.

Yet this rationalist process achieves the curious conjunction of being both dominant and disparaged. Few firms, or their advisers, approach the strategy process in any different way. But most senior managers are also critical of the rationalist approach. They sense that rationalism undervalues people, and underestimates implementation, and feel that new and more behaviourally orientated approaches are required. But there is little consensus on what these alternative approaches are, or might be.

21

A Brief History of Business Strategy

Much has been written about the strategies that firms aiming at corporate success should adopt. My objective in this chapter is to describe the evolution of thinking about business strategy over the thirty years in which it has been identified as a distinct subject of study, and the relationship of that thinking to the analysis presented here. I begin from the 1960s' perspective in which strategy was largely equated with corporate planning, describe the 1970s' emphasis on diversification and portfolio planning, and observe concern in the 1980s for concentration on the core business and the development of less analytic, more people-orientated approaches to management. I outline the conventional, now unfashionable, but nevertheless still dominant rationalist approach to strategic thinking—scan the environment, formulate the strategy, and then go on to secure its implementation. But I also register the principal criticisms made of that approach. A common view today is that the formulation of strategy is easy, but the real issues and problems are those of implementation, and that the conventionally prescriptive approach to strategy ignores the degree to which strategy in real businesses is emergent rather than directed.

I argue that this is a justified critique of standard approaches to strategy, but that these approaches are themselves based on a misconception of what strategy for a business really involves. Such criticisms are appropriately directed at a wish-driven view of strategy which emphasizes leadership, visions, and missions. If this is strategy, then it should be no surprise that formulation is easy and implementation difficult, and also unsurprising that such 'strategy' has limited impact on what operating businesses actually do. Meaningful strategy is not a statement of corporate aspirations, but is rooted in the distinctive capabilities of the individual firm. When strategy is emergent in this sense, the distinction between formulation and implementation largely falls away.

I also comment more generally on the nature of research and thinking in the field of strategy, and suggest that the inability to distinguish sufficiently clearly between taxonomy, deductive logic, and empirical observation is responsible for the limited progress which has been made in the development of an organized framework for the study of business behaviour.

General Electric

If the evolution of business strategy in the West was to be told by reference to the history of a single company, that company would be the General Electric Company of the United States (GE). GE has both led and followed every major development in strategic management over the last four decades. This evolution is closely associated with the four chief executives of the company over the period, each of whom has imposed his own personal sense of strategic direction on the company.

GE emerged from the genius of Thomas Edison, who made electricity a commercial product. By 1900 the company was involved in every aspect of the electrical business. Throughout the first half of the century GE was responsible for an outstanding range of technical and product innovations, which led to the development of national broadcasting, the peaceful application of nuclear power, and the creation of a market in domestic electrical appliances. Today the company is a widely diversified conglomerate. Its largest business is aircraft engines, but it is also a major bank and financial services firm and is owner of one of the major US television networks, NBC.

In the 1950s and 1960s, GE's philosophy was one of decentralization to individual operating businesses. The departments, the critical unit of this decentralized management, were to be of 'a size that a man could get his arms around' (Ralph Cordiner, chief executive, 1953–60). GE established a large management training centre at Crotonville, designed to create general managers who would transcend functional specialisms, and the principles of general management were enshrined in the company's famous 'blue books'.

Towards the end of the 1960s, some weaknesses in this system were identified. In particular, the planning functions of the corporate centre were poorly related to the activities of the operating businesses, the centre's capacity to review their plans effectively was very limited, and the attempt by each departmental head to expand the size of his own empire was seen as having led to profitless growth for the corporation as a whole. Following a McKinsey report in 1969, GE created 'strategic business units'. A smaller number of operating businesses were each to be responsible for their own strategic planning.

The central function was now to be portfolio planning—the allocation of resources between strategic business units. A fresh group of consultants created the 'GE screen', a matrix in which businesses were ranked by market share and market growth prospects. This was designed to structure that resource allocation process. GE became one of the first diversified businesses to divest as well as to acquire, although the purchase of new businesses was also a key part of the portfolio planning approach. In 1976 GE made what was then the largest acquisition by a US company, with the purchase of Utah

International, itself a diversified energy and resources business. (Utah was sold eight years later, for about the same price as GE had paid.) With strategic planning at the centre of the agenda for each of forty-three business units, the day of the strategic planner, and the strategy consultant, had truly arrived.

But there were still limitations on the capacity of GE's corporate centre to review forty-three strategic business units. Nor was it clear where in the organization major new business opportunities were to be identified. So in 1977 the strategic business units were consolidated into six sectors. The centre was to take more responsibility for corporate planning, layers of planning staff were removed, and 'arenas' of business development were identified. In acknowledgement of the force of Japanese competition, the international arena was given particular emphasis.

For Jack Welch, who became chief executive in 1981, vision was central to strategy. 'Good business leaders create a vision, articulate the vision, passionately own the vision, and relentlessly drive it to completion' (quoted in Tichy and Charan, 1989: 113). The key elements in Welch's own vision were two: 'We will run only businesses that are number one or number two in their global markets', and 'In addition to the strength, resources and reach of a big company . . . we are committed to developing the sensitivity, the leanness, the simplicity and the agility of a small company' (GE annual report, 1988). In pursuit of these objectives, GE rearranged the corporate portfolio. 'We started out with 411,000 employees. We acquired an additional 111,150 employees. Through divestitures, we reduced 122,700 employees. We restructured, or down-sized to get more efficient, reducing some 123,450 employees. Now we have 276,000. Enormous in and out' (Welch, quoted in HBS, 1989). Welch acquired the nickname 'Neutron Jack' after the neutron bomb, which destroys people but preserves property.

In 1988, however, Welch felt that the stock market was insufficiently appreciative of the company's performance. 'We're not sure why this is the case, but it occurs to us that perhaps the pace and variety of our activity appear unfocused to those who view it from the outside' (GE annual report, 1988). The company began a programme of repurchasing its shares, but more important for strategy was a new Welch initiative, 'Work-out at GE'. 'Work-out is allowing self-confidence to flourish around our company. As that self-confidence grows, the boundaries are beginning to fall; and as they fall, GE is picking up speed, and with that speed a competitive advantage. Some people are uncomfortable with this soft stuff and press us to quantify it . . .'. 'In a boundaryless company, suppliers aren't outside. They are drawn closer and become trusted partners in the total business process . . . in a boundaryless company, internal functions begin to blur' (GE annual report, 1990). Behind the florid metaphor and business buzzwords, there is a recognition of the role of relational contracting in facilitating flexible response and the development of organizational knowledge.

These themes that run through GE's development—the cycles of centralization and decentralization, the shifting role of the corporate centre, the steady move from 'hard', quantified concepts of planning to looser, organizationally based ones, are exactly paralleled in the literature of business strategy. Has the result been a more successful company?

There are two perspectives on GE's performance. Over a long period, the GE share price tracks the Standard and Poor's index extremely closely, but on balance there is evidence of slight outperformance. As managers of a diversified portfolio of US businesses, GE is ahead of the market and the executives of GE have beaten the average mutual fund.

There is a different view. Computers and consumer electronics have been among the fastest growing and exciting new business opportunities of the last fifty years, and GE, once dominant in US markets for all kinds of electrical equipment, has failed in both of them. Perhaps the company enjoyed no relevant distinctive capabilities; or perhaps, despite the unquestioned abilities and sophistication of its managers and management systems, it failed fully to identify and exploit them. 'When Japanese managers come to visit us, they don't ask to see our research centers or manufacturing facilities. All they want to know about is our management systems' (anonymous GE executive, quoted in HBS, 1981). This chapter describes the thinking behind the management systems that GE has successively adopted.

The rationalist school: assessing the environment

The sheer volume of information which a company can assemble, both about its environment and about itself, is daunting. The first problem which the descriptive phase of strategy formulation must confront is how to organize this mass of data (Houlden, 1980). The earliest processes of strategy formulation were closely linked to corporate planning.

These formal planning procedures typically grew out of the budgeting process, which is a key control mechanism in most firms. The budget normally covers revenues and expenditures, cash incomes and outgoings, requirements of labour and of materials. The plan extends these projections forward. In the earliest days of planning, this was often done by simple extrapolation. More sophisticated planning procedures were then developed to take account of the firm's expectations of economic growth, the probable development of its markets, and its own established plans and intentions. (Brandenburg and Gilmore, 1962, and Anthony, 1965, are good expositions of these models of strategy as planning.)

Any well-run firm must have some planning process of this kind. Many important corporate inputs—people, plans, accommodation, finance—cannot be turned on and off as markets evolve, but have to be projected, determined, negotiated years ahead. The firm needs forecasts of these requirements and these forecasts are an essential input to management decisions. (Argenti, 1965, 1968, and 1980 describes these procedures.) But planning is not strategy, and those firms which believed that by describing the future—often in very considerable detail—they had taken major steps towards making it happen often found the results of their planning rounds a disappointment. Elaborately quantified corporate plans lay gathering dust on the shelves of managers who went on making the decisions they would have made had the plan never existed. Increasingly sceptical appraisals can be found: Brown *et al.* (1969), Ansoff (1970), Lorange (1979), Armstrong (1982).

The heyday of such corporate planning in business—the 1960s—was also the time when similar processes were adopted by governments in many countries. French planning was widely admired, Britain adopted a National Plan for its economy, and every newly independent LDC saw economic planning as the key to future development. The results were, in the main, as unsatisfactory for governments as for corporations.

Planning goes beyond forecasting and begins to become a basis for strategic choices when it encompasses a variety of possible outcomes. One very deliberate approach to this issue is *scenario* planning (McNulty, 1977; Grant and King, 1979; Zentner, 1982; Wack, 1985), a widely used technique but one particularly associated with Shell (Beck, 1981; de Geus, 1988). The company invites its group planners to speculate freely on diverse, internally consistent views of the future of the business within the world economy. For Shell, as for other corporations which adopt similar approaches often in a less formal way, scenarios are a means of organizing their thinking about the environment they face and of beginning to formulate an agenda of strategic alternatives. What would the company do if the oil price fell to $10 per barrel? How would it react if economic growth were much slower in the 1990s than in earlier decades?

The development of a model of the business environment is a means both of forecasting the future of the business and assessing how that future might be influenced by internal or external developments (Lyles, 1981). These types of model, which are designed to simulate the functionings of a complete system, may describe an operating business, or the firm itself, or even (as with large macroeconomic models) a whole economy. The objective of these models is to describe a more complex set of interactions and feedbacks than can be handled intuitively or with the aid of *analytic* models (which are discussed more fully below). In this way a simulation model can allow the free-ranging speculation of alternative scenarios to be combined with the apparent precision of outcomes associated with the corporate plan. The relationships of the model may be deterministic (as in a financial planning model, where many of them will be dictated by accounting identities). They may simply be imposed (as in the style of modelling associated with System Dynamics (Forrester, 1961)). They may be estimated, statistically or econometrically, from extended time series of data (as in macroeconomic models and their business counterparts).

Such modelling began in the 1960s but has become increasingly widespread as databases and spreadsheets, sophisticated specialist modelling languages, and the universal availability of computers have made it possible for

Fig. 21.1. The Evolution of Strategy: Assessing the Environment

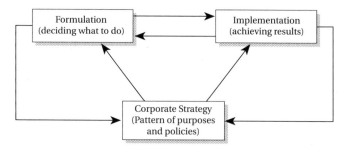

The stages of strategy

Origin: Based on Andrews (1971)

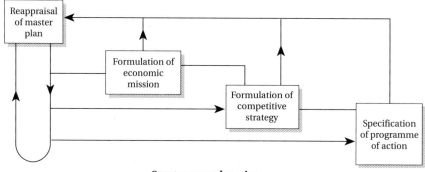

Strategy as planning

Origin: Simplified from Brandenburg (1992)

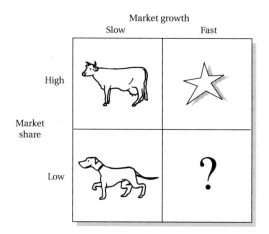

The portfolio planning matrix

Origin: Boston Consulting Group

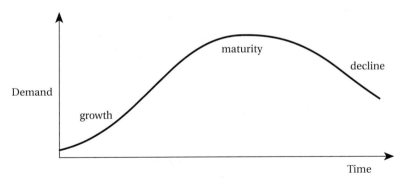

The product life cycle

Origin: Unknown

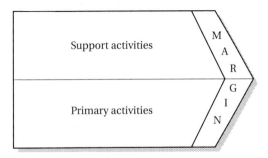

The value chain

Origin: Based on Porter (1985)

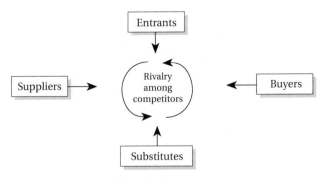

The five forces

Origin: Based on Porter (1985)

every executive to be his own model builder. But these models are no more than ways of assembling data and analysis as a background to strategic decisions. Models cannot be relied on to forecast the future and even large econometric forecasting models, whose results are widely used even if widely disparaged, are essentially systems of managing information and making judgements rather than true representations of real economies.

The technological optimism of the 1960s—the belief that management was a process which could one day be defined with sufficient precision to be entrusted to a computer—has now sharply diminished. Yet the role which information technology in general and modelling in particular can play in business is still widely misunderstood. The world of business is too complex ever to be adequately described by any model. This observation, trite and obvious as it is, prompts two opposed, but equally mistaken, reactions.

The simpler response is to reject the analytic model altogether. But intuitive responses and judgements are not always right, and whether they are right or wrong they are always the product of some implicit model. Typically that model or theory is based on a previous experience of an analogous situation, or series of situations, or some incompletely articulated view of competitive behaviour or supplier response. The merit of the model—the explicit process of deductive reasoning—is that it forces this process into the open, spells out the assumptions on which it is based, and identifies those features of reality to which its conclusions may be sensitive. This process may reinforce or reject the initial judgement, or more often facilitate a better appreciation of what it involves.

An alternative, and more subtle, error is the successive complication of the model in an endeavour to capture a larger fraction of the complex reality. The weakness of this approach is that beyond a certain, quickly reached, point the additional descriptive value is slight while the cost in terms of the real objective—a better appreciation of the analytic structure of the relevant relationships—is high. The model which requires many hours to run and which neither forecasts reality in a way which users find credible nor describes a set of relationships which they can readily understand falls squarely, and uselessly, between two stools.

Such formal approaches to analysis of the environment proved unattractive to many managers. Some were simply frightened of technique, others sensed its limitations. Corporate plans seemed sterile documents, irrelevant to daily operating decisions, scenarios the province of distrusted eggheads, models the playthings of computer buffs. More qualitative ways of organizing relevant data were needed (Mintzberg, 1973, in an early, wide-ranging critique). Many of these techniques were provided by consultants.

The portfolio planning matrix (Day, 1977; Hedley, 1977) and the product life cycle (Levitt, 1965; Rink and Swan, 1979) are examples of these tools. They enable managers to categorize their business as cows, dogs, or stars, to identify phases of growth, maturity, and decline. They are organizing frameworks which facilitate comparison of the different businesses in a corporate portfolio or different products in a business portfolio. Portfolio planning and the product life cycle are means of organizing information about markets and about demand. Other tools are relevant to production and supply. The McKinsey business system, later to be developed as Porter's value chain (Porter, 1985), is a means of describing the successive phases of a production process and analysing the determinants of costs (cost drivers) in a framework whose objective is support for commercial decision-making rather than accounting allocation. Such techniques were used to identify key success factors—points in the production process at which the firm might succeed, or fail, in adding value to its output.

The corporate planners of the 1960s and 1970s were much concerned with issues such as the market and macroeconomic environment, the product portfolio, and the product life cycle. All of these emphasize characteristics of industry or sector and market. They tended to underplay the role of competitors and competitive behaviour in influencing outcomes (Rothschild, 1979a, 1979b). Indeed, it is still common to see plans which base output growth on forecasts of the market, or to observe industries in which each individual firm extrapolates its own experience to give overall results which everyone knows are incapable of realization.

Porter's (1979, 1980) 'five forces'—of competition, entry, substitution, suppliers, and customers—offered a more comprehensive checklist of environmental factors (Porter, 1981). By the early 1980s, competitor analysis had often replaced, or at least supplemented, environmental analysis. The BCG portfolio matrix, whose dimensions in the 1970s were market growth and market share, was transformed in the 1980s into the strategic environment matrix, which mapped the number of sources of competitive advantage against the size of that advantage.

The rationalist school: formulating a strategy

Having reviewed the business environment and its competitive position, the firm must go on to formulate its strategy. The rationalist school sees the definition of the objectives of the firm as the key element in strategy formulation. That view, which owes much to the continuing influence of Drucker[1] on management thinking, is in itself relatively uncontroversial, but the subject of considerable operational difficulty. A firm needs both corporate objectives—what business should we be in?—and business unit objectives—how should the firm position itself relative to its competitors in its chosen markets?

There are two distinct historical phases in the evolution of thought on *corporate* strategy. Until the early 1980s, the primary aim of corporate strategy was the creation of a diversified business portfolio. Such a portfolio might

---

1 P. F. Drucker has been one of the most eloquent, and prolific, writers on management issues over 50 years. A survey of his contributions is Drucker (1977).

encompass related diversification—motivated by synergy between old and new businesses—and unrelated diversification—supported by portfolio planning techniques. But by the early 1980s, evidence had accumulated that unrelated diversification added little value (Chapter 10) and many of the conglomerates created in these earlier decades had succumbed to financial pressures. (TRW and Litton Industries were singled out for special praise in Ansoff's readings on business strategy (Ansoff, 1969), and ITT was perhaps the most widely admired of conglomerates. By 1980, Litton was broke and TRW and ITT decidedly out of fashion and favour).

Attitudes changed. The trend of the 1980s was one for focus on the core business; 'stick to the knitting', in the graphic phrase used by Peters and Waterman (1982). Debate on corporate strategy then centred on a view of what the core business is. Is a computer company a manufacturing business, or a provider of information management systems? Is a brewer in beer or in leisure? Oil companies have burnt their fingers in the resource business and railroads no longer wish to be seen as transportation companies. Yet the criteria of relatedness have remained poorly defined. Indeed, one influential contribution (Prahalad and Bettis, 1986) proffers 'dominant logic' as the key criterion; loosely interpreted, a business is related if you think it is.

In formulating business strategy, the 'experience curve' popularized by the Boston Consulting Group (BCG 1968, 1972; Yelle, 1979) led firms to focus on the critical importance of market share. This emphasis was reinforced by the observation in the PIMS database of a strong positive correlation between market share and returns (Buzzell, Heany, and Schoeffer, 1974; Buzzell, Gale, and Sultan, 1975). PIMS also identified a correlation between relative product quality and return on investment (Buzzell and Gale, 1987). With the awakened, or renewed, emphasis on competitive issues, the choice market position was seen as a central element in strategic decision-making. Quality, it was perceived, had been a key ingredient in Japanese success. Over time most markets moved up the quality spectrum. With the aid of phrases such as 'quality is free' (Crosby, 1979) 'total quality management' became a preoccupation of the later 1980s.

Many authors offered taxonomies of generic strategies—checklists from which corporations could choose the most relevant objectives for particular markets. One early list was proposed by Ansoff (1965), who identified market penetration, product development, market development, and diversification as alternative strategic objectives. The Boston Consulting Group's alternatives are invest, hold, harvest, divest, and Arthur D. Little offers a list of no less than twenty-four strategic options (Wright, 1974). Porter's (1980) classification of generic strategies proved particularly influential. In Porter's framework there are two dimensions of choice. Firms can pursue either cost leadership—the same product as competitors but at lower cost—or differentiation. They can range narrowly, or broadly, thus generating a range of alternatives encompassing cost leadership, differentiation, and focus. (Pearce, 1983; Galbraith and Schendel, 1983; Karmani, 1984; White, 1986, are surveys of generic strategies.)

Thinking in the 1980s came to support simple crisp statements of objectives in terms of the corporate vision (Campbell and Yeung, 1990) or an assertion of 'strategic intent' (Prahalad and Hamel, 1985). Today, a debate on the content of the corporate mission is a common starting-point for a discussion of strategy. Such a statement can cover objectives in both corporate and business strategy. The mission statement is intended to provide a link between the broad objectives of the firm (which may focus exclusively on profit maximization, or may assert concern for other stakeholders) and its specific commercial activities.

A rather different critique of these processes of rationalist strategy formulation—yet one still very much within the rationalist framework—is provided by the shareholder value movement. As with many shifts in thinking about strategy, this is found more or less simultaneously in the thinking of practitioners and the writings of business school academics. American business was stunned in the 1980s by the emergence of a group of corporate raiders. Figures like T. Boone Pickens and the partners of Kohlberg Kravis Roberts, with little in the way of resources of their own, but with the aid of the 'junk bond' financing pioneered by Michael Milken, could make credible bids for some of the largest corporations in the United States. This threat to incumbent managers led to anxious re-emphasis on major companies' concerns for 'shareholder value'. Academics (Rappaport, 1986; Jensen, 1988) were led to explain and justify it, providing both a critique of accounting earnings as a focus of corporate attention and a rationale of the public benefits of exclusive focus on the interests of shareholders.

The most important practical consequence of this activity was to give further impetus to the break-up of conglomerate firms. The grouping of unrelated businesses tended, it was argued, to conceal the potential strategic value of individual components to specific purchasers. That message for corporate strategy was clear, but for business strategy shareholder value had few clear implications. Proponents stressed the need to evaluate investment and acquisitions by reference to their expected cash flows—but this is a theme familiar from every elementary text in corporate finance—and texts on strategy in a shareholder value framework (such as Reiman, 1989) do no more than juxtapose Rappaport's critique with Porter's taxonomies of competitive forces and generic strategies.

The threat to established US corporations in the 1980s did not only come from changes in the capital market. American business attitudes were also transformed by the force of competition from Japan, particularly in automobiles and consumer electronics but across an increasingly wide range of products. For some writers, this penetration itself reflected the malign effect of rationalist strategy on US business (Abernathy *et al.*, 1983). The globalization of markets (Levitt, 1983) was a reiterated theme and no self-respecting corporation could be without its global strategy (Prahalad and Hamel, 1985). International management became a subject in its own right (Ohmae, 1985; Bartlett and Ghoshal, 1986, 1989; Porter (ed.), 1986).

Fig. 21.2. Formulating the Strategy

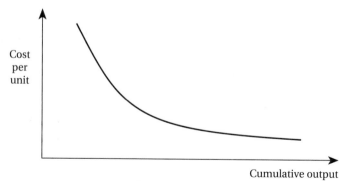

The experience curve

Origin: Boston Consulting Group

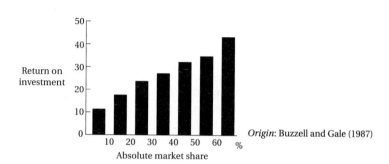

The importance of market share

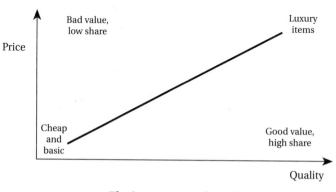

The importance of quality

Origin: Davis (1990)

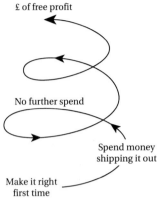

£ of free profit

No further spend

Spend money
shipping it out

Make it right
first time

Quality is free

Origin: Price (1990)

Generic strategies

invest

hold

harvest

divest

A. D. Little generic strategies

Origin: Ansoff (1955)

Advantages

Cost　　　Differentiation

	Cost	Differentiation
Broad	Cost leadership	Differentia-tion
Scope		
Narrow	Focus	

Porter generic strategies

Origin: Porter (1980)

Mission statement

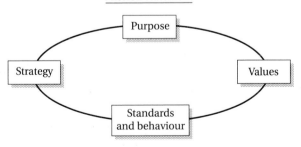

Purpose

Strategy

Values

Standards
and behaviour

Formulating the mission

Origin: Campbell and Young (1990)

As the 1990s began, the state of the art in rationalist strategy involved the formulation of a statement of company objectives, often encapsulated in a 'mission statement' and encompassing both corporate strategic objectives—what sort of business are we in—with business strategic objectives—expressed in terms of plans for market share, product quality, and geographical scope. It is not surprising that attention was moving from the problems of formulating strategy to issues of implementation.

Copycat strategy

There is a mechanism for formulating strategy which is apparently simpler than selecting from a menu of generic strategies in the light of a well-formulated assessment of the business environment. That is to look at what other firms do, and copy it. This strategy is more felicitously expressed as adopting best practice.

This strand of strategy has two primary threads. One is the product of Western concern, and admiration for, the success of Japan in certain manufacturing sectors. Observers are inclined to seize on some particular characteristic of Japanese practice—just in time management of inventories, for example—and advocate its widespread adoption. The current management preoccupation with quality owes much to this. The other thread results from the inevitable desire of the number two, or number three, firm in an industry to be number one. How better to become number one than to be like number one?

But copycat strategy encounters fundamental problems. The Japanese comparison makes one particularly evident. There are many features—some cosmetic and peripheral, some fundamental—which distinguish the functioning of Japanese and European industry. But which are which? And which superficially cosmetic factors are truly supportive of fundamental ones? Someone aspires to be a great violinist. He goes to a concert, and sees a great violinist in evening dress, with an expensive violin, drawing a bow across it. So he dons evening dress, buys an expensive violin, and draws a bow across it. The factors that truly make the great violinist great are not those which are most apparent to the casual observer.

Any attempt at imitation faces that issue but there is also a second problem which is particular to business strategy. In most fields of human endeavour, one person can do something well without inhibiting the ability of anyone else to do the same thing equally well. I can be a good driver, or golfer, or singer without any detriment to your ability to drive, or golf, or sing. Indeed, these skills are usually mutually enhancing. But successful strategies are—necessarily—individual to the particular firms which adopt them.

The rationalist school: implementing strategy

Chandler's findings addressed the implementation of strategy directly. Structure follows strategy, he argued, and since then corporation after corporation has rearranged its structure, and rearranged its structure again, in line with changes in its own strategy and in response to changing patterns of strategic thought.

Chandler drew particular attention to the development of multi-divisional forms of organization in response to the increased complexity and diversity of large corporations with multiple activities. Traditionally, firms had decentralized functionally, to accounts departments, marketing groups, and other collections of specialist skills. The multi-divisional firm decentralized by type of business activity, so that each operating business would have its own accountants, and its own marketeers.

But if operating businesses are treated as independent units, what is the corporate centre for? There are several answers. One sees strategy as the key central function. The corporate centre may act, in effect, as an internal consultancy unit on business level strategy. Or its primary concern may be with corporate strategy. Here the task of the centre is to identify and derive synergies from the distinct divisional activities. While Sloan's General Motors sought to exert both functions centrally, more recently, as in General Electric, business unit strategy was pushed down to business unit level. If there are also substantive interactions between these distinct divisions, the company is driven towards a matrix form of organization (Knight, 1976), in which functional groupings coexist with, and across, divisional boundaries.

The diversification of the 1960s and 1970s led many more companies to pursue multi-divisional structures. As in General Electric, the degree of central control exercised was sometimes tightened, sometimes relaxed, in ways which sometimes reflected simply a desire for change, sometimes a revised assessment of the balance of advantages. In the 1980s, the very clear tendency was to decentralize, stripping back the corporate centre to minimal levels, even to that of a passive holder of shares in operating businesses. Traditionally central functions—like finance, treasury, and planning—were pushed down to lower levels. These moves cast further doubt on the value of the centre and often firms concluded that there were parts of their business to which the corporate function could add no value. Divestment of peripheral businesses became common.

But the implementation of strategy is concerned not only with the structure of a firm's activities, but with their style. Burns and Stalker (1966) associated relatively mechanistic, routinized management regimes and well-organized reporting lines with stable strategies and environments, contrasting these with more organic, confused management approaches relevant to more rapid change. These links between strategy and structure have been explored further by many other writers. Mintzberg (1979, 1983*a*) identifies five broad organizational categories—simple structure, machine bureaucracy,

Fig. 21.3. Implementing Strategy

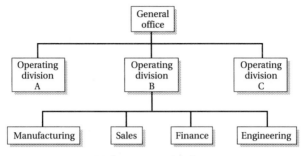

M-form organization

Origin: Williamson (1975)

Central influence and control

Origin: Based on Goold and Campbell (1987)

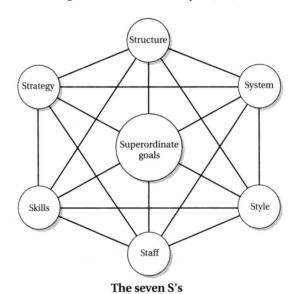

The seven S's

Origin: McKinsey & Co

The simple structure

The machine bureacracy

Visualising organisations

Origin: Mintzberg (1979)

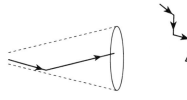

Entrepreneurial mode

Adaptive mode

Planning mode

Planning styles

Origin: Mintzberg (1973)

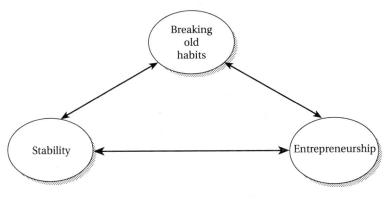

Implementing strategy

Origin: Peters and Waterman (1982)

divisionalized form, professional bureaucracy, and adhocracy, effectively adding simple structure (typically the small owner-managed firm) to Burns and Stalker's classification and subdividing their mechanistic style.

As these typologies became elaborated, there was increasing recognition that structure does not only follow strategy. Structure is itself a determinant of strategy. The essentially interactive nature of this relationship is a theme of Child's (1974, 1975) and is one developed in Miles and Snow (1978), who distinguish prospectors and defenders. The prospector seeks out a changing environment, the defender looks to a stable one. From a quite different perspective, the work of Nelson and Winter (1982) reaches analogous conclusions. They envisage the evolution of business as essentially a process of natural selection, in which only structures well adapted to their environment survive.

From these perspectives, however, strategic thinking no longer runs unambiguously from environmental assessment through strategy formulation to the process of implementation. If the causal relationship between strategy and structure works in both directions, it may be as feasible to determine the strategy by defining the structure as it is to choose the structure to match the strategy. This is implicit in the 'excellence' identified by Peters and Waterman (1982), who focus on the internal attributes of the organization—shared values, 'loose-tight' organization—and anticipate that the excellent firm will find environments appropriate to the exploitation of its excellence. It is a line of thinking developed in the burgeoning literature on corporate culture. At this point, the rationalist approach in which strategy is devised for the organization gives way to a view of strategy which sees it as derived from the organization.

Critics of rationalism

Dissatisfaction with the rationalist school is widespread. That dissatisfaction centres, in one way or another, around issues of implementation and there is a growing literature on that topic (Bourgeois and Brodwin, 1984; Hrebiniak and Joyce, 1984; Hamermesh, 1986). The agendas of fashionable consultants and trendier business schools are increasingly filled with related issues—the management of change, the evolution of corporate culture, coping with a turbulent environment, the institution of programmes of total quality management. Rationalism is in retreat, but by no means routed, principally because of the absence of equally well-articulated alternative frameworks. The management of change is important, to be sure, but there are logically precedent questions of what change, and why.

One expression of this dissatisfaction is the commonly expressed view that 'strategy formulation is easy, it is implementation that is difficult'. Such a statement reveals much about the weaknesses of the ways in which rationalist strategy has developed. This implied distinction between strategy and implementation rests on a misconception, as the military analogy reveals. Was Napoleon's defeat in Russia a failure of strategy or of implementation? It hardly makes sense to ask the question, because in the hands of a skilled strategist formulation and implementation are inextricable. But if strategy is nothing more than a vision, a mission statement, an expression of aspiration—and that is often what it is—then it is hardly surprising that it seems easy to formulate strategy and hard to implement it. One might as well say that Saddam Hussein had a fine strategy—defeat the United States Army in pitched battle and so conquer the oil reserves of the Middle East—but there were failures in implementation; and that is what he did say to his unsuccessful generals before he murdered them. If the formulation of strategy amounts to little more than the statement of objectives, then all the interesting and important issues of strategy have been redefined as problems of implementation. But this results from a misunderstanding of what strategy is, not from a real characteristic of the business environment.

A related critique is particularly associated with Mintzberg. It stresses the need to consider the strategy process, rather than to address the choice of strategy itself. Thus, 'One cannot decide reliably what should be done in a system as complicated as a contemporary organization without a genuine understanding of how that organization really works. In engineering, no student ever questions having to learn physics; in medicine, having to learn anatomy. Imagine an engineering student's hand shooting up in a physics class. "Listen, prof, it's fine to tell us how the atom does work. But what we want to know is how the atom *should* work"' (Quinn, Mintzberg, and James, 1988).

The analogy is instructive both for the elements in it which are right and for those which are wrong. It is right to emphasize that fundamental knowledge is a prerequisite to practical application. A competent engineer must first learn physics. Imagine the student who shouts, 'Stop wasting our time with the theory of the atom, we came here to learn how to make nuclear bombs,' and then note that equivalent statements are made every day by managers and business school students impatient for what they suppose to be practical knowledge. The position is aggravated by the high reputation of many educators who are happy to illustrate the relevance of their material by showing their classes exciting pictures of nuclear explosions, winning their approbation but communicating nothing of any value. Practical knowledge which is not based on some more fundamental analysis is usually knowledge of only the most superficial kind.

But although it contains that element of truth, the analogy above is essentially false. The views of the student, or the instructor, on what the structure of the atom *should* be like are matters of no conceivable interest since neither of them has any power to influence it. It is quite realistic, however, to suppose that businessmen can influence strategy and it is the prospect that they might do so which is their principal reason for studying it. Observation of the strategy process, and the prescriptive analysis of what strategy should be, are both proper questions, and legitimate subjects of study, but they are distinct questions. In just the same way, the issue of how the European Community makes its decisions through the mechanisms of the Commission, Parliament, and Council of Ministers, is distinct from the issue of what its decisions should be. And while you must understand both if you are to influence policy, it is the second group of questions—what the decisions should be—which are of most general interest. The same is true of strategy.

Emergent strategy

But the study of the strategy process does give further insight into the failings of rationalist strategy. Successful firms often seem to have achieved their position without going through the processes of analysis, formulation, and implementation that the rationalist school implies. Indeed, the story of Honda's attack on the US cycle market, described in Chapter 1, is often used to illustrate precisely that point.

The notion that successful strategies are often opportunistic and adaptive, rather than calculated and planned, is a view as old as the subject of business strategy itself. One of the best expressions of it is Lindblom's (1959) exposition of 'the science of muddling through'. Lindblom wrote from a perspective of public administration, rather than business administration, and stressed how the political constraints on policy make a rationalist approach impossible. He argued that the range of options attainable at any time was necessarily limited, and contrasted what he called the 'branch' method of 'successive limited comparison' with the 'root' method of comprehensive optimization.

In his popular volume of readings, Ansoff reprinted Lindblom's views, but more, it appears, to expose heresy than to commend it. 'Lindblom is wrong when he claims the "root" method to be "impossible". . . . The TRW reading shows how one of the world's most dynamic corporations goes about a methodical exploration of wide vistas . . . nevertheless, Lindblom's article is instructive, since it describes a widely prevalent state of practice in business and government organisations' (Ansoff (ed.), 1969: 10). Twenty years later, that widely prevalent state of practice is still with us, but the argument perhaps more open than it was.

Lindblom's perspective is most extensively developed by Simon (1961) and by Cyert and March (1963). They deny that organizations can sensibly be viewed as entities with personalities and goals like those of individuals. Firms are better seen as shifting coalitions, in which conflicting demands and objectives are constantly but imperfectly reconciled, and all change is necessarily incremental. In this framework, rationalist strategy—in which senior management chooses and imposes a pattern of behaviour on the firm—denies the reality of organizational dynamics.

The implications of this for strategy are developed by Mintzberg (1972, 1978), who contrasts *deliberate* and *emergent* strategy. The former is the realization of the rationalist approach, the latter the identification of relatively systematic patterns of behaviour in what the organization actually does. Essentially, the same features distinguish the adaptive mode of strategic decision-making from the planning mode. In the former, 'Clear goals do not exist . . . the strategy-making process is characterised by the reactive solution to existing problems . . . the adaptive organization makes its decisions in incremental, serial steps' (Mintzberg, 1973). By contrast, planning involves, 'Anticipating decision-making . . . a system of decisions . . . a process that is directed towards producing one or more future states' (Mintzberg, 1973, from Ackoff, 1970).

As a description of how real organizations operate, this critique is so obviously compelling that at first it is hard to see why the rationalist school of strategy remains influential. But the reasons why it does are clear enough. Apart from a few disinterested scholars, people study and analyse strategy because they want to know what to do. To observe that organizations are complex, that change is inevitably incremental, and that strategy is necessarily adaptive, however true, helps very little in deciding what to do. Managers wish to be told of a process which they can at least partially control and, whatever its weaknesses, that is what rationalist strategy appears to offer.

For some, the nihilist conclusion of the critics deals with the matter. Firms do what they do because they are what they are, and the strategy process is one which one can observe, describe, but for which it is not possible to prescribe. This seems to be the view taken by Pettigrew in his theoretical argument (Pettigrew, 1977) and in his massive history of ICI (Pettigrew, 1985). Mintzberg offers at least a partial answer—crafting strategy. 'Imagine someone *planning* strategy. What likely springs to mind is an image of orderly thinking; a senior manager, or a group of them, sitting in an office formulating courses of action that everyone else will implement on schedule. The keynote is reason—rational control, the systematic analysis of competitors and markets, or company strengths and weaknesses. . . . Now imagine someone *crafting* strategy. A wholly different image likely results, as different from planning as craft is from mechanization. Craft involves traditional skill, dedication, perfection through the mastering of detail' (Mintzberg, 1987: 66). The metaphor has further implications. The skills of the craftsman are acquired, not from books or lectures, but from observation of the behaviour of established craftsmen. The case-study technique of the business school even finds its parallel in the minor works of the apprentices which preceded the master pieces of the skilled craftsmen.[1]

Yet at this point the use of metaphor has got wholly out of hand. Strategy is necessarily incremental and adaptive, but that does not in any way imply that its evolution cannot be, or should not be, analysed, managed, and controlled.

1 The case—in which the student is presented with a quantity of (largely unstructured) information and asked to read a decision in class discussion—is a common teaching technique in business schools. In some institutions—notably Harvard—it is essentially the only method of formal instruction.

Neither Lindblom nor Cyert and March had any doubts on that score, and the process of 'successive limited comparison' which Lindblom described is a highly rational process; he underplayed his argument, and perhaps misled some readers by describing it as 'muddling through'. Indeed, it may be that we are, at least subconsciously, under the grip of a more powerful metaphor—the contrast between grand design and natural selection as accounts of the origin of species. Thus there is an artificial polarization between a view of the world which sees it as potentially wholly receptive to rational control and planning and one in which events fall as they will. Although biological evolution is not one, the world is full of adaptive, incremental processes where that adaptation is subject to partial, but imperfect, control-processes ranging from travelling in space to boiling an egg. If we must use analogies we should look there, and learn about guided adaptation and managed incrementalism. In this framework, the false dichotomies between the implementation and the formulation of strategy, between rational analysis and incremental evolution, and between analytic and behavioural approaches, quickly fall away.

The content of business strategy

The subject of strategy which I have described falls a long way short of an established discipline, characterized by a widely accepted organizing structure and a growing body of empirical knowledge. Indeed, the strongly commercial orientation of the strategy business itself conflicts directly with this objective. The traditions of scholarship demand that each author should explain carefully how his contribution relates to all that has gone before; the dictates of profit suggest that each consultant should dismiss as bunkum the theories of his rivals and proffer his own nostrums as the one true solution.

The best and most familiar example of an organizing framework is SWOT analysis—the definition of the strengths, weaknesses, opportunities, and threats which the business faces. SWOT is simply a list. It conveys no information in itself, but it is a way of helping us to think about the information we already have. And for a busy manager, confronted by endless everyday pressures and unused to standing back to think about longer-term issues, it is a particularly useful list, as demonstrated by its continued popularity.

It is easy to generate lists, and the literature of business strategy is full of them, few of which stand the test of time. An organizing framework can never be right, or wrong, only helpful or unhelpful. A good organizing framework is minimalist—it is as simple as is consistent with illuminating the issues under discussion—and it is memorable. That is why alliteration is favoured (the seven S framework of McKinsey, or the five forces of Porter). A good list is usually between three and five items long (two is hardly a list, six is too many to remember).

A model is a more sophisticated organizing framework. It goes beyond mere listing of items and contains premises and deductions. The Prisoner's Dilemma is such a model. It, too, is minimalist—it focuses starkly on the problem of co-operation, and all real life problems are more complex. Because of its deductive structure, this model—and even the simplest of models—is more complex than a list. But in a good model, such as the Prisoner's Dilemma, the additional complexity is compensated by the greater insight it conveys. A useful model is a way of learning about processes and interrelationships and so goes beyond the mere structuring of existing knowledge. The suitability of the model, like the value of the list, is determined by the extent of its application, and it is the continued and widespread use of the Prisoner's Dilemma framework across biology, economics, sociology, and psychology after thirty years which indicates that this is, indeed, a good model. Like a useful list, a useful model is also memorable, and memorability is achieved here by the ludicrous but colourful story of the two prisoners in separate cells.

The organizing framework provides the link from judgement through experience to learning. A valid framework is one which focuses sharply on what the skilled manager, at least instinctively, already knows. He is constantly alive to the strengths, weaknesses, opportunities, threats, which confront him. She understands that co-operative behaviour cannot simply be assumed, or exhorted, but requires the support of an explicit incentive structure or the expectation of a continued relationship. For both, a successful framework formalizes and extends their existing knowledge. For the less practised, an effective framework is one which organizes and develops what would otherwise be disjointed experience.

Business strategy also benefits from the accumulation of empirical knowledge. Chandler's hypothesis—that organizational structure follows strategy—falls into this category. As framed by Chandler—reflecting the histories of a limited number of US corporations—it must remain a hypothesis. Validation can be achieved only by reference to a much wider body of data but, as subsequent research has deepened our understanding of the evolution of modern business, Chandler's hypothesis has stood up well. There are many other ways of testing arguments. The most extensive body of empirical information on strategic issues is the PIMS database, which reflects the anonymous experience of over 7,000 business units. Two empirical findings stand out from that research—the association between profitability and market share, and that between quality and return on investment.

The development of frameworks and the accumulation of empirical knowledge go together. There is simply too much information about business available for it to be interpreted without some extensive conceptual structure. So the PIMS observation on the association of high profitability with high market share cannot be interpreted without a view of what defines a market, and it is to the credit of the PIMS researchers that they have a clearly specified view on this. The 'served market' is what is supplied by the group of firms which the business, subjectively, perceives as its competitors. The term 'market' is used in many other ways, by different writers, and its use in this book emphasizes the importance of the consumer perspective, and employs the term strategic group in a sense rather similar to the PIMS market. Neither this usage nor that of PIMS is right or wrong; the important issue is to understand the difference and be clear about which term, and which sense, is being applied in any particular case.

But the valid interpretation of empirical data in a complex world also requires the support of a model and a theory. Certainly it would be wrong to infer from the PIMS findings that increasing market share is either necessary or sufficient to increase profitability. This issue was discussed at length in Chapter 11, and the conclusion drawn there was that competitive advantage tended to be associated with both high return on investment and high market share—that the relationship was indirect rather than causal. But the same relationship could be interpreted in many other ways. The choice between these interpretations depends on specifying hypotheses and testing them by reference to other observations and further data.

Frameworks, models, and taxonomies can never, in themselves, be prescriptive. We may note that men are either fat or thin as we can identify decentralized or matrix organization, and while these are often helpful ways of describing the world, neither observation tells us what any individual or firm should do. If we add the empirical finding that fat men die prematurely, or that matrix organization is unsuccessful in particular types of industry, then we have findings we can apply in practical situations.

These observations about the nature of knowledge are scarcely new. It is more than two centuries since the Scottish philosopher David Hume spelt them out.

If we take in our hand any volume . . . let us ask, 'Does it contain any abstract reasoning concerning quantity or number?' No. 'Does it contain any experimental reasoning concerning matter of fact or existence?' No. Commit it then to the flames; for it can contain nothing but sophistry and illusion. (Hume, 1748.)

Yet it is clear even today that there is much in the literature of business strategy that Hume would have consigned to the flames. Most of all, the view that the construction of lists—the dominant methodology of strategy—is an activity which has empirical content or can form the basis of recommendations for action is one which is widely held and clearly erroneous.

In this book I have tried to avoid making or reproducing statements unless they follow as a result of explicit deduction from stated premises or are potentially verifiable claims about the empirical world. I do not claim invariably to have succeeded, but if the study of business is to develop in any scientific manner that objective is one which needs to be widely shared.

Contingency and resource based approaches to strategy

The analysis presented in this book derives from the contingency theory which is the dominant strand of thought in organizational behaviour. Starting from the original work of Burns and Stalker (1966) and Woodward (1965), contingency theory (Steiner, 1979; Grinyer *et al.*, 1986) emphasizes that there is no best form of organization and that organizational success rests on matching the organization to its environment. There is a striking congruence here between the sociological tenets of contingency theory and the financial economist's efficient market perspective, which argues that there can be no universal prescriptions for success since, if there were, their general adoption would reduce their value to everyone. These two approaches taken together lead directly to the conclusion that it is the creation and maintenance of distinctive capabilities which is at the heart of successful strategy.

The successful match of organizational structure and environment is not, in itself, a source of competitive advantage; it is a necessary, but not sufficient condition. Banking demands a mechanistic structure—the decentralized processing of millions of daily transactions under common procedures simply cannot be managed in any other way. But the sources of competitive advantage in banking are to be found elsewhere, in reputation and in the architecture of lending relationships. Mechanistic structures are, by their very nature, replicable, but certain types of organic structure—those here identified with architecture—are not. Contingency theory, given its origins, naturally stresses the organizational contribution to distinctive capabilities.

The contribution of economics to our understanding of distinctive capabilities is both to broaden and to narrow the range. It broadens it in importing factors which are not behavioural but which none the less contribute to competitive advantage, emphasizing particularly the role of strategic assets. It narrows it by focusing attention on characteristics of the organization which are both appropriable and irreproducible. This latter emphasis is missing in the very wide range of distinctive competencies identified by Snow and Hrebiniak (1980).

The necessary irreproducibility of capabilities which yield sustainable competitive advantage has been developed by a number of authors. Teece (1986) draws particular attention to the appropriability problem associated with innovation. Prahalad and Hamel (1990) are concerned with similar issues in the context of organizational knowledge, and Oster (1990) is particularly effective in stressing the efficient market perspective in this context. Lippman and Rumelt (1982) review the issue more generally and the concept of architecture owes much to their 'uncertain imitability' (usefully developed by Reed and De Filippi (1990) and Barney (1991))—copycat strategies fail because, as I suggested at p. 350, the potential copier cannot easily identify what it is that it is necessary to copy. Grant (1991) usefully draws a number of these themes together.

An emphasis on the creation and maximization of rents as the engine of commercial activity is, of course, hardly a new idea. Elements of it can be found in Ricardo (1819), to whom the concepts of rents and quasi-rents are due, but by far the most forceful exposition of this perspective remains that of Schumpeter (1934). Yet this work has not been in the mainstream of economic thought. Industrial economics has followed broadly the traditions of Alfred Marshall, whose primary unit of analysis was 'the representative firm', and in subsequent models of competition firms differed not at all from each other or did so in essentially trivial ways (see Kay, 1991a, for an elaboration of these points). It is, indeed, this perspective which justified Ansoff's rejection of microeconomics as a basis for strategy—'microeconomic theory provides for no differentiation of behaviour among firms . . . as a result, the traditional microeconomic theory is neither rich nor extensive enough for our purpose' (Ansoff, 1969). Although these criticisms are much less valid as applied to microeconomic theory today, the contribution of economics to strategy has remained slight.

Looking to the future

Yet it is clear that the subject of strategy has suffered from this neglect of obvious roots in sociology and in economics. Too much of what is offered as strategy consists of lists or platitudes. The value of these is not negligible. Lists are aids to structured thought. Platitudes are often platitudes because they are necessary reassertions of important truths. But the claims which can be made for knowledge of this kind are modest indeed.

For centuries, the subject of medicine was mostly nonsense. Doctors applied fashionable nostrums, sometimes bleeding their patients, sometimes starving them. Generally these remedies were useless, sometimes they were fortuitously beneficial, at other times unintendedly harmful. States of health were defined by reference to ascientific categorization, such as the humours or the elements. The prestige of a doctor rested more on the status of his patients and the confidence of his assertions than on the evidence of his cures.

The parallels are obvious, if not exact, and the reasons for the parallels are obvious too. Both medicine and management deal with urgent and pressing problems. The demand for a cure is so pressing that critical faculties are suspended. The quack who promises relief often receives a warmer welcome than the practitioner who recognizes the limitations of his own knowledge, and since it is difficult to measure the effectiveness of treatment, this impression may persist even after it is over.

But in the last fifty years, the application of scientific method to medical subjects, and the development and adoption of knowledge gained in physics, chemistry, and biology, has transformed their effectiveness. Medicine remains a practical subject. The experience and judgement of a good doctor is as important as the extent of his knowledge and the quality of his training.

Untrained individuals continue to express opinions on medical matters, not all of which are wrong. But few of us would now wish to put ourselves in the hands of doctors who had no such knowledge or training, or who professed to despise it.

The subject of management has far to go before it can claim the scientific status achieved by modern medicine. The objective of this book has been to take one or two faltering steps on the road towards that goal.

T he best introduction to what has been written on business strategy is Quinn, Mintzberg, and James (1988), which is not only a useful textbook but reproduces or extracts many of the most important or widely cited writings in the field. The *Harvard Business Review* is a reliable guide to current fashions in business thought.

On General Electric, see Springer and Hofer (1978), Hamermesh (1986), Potts and Behr (1987), Tichy (1989), Tichy and Charan (1989).

22

....

Conclusions

It is easy to see why the military analogy continues to exercise such a powerful hold on thinking about corporate strategy. What boy (and most chief executives are men) has not dreamt of destroying his opponents with his new technology or his ingenuity? What youth has not identified with the great field generals of history, alone with their troops, placing divisions here, battalions there, and inspiring their men to heroic feats with a few well-chosen words of encouragement and inspiration?

There is something in the military analogy, of course, but it is as misleading as it is helpful. It is, I believe, directly responsible for two of the most widespread fallacies in the interpretation of business behaviour and economic performance. One is the almost universal overestimation of the importance of size and scale. Modern warfare is based on the destruction of opposing forces. Success derives directly from the power to impose such destruction on others and the capacity to bear it oneself. The United States was the almost inevitable victor in the two world wars this century, because of its resources of men and materials that were essentially limitless relative to those of its opponents. The same phenomenon is seen in the defeat of Europe's two greatest military machines, those of Hitler and Napoleon, by the vast inhospitable scale of Russia, the worst governed of European countries.

Business is not like that at all. Success in business derives from adding value of your own, not diminishing that of your competitors, and it is based on distinctive capability, not destructive capacity. Distinctive capability becomes harder, not easier, to maintain as size increases. Yet in descriptions of both business and public policy, the equation of scale, power, and effectiveness is often simply assumed. Nowhere is this more apparent than in discussion of Europe after 1992, where the effects of integration are repeatedly described in terms that would be appropriate to a military alliance.

Separately, each nation represents only a statistical blip in global accounting. But united as the EC they become an economic powerhouse that dwarfs Japan and directly challenges the heretofore unchallengeable economic output of the United States. (Silva and Sjogren, 1990: pp. viii–ix.)

The generalization from the military to the economic sphere is often assumed to be so obvious as not to require specific elaboration.

But it is wholly false. While military power is directly related to the scale of resources that underpin it, economic power (whatever that means) is not. If economic strength is competitiveness—and it is hard to see what else it could sensibly mean—then the competitiveness of European industry is related to the aggregate size of the resources of labour, capital, and other factors in the European economies only in the most tenuous and indirect of ways. A 'home market of 320 million people' in no sense resembles an army of 320 million people in the service of European industry. Yet the phrase is used in ways that invite precisely that comparison.

The loosely formulated analogy distracts attention from the real benefits of European integration. These come from specialization—the ability to deploy specific distinctive capabilities more readily in different geographic markets. The metal-workers of Lumazzone illustrate the opportunity well. They are now able to use their particular skills in a global rather than a national market and hence sell greater volumes and obtain higher price premiums in markets that are better served than before. And there are substantial gains from integration through the introduction of competitive forces into sectors of European industry where inefficiency has survived because of regulation, public procurement rules, or other protectionism.

The second area in which the military analogy misleads is inviting excessive emphasis on leadership, vision, and determination. Military history abounds with stories of heroism in the face of adversity—Horatio defending the bridge, Custer's last stand, the charge of the Light Brigade. It is easy to see why these images are important in a military context. But if General Custer or Lord Raglan had been businessmen, we would not wish to have been their employees or to have bought their shares, and I would not myself have wished to invest much in Horatio either. Fighting against overwhelming odds may sometimes be a necessary military strategy. It is almost never a sensible business strategy.

These attitudes relate directly to the rationalist view of strategy which sees it as something devised for the corporation by its most senior executives. It is commonplace for them to distance themselves physically from the organization to contemplate strategy in weekend retreats. They return refreshed and inspired, to mould the company in the light of the strategy they have conceived. Strategy is something which is imposed on the company, and the chief executive is the man who imposes it.

The Anglo-American business environment has particularly developed this personalization of the role of the chief executive, who has come to enjoy the status of the commanding general. His authority is (for so long as he remains in office) unquestioned. The vision of the organization is his. His primary task is to frame that vision and to inspire his staff and employees with it. If a new chief executive takes the helm, it is possible, indeed often expected, that this will lead to a change in the strategic goals of the firm. A business school case in strategy will characteristically feature a named CEO struggling, frequently alone, to resolve the fundamental issues of his company's strategic direction.

The focus on issues of leadership and the management of change in courses and seminars for senior executives follows directly from this view of the world.

The emphasis on merger, acquisition, divestment, and the management of the corporate portfolio in the business environment of English-speaking countries is a closely related phenomenon. These mechanisms are the fastest and most effective ways of engineering changes in strategic direction and accomplishing strategic goals. It is quite common to encounter senior executives who see the question, 'What should our strategy be?' as virtually interchangeable with the question, 'What companies should we buy?'

The views I have described are the product of the ways in which the subject of strategy has been pursued in the last three decades, principally in the United States. They also reflect the financial systems of these countries, which emphazise equity investment and allow hostile take-over and the free operation of the market for corporate control. But this approach is not shared in Japan—as has often been noted, the Japanese find the rationalist model of strategy a peculiar one. Nor has it been pursued to the same degree in much of continental Europe. In France, however, the PDG has increasingly come to enjoy the same role as the American CEO, and the dramatic surge in acquisition activity by French companies is a close consequence. A Japanese manager who had proposed in the late 1980s that shareholder value would be enhanced by breaking up the corporation and disposing of its assets (as would often have been the case) would have been regarded in much the same light as the new master of an Oxford college who, observing that the historic buildings were quite unsuitable for the needs of modern education (as they mostly are), proposed that they be sold and the proceeds invested in new purpose-built facilities. Each of them would be seen as the victim of a misunderstanding of what it was their job was about, and of the purposes of an organization for which they are trustee as well as manager. Outside the English-speaking world, the corporation is seen in an organic rather than an instrumental way, as an organization with a character of its own and its own internal purposes and dynamism.

This dichotomy is reflected in the ways in which added value is created, and the ways in which it is distributed. The United States is at one extreme. Appropriation of added value for shareholders is seen as the principal, even the sole, objective of the corporation. This position has legal support and is enforced, in practice, through the threat of take-over. In Japan, at the opposite end of the spectrum, managers see shareholders as only one of a number of stakeholder groups, and by no means the most important. Odagiri, explaining why mergers and acquisitions are not an important component of the strategies of Japanese corporations, brings out this difference, and its consequences, clearly:

The executives of Japanese firms are mostly internally promoted and are less constrained by the stock market's evaluation. Corporate growth is appreciated and sought after primarily for its contribution to utilising the enriching human resources and in creating

promotion opportunities. . . . Obviously, only internal growth contributes to this purpose
. . . workers identify their interests with those of the company which, as a consequence, is
regarded as a sort of community. Any offer to acquire the company is therefore likely
taken as an intrusion . . . because labour practices are in many ways firm-specific, unify-
ing the practices of two different firms tends not only to be costly but also to create
uneasiness and conflicts of interest (1991, p. 106).

The paradox in this comparison, of course, is that the different objectives of
Japanese managers do not appear to have worked to the detriment of
investors in Japanese securities. Despite low dividend yields on Japanese
shares, total returns from investment in Japan have been outstanding in the
long term. For reasons described in Chapter 12, an exclusive preoccupation
with the interests of one stakeholder group may not serve the interests even of
that group if it inhibits the formation of relational contracts within the corporation. In US companies, by contrast, strategic bargaining between stakeholder groups is assumed to be central to all commercial activity. Such
bargaining took a new twist in the 1980s when senior management appreciated that, given the high costs of removing them, they themselves could negotiate for a material share of the added value created by the firm. The extreme
case is the well-documented tale of Ross Johnson of RJR Nabisco, who, not
content with surrounding himself by corporate jets and America's leading
sportsmen, attempted to restructure the company to yield $100 million for
himself.

In all this, European business lies, as it often does, in an intermediate position. Britain's financial markets, and systems of corporate governance, are
close to those of the United States. Italy, in which a large part of effective business is conducted in smaller firms in which proprietorial influences are dominant, occupies rather different ground, while France and Germany pursue the
'Rhenan model' described by Michel Albert, in which the firm is perceived as
operating within a wider social context.

The central theme of this book is that competitive advantages are generally
based on stability and continuity in relationships. It is a theme which has
been developed in many different ways. It began (in Chapters 1 and 2) with a
view of what success in business meant, and with the identification of companies which had achieved such success—BMW and Glaxo, Honda and IBM,
Benetton and Marks & Spencer—companies whose names have recurred
throughout. They are companies with a strong sense of vision and mission,
but with a sense of vision and mission which has arisen from within the company and from a recognition of its strengths, not one which has been imposed
from outside or created by a corporate communications programme. These
are all businesses which are clearly focused around that recognition of
strengths, and if there is one company on that list which is evidently faltering
it is Benetton, which has drifted from a strong sense of its own identity in the
market-place.

These issues were developed in Chapters 4 and 5, which explained the role
of relational contracting and described how a network of relational con-

tracts—the architecture of the firm—often formed the basis of competitive advantage. Chapter 9 described how competitive advantages are created by the application of distinctive capabilities in particular markets. It follows that added value will normally arise at the level of the individual operating business. Chapter 10 reviewed the disappointing record of merger and acquisition activity, and Chapter 11 explained how size and scale rarely form the basis of sustainable competitive advantage, and why there are rarely gains from portfolio planning. Chapter 13 reinforced the argument that firm performance depends on the creation of added value in operating businesses. Financial engineering contributes nothing to corporate success in the long run.

How is the need for stability and continuity in relationships to be reconciled with the equal need for change and flexibility which confront every organization in business today? If there is a single central lesson from the success of Japanese manufacturing industry, or from Benetton, or from many others of the cases developed in this book, it is that the stability of relationships and the capacity to respond to change are mutually supportive, not mutually exclusive, requirements. It is within the context of long-term relationships, and often only within that context, that the development of organizational knowledge, the free exchange of information, and a readiness to respond quickly and flexibly can be sustained.

So the most important challenge for European business is to maintain, and enhance, those competitive advantages which are based on architecture. Of the three major economic areas of the world, one—North America—has developed a business culture which offers little support for structures of relational contracts, and the competitive advantages of US firms are mostly to be found elsewhere—in innovation, in branding and reputation, and through the exploitation of strategic assets. Firms in Japan and the Far East have made much of the sources of competitive strength which I have identified with architecture. Yet the pressures on European companies are principally to move in a trans-Atlantic direction. This is reflected in an increasing pace of merger and acquisition activity, a more American approach to corporate strategy, and a more aggressive business environment characterized by tighter financial controls, more specific monitoring of performance, and less emphasis on long-term relationships with contractors or with employees. In public policy, and in business policy, the potential losses from these developments far outweigh the potential gains.

The foundations of corporate success are built on the identification and exploitation of distinctive capabilities. The distinctive capabilities of Glaxo and of Benetton, of Reuters and of BMW, could hardly be more different. And there is a general lesson here. The search for generic strategies, for recipes for corporate success, is doomed to failure. There can be no such recipes because their value would be destroyed by the very fact of their identification.

VALUE OF THE ECU

Value of the Ecu at 1st January 1992

Australia	$1.76
Austria	14.3 Sch.
Belgium	41.9 Fr.
Canada	$1.55
Denmark	7.93 Kr.
France	6.95 FF
Germany	2.04 DM
Greece	235 Dr.
Ireland	£0.766
Italy	1542 Lire
Japan	Y169
The Netherlands	2.29 Guilder
New Zealand	$2.48
Norway	8.02 Kr.
Spain	130 Peseta
Sweden	7.45 Kr.
Switzerland	1.82 SFr.
UK	£0.716
USA	$1.34

GLOSSARY

Activity Based Costing The analysis of costs by reference to the purposes for which they are incurred.

Adaptive Strategy Strategy that responds incrementally to changes in the external environment.

Added Value The difference between the market value of a firm's output and the value which its inputs would have in comparable activities undertaken by other firms.

Aggregated Rebate A discount related to the totality of purchases from a particular supplier.

Appropriability The ability to realize the benefits of a distinctive capability or competitive advantage for the benefit of the firm itself rather than its customers, suppliers, or competitors.

Arbitrage Buying a commodity or security in a low price market to sell unchanged in a higher price one.

Architecture A distinctive collection of relational contracts. The benefits of architecture typically rest in the development of organizational knowledge, flexibility in response and information exchange within or between organizations. A primary *distinctive capability*.

Articles 85/86 The provisions of the Treaty of Rome dealing with competition policy. Article 85 covers restrictive agreements, Article 86 the abuse of a dominant position.

Asset Specificity A characteristic of tangible or intangible assets which have value only in the context of a particular business relationship.

Auction An auction is *open* when bidders know, and can respond to, other bids. A *sealed bid* auction is one in which each bid is made in ignorance of others.

Battle of the Sexes A game in which satisfactory outcomes depend on the co-ordination of responses.

BCG The Boston Consulting Group. (One of the leading firms of strategic consultants.)

BCG Matrix A scheme for categorizing business units by reference to their market share and the expected growth of their markets.

Business Strategy See *Strategy*.

Business System See *Value Chain*.

Capital Asset Pricing Model A theory of capital markets in which the returns to risk are based on the relationship between individual security risk and overall market volatility.

CEO Chief Executive Officer. US term for the most senior employee engaged in line management. Chief executive (UK), président-directeur général (France) have similar meanings but there are significant differences between companies and business environments in their use of the terms.

Chaos, Chaotic System A system of non-linear differential equations which has the property that its evolution may be very sensitive to small changes in initial conditions.

Chicken A game in which satisfactory outcomes depend on differentiation.

Classical Contract A long-term contract whose terms are fully spelled out in a legal relationship. Cf. *relational contract*.

Cold Wars See *Competitive Environments*.

Commitment An action taken with the intention of restricting the range of actions which are subsequently possible or profitable. See *Credible Commitment*.

Competitive Advantage The ability of a firm to add more value than another firm in the same market.

Competitive Environments—Stable and Unstable A competitive environment is stable if firms sacrifice short-term competitive gains in the expectation of larger returns from reciprocal behaviour by competitors. In unstable competitive markets, firms engage in short-run profit maximization.

Competitive Strategy See *Strategy*.

Complementary Asset An asset necessary to the exploitation of a distinctive capability.

Concentration A measure of the dominance of a market by few firms.

Conglomerate A multi-divisional firm in which there are few transactions between divisions.

Consummate Co-operation Co-operative action which fully utilises joint resources and information.

Contestable market A market characterized by free entry and low sunk costs, which is constantly disciplined by the threat of entry.

Contingency Theory The hypothesis that the best organizational structure is unique to the particular environment the firm faces.

Contingent Contract A long-term contract in which some contract provisions are conditional on future unknown events.

Contingent Strategy Strategy which is distinctive both to the firm and to its economic environment.

Contract A legal agreement for exchange. See *Classical Contract, Spot Contract*.

Co-operation Actions by two, or more, firms which maximize the joint product of a relationship rather than the individual returns. See *Perfunctory Co-operation* and *Consummate Co-operation*.

Co-operative Ethic A systematic pattern of *consummate co-operation* within an organization.

Co-ordination The simultaneous adoption of identical or complementary strategies by independent agents. See *Differentiation*.

Core Outcomes of negotiation which all parties would prefer to the absence of a general agreement.

Core Business The set of markets in which the firm's *distinctive capability* is likely to yield *competitive advantage*.

Corporate Control, Market for The process by which capital markets encourage competition for the control of companies.

Corporate Strategy See *Strategy*.

Cost Driver Factors (either activities within the firm or events external to it) which determine costs.

Cost Leadership The lowest cost producer in a market. (Possibly after adjustment for differences in product quality.)

Cost of Capital The return which a firm must earn on incremental investment if the value of existing equity is not to be reduced.

Credible Commitment A promise to engage in a subsequent course of behaviour which is accompanied by actions which increase the profitability of that course or reduce the profitability of alternatives.

Current Cost Accounting System of inflation accounting in which asset values and depreciation are based on the replacement cost of assets.

Differentiation The simultaneous adoption of distinct strategies by independent agents.

Distinctive Capability The features of a firm's position or organization which cannot readily be reproduced by competitors. Generally based on *architecture, innovation, reputation,* or the ownership of *strategic assets.*

Dominant Strategy An action which is best regardless of the action of any other player. (Contrast with *Nash Equilibrium.*)

Dominant Strategy Equilibrium An outcome of a game in which all players have dominant strategies.

Economic Market A range of strongly substitutable methods of meeting consumer needs.

Economies of Scale, Scope See *Scale Economies, Scope Economies.*

Emergent Strategy Strategy which is inferred from patterns of behaviour rather than consciously adopted.

Engineering Method A means of measuring *scale economies* by assessing the costs of hypothetical alternative plants.

Entry The process by which a firm comes to a new market.

EPS Earnings Per Share. Post-tax profits per unit of equity capital.

Equilibrium (in *Game Theory*) See *Nash Equilibrium, Dominant Strategy Equilibrium.*

Equity, Equity Capital Capital provided for the firm by its shareholders. May be measured by reference either to the value of the company's assets or the market value of its shares

Excess Return Return to shareholders in excess of the cost of capital.

Experience Curve The relationship between costs and cumulative output.

Experience Good A commodity whose most important characteristics can only be ascertained after purchase. A long-term experience good is one for which they emerge only after repeated purchase or long interval.

Extensive Form Game (in *Game Theory*) A game in which players respond to earlier moves by other players.

Externalities Actions which affect other agents directly (and not through market behaviour).

FASB Federal Accounting Standards Board.

Focal Points Intuitively attractive outcomes to games or negotiations (equal sharing, round numbers, etc.).

Focus Structuring the different characteristics of a multiple attributes commodity in combinations that reflect market demand.

Game Theory The formal study of structures in which the returns to any individual agent depend both on the strategy chosen and on the response of other parties.

Gearing The proportion of a company's assets which are financed by debt. (UK usage: see *Leverage.*)

GDP (Gross Domestic Product) The total of incomes (net output) accruing in a country.

GE Screen (General Electric) A system of *portfolio planning*. See also *BCG Matrix*.

Gross Output The aggregate value of sales. Cf. *Net Output*.

Hedging The deliberate assumption of a risk which offsets a pre-existing risk.

Historic Cost Generally accepted accounting principles in which asset values are entered at historic cost.

Horizontal Product Differentiation See *Product Differentiation*.

Hot Wars See *Competitive Environments*.

Hub and Spoke (in civil aviation) A pattern of operation in which many journeys are made by *interlining* through a centrally located airport.

Implicit Contract See *Relational Contract*.

Incremental Cost The additional cost of undertaking an activity or producing a unit of output. Differs from average cost when there are economies of scope or scale.

Incumbency An established presence in a market.

Industry A group of firms producing technically related products.

Informal Contract See *Relational Contract*.

Innovation New products, processes, or styles of relationship. A primary *distinctive capability*. Innovation is often used mainly to refer to technological innovations, but here it is used in a much more general sense.

Interlining (in civil aviation) Transfer at an airport which is not the final destination.

Just in Time See *Kanban*.

Kanban 'Just in time' management. A system (pioneered by Toyota) of managing production processes with minimal inventory.

Keiretsu Network of Japanese customer–supplier relationships, e.g. those around Toyota (distinguished from *Kigyo-Shudan*).

Kigyo-Shudan Loosely affiliated group of Japanese companies in different industries. (Successor to more tightly organized *Zaibatsu*.)

LBO Leveraged Buy Out. A highly *geared* restructuring of a company's capital structure to increase the equity stake held by management.

Leverage The proportion of a company's assets which are financed by debt. (US usage: see *Gearing*.)

Market See *Economic Market, Strategic Market*.

Market Segmentation The adoption of price and other strategies to distinguish related markets. See *Price Discrimination*.

Matrix Organization A multi-divisional organization which links the various functional activities across divisions.

Mission Statement A brief expression of corporate objective.

Model Algebraic or arithmetic specification of a set of relationships. A model may be a representation of a firm or part of a firm, or of the interactions between firms.

Nash Equilibrium (in *Game Theory*) An outcome in which each player's strategy is best given the strategies adopted by other players.

Natural Monopoly A market in which only one firm can be viable

Net Cash Flow Pre-tax profit plus depreciation but minus capital expenditure.

Net Output Aggregate value of sales less the cost of materials (but not the costs of labour or capital).

Niche Player A company focusing on a limited market or market segment.

Oligopoly A market dominated by a small number of firms.

Opportunism One party attempts to gain from *asset specificity* by driving a harder bargain after the other party has invested in the assets concerned.

Organizational Knowledge Systems, routines, data within an organization which are only imperfectly understood by any individual member. Their value is therefore partly appropriable by the organization.

Pay-off Matrix (in *Game Theory*) A description of the returns to each strategy given the strategies adopted by other players.

PDG Président-Directeur Général (France). See *CEO*.

PE Ratio See *Price–Earnings Ratio*.

Perfunctory Co-operation The degree of *co-operation* between two or more parties which can be enforced by formal agreement.

PIMS Profit Impact of Market Strategy. An extensive database on the market performance and other characteristics of business units supplied anonymously by 7,000 companies.

Portfolio Planning A system of grading business units by reference to market share, market growth, or similar variables. See *BCG Matrix, GE Screen*.

Positioning Product positioning is the relationship between a firm's products and those of its competitors in commodity space. (Positioning is also often used to refer to a firm's overall strategy relative to its competitors.)

Predation A pricing strategy whose objective is the elimination of a competitor.

Price Discrimination Price differences between related commodities which reflect differences in value rather than cost. See *Market Segmentation*.

Price–Earnings Ratio Share price as a multiple of after-tax earnings.

Prisoner's Dilemma A game with an inferior *dominant strategy equilibrium*.

Product Differentiation Differences between related products. Product differentiation is 'vertical' when quality based and 'horizontal' when it reflects differences in tastes.

Product Life Cycle Successive phases of evolution of demand for a product.

Relational Contract An exchange relationship between two parties which is not fully articulated. The rules of behaviour are implicit and the enforcement mechanism is the value of the continuing relationship between the parties.

Relationship An agreement for exchange. Includes both fully specified legal relationships and relational contracts. See *Relational Contract*.

Reputation A name for high quality in characteristics that cannot easily be monitored. Enables contracts to be made, or made on more favourable terms, than would otherwise be possible. A primary *distinctive capability*.

ROE Return on Equity. Profits as a percentage of the value of shareholders' assets.

ROI Return on Investment. Profits as a percentage of the value of all corporate assets.

ROS Return on Sales. Profits as a percentage of turnover

Scale Economies Cost reductions attributable to increases in the rate of output.

Scope Economies Cost savings arising where the cost of producing two products together is less than the sum of the costs of producing them separately.

Search Good A commodity for which consumers can establish most relevant characteristics of the product before purchase. See *Experience Goods*.

Shareholder Value An approach to business planning which stresses maximization of the value of shareholders' equity and discounted cash flow methods of investment appraisal.

Sogo Shosha General (largely overseas) trading company within a Zaibatsu (pre-WW II) or a Kigyo-Shudan (today), e.g. Mitsui and Co., C. Itoh.

Spot Contract An immediate bilateral exchange.

SSAP Statement of standard accounting practice (UK).

Strategic Asset A source of *competitive advantage* which is derived from factors external to the firm rather than from its own *distinctive capabilities*.

Strategic Business Unit The level of a multi-divisional organization at which strategy is determined.

Strategic Group Firms which adopt similar strategies and hence see themselves as in direct competition.

Strategic Market The smallest range of activities across which a firm can viably compete.

Strategy Corporate strategy is concerned with the firm's choice of markets. Business or competitive strategy is concerned with its relationships with customers, distributors, suppliers, and competitors within those markets.

Sunk Costs Costs incurred in entering a market which cannot be recouped on exit.

Survivor Method A means of measuring *scale economies* by reference to changes in the size and distribution of firms and plants over time.

Sustainable (of *distinctive capability* or *competitive advantage*) Capable of being maintained over time despite market entry and competitor attempts at replication.

SWOT Analysis The discussion of a firm's prospects by reference to strengths, weaknesses, opportunities, and threats.

Synergy Added value created by joining two distinct firms.

Value Added As *Net Output*. Differs from *Added Value* which deducts the cost of all inputs, including those of labour and capital. Value added tax liability is compiled after deducting the cost of capital inputs on a cash basis, but without deduction for labour cost.

Value Chain A breakdown of the production process into segments and functional activities.

Vertical Integration Entry by a firm into the markets served by its suppliers or distributors.

Vertical Product Differentiation See *Product Differentiation*.

Vertical Relationships Relationships between a firm and its suppliers and distributors.

Winners Curse A feature of auction behaviour in which successful bidders are likely to be those who have overestimated its value.

Wish-Driven Strategy Strategy directed towards aspirations that are not unique to the firm's distinctive capabilities.

Yield Curve The relationship between interest rates on debt and the length of time for which the debt is incurred.

Zaibatsu Close-knit group of Japanese companies (e.g. Mitsui, Mitsubishi), dissolved by Allies after the Second World War.

BIBLIOGRAPHY

Aaker, D. A. and Keller, K. L. (1990), 'Consumer evaluations of brand extensions', *Journal of Marketing*, 54 (Jan.), 27–41.

Abbott, K. and Thompson, D. J. (1991), 'De-regulating European aviation: The impact of bilateral liberalisation', *International Journal of Industrial Organisation*, 9: 125–40.

Abell, D. F. (1980), *Defining the Business*, Prentice-Hall.

—— and J. S. Hammond (1988), 'Cost dynamics: scale and experience effects', in Quinn, Mintzberg, and James (eds.) (1988).

Abernathy, W. J. and Hayes, R. H. (1980), 'Managing our way to economic decline', *Harvard Business Review* (July–Aug.), 67–77.

—— and Utterback, J. M. (1978), 'Patterns of technological innovation', *Technology Review*, 80: 40–7.

—— and Wayne, K. (1974), 'Limits of the learning curve', *Harvard Business Review*, (Sept.–Oct.), 109–19.

—— Clark, K. B. and Kantrow, A. M. (1983), *Industrial Renaissance: Producing a Competitive Future for America*, Basic Books.

Ackoff, R. L. (1970), *A Concept of Corporate Planning*, John Wiley.

Advisory Committee on Science and Technology (1990), *The Enterprise Challenge—Overcoming Barriers to Growth in Small Firms*, HMSO.

Agnew J. H. (1986), *Worlds Apart: The Market and the Theatre in Anglo-American Thought, 1550–1750*, Cambridge University Press.

Akerlof, G. A. (1970), 'The market for "lemons": Quality, uncertainty and the market mechanism', *Quarterly Journal of Economics* (Aug.), 488–500.

—— (1976), 'The economics of caste and of the rat race and other woeful tales', *Quarterly Journal of Economics*, 90: 599.

Albert, M. (1991), *Capitalisme contre capitalisme*, Seuil.

Alberts, W. W. (1989), 'The experience curve doctrine reconsidered', *Journal of Marketing*, 52/3: 36–49.

Alchian, A. and Demsetz, H. (1972), 'Production, information costs, and economic organization', *American Economic Review*, 62 (Dec.), 777–95.

—— Crawford, R. and Klein, B. (1978), 'Vertical integration, appropriable rents, and the competitive contracting process', *Journal of Law and Economics*, 21 (Oct.), 297–326.

Allen, F. (1984), 'Reputation and product quality', *Rand Journal of Economics*, 15: 311–27.

Andrews, K. R. (1980), *The Concept of Corporate Strategy*, rev. edn., Richard D. Irwin Inc.

Anschen, M. (1960), 'The manager and the black box', *Harvard Business Review*, 38/6: 85.

Ansoff, H. I. (1965), 'The firm of the future', *Harvard Business Review*, 43/5 (Sept.–Oct.), 162–78.

—— (ed.) (1969), *Corporate Strategy*, McGraw-Hill.

—— (1970), 'Does planning pay?', *Long Range Planning*, 3/2: 2–7.

Anthony, R. N. (1965) *Planning and Control Systems: A Framework for Analysis*, Division of Research, Harvard Business School.

Aoki, M., Gustaffson, B., and Williamson, O. E. (1990), *The Firm as a Nexus of Treaties*, Sage Publications.

Argenti, J (1965), *Corporate Planning*, Allen and Unwin.

—— (1968), *Corporate Planning—A Practical Guide*, Allen and Unwin.

—— (1980), *Practical Corporate Planning*, Allen and Unwin.

Armstrong, J. S. (1982), 'The value of formal planning for strategic decisions—a review of empirical research', *Strategic Management Journal*, 3: 197–211.

Arrow, K. J. (1952), 'An extension of the basic theorems of welfare economics', *Proceedings of the Second Berkeley Symposium on Mathematical Statistics and Probability*, University of California Press.

—— (1974), *The Limits of Organisation*, W. W. Norton.

Ashworth, M. H. and Forsyth, P. (1984), 'Civil aviation policy and the privatisation of British Airways', *IFS Report Series*, 12, The Institute for Fiscal Studies, London.

Aston, B. (1991), 'Unlimited horsepower: innovation at Cosworth Engineering', *Technology Project Paper*, 10, Centre for Business Strategy, London Business School.

Axelrod, R. (1984), *The Evolution of Co-operation*, Basic Books Inc.

Bailey, E. E., Graham, D. R., and Kaplan, D. P. (1985), *Deregulating the Airlines*, MIT Press.

Bain, J. S. (1956), *Barriers to New Competition*, Cambridge University Press.

Ball, B. C. (1987), 'The mysterious disappearance of retained earnings', *Harvard Business Review*, (July—Aug.), 56–63.

Bannock, G. and Peacock, A. T. (1991), *Corporate Takeovers and the Public Interest*, Aberdeen University Press.

Barney, J. (1991), 'Firm resources and sustained competitive advantage', *Journal of Marketing*, 17/1: 99–120.

Barry, N. (1992), *The Morality of Business Enterprise*, David Hume Institute, Aberdeen University Press.

Bartlett, C. A. and Ghoshal, S. (1986), 'Tap your subsidiaries for global reach', *Harvard Business Review*, (Nov.–Dec.), 87–94.

—— —— (1989), *Managing Across Borders: The Transnational Solution*, Harvard Business School Press.

Barwise, P., Higson, C., Likierman, A., and Marsh, P. (1989), *Accounting for Brands*, London Business School and Institute of Chartered Accountancy, England and Wales.

Bator, F. M. (1957), 'The simple analytics of welfare maximisation', *American Economic Review*, 47: 22–59, in H. Townsend (ed.) (1971).

Baumol, W. J. (1959), *Business Behaviour, Value and Growth*, Macmillan.

—— (1982), 'Contestable markets: An uprising in the theory of industry structure', *American Economic Review*, 72: 1–15.

—— Panzer, J. C. and Willig, R. D. (1982), *Contestable Markets and the Theory of Industry Structure*, Harcourt, Brace Jovanovich.

Beauchamp, T. and Bowie, N. (eds.) (1988) *Ethical Theory and Business*, Prentice-Hall.

Beck, P. (1981), *Corporate Plans for an Uncertain Future*, Shell UK.

Bellamy C. and Child, G. D. (1987), *Common Market Law of Competition*, 3rd edn., Sweet and Maxwell.

Benham, L. (1972), 'The effect of advertising on the price of eyeglasses', *Journal of Law and Economics*, 15/2, 337–52.

Bevan, A. (1974), 'The UK potato crisp industry 1960–72: A study of new entry and competition', *Journal of Industrial Economics*, 22: 281–97.

Binmore, K. and Dasgupta, P. (eds.) (1987), *The Economics of Bargaining*, Basil Blackwell.

Bishop, M. and Kay, J. A. (1988), *Does Privatisation Work? Lessons from the UK*, Centre for Business Strategy Report Series, London Business School.

—— —— (eds.) (1993), *European Mergers and Merger Policy*, Oxford University Press.

Blois, K. J. (1990), 'Transaction costs and networks', *Strategic Management Journal*, 11/6: 497–9.

Blyth, M. L., Friskey, E. A., and Rappaport, A. (1986), 'Implementing the shareholder value approach', *Journal of Business Strategy* (Winter), 48–58.

Bork, R. H. (1978), *The Anti Trust Paradox: A Policy at War with Itself*, Basic Books.

Boston Consulting Group (1968) 'Perspectives on Experience', *Boston Consulting Group*, Boston, Mass.

—— (1972), *Perspectives on Experience*, Boston Consulting Group.

—— (1975), *Strategy Alternatives for the British Motor-cycle Industry*, HMSO.

Bourgeois, L. J. and Brodwin, D. R. (1984) 'Strategic implementation: Five approaches to an elusive phenomenon', *Strategic Management Journal*, 5: 2412–64.

Bradach, J. L. and Eccles, R. G. (1989), 'Price authority and trust: from ideal types to plural forms', *Annual Review of Sociology*, 97–118.

Brealey, R. and Myers, S. (1991), *Principles of Corporate Finance*, McGraw-Hill.

Brown, J. K., *et al.* (1969), 'Long range planning in the USA', *Long Range Planning*, 1/3: 44–51.

Bruck, C. (1989), *The Predator's Ball*, Simon & Schuster.

Buday, T. (1989), 'Capitalising on brand extensions', *Journal of Consumer Marketing*, 6/4 (Fall), 27–30.

Bulow, J. and Roberts, J. (1989), 'The simple economics of optimal auctions', *Journal of Political Economy*, 97: 1060–90.

Burns, T. and Stalker, G. M. (1966), *The Management of Innovation*, Tavistock.

Burrough, B. and Helyar, J. (1990), *Barbarians at the Gate*, Jonathan Cape.

Bursi, T. (1989), *Piccola e media impresa e politiche de adattamento: Il distretto della maglieria di Carpi*, Agneli.

Butler, J. E. (1988), 'Theories of technological innovation as useful tools for corporate strategy', *Strategic Management Journal*, 9/1 (Jan.–Feb.), 15–30.

Buzzell, R. D. (1983), 'Is vertical integration profitable?', *Harvard Business Review*, 61: 92–102.

—— and Gale, B. T. (1987), *The PIMS Principles—Linking Strategy to Performance*, Free Press.

—— —— and Sultan, R. (1975), 'Market share—a key to profitability', *Harvard Business Review* (Jan.–Feb.), 97–106.

—— Heany, D. F. and Schoeffer, S. (1974), 'Impact of strategic planning on profit performance', *Harvard Business Review*, 52/2: 137–45.

Calori, R. and Lawrence, P. (1991), *The Business of Europe: Managing Change*, Sage Publications.

Camerer, C. and Vepsalainen, A. (1991), 'The economic efficiency of corporate culture', *Strategic Management Journal*, 12: 115–26.

Camp, R. C. (1989), *Benchmarking*, ASQS Quality Press, Milwaukee, referred to in Eccles (1991).

Campbell, A. and Yeung, S. (1990), 'Do You Need a Mission Statement?', Economist Publications.

Campbell-Smith, D. (1986), *Struggle for Takeoff*, Coronet.

Carney, M. and Gedajlovic, E. (1991), 'Vertical integration in franchise systems: Agency theory and resource explanations', *Strategic Management Journal*, 12/8: 607–30.

Chandler, A. D. (1962), *Strategy and Structure*, MIT Press.

Child, J. (1974), 'Part I: Management and organisational factors associated with company performance', *Journal of Management Studies*, 11 (Oct.), 175–89.

—— (1975), 'Part II: A contingency analysis', *Journal of Management Studies*, 12 (Feb.), 12–27.

—— (1984), *Organisation: A Guide to Problems and Practice*, Harper and Row.

Chipman, J. S. (1965), 'The nature and meaning of equilibrium in economic theory', in Townsend (1971).

Coase, R. H. (1937), 'The nature of the firm', *Economica*, 4: 386–405, repr. in G. J. Stigler and K. E. Boulding (eds.) (1952), *Readings in Price Theory*, Homewood, Ill.

—— (1988), *The Firm, The Market and The Law*, University of Chicago Press.

Coate, M. B. (1983), 'Pitfalls of portfolio planning', *Long Range Planning*, 16/3: 47–56.

Comanor, W. S. Jnr. and French, H. E. III (1985), 'The competitive effects of vertical agreements', *American Economic Review*, 75: 539–46.

—— and Wilson, T. A. (1979), 'The effect of advertising on competition: A survey', *Journal of Economic Literature*, 17: 453–76.

Commission of the European Communities (1988), 'The economics of 1992', *European Economy*, 35 (Mar.).

Connors, T. D. (ed.) (1980), *The Non Profit Organisation Handbook*, McGraw-Hill.

Cooke, T. E. (1986), *Mergers and Acquisitions*, Basil Blackwell.

Cooper, R., de Jong, D. V., Forsythe, R., and Ross, T. W. (1989), 'Communication in the battle of the sexes game: Some experimental results', *Rand Journal of Economics*, 20/4 (Winter), 568–87.

Copeland, T., Kotler, T., and Murrin, J. (1990), *Valuation: Measuring and Managing the Value of Companies*, Wiley/McKinsey.

Cosh, A. D., *et al.* (1990), *Predicting Success: Pre-Merger Characteristics and Post-Merger Performance*, University of Cambridge Small Business Research Centre Working Paper, Series 6.

Cowling, K., *et al* (1980), *Mergers and Economic Performance*, Cambridge University Press.

Cronshaw, M. and Kay, J. (1991), 'Whatever Next?', Centre for Business Strategy Mimeo, London Business School.

Crosby, P. B. (1979), *Quality is Free: The Art of Making Quality Certain*, McGraw-Hill.

Cubbin, J. and Geroski, P. (1987), 'The convergence of profits in the long run: Inter-firm and inter-industry comparisons', *Journal of Industrial Economics*, 35: 427–42.

Curran, J. G. M. and Goodfellow, J. H. (1990), 'Theoretical and practical issues in the determination of market boundaries', *European Journal of Marketing*, 24/1: 16–28.

Cyert, R. and March, J. (1963), *A Behavioural Theory of the Firm*, Prentice-Hall.

Dale, B. G. and Plunkett, J. J. (eds.) (1990), *Managing Quality*, Philip Allan.

Dasgupta, P. (1988), 'Patents, priority and imitation, or the economics of races and waiting games', *Economic Journal*, 98: 66–80.

David, P. A. (1986), 'Understanding the economics of QWERTY: The necessity of history', in W. N. Parker (ed.), *Economic History and the Modern Economist*, Basil Blackwell.

—— and Greenstein, S. (1990), 'The economics of compatibility standards: An introduction to recent research', *Economics of Innovation and New Technology*, 1/1–2: 3–42.

Davies, G. J. and Brookes, J. M. (1989), *Positioning Strategy in Retailing*, Paul Chapman Publishing Ltd.

Davies, S., *et al.* (1991), *The Dynamics of Market Leadership in the UK Manufacturing Industry 1979-1986*, Centre for Business Strategy Report Series, London Business School.

Davis, E. (1990), 'High quality positioning and the success of reputable products', *Business Strategy Review*, 1/2, Centre for Business Strategy, London Business School, 61–75.

—— and Bannock, G. (1991), 'The Nestlé takeover of Rowntree', *Hume Occasional Paper*, 30: The David Hume Institute.

—— and Kay, J. (1990), 'Assessing corporate performance', *Business Strategy Review*, 1/2, Centre for Business Strategy, London Business School, 1–16.

—— Flanders, S. and Star, J. (1991), 'Who are the World's most successful companies?', *Business Strategy Review*, 2/2, Centre for Business Strategy, London Business School, 1–33.

—— Hanlon, G. and Kay, J. (1992), 'What internationalisation in services means: the case of accountancy in the UK and Ireland', in J. Clegg, H. Cox, and G. Ietto-Gillies (eds.), *The Growth of Global Business: New Strategies*, Routledge.

—— Kay, J. and Star, J. (1991), 'Is advertising rational?', *Business Strategy Review*, 2/3, Centre for Business Strategy, London Business School, 1–23.

—— *et al.* (1989), *1992: Myths and Realities*, Centre for Business Strategy Report Series, London Business School.

Day, G. S. (1977), 'Diagnosing the product portfolio', *Journal of Marketing*, 41: 29–38.

—— (1990), *Market Driven Strategy*, Free Press.

Debreu, G. (1954), 'Valuation equilibrium and Pareto optimum', *Proceedings of the National Academy of Sciences*, 40/7 (July), 588–92.

de Geus, A. (1988), 'Planning as learning', *Harvard Business Review* (Mar.–Apr.), 70–4.

Delamarter, R. T. (1986), *Big Blue: IBM's Use and Abuse of Power*, Dodd, Mead & Company.

dell'Osso, F. (1990), 'Defending a dominant position in a technology led environment', *Business Strategy Review*, 1/2, Centre for Business Strategy, London Business School, 77–86.

—— and Szymanski, S. (1991), 'Who are the champions? (An analysis of football and architecture)', *Business Strategy Review*, 2/2, Centre for Business Strategy, London Business School, 113–30.

Demsetz, H. (1973), 'Industry structure, market rivalry and public policy', *Journal of Law and Economics*, 16: 1–9.

—— (1988), *Ownership, Control and the Firm*, Basil Blackwell.

Dermine, J. (ed.) (1990), *European Banking in the 1990s*, Basil Blackwell.

Devinney, T. M. (1988), *Issues in Pricing: Theory and Research*, Lexington Books.

Dixit, A. and Nalebuff, B. (1991), *Thinking Strategically: The Competitive Edge in Business, Politics and Everyday Life*, W. W. Norton.

Dore, R. (1973), *British Factory—Japanese Factory: The Origins of National Diversity in Industrial Relations*, University of California Press.

Drucker, P. F. (1977), *People and Performance: The Best of Peter Drucker on Management*, Heinemann.

Dunning, J. H. (1986), *Japanese Participation in British Industry*, Croom Helm.

Dyerson, R. and Roper, M. (1991), 'When expertise becomes know-how: Technology management in financial services', *Business Strategy Review*, 2/2, Centre for Business Strategy, London Business School, 55–73.

Eaton, B. C. and Lipsey, R. G. (1975), 'The principle of minimum differentiation reconsidered: Some new developments in the theory of spatial competition', *Review of Economic Studies*, 42: 27–49.

Eccles, R. G. (1991), 'The performance measurement manifesto', *Harvard Business Review*, (Jan.–Feb.), 131–7.

Edwards, J., Kay, J., and Mayer, C. (1987), *The Economic Analysis of Accounting Profitability*, Clarendon Press.

Ehrenberg, A. S. C. and Goodhart, G. J. (1980), 'How Advertising Works', in *Understanding Buyer Behaviour*, J. Walter Thompson, Market Research Corporation of America, New York.

Eisenhardt, K. (1989), 'Agency theory: an assessment and review', *Academy of Management Review*, 14/1: 57–74.

Emerson, M., *et al.* (1988), *The Economics of 1992: The EC Commission Assessment and the Economic Effects of Completing the Internal Market*, Oxford University Press, for the Commission of the European Communities.

Emmott, W. (1989), *The Sun Also Sets*, Simon & Schuster.

Engelbrecht-Wiggins, R. (1980), 'Auction and bidding models: A survey', *Management Science*, 26: 119–42.

—— Shubik, M. and Stark, R. M. (1983), *Auctions, Bidding and Contracting: Uses and Theory*, New York University Press.

Espy, S. N. (1986), *Handbook of Strategic Planning for Non Profit Organisations*, Praeger.

Eurostat (1990), *Employment and Unemployment*, UN Industrial Statistics.

Evered, R. (1983), 'So what's strategy?', *Long Range Planning*, 16/3: 57–72.

Fallon, I. (1988), *The Brothers: The Rise and Rise of Saatchi & Saatchi*, Contemporary Books.

Fama, E. F. (1970), 'Efficient capital markets: A review of theory and empirical work', *Journal of Finance*, 25: 383–417.

—— (1980), 'Agency problems and the theory of the firm', *American Economic Review*, 76: 971–83.

—— and Jensen, M. C. (1983), 'Agency problems and residual claims', *Journal of Law and Economics*, 26: 327–49.

Farrell, J. (1990), 'The economics of standardisation: A guide for non-economists' in J. Berg and H. Shummy (eds.), *An Analysis of the Information Technology Standardisation Process*, Elsevier.

Financial Times (1989), 'Taking Groupe Bull by the horns', 30 June, p. 29.

Fisher, F. M. (1989), 'Games economists play: A non-cooperative view', *Rand Journal of Economics*, 20: 113–24.

—— and McGowan, J. J. (1983), 'On the misuse of accounting rates of return to infer monopoly profits', *American Economic Review*, 73: 82–97.

—— and Ury, W. (1982), *Getting to Yes*, Hutchison.

Flanders, S. and Thiry, B. (1991), 'Who should get the champagne spoils?', *Business Strategy Review*, 2/3, Centre for Business Strategy, London Business School, 91–112.

Forrester, J. (1961) *Industrial Dynamics*, MIT Press.

Fox, A. (1974), *Beyond Contract: Work, Power and Trust Relations*, Faber and Faber.

Franks, J. and Harris, R. (1986), 'Shareholder wealth effects of corporate takeovers: the UK experience, 1955–1985', *Journal of Financial Economics*, 225–49.

—— —— and Mayer, C. (1988), 'Means of payment in takeovers: Results for the United Kingdom and the United States', in A. J. Auerbach (ed.), *Corporate Takeovers: Causes and Consequences*, National Bureau of Economic Research, University of Chicago Press.

Friedman, M. (1970), 'The social responsibility of business is to increase its profits', in Beauchamp and Bowie (eds.) (1988).

Fudenberg, D. and Tirole, J. (1987), 'Understanding rent dissipation: On the use of game theory in industrial organization', *American Economic Review*, 77: 176–83.

Gabel, L. (ed.) (1987), *Product Standardisation as Tool of Competitive Strategy*, INSEAD Symposium, Paris.

Gabor, A. (1977), *Pricing: Principles and Practices*, Heinemann Education Books.

Galbraith, C. and Schendel, D. (1983), 'An empirical analysis of strategy types', *Strategic Management Journal*, 4: 153–73.

Galbraith, J. K. (1958), *The Affluent Society*, Hamish Hamilton.

—— (1986), *The Anatomy of Power*, Hamish Hamilton.

Gambetta, D. (ed.) (1990), *Trust: Making and Breaking Cooperative Relations*, Basil Blackwell.

GE Annual Report (1988) and (1990).

Geneen, H. (1984), 'The strategy of diversification', in Lamb (ed.) (1984), 395–414.

Gerlach, M. (1987), 'Business alliances and the strategy of the Japanese firm', *California Management Review*, 30 (Fall), 126–42.

Geroski, P. (1993), 'Technology and markets', in P. Stoneman (ed.), *Handbook of the Economics of Innovation and Technical Change*, Basil Blackwell.

—— and Vlassopoulos, A. (1990), 'European merger activity: A response to 1992', in *Continental Mergers Are Different*, Centre for Business Strategy, London Business School.

Ghemawat, P. (1986), 'Sustainable advantage', *Harvard Business Review*, (Sep.–Oct.), 53–8.

—— (1991), *Commitment: The Dynamic of Strategy*, Free Press.

—— and Nalebuff, B. (1985), 'Exit', *Rand Journal of Economics*, 16: 184–94.

Gilmore, F. F. and Brandenburg, R. G. (1962), 'Anatomy of Corporate planning', *Harvard Business Review* (Nov.–Dec.), 61–9.

Gleick, J. (1988), *Chaos*, Penguin.

Goldenberg, N. (1989), *Thought for Food: A Study of the Development of the Food Division, Marks & Spencer: An Autobiography*, Food Trade Press, Orpington.

Goold, M. and Campbell, A. , (1987), *Strategies and Styles*, Basil Blackwell.

Gordon, D. D. (1988), *Japanese Management in America and Britain*, Gower.

Granovetter, M. (1985), 'Economic action and social structure: The problem of embeddedness', *American Journal of Sociology*, 91 (Nov.), 481–501.

Grant, J. H. and King, W. R. (1979), 'Strategy formulation: Analytical and normative', in C. W. Hofer and D. E. Schendel (eds.), *Strategic Management*, Little Brown.

Grant, R. M. (1986), 'The effects of product standardisation on competition: The case of octane grading of petrol in the UK', *Centre for Business Strategy Working Paper*, 11: London Business School.

—— (1991), *Contemporary Strategy Analysis*, Basil Blackwell.

Griliches, Z. (ed.) (1984), *R&D, Patents, and Productivity*, National Bureau of Economic Research, University of Chicago Press.

Grindley, P. (1990), 'Winning standards contests: using product standards in business strategy', *Business Strategy Review*, 1/1, Centre for Business Strategy, London Business School, 71–84.

Grinyer, P. H., Al-Bazazz, S., and Yasai-Ardekani, M. (1986), 'Towards a contingency theory of corporate planning: Findings in 48 UK companies', *Strategic Management Journal* (Jan.–Feb.), 3–28.

Grossman, S. (1981), 'The information role of warranties and private disclosure about product quality', *Journal of Law and Economics*, 24: 461–83.

—— and Hart, O. (1983), 'An analysis of the principal-agent problem', *Econometrica*, 51/1 (Jan.), 7–45.

—— —— (1986), 'The costs and benefits of ownership: A theory of vertical and lateral integration', *Journal of Political Economy*, 94 (Aug.), 691–719.

Hamel, G., Doz, Y., and Prahalad, C. K. (1989), 'Collaborate with your competitors— and win', *Harvard Business Review* (Jan.–Feb.), 133–9.

Hamermesh, R. G. (1986), *Making Strategy Work: How Senior Managers Produce Results*, John Wiley.

Hampden-Turner, C. (1990a), *Corporate Culture for Competitive Edge: A User's Guide*, Economist Publications.

—— (1990b), *Charting the Corporate Mind: From Dilemma to Strategy*, Basil Blackwell.

Hannah, L. (1976), *The Rise of the Corporate Economy*, Methuen.

Hapselagh, P. (1982), 'Portfolio planning: Uses and limits', *Harvard Business Review* (Jan.–Feb.), 58–72.

Harcourt, G. C. (1965), 'The accountant in a golden age', *Oxford Economic Papers*, 17: 66–80.

Harrigan, K. R. (1983), *Strategies for Vertical Integration*, Lexington Books.

—— (1986), *Managing for Joint Venture Success*, Lexington Books.

—— (1988), 'Joint ventures and competitive strategy', *Strategic Management Journal*, 9/2: 141–58.

Harris, C. and Vickers, J. (1985), 'Patent races and the persistence of monopoly', Journal of Industrial Economics, 33, 461–481.

Harsanyi, J. and Selten, R. (1988), *A General Theory of Equilibrium Selection in Games*, MIT Press.

Hart, O. (1988), 'Incomplete contracts and the theory of the firm', *Journal of Law, Economics and Organization*, 4 (Spring), 119–40.

—— and Moore, J. (1990), 'Property rights and the nature of the firm', *Journal of Political Economy*, 98: 1119–58.

—— and Tirole, J. (1990), 'Vertical integration and market foreclosure', *Brookings Papers on Economic Activity*, 205–76.

HBS (1978), *Notes on the Motorcycle Industry—1974*, Case 578–210.

—— (1980), *General Electric vs Westinghouse in Large Turbine Generators (A)*, Case 9–380–128.

—— (1981), *General Electric—Strategic Position 1981*, Case 381–174, p. 1.

—— (1983a), *Honda (A)*, Case 9–384–049.

—— (1983b), *Honda (B)*, Case 9–384–050.

—— (1985), *Komatsu Ltd*, Case 9–385–277.

—— (1989), *GE—Preparing for the 1990s*, Case 9–390–091, p. 7.

—— (1990), *Komatsu: Ryoichi Kawai's Leadership*, Case 9–390–037.

Hedley, B. (1977), 'Strategy and the business portfolio', *Long Range Planning*, February 1977, 9–15.

Heil, O. and Robertson, T. S. (1991), 'Towards a theory of competitive market signalling', *Strategic Management Journal*, 12: 403–18.

Henderson, B. D. (1973), *The Experience Curve Reviewed*, Boston Consulting Group.

Henwood, F. and Thomas, H. (compilers) (1984), *Science, Technology and Innovation: A Research Bibliography*, SPRU, Wheatsheaf Books.

Hill Samuel (1990), *Mergers, Acquisitions and Alternative Corporate Strategies*, Mercury Books and Confederation of British Industry.

Hirschman, A. O. (1982), 'Rival interpretations of market society: civilising, destructive, or feeble?',*Journal of Economic Literature*, 20: 1463–84.

Hitchens, R. E., Robinson, S., and Wade, D. P. (1978), 'The directional policy matrix', *Long Range Planning*, 11: 8–15.

Hotelling, H. (1929), 'Stability in competition', *Economic Journal*, 39 (Mar.), 41–52.

Houlden, B. T. (1980), 'Data and effective corporate planning', *Long Range Planning*, 13: 106–11.

Hrebiniak, L. G. and Joyce, W. F. (1984), *Implementing Strategy*, Macmillan.

Hughes, A. (1990), *Industrial Concentration and the Small Business Sector in the UK: The 1980s in Historical Perspective*, University of Cambridge Small Business Research Centre, Working Paper, 5.

—— (1993), 'Mergers and economic performance in the UK: A survey of the empirical evidence 1950–1990', in Bishop and Kay (eds.) (1993).

Hume, D. (1748), *An Enquiry Concerning Human Understanding*.

Hunt, J. W., Lees, S., Grumbar, J. J., and Vivian, P. D. (1987), *Acquisitions: The Human Factor*, Egon Zehnder International.

Interbrand (1990), *Brands: An International Review*, Mercury, Interbrand Group, London.

Ireland, N. J. (1987), *Product Differentiation and Non-Price Competition*, Basil Blackwell.

Jacobsen, R. (1988), 'The persistence of abnormal returns', *Strategic Management Journal*, 9/5: 415–30.

—— and Aaker, D. A. (1987), 'The strategic role of product quality', *Journal of Marketing*, 51/4: 31–44.

James, B. G. (1985), *Business Wargames*, Penguin.

Jarillo, J. C. (1988), 'On strategic networks', *Strategic Management Journal*, 9: 33–41.

—— (1990), 'Comments on transactions costs and networks', *Strategic Management Journal*, 11/6: 497–9.

Jensen, M. C. (1984), 'Takeovers—folklore and science', *Harvard Business Review*, (Nov.–Dec.), 109.

—— (1986), 'The takeover controversy: analysis and evidence', *Midland Corporate Finance Journal*, 4/2 (Summer), 6–32.

—— (1988), 'Takeovers: Their causes and consequences', *Journal of Economic Perspectives*, 2/1: 21–48.

—— (1989), 'Eclipse of the public corporation', *Harvard Business Review* (Sept.–Oct.), 61–74.

Jensen, M. C. and Meckling, W. H. (1976), 'Theory of the firm, managerial behaviour, agency costs and ownership structure', *Journal of Financial Economics*, 3: 305–60.

—— and Ruback, R. (1983), 'The market for corporate control', *Journal of Financial Economics*, 11: 5–50.

Jevons, W. S. (1871), *The Theory of Political Economy*, Augustus M. Kelley.

Johanson, J. and Mattson, L. G. (1987), 'Interorganisational relations in industrial systems: a network approach compared with the transactions-cost approach', *International Studies in Management and Organisation*, 17/1: 34–48.

Johnston, R. and Lawrence, P. R. (1988), 'Beyond vertical integration—the rise of the value-adding partnership', *Harvard Business Review* (July–Aug.), 94–104.

Jones, J. P. (1986), *What's in a Name? Advertising and the Concept of Brands*, Lexington Books.

Jordan, A. G. and Richardson, J. J. (1987), *Government and Pressure Groups in Britain*, Clarendon Press.

Journal of Financial Economics (1977), 'Symposium on some anomalous evidence on capital market efficiency' (Special issue).

Kahn, A. E. (1988), 'Some surprises of airline deregulation', *American Economic Review*, 78: 316–22.

Kaikati, J. G. (1987), 'Celebrity advertising: A review and synthesis', *International Journal of Advertising*, 6: 93–105.

Kaplan, S. (1989), 'The effects of management buy-outs on operating performance and value', *Journal of Financial Economics*, 24: 217–54.

Karmani, A. (1984), 'Generic competitive strategies—an analytical approach', *Strategic Management Journal*, 5/4: 367–80.

Kay, J. A. (1990), 'Identifying the strategic market', *Business Strategy Review*, 1/1, Centre for Business Strategy, London Business School, 2–24.

—— (1991*a*), 'Economics and Business', *Economic Journal* (Special issue), 57–63.

—— (1991*b*), 'The economics of mutuality', in D. Heald (ed.), *Demutualization of Financial Institutions—Annals of Public and Cooperative Economics* (Special issue), 62/3, De Boeck Université, Brussels, pp. 309–18.

—— and Mayer, C. P. (1986), 'On the application of accounting rates of return', *Economic Journal*, 96: 199–207.

—— and Willman, P. (1991), 'Managing technological innovation: architecture, trust and organisational relationships in the firm', *Centre for Business Strategy Working Paper*, 102: London Business School.

—— Manning, A., and Szymanski, S. (1990), 'Pricing a new product: Eurotunnel', *Business Strategy Review*, 1/1, Centre for Business Strategy, London Business School, 37–56.

—— Mayer, C. P. and Thompson, D. J. (eds.) (1986), *Privatisation and Regulation: The UK Experience*, Clarendon Press.

Kihlstrom, R. E. and Riordan, M. H. (1984), 'Advertising as a signal', *Journal of Political Economy*, 92/3: 427–50.

Kirzner, I. M. (1973), *Competition and Entrepreneurship*, University of Chicago Press.

—— (1989), *Discovery, Capitalism and Distributive Justice*, Basil Blackwell.

Klein, B. (1983), 'Contracting costs and residual claims', *Journal of Law and Economics*, 26/2, 367–74.

—— and Leffler, K. (1981), 'The role of market forces in assuring contractual performance', *Journal of Political Economy*, 89: 615–41.

Knight, K. (1976), 'Matrix organisation—a review', *Journal of Management Studies* (May).

Kono, T. (1990), 'Corporate culture and long range planning', *Long Range Planning*, 23/4: 9–19.

Kotler, P. (1991), *Marketing Management*, Prentice-Hall.

—— and Armstrong, G. (1991), *Principles of Marketing*, Prentice-Hall.

Kreps, D. and Wilson, R. (1982), 'Reputation and imperfect information', *Journal of Economic Theory*, 27: 253–79.

Lamb, R. (ed.) (1984), *Competitive Strategy Management*, Prentice-Hall.

Landes, D. (1969), *The Unbound Prometheus*, Cambridge University Press.

Landes, W. M. and Posner, R. A. (1981), 'Market Power in Anti Trust Cases', *Harvard Law Review*, 94: 937.

Lauderdale, Earl of (1804), *An Inquiry into the Nature and Origin of Public Wealth*, Constable, cited in G. J. Stigler, *The Theory of Price*, 3rd edn., Macmillan, 1966.

Law Society (1991), *Maintenance and Capital Provision on Divorce*, The Law Society, London.

Leavitt, H. J. and Whisler, T. L. (1958), 'Management in the 1980s', *Harvard Business Review*, 36/6: 41.

Levin, R. C., Cohen, W. M., and Mowery, D. C. (1985), 'R & D, appropriability and market structure: New evidence on some Schumpeterian hypotheses', *American Economic Review*, 75: 20–4.

Levine, M. E. (1987), 'Airline competition in deregulated markets: Theory, firm strategy and public policy', *Yale Journal of Regulation*, 4: 393.

Levitt, T. (1965), 'Exploit the product life cycle', *Harvard Business Review* (Nov.–Dec.), 81–94.

—— (1983), 'The globalisation of markets', *Harvard Business Review*, 1 (May–June), 92–102.

—— (1986), *The Marketing Imagination*, Free Press.

Lewis, Michael (1989), *Liars Poker: Two Cities, True Greed*, Hodder & Stoughton.

Liddell Hart, B. H. (1968), *Strategy*, Praeger.

Lieberman, M. B. and Montgomery, D. B. (1988), 'First mover advantages', *Strategic Management Journal*, 9 (Special issue), 41–58.

Lindblom, L. E. (1959), 'The science of muddling through', *Public Administration Review*, 19 (Spring), 79–88.

Lippman, S. A. and Rumelt, R. P. (1982), 'Uncertain imitability: An analysis of inter-firm differences in efficiency under competition', *Bell Journal of Economics*, 23: 418–38.

Lloyd, T. (1990), *The Nice Company*, Bloomsbury.

Lockwood, B. (1992), *The Social Cost of Electricity Generation*, Centre for Social and Economic Research on the Global Environment, Discussion Paper GEC 92–09.

Lorange, P. (1979), 'Formal planning systems: Their role in strategy formulation and implementation', in D. E. Schendel and C. W. Hofer (eds.), *Strategic Management*, Little Brown.

Lorenz, E. (1991), 'Neither friends nor strangers: Informal networks of subcontracting in French industry', in G. Thompson *et al.* (eds.) (1991).

Lorenzoni, G. (1979), *Una politica innovativa nelle piccole e medie imprese: L'analisi del cambiamento nel sistema industriale pratese*, Etas Libri, Milan.

—— (1988), 'Benetton', *Centre for Business Strategy Case Series*, 4: London Business School.

Luce, D. R. and Raiffa, H. (1957), *Games and Decisions: Introduction and Critical Survey*, Wiley.

Lutz, N. A. (1989), 'Warranties as signals under consumer moral hazard', *Rand Journal of Economics*, 20: 239–255.

Lyles, M. A. (1981), 'Formulating strategic problems: Empirical analysis and model development', *Strategic Management Journal*, 2: 61–75.

Lynn, M. (1991), *Merck vs Glaxo: The Billion Dollar Battle*, Heinemann.

Lyons, B. (1980), 'A new measure of minimum efficient plant size in UK manufacturing industry', *Economica*, 47: 19–34.

Lyons, M. P. (1991), 'Joint ventures as strategic choice—a literature review', *Long Range Planning*, 24/4: 130–44.

McAfee, R. P. and MacMillan, J. (1987), 'Auctions and bidding', *Journal of Economic Literature*, 25: 699–738.

McArthur, B. (1988), *Eddie Shah, Today and the Newspaper Revolution*, David & Charles.

MacAuley, S. (1963), 'Non-contractual relations in business: A preliminary study', *American Sociological Review*, 28: 55–67.

McCann, J. E. (1991), 'Design principles for an innovating company', *Academy of Management Executive*, 5/2: 76–93.

Macneil, I. R. (1974), 'The many futures of contract', *Southern California Law Review*, 47: 691–738.

—— (1978), 'Contracts: Adjustment of long term economic relations under classical, neoclassical and relational contract law', *Northwestern University Law Review*, 72: 854–905.

—— (1980), *The New Social Contract: An Inquiry into Modern Contractual Relations*, Yale University Press.

McNulty, C. A. R. (1977), 'Scenario development for corporate planning', *Futures*, 9 (Apr.), 128–38.

Manne, H. G. (1965), 'Mergers and the market for corporate control', *Journal of Political Economy*, 73: 110–20.

Marris, R. (1966), *The Economic Theory of Managerial Capitalism*, Macmillan.

Marschak, J. and Radner, R. (1972), *Economic Theory of Teams*, Yale University Press.

Marsh, P. (1990), *Short-Termism on Trial*, International Fund Managers Association.

Marshall, Alfred (1890), *Principles of Economics*, 8th edn., Macmillan.

Mathias, P. and Davis, J. A. (eds.) (1991), *Innovation and Technology in Europe*, Basil Blackwell.

Mayer, C. (1987), *The Real Value of Company Accounts*, University of Leeds.

Meeks, G. (1977), *Disappointing Marriage: A Study of the Gains from Merger*, Cambridge University Press.

Mercer, D. (1987), *IBM: How the World's Most Successful Corporation is Managed*, Kogan Page.

Miles, R. E. and Snow, C. C. (1978), *Organizational Strategy, Structure and Process*, McGraw-Hill.

—— —— (1986), 'Network organizations: New concepts for new forms', *California Management Review*, 28: 62–73.

Milgrom, P. R. and Roberts, J. (1986), 'Price and advertising signals of product quality', *Journal of Political Economy*, 96/4: 796–821.

—— —— (1992), *The Economics of Organisation and Management*, Prentice-Hall.

Miller, C. (1990), *Lobbying: Understanding and Influencing the Corridors of Power*, 2nd edn., Basil Blackwell.

Mintzberg, H. (1972), 'Research on strategy making', *Academy of Management Proceedings*, 90–4.

—— (1973), 'Strategy making in three modes', *California Management Review*, 16/2: 44–53.

—— (1978), 'Patterns in strategy formation', *Management Science*, 934–48.

—— (1979), *The Structuring of Organisations: A Synthesis of the Research*, Prentice-Hall.

—— (1983*a*), *Power In and Around Organizations*, Prentice-Hall.

—— (1983*b*), 'The case for corporate social responsibility', *Journal of Business Strategy*, 4/2: 3–15.

—— (1987), 'Crafting strategy', *Harvard Business Review* (July–Aug.), 66–75.

Mönnich, M. (1989), *BMW, Eine Deutsche Geschichte*, Zsolnay, Vienna.

—— (1991), *The BMW Story—A Company in its Time*, Sidgwick & Jackson.

Monopolies & Mergers Commission (1988), *Gas: A Report on the Matter of Existence or Possible Existence of a Monopoly Situation in Relation to the Supply in Great Britain of Gas to Persons other than Tariff Customers*, Cmnd. 500, HMSO.

Monteverde, K. and Teece, D. J. (1982), 'Supplier switching costs and vertical integration in the US auto industry', *Bell Journal of Economics*, 13/1: 206–13.

Morgan, G. (1986), *Images of Organisation*, Sage Publications.

Mueller, D. C. (ed.) (1980), *The Determinants and Effects of Merger: An International Comparison*, Oelschlager, Gunn and Hain.

—— (ed.) (1986), *Profits in the Long Run*, Cambridge University Press.

Murphy, J. (ed.) (1991), *Brand Valuation*, Business Books.

Nagle, T. T. (1988), *The Strategy and Tactics of Pricing*, McGraw-Hill.

Nash, J. F. (1950), 'The bargaining problem', *Econometrica*, 18: 155–62.

—— (1953), 'Two-person co-operative games', *Econometrica*, 21: 128–40.

Nelson, P. (1970), 'Information and consumer behaviour', *Journal of Political Economy*, 78/2: 311–29.

—— (1974), 'Advertising as information', *Journal of Political Economy*, 81/3: 729–54.

—— (1975), 'The economic consequences of advertising', *Journal of Business*, 48: 213–45.

Nelson, R. R. and Winter, S. G. (1982), *An Evolutionary Theory of Economic Change*, Harvard University Press.

Nicolaides, P. and Baden Fuller, C. (1987), *Price Discrimination and Product Differentiation in the European Domestic Appliance Market*, Centre for Business Strategy, London Business School, paper given to Cescom Conference (Milan, July 1987).

Norburn, D. and Schoenberg, R. (1990), 'Acquisitions and joint ventures—similar arrows in the strategic quiver', *Business Strategy Review*, 1/3, Centre for Business Strategy, London Business School, 75–90.

Odagiri, H. (1991), *Growth Through Competition: Competition Through Growth*, Clarendon Press.

—— and Yamawaki, H. (1990), 'The persistence of profits: international comparison', in D. C. Mueller (ed.), *The Dynamics of Company Profits*, Cambridge University Press.

OECD (annual), 'Competition policy in OECD countries', *Annual Report of the OECD Committee on Competition Law and Policy*.

Ohmae, K. (1985), *Triad Power: The Coming Shape of Global Competition*, Free Press.

—— (1989), 'The global logic of strategic alliances', *Harvard Business Review*, (Mar.–Apr.), 143–54.

Olson, M. (1965), *The Logic of Collective Action*, Harvard University Press.

Olson, M. (1982), *The Rise and Decline of Nations: Economic Growth, Stagflation, and Social Rigidities*, Yale University Press.

O'Reilly, C. (1989), 'Corporations, culture and commitment: Motivation and social control in organisations', *California Management Review*, 31/4: 9–25.

Oster, S. (1990), *Modern Competitive Analysis*, Oxford University Press.

Ouchi, W. G. (1981), *Theory Z: How American Business Can Meet the Japanese Challenge*, Addison-Wesley.

Packard, V. (1957), *The Hidden Persuaders*, Penguin Books.

Pascale, R. T. (1984), 'Perspectives on strategy: The real story behind Honda's success', *California Management Review*, 26/3: 47–72.

Pearce, J. A. II (1983), 'Selecting among alternative grand strategies', *California Management Review*, 14/3: 23–31.

Pepall, L. (1990), 'Market demand and product clustering', *Economic Journal*, 100: 195–205.

Perrow, C. (1986), *Complex Organisations: A Critical Essay*, Scott, Foresman.

Peters, T. J. and Waterman, R. H. (1982), *In Search of Excellence*, Harper and Row.

Pettigrew, A. M. (1977), 'Strategy formulation as a political process', *International Studies of Management and Organisation*, 7/2: 78–87.

—— (1985), *The Awakening Giant: Continuity and Change in Imperial Chemical Industries*, Basil Blackwell.

Pfeffer, J. and Nowak, P. (1976), 'Joint ventures and interorganizational interdependence', *American Science Quarterly*, 21: 398–418.

Phlips, L. (1983), *The Economics of Price Discrimination*, Cambridge University Press.

—— and Thisse, J. F. (1982), 'Spatial competition and the theory of differentiated markets: An introduction', *Journal of Industrial Economics*, 31: 1–9.

Piesse, J. (1991), 'Retail banking', in Calori and Lawrence (eds.) (1991).

Pigou, A. C. (1920), *The Economics of Welfare*, Macmillan.

Piore, M. and Sabel, C. (1984), *The Second Industrial Divide*, Basic Books.

Porter, M. E. (1979), 'How competitive forces shape strategy', *Harvard Business Review* (Mar.–Apr.), 137–45.

—— (1980), *Competitive Strategy: Techniques for Analyzing Industries and Competitors*, The Free Press.

—— (1981), 'The contributions of industrial organisation to strategic management', *Academy of Management Review*, 4: 609–20.

—— (1985), *Competitive Advantage: Creating and Sustaining Superior Performance*, The Free Press.

—— (ed.) (1986), *Competition in Global Industries*, Harvard Business School Press.

—— (1990), *The Competitive Advantage of Nations*, Macmillan.

Posner, R. A. (1975), 'The social costs of monopoly and regulation', *Journal of Political Economy*, 83: 807–27.

Potts, M. and Behr, P. (1987), 'General Electric: Charting a fast new course for a once stodgy corporate giant', in M. Potts and P. Behr, *The Leading Edge: CEOs Who Turned their Companies Around*, McGraw-Hill.

Prahalad, C. K. and Bettis, R. A. (1986), 'The dominant logic: A new linkage between diversity and performance', *Strategic Management Journal*, 7/6: 485–502.

—— and Hamel, G. (1985), 'Strategic intent', *Harvard Business Review* (May–June), 63–76.

—— —— (1990), 'The core competence of the corporation', *Harvard Business Review* (May–June), 79–91.

Pratt, J. W. and Zeckhauser, R. J. (1985), *Principals and Agents: The Structure of Business*, Harvard Business School Press.

Pratten, C. (1988), 'A survey of the economics of scale', in *Research on the Cost of Non-Europe*, 2, Commission of the European Communities.

Price, F. (1990), *Right Every Time*, Gower.

Quinn, J. B., Mintzberg, H., and James, R. M. (1988), *The Strategy Process*, Prentice-Hall.

Radner, R. (1985), 'The internal economy of large firms', *Economic Journal Supplement*, 96–1–22.

Rappaport, A. (1986), *Creating Shareholder Value: The New Standard for Business Performance*, Free Press.

—— (1990), 'The staying power of the public corporation', *Harvard Business Review* (Jan.–Feb.), 96–104.

Rasmusen, E. (1989), *Games and Information: An Introduction to Game Theory*, Basil Blackwell.

Ravenscraft, D. J. and Scherer, F. M. (1987), *Mergers, Sell-Offs and Economic Efficiency*, Brookings Institution.

—— —— (1989), 'The profitability of mergers', *International Journal of Industrial Organisation*, 7/1 (Mar.), 101–16.

Reed, R. and De Filippi, R. J. (1990), 'Causal ambiguity, barriers to imitation and sustainable competitive advantage', *Academy of Management Review*, 15 (Jan.), 88–102.

Rees, G. (1973), *St. Michael: A History of Marks & Spencer*, Pan Books.

Rees, R. D. (1973), 'Optimum plant size in UK industries: Some survivor estimates', *Economica*, 40: 394–401.

Reidenback, R. and Robin, D. P. (1989), *Ethics and Profits*, Prentice-Hall.

Reiman, B. C. (1989), 'Creating value to keep the raiders at bay', *Long Range Planning*, 22/3: 18–27.

Reve, T. (1990), 'The firm as a nexus of internal and external contracts', in Aoki, Gustaffson, and Williamson (eds.). (1990).

Rey, R. and Tirole, J. (1986), 'The logic of vertical restraints', *American Economic Review*, 76: 921–39.

Reynolds, B. (1989), *The 100 Best Companies to Work for in the UK*, Fontana/Collins.

Ricardo, David (1819), *The Principles of Political Economy and Taxation*.

Richardson, G. B. (1972), 'The organization of industry', *Economic Journal*, 82: 883–96.

Ries, A. and Trout, J. (1981), *Positioning—the Battle for Your Mind*, McGraw-Hill.

Rink, D. R. and Swan, J. E. (1979), 'Product life cycle research: A literature review', *Journal of Business Research*, (Sept.), 219–42.

Rodgers, F. G. (1986), *The IBM Way*, Harper and Row.

Rogerson, W. (1983), 'Reputation and product quality', *Bell Journal of Economics*, 14: 508–16.

Rothschild, W. E. (1979*a*), 'Competitor analysis', *Management Review* (July), 22–8, 37–9.

—— (1979*b*), 'Competitor analysis—the missing link in strategy', *McKinsey Quarterly* (Autumn), 42–53.

Ruggles, R. L. and Smalter, D. J. (1966), 'Six business lessons from the Pentagon', *Harvard Business Review*, 44/2 (Mar.–Apr.), 64–75.

Rumelt, R. P. (1991), 'How much does industry matter?', *Strategic Management Journal*, 12/3 (Mar.), 167–86.

Saatchi & Saatchi (1984), *Annual Report*.

Salop, S. (1979), 'Strategic entry deterrence', *American Economic Review*, 335–8.

Schapiro, C. (1982), 'Consumer information, product quality and seller reputation', *Bell Journal of Economics*, 13: 20–35.

Scheffman, D. T. and Spiller, P. T. (1987), 'Geographic market definition under the US Department of Justice Merger Guidelines', *Journal of Law and Economics*, 30: 123–48.

Schelling, T. C. (1956), 'An essay on bargaining', *American Economic Review*, 46: 281–306.

—— (1960), *The Strategy of Conflict*, Harvard University Press.

Scherer, F. M. and Ross, D. (1990), *Industrial Market Structure and Economic Performance*, 3rd edn., Houghton Mifflin.

Schleifer, A. and Summers, L. H. (1988), 'Breach of trust in hostile takeovers', in A. J. Auerbach (ed.), *Corporate Takeovers: Causes and Consequences*, National Bureau of Economic Research, Chicago.

Schmalensee, R. (1978), 'A model of advertising and product quality', *Journal of Political Economy*, 86: 485–503.

—— (1981), 'Economics of scale and barriers to entry', *Journal of Public Economics*, 89: 1228–38.

Schumpeter, J. A. (1934), *The Theory of Economic Development*, Harvard University Press.

—— (1943), *Capitalism, Socialism and Democracy*, Unwin.

—— (1961), *The Theory of Economic Development*, Oxford University Press.

Schwartz, A. and Wilde, L. (1985), 'Product quality and imperfect information', *Royal Economic Studies*, 52 (Apr.), 251–62.

Sharkey, W. W. (1982), *The Theory of Natural Monopoly*, Cambridge University Press.

Sharpe, W. F. (1964), 'Capital asset prices: a theory of market equilibria under conditions of risk', *Journal of Finance*, 19 (Sept.), 425–42.

Shaw, W. (1990), 'An empirical analysis of organisational strategies by entrepreneurial high technology firms', *Strategic Management Journal*, 11/2: 129–40.

Shepherd, W. (1984), 'Contestability vs competition', *American Economic Review*, 74: 572–87.

Sieff, M. (1990), *Management the Marks & Spencer Way*, Fontana.

Silva, M. and Sjogren, B. (1990), *Europe 1992 and the New World Power Game*, Wiley.

Simon, H. A. (1960), 'The corporation: Will it be managed by machines?', in M. Anschen and G. L. Back (eds.), *Management and Corporations*, McGraw-Hill.

—— (1961), *Administrative Behaviour*, 2nd edn., Macmillan.

—— (1964), 'On the concept of the organizational goal', *American Science Quarterly*, 9 (June), 1–22.

Sloan, A. (1963), *My Years at General Motors*, Doubleday.

Smith, Adam (1776), *An Inquiry into the Nature and Causes of the Wealth of Nations*, repr. 1925, G. Bell & Sons.

Smith, W. P. (1987), 'Conflict and negotiation: trends and emerging issues', *Journal of Applied Social Psychology*, 17: 641–67.

Snow, C. C. and Hrebiniak, L. G. (1980), 'Strategy, distinctive competence, and organisational performance', *American Science Quarterly*, 25: 317–36.

Sobel, R. (1981), *IBM: Colossus in Transition*, Times Books.

Spence, M. (1973), 'Job market signalling', *Quarterly Journal of Economics*, 87 (Aug.), 355–74.

—— (1977), 'Entry, capacity, investment and oligopolistic pricing', *Bell Journal of Economics*, 8 (Autumn), 534–44.

Springer, C. and Hofer, C. W. (1978), 'General Electric's evolving management system', in C. W. Hofer, E. A. Murray Jnr, R. Charan, R. A. Pitts (eds.) (1980), *Strategic Management: A Casebook in Business Policy and Planning*, West Publishing Company.

Steer, P. S. and Cable, J. (1978), 'Internal organization and profit: An empirical analysis of large UK companies', *Journal of Industrial Economics*, 27: 13–30.

Steiner, G. (1979), 'Contingent themes of strategy and strategic management', in D. Schendel and C. W. Hofer (eds.), *Strategic Management*, Little Brown, 403–16,.

Stewart, G. B. (1991), *The Quest for Value: A Guide for Senior Managers*, Harper Collins.

Stigler, G. J. (1966), *The Theory of Price* (3/e). Macmillan.

—— and Sherwin, R. A. (1985), 'The Extent of the Market', *Journal of Law and Economics*, 28: 555–86.

Stoneman, P. (1983), *The Economic Analysis of Technological Change*, Cambridge.

Sutton, J. (1991), *Sunk Costs and Market Structure*, MIT Press.

Sun (1991), 11 Nov. p. 9.

Tauber, E. M. (1981), 'Brand franchise extensions: New products benefit from existing brand names', *Business Horizons*, 24/2: 36–41.

Teece, D. J. (1986), 'Profiting from technological innovation: Implications for integration, collaboration, licensing and public policy', *Research Policy*, 15: 285–305.

—— (1987), *The Competitive Challenge: Strategies for Industrial Innovation and Renewal*, Mosi Balinger.

Thompson, D. and Meadowcroft, S. (1987), 'Partial integration: A loophole in competition law', *Fiscal Studies*, 8/1: 24–47.

Thompson, G., *et al.* (eds.) (1991), *Markets, Hierarchies & Networks: The Coordination of Social Life*, Open University, Sage Publications.

Thorelli, H. B. (1986), 'Networks: Between markets and hierarchies', *Strategic Management Journal*, 1/7: 37–52.

Tichy, N. (1989), 'GE's Crotonville: A staging ground for corporate revolution', *Academy of Management Executive*, 3/2: 99–106.

—— and Charan, R. (1989), 'Speed, simplicity and self-confidence: An interview with Jack Welch', *Harvard Business Review* (Sept.–Oct.), 112–20.

Tirole, J. (1988), *Theory of Industrial Organisation*, MIT Press.

Townsend, H. (ed.) (1971), *Price Theory*, Penguin.

Tse, K. K. (1985), *Marks & Spencer: Anatomy of Britain's Most Efficiently Managed Company*, Pergamon Press.

Tynan, A. C. and Drayton, J. (1987), 'Market segmentation', *Journal of Marketing Management*, 2/3: 301–35.

van Fleet, D. D. (1984), 'Organisational differences in critical leader behaviours: Industrial and military', in R. L. Taylor and W. E. Rosenbach (eds.) *Military Leadership: In Pursuit of Excellence*, Westview Press.

Veblen, T. (1899), *The Theory of the Leisure Class*, Penguin Books.

Vickers, J. (1985) 'Strategic competition among the few—some recent developments in the economics of industry', *Oxford Review of Economic Policy*, 1/3: 39–62.

—— and Yarrow, G. (1988), *Privatization—An Economic Analysis*, The MIT Press.

Vickrey, W. (1961), 'Counter speculations, auctions and competitive sealed tenders', *Journal of Finance*, 16: 8–37.

Von Hayek, F. A. (1944), *The Road to Serfdom*, University of Chicago Press.

—— (1948), *Individualism and Economic Order*, Gateway.

—— (1960), *The Constitution of Liberty*, University of Chicago Press.

von Neumann, J. and Morgernstern, O. (1944), *Theory of Games and Economic Behaviour*, Princeton University Press.

Von Weizsacker, C. C. (1980), *Barriers to Entry: A Theoretical Treatment*, Springer-Verlag.

Wack; P. (1985), 'Scenarios, shooting the rapids', *Harvard Business Review*, (Nov.–Dec.), 139–50.

Wall, J. A. Jnr and Blum, M. W. (1991), 'Negotiations', *Journal of Management*, 17: 273–303.

Water Services Association and Water Companies Association (1991), *The Cost of Capital in the Water Industry*, Water Services Association, London.

Weber, M. (1925), *The Theory of Social and Economic Organization*, Free Press.

Weigelt, K. and Camerer, C. (1988), 'Reputation and corporate strategy: A review of recent theory and applications', *Strategic Management Journal*, 9: 443–54.

Weintraub, R. (1975), *Conflict and Cooperation in Economics*, Macmillan.

Wernerfelt, B. (1988), 'Umbrella Branding as a signal of new product quality: An example of signalling by posting a bond', *Rand Journal of Economics*, 19: 458–66.

White, L. J. (1981), 'Vertical restraints in anti-trust law: A coherent model', *The Antitrust Bulletin*, 26: 327–45.

White, R. E (1986), 'Generic business strategies, organisational content and performance: An empirical investigation', S*trategic Management Journal*, 7: 217–31.

Whittington, G. (1983), *Inflation Accounting: An Introduction to the Debate*, Cambridge University Press.

Williamson, O. E. (1975), *Markets and Hierarchies: Analysis and Antitrust Implications*, The Free Press.

—— (1983), 'Hostages—using credible commitments to support exchange', *American Economic Review*, 73: 519–40.

—— (1985), *The Economic Institutions of Capitalism: Firms, Markets and Relational Contracting*, The Free Press.

—— (1986), *Economic Organisation*, Wheatsheaf Books.

—— (1987), *Antitrust Economics: Mergers, Contracting and Strategic Behaviour*, Basil Blackwell.

—— and Winter, S. G. (1991), *The Nature of the Firm*, Oxford University Press.

Willman, P. (1986), *Technological Change, Collective Bargaining and Industrial Efficiency*, Clarendon Press.

Woodward, J. (1965), *Industrial Organisation: Theory and Practice*, Oxford University Press.

—— (1982), *Science in Industry: Science of Industry*, Aberdeen University Press.

Wright, M., Chiplin, B., and Thompson, S. (1993), 'The market for corporate control: Divestments and buy-outs', in Bishop and Kay (eds.) (1993).

Wright, R. V. C. (1974), *A System for Managing Diversity*, A. D. Little.

Yao, D. A. (1988), 'Beyond the reach of the invisible hand: Impediments to economic activity, market failures and profitability', *Strategic Management Journal*, 9 (Special issue), 59–70.

Yelle, L. E. (1979), 'The learning curve: Historical review and comprehensive survey', *Decision Sciences*, 10: 302–28.

Zentner, R. D. (1982), 'Scenarios, past, present and future', *Long Range Planning*, 15/3: 12–20.

Zucker, L. G. (1986), 'Production of trust: Institutional sources of economic structure, 1840–1920', *Research in Organizational Behaviour*, 8: 53–111.

INDEX OF COMPANIES

Rowntree 145, 149
Royal Dutch Shell 20, 29, 53, 99, 168
RWE (Rhein Westfälische Electrik) 168, 323
Ryanair 116, 308

Saatchi & Saatchi 3, 4, 12–13, 149, 252, 332
Sabena 287
Safeway Corporation 21
Sainsbury's 20, 21, 22, 23, 24, 26, 78, 137, 167, 168, 193, 194, 195, 246, 247, 290, 322
Salomon Brothers 106, 332
SAS (Scandinavian Airlines System) 232, 287, 309
Sears Roebuck 8, 335
Shandwick 213–14
Shell, *see* Royal Dutch Shell
Siemens 10, 151, 163, 168, 332
Sinclair 102
Sky Television 109, 115
Smith's Crisps 145
SNCF (Société Nationale des Chemins de Fer) 229, 236
Société Générale de Belgique 82, 156, 171
Solid State Logic 110
Sony 15, 106, 107, 108, 109, 110, 112, 115, 116, 135, 145, 152, 181
Southalls 94
Sprint 115
SR Gent 311
Statoil 183, 184, 185, 186, 189, 212, 213, 214
Stefanel 287, 293, 315, 317
Stella Artois 232
Studebaker 175
Sumitomo 171
Swissair 294, 295, 312, 315

3M (Minnesota Manufacturing and Mining) 134

Tabacelara 29
Tarmac 76
Ted Bates 13, 149
Tesco 20, 21, 22, 23, 193, 194, 195, 246, 247
Texas Instruments 102
Thyssen (ATH) 168
Toyota 83, 98, 170, 175, 196, 197
TRW 346
TWA (Transworld Airlines) 98, 164, 188, 305, 308, 313

Unilever 29, 82, 165, 168
United Airlines 304, 305, 308, 310, 313, 319
United Alkali 156
United Brands 82
Utah International 338–9

Veba 168
Veuve Cliquot 289
Virgin 280, 305, 308, 312
Visa 107
Volkswagen 120, 168, 183, 197, 255

Wallenberg group 331
Warburg Securities 209, 210 n.
Water Companies Association 218 n.
Water Services Association 218 n.
Wella 29
Western Bankcorp 171
Westin Hotels 308
Westinghouse 238, 250 n.
Wilkinson Sword 148
Woolworth 136, 246

Xerox (*see* Rank Xerox) 102, 104, 163

Zanussi 162

GENERAL INDEX

Note: Entries in **bold** type are also listed in the Glossary (pp. 371–6)

Alexander, Anthony 76
Allen, F. 100 n.
alliances 40, 144, 300, 310
  strategic 85 n., 151–2, 159 n.
amalgamations 20–1, 156, 171
Amsterdam 288
Andrews, K. R. 124 n.
Anschen, M. 336
Ansoff, H. I. 336, 341, 346, 356, 362
Anthony, R. N. 340
anti-trust legislation 157, 236, 304, 317, 327 n.
  investigation 281
  policies 114, 121–4, 165
  restrictions 115
anti-ulcerants, *see* drugs
Antwerp 81
Aoki, M. 60 n.
appellation contrôlée 261, 289, 296, 299, 301
appropriability 105, 106, 149, 181–91, 330, 361
  added value 181–3, 322, 332, 366
  high 112
  poor 329
  problem of 102
  returns to **innovation** 323
  sustainability and 13–14
  tight 163
Arab–Israeli war (1973) 129
arbitrage 232, 233, 234, 324
architecture 14, 66–86, 145, 149, 309, 311, 329–31
  added value the product of 322, 327
  and brand advantages 313
  as a characteristic of the organization 69–70
  competitive advantage and 65, 114, 141,
    163, 186, 297, 368
  developing 254
  distinctive capability based on 15, 138, 160,
    161, 178, 181
  exploitation of 333
  external 64, 82, 137, 186, 247; and networks
    80–2
  financial 331–2, 333, 334 n.
  innovation and 105, 106, 110–11
  internal 64, 78–9, 82, 247, 299
  social context of 84–5
  sources of 77–8
  sustainability of 150, 164
Argenti, J. 340
Armstrong, J. S. 266 n., 341
Arrow, K. J. 49 n., 85 n., 334 n.
artificial sweeteners 106
Ashworth, M. H. 319 n.
Asolo hiking boots 310
aspartame 106
asset specificity 54
assets:
  capital, depreciation of 24
  complementary 152, 163
  fixed 21, 198
  infrastructure 295
  intangible 71
  operating, rate of return on 24 n.
  principal 20
  transaction-specific 83
  see also **strategic assets**

Atlanta 262, 288
Atlantic City 98
auctions 189, 272, 281 n.
audio cassettes 101
  see also compact cassettes; VCRs
Austen, Jane 135
Australia 188, 242, 311
automobiles 5–10, 91, 131, 139–41 *passim*, 264,
    347
  distribution 280
  high-performance 330
  industry 105, 165, 202, 230
  markets 196, 236; international 171
Axelrod, R. 49 n., 249 n.

Baden Fuller, C. 131
Bailey, E. E. 319 n.
Bain, J. S. 124 n.
Ballantyne 313
Ballesteros, Seve 95
Ball, B. C. 218 n.
Bangladesh 328
banks 92, 277, 294–6, 331, 338, 361
  absence of much competition between 291
  British 111, 295
  contracts 280
  European 196–7, 292, 319 n.
  finance 279
  internal **architecture** 299
  investment 330
  Japanese 170
  major 46
  retail 146, 163, 197, 238, 288–9, 291–2, 293,
    296, 298–9, 300–1; **added value** in 198;
    attempts to build networks 140
  Spanish 146, 197, 198, 202
  Swiss 329
  world's largest (1970–90) 171
Bannock, G. 159 n.
Barney, J. 361
barriers 156, 165, 232, 233
Barry, N. 334 n.
Bartlett, C. A. 347
Barwise, P. 266 n.
Basle agreements 288
Bates, Ted 13
Bator, F. M. 334 n.
batteries 132, 133, 149, 157
Battle of the Sexes 41–3, 46, 47, 49 n., 51, 107–9
Baumol, W. J. 124 n., 191 n.
Beauchamp, T. 334 n.
Beck, P. 341
beer 129, 157, 172, 281, 346
  advertising 263
  exclusive supply arrangements 280
  foreign, **entry** inhibited 146
  quantity sold 269
Behr, P. 363 n.
Belgium 27, 82, 131
Bell's whisky 252, 253, 255, 257
Bellamy, C. 124 n.
Benedetti, Carlo de 82, 156
Benelux countries 29
Benetton, Carlo, Giuliana, and Luciano 304

classical contracts 53, 59, 72, 85, 325
  allocation of risks defined in 276
  long-term 268
  long-term **relationships** best established
    through 54–5
  means of enforcement 152
  most keenly negotiated 317
  no room for team spirit in 77
  serious business and 269
  toughly negotiated 298
  versus **relational contracts** 51, 57–8, 278–80,
    331
clothes/clothing 137, 244, 262–3, 311, 313
  fashionable 179
clustering behaviour 242, 246, 330, 331
Clydebank 79
Coase, R. H. 49 n., 60 n.
Coate, M. B. 180 n.
Cohen, Jack, Lord 20
cold wars 224, 226, 227, 249 n.
Columbus, Christopher 152
Comanor, W. S. 266 n., 281 n.
commercial property lease 276
commercial secrecy 106
commitment 21, 43–6, 48, 49 n., 92, 104, 109,
    317
  answers to the problems of 68
  binding 44, 330
  brand 318
  key element in **Chicken** games 116
  long-term 95
  maintenance of knowledge base 71
  market 94, 257, 258
  mutual 14, 54
  not credible 45
  prior 42–3
  relational contracts 154
  rewards of collective achievement 77
  tangible 45
  very strong 76
  voluntary 45
commodity bundling 230
commodity markets 115, 130
communication 34, 41, 42, 47, 173, 324
  one-way preferable to two-way 43
compact cassettes 27
compact discs 27, 101, 152
competition 161, 170, 194, 316
  between banks 291
  damage to 158
  degree of 231
  different strengths of 296
  disciplined 242
  distortion of 123
  force of 347
  functionally equivalent 262
  greater 146
  instability in 226
  insufficient 323
  intense 163
  international 67
  Japanese 339
  low-cost 112
  muted 294

mutually destructive 104
in network provision 115
perceived 176
policy 224, 318
price-based 136
restricted 123, 197
stability in 226, 238, 239
unstable 242
competitive advantage 12, 64, 125–218, 222,
    248, 286, 291, 297, 307–11 *passim*, 319, 322,
    327–31, 334, 360, 367
  advertising and branding 254
  architecture and 68, 79, 81, 82, 84, 85, 163
  basis of 368; different 247
  changing 316
  copycat **strategy** and 332
  distinctive capability and 4, 14–16, 27, 333
  incumbency and 262
  innovation as 102, 106, 110, 111–12
  large 74
  limited 77
  market share as 176
  matching to geographic market 140–1
  measurement of 193–5
  nature of 296–9
  relational contracts and 60
  reputation and 70, 89, 90
  scale as 170–5
  sources of 65, 94, 179, 345, 361
  strategic assets and 113, 114, 119, 120
  strength of 24, 26, 296,
  substantial and sustained 92
  sustainable 17, 101, 105, 116
  sustaining 162–4, 313–15
  technology central to 110
  value of 192–218, 303, 310
competitive disadvantage 325
competitive environments 31, 249
  intensity of 226
  nature of 223–6
  stable/unstable 236–9
competitive strategy 3, 4, 8, 128, 142, 219–81
  role of advertising in 255
competitive success 71
competitiveness 333, 365
Compton, Denis 95
computerization 75
computers 101, 102, 109, 136, 224, 238,
    340
  huge and fast–growing market 161–2
  modelling with 341
  operating systems 107
  subsectors of market 10
  see also airlines (CRSs)
condoms 94
conglomerates 20, 27, 149, 150, 203, 346
  acquisition 154, 158
  breakup of 347
  retail 21
  widely diversified 338
  wide-ranging manufacturing 27
Connors, T. D. 191 n.
Conservative government 120, 304
consumer goods 231, 237, 238, 265

games (*cont.*):
    worse standards 108
    see also **Battle of the Sexes; Chicken;**
        Criminal's Revenge; **Prisoner's Dilemma**
Gatiss, Dean 96
Gatwick 305, 310, 311, 313
Gaulle, Charles de 10
'Gazza' (Paul Gascoigne) 96
GDP (gross domestic product) 327–8
gearing 217
Gedajlovic, E. 281 n.
Geneen, Harold 150
geographical concentration 78
Gerlach, M. 86 n.
Germany 43, 140, 162, 233, 290, 293, 299, 321,
        328–33 *passim*, 367
    above-average profitability 166
    anti-trust legislation 123, 236
    Cartel Office 158
    East 321
    educational system/technical skills 5
    government-owned firms 120
    influence of shareholders 217
    kitchen furniture manufacture 134, 330, 331
    leading companies 29
    major banks 171, 196, 198, 288
    manufacturing industry 5
    merger control 158
    prices 131, 231, 232
    size of firms 169, 170
    ten largest companies (1962–91) 167, 168
    textiles 286, 287
    wine 289
Geroski, P. 112 n., 147, 159 n., 167, 179 n.
Ghemawat, P. 49 n., 124 n., 179 n.
Ghoshal, S. 347
Gilmore, F. F. 340
Gleick, J. 18 n.
global warming 190
globalization 131, 239, 339, 347
Goldenberg, N. 18 n.
Goodfellow, J. H. 143 n.
Goold, M. 76
Gordon, D. D. 86 n.
governments 332
    and the **appropriability** of **added value** 183–6
    firms in **competitive markets** 120
    influence 184, 185, 231, 232
    sponsorship 171
    Third World 188
Granovetter, M. 60 n.
Grant, J. H. 341
Grant, R. M. 99 n., 361
Greece 69, 77, 288
greenfield sites 67, 75, 188
Greenstein, S. 112 n.
Griliches, Z. 112 n.
Grindley, P. 112 n.
Grinyer, P. H. 361
gross output 24, 25, 195, 212
    ratio of net output to 214
Grossman, S. 60 n., 100 n.
Guardian, The 245
Gustaffson, B. 60 n.

Hailey, Arthur 135
Halsbury's Laws of England 99
Hamburg 291
Hamel, G. 85 n., 347, 361
Hamermesh, R. G. 354, 363 n.
Hampden-Turner, C. 85 n.
Hanlon, G. 88
Hannah, L. 159 n.
Hapselagh, P. 180 n.
Harrigan, K. R. 159 n., 281 n.
Harris, R. 112 n., 148, 159 n.
Harsanyi, J. 49 n.
Hart, O. 60 n., 61 n., 281 n.
Harvard Business Review 12, 363 n.
Hauer, Rutger 96
Hayek, F. von 321, 334 n.
Hayes, R. H. 112 n.
HBS (Harvard Business School) 18 n., 250 n.,
        335, 339, 340
Heany, D. F. 346
Heathrow Airport 225, 239, 291, 305–8 *passim*,
        310, 313
hedging 275
Hedley, B. 180 n., 344
Heidsieck 290
Heil, O. 100 n.
Hello 222
Helyar, J. 159 n.
Henderson, B. D. 124 n.
Henwood, F. 112 n.
hereditary authority 43
hierarchies 42, 43, 85 n., 109
hi-fi equipment 136
high-quality mass production 134
Hirschman, A. O. 49 n., 85 n.
historic costs 199–202, 204–9, 215
Hitchens, R. E. 180 n.
Hitler, A. 152, 321, 364
Hofer, C. W. 363 n.
Honda, S. 7
Hong Kong 27, 287, 306
hostages 45, 46
hostile bids 218 n.
    see also take-overs
hot wars 224, 226–7, 238, 249 n.
Hotelling, H. 249 n.
hotels 136, 140
    international 98
Houlden, B. T. 340
Houndsfield, Geoffrey 17
Hrebiniak, L. G. 354, 361
Hughes, A. 159 n.
Hume, David 360
Hunt, J. W. 148, 159 n.

Icahn, Carl 164
identity 132
Imigran 161
incentives 268, 277–8, 280, 331
incumbency 65, 104, 129, 165, 187, 196, 222,
        224, 264–6 *passim*, 316–17
    competitive advantage based on 113–14,
        262, 264
    competitive disadvantage relative to 197

decentralized 338
decision-making 74
deficiencies in systems 111
good 9
incumbent 156, 157
international 347
inventory, **just in time** 83, 350
lacking skills 146
local 76
multi-team 75
preoccupation with quality 350
public policy 179 n.
regulation 165
role of networks in 86 n.
senior 164
store, manual on 307
strategic assets 327
styles of 67, 68
total quality 346, 354
Management Today 18 n.
Manhattan 84
Manne, H. G. 159 n.
Manning, A. 250 n.
manufacturing **industry** 5, 91, 156, 174, 368
    automobiles 142, 277
    capabilities 107
    distinction between retailing and 281
    kitchens 134, 330, 331
    metal 68
    motor cycles 8 n.
    output 169
    soap and margarine 82
    wide-ranging 27
    workers in 174
March, J. 85 n., 191 n., 356, 358
marginal firms 195–6, 216, 311, 327
margins 21, 77
market segmentation 175, 222, 291, 297
    automobiles 4, 6, 15, 139,
    central to airline economics 315
    geographical 231–2, 234, 249 n.
    new, soft drink 106
    product proliferation and 229, 230
    supermarkets 26, 194, 195, 228,
    sustainability of 232
    techniques of 233
    temporal 231
market share 20, 21, 132, 174, 177, 247, 315
    as **competitive advantage** 176
    critical importance of 346
    evolution of 167
    greater security of 280
    high profitability and 359
    importance of 179 n.
    individual, instability of 238
    loss of 240
marketing 100 n., 228, 250 n., 258, 317
    champagne 290
    global 67
markets 14–15, 127–43, 323, 360
    attractive, and market positions 176–9
    barriers to **arbitrage** between 233
    boundaries of 130–2
    cartelized 232

chaotic 173
choice of, key issue for the firm 127, 230
commitment to 94, 257, 258
commodity 115, 130
competitive 27, 326; government-owned
    firms in 120; highly, strong position in
    212–13
contestable 124 n., 196, 202
continuing 99
core 142
declining 177
demand and 286, 290–3
development of 340
domestic 301
dominance 114, 121, 340
economic 142, 169, 228, 229
efficient 63, 64, 93, 178
financial 27, 63, 162; deregulation of 46, 292
geographic 140–1, 232–4; new 300
globalization of 131, 239, 339, 347
history of 143 n.
insurance, world 81
international 68, 171; *see also* under
    globalization
liberalization 165
matching to **distinctive capabilities** 17,
    132–4, 307–10
mature, low-technology 149
means of organizing information about 345
more fragmented 76
narrow 15
new, most common means of **entry** into
    144
niche 114, 179, 194, 318
oligopolistic 249 n.
prime position in 106
profitable 10
regulated, licences in 65
restrictions 113
saturation 319
second-hand 234
served 359
strategic 128, 141–2
strong, established **reputation** 18
structure of 162; vertical **relationships** and
    280–1
Western, archetype of Japanese penetration
    of 7
wholesale money 140
young adult 317–18
see also **market segmentation; positioning;**
    stock markets
Marks, Michael 67
Marlboro cigarettes 255, 258, 264, 329
Marris, R. 191 n.
Marschak, J. 85 n.
Marsh, P. 159 n.
Marshall, Alfred 81, 131, 217 n., 362
Mathias, P. 112 n.
Mattson, L. G. 49 n.
Maxwell House 244
Mayer, C. 124 n., 148, 218 n., 334 n.
Meadowcroft, S. 159 n.
Meckling, W. H. 61 n.

Packard, V. 266 n.
Padua 305
Pakistan 328
Palma 307
Panzer, J. C. 124 n.
Paris 89, 130, 140, 224, 225, 259, 316
    Bourse 209
partnerships 69, 107
    fundamentally incompatible 151
Pascale, Richard 7–8, 18 n.
patents 105, 106, 162, 163, 231
    protection 236, 262
pay-off matrix 35–6, 40, 41–2
pay-offs 39, 47, 152
    structure 51, 91, 256, 277
PE (price-earnings) ratio 22, 23, 151, 201
Peacock, A. T. 159 n.
Pearce, J. A. 346
Pedigree Chum 262, 264
Pepall, L. 249 n.
Perrow, C. 49 n.
Persil 258, 264
pest control services 94
Peters, T. J. 69, 85 n., 143 n., 346, 354
petrol 99, 238, 280
    retail market 239
Pettigrew, A. M. 357
Pfeffer, J. 85 n.
pharmaceuticals 18, 20, 142, 161, 226, 231–4
    passim
    industry 134, 177, 262
    producers 17
    products 236
Phlips, L. 249 n.
photocopiers 102, 141, 230
Pickens, T. Boone 183, 347
Piesse, J. 319 n.
Pigou, A. C. 249 n.
PIMS database 143 n., 176–8 passim, 187, 229,
    254, 346, 359–60
Piore, M. 86 n.
planning 340
    central 173
    scenario 341
    strategic 6–7, 338–9
    see also portfolio planning approach
Plunkett, J. J. 143 n.
political corruption 85
Porter, M. E. 81, 86 n., 135, 217 n., 249 n.,
    250 n., 330, 334 n., 345, 346, 347, 358
Porter value chain 217 n., 345
portfolio planning approach 64, 176–7, 180 n.,
    338–9, 344–6
Portugal 29, 327, 328, 330
positioning:
    competitive 111
    down-market 138
    market 9, 20, 65, 106, 134, 176–9; dominant
        123, 149
    in newspaper and food retailing 244–7
    pricing and 221–50, 303
    product 15, 134–6; when products have
        many attributes 138–40
    up-market 21, 143 n., 161

Posner, R. A. 30 n., 143 n.
Post-it notes 134
Potts, M. 363 n.
power generation 120, 151, 175
Prahalad, C. K. 85 n., 346, 347, 361
Pratt, J. W. 61 n.
Pratten, C. 174
price discrimination 228, 229–30, 249 n., 250 n.,
    291
price premiums 88, 137, 266, 318, 365
prices 190, 222–3, 231, 236
    competitive 12, 20
    contract 268, 269–73, 275
    higher 20, 64, 93, 135
    how costs influence 226–8
    how values influence 228–31
    low, branded goods at 21
    market 50, 323
    premium 293
    share 13
    value for money 29
    see also price discrimination; price
        premiums
pricing 6, 221–50, 303, 318, 316
    predatory 123
Pringle 313
Prisoner's Dilemma 43–5 passim, 47, 51, 58–9,
    95, 99, 164, 223–4, 238, 249 n., 277, 326, 359
    archetypal 301
    characteristic of the passing game 77
    described 34, 35–9
    difference between Criminal's Revenge and 41
    experiments and applications 49 n.
    low-level equilibrium 256
    pessimistic view of outcome 152
    reiterated 330
    signalling quality 90–2
privatization 120, 124 n., 165, 304
product differentiation 134, 174, 175, 231,
    294 n.
    highly differentiated 211
    horizontal and vertical 244
productivity 67, 311
product quality 6, 20, 87, 91, 93, 95
    advertising and 255, 256–8
    uncertainty about 265
products 21, 68, 236
    availability 255, 256, 258
    characteristics 90
    down-market 136
    focused 230
    innovative 110, 262, 298
    life cycles 119, 344, 345
    niche 232
    premium 232
    proliferation 229, 230
    specification 255, 256, 258, 262
    standardization 134
    see also product differentiation; product
        quality
professional services 140
professors 69
profitability 15–16, 82, 133, 139, 177–8, 183,
    192–3

United States (*cont.*):
    political opportunities offered by democratization 12
    protectionist reactions to Japanese firms 67
    savings and loan industry 275
    shareholders 181, 190, 203, 217
    size of firms 170
    stock exchange obligations 30 n.
University of Sussex 112 n.
unwritten codes/rules 77
up-market moves/positions 21, 143 n., 161
Ury, W. 281 n.
used cars 88, 91
utilities 114, 175, 214, 265
    monopolistic 16
    regulated 325
Utterback, J. M. 112 n.

Valium 17, 161
value added 149, 178
    see also **added value**
value chains 25, 189, 212–13, 227, 306
    for champagne (UK) 296
    for various products 293
values:
    diverse 325
    individualistic 60
    market 200, 201, 204, 207, 209, 215, 234
    prices influenced by 228–31
van Fleet, D. D. 72
Vauxhall 130
VCRs (video cassette recorders) 15, 27, 101, 107, 109
    battle 116
    standards war 115
Veblen, T. 266 n.
Veneto region 304
Vepsalainen, A. 85 n.
vertical integration 158, 294
VHS recorders 115
Vickers, J. 49 n., 112 n., 124 n.
Vickrey, W. 281 n.
video equipment 67
    see also VCRs
vision and mission 367
Vlassopoulos, A. 147, 159 n.
'voodoo economics' 203

Wack, P. 341
Walkman 106
Wall, J. A. 281 n.
Wall Street 182, 330

Wall Street Journal 114
war of attrition 46
warranties 91–2, 100 n., 133
Washington 310
Waterman, R. H. 69, 85 n., 143 n., 346, 354
Watson, Thomas 67
Wayne, K. 124 n.
wealth creation 322–4, 326, 330
Weber, M. 85 n.
Weigelt, K. 100 n.
Weinstock, Lord 76
Weintraub, R. 281 n.
Weizsacker, C. C. von 124 n.
Welch, Jack 339
Wernerfelt, B. 100 n.
What's On TV 222
Whisler, T. L. 336
Which? magazine 260 n.
White, L. J. 281 n., 346
Whittington, G. 218 n.
Williamson, Oliver E. 49 n., 60 n., 61 n., 85 n., 100 n.
Willig, R. D. 124 n.
Wilson, R. 100 n.
Wilson, T. A. 266 n.
wines 135, 261, 289, 296
    see also champagne
winner's curse 272–3
Winter, S. G. 49 n., 85 n., 354
Woodward, J. 112 n., 361
Wright, M. 155, 159 n.
Wright, R. V. C. 346

Yamawaki, H. 166 n.
Yao, D. A. 124 n.
Yarrow, G. 124 n.
Yelle, L. E. 346
Yeung, S. 347
yield curve 215

Zaibatsu 83
Zaïre 189
Zantac 4, 17, 18, 26, 64, 65, 94, 137, 152, 161, 204, 205, 262
Zeckhauser, R. J. 61 n.
Zeebrugge 239
Zentner, R. D. 341
zero sum game 269
Zucker, L. G. 60 n., 85 n.

Index compiled by Frank Pert